MW00573943

Tableau 2019.x Cookbook

Over 115 recipes to build end-to-end analytical solutions using Tableau

Dmitry Anoshin
Teodora Matic
Slaven Bogdanovic
Tania Lincoln
Dmitrii Shirokov

BIRMINGHAM - MUMBAI

Tableau 2019.x Cookbook

Commissioning Editor: Sunith Shetty
Acquisition Editor: Yogesh Deokar
Content Development Editor: Nathanya Dias
Technical Editor: Vibhuti Gawde
Copy Editor: Safis Editing
Project Coordinator: Kirti Pisat
Proofreader: Safis Editing
Indexer: Rekha Nair
Graphics: Jisha Chirayil
Production Coordinator: Deepika Naik

First published: January 2019

Production reference: 1310119

Published by Packt Publishing Ltd.
Livery Place
35 Livery Street
Birmingham
B3 2PB, UK.

ISBN 978-1-78953-338-5

www.packtpub.com

`mapt.io`

Mapt is an online digital library that gives you full access to over 5,000 books and videos, as well as industry leading tools to help you plan your personal development and advance your career. For more information, please visit our website.

Why subscribe?

- Spend less time learning and more time coding with practical eBooks and Videos from over 4,000 industry professionals

- Improve your learning with Skill Plans built especially for you

- Get a free eBook or video every month

- Mapt is fully searchable

- Copy and paste, print, and bookmark content

Packt.com

Did you know that Packt offers eBook versions of every book published, with PDF and ePub files available? You can upgrade to the eBook version at `www.packt.com` and as a print book customer, you are entitled to a discount on the eBook copy. Get in touch with us at `customercare@packtpub.com` for more details.

At `www.packt.com`, you can also read a collection of free technical articles, sign up for a range of free newsletters, and receive exclusive discounts and offers on Packt books and eBooks.

Foreword

This book is different from most Tableau books. Previuosly, Tableau books tried to cover the default Tableau functionality with simple examples, or covered the principles of data visualization. This book focuses on end-to-end BI solutions based on Tableau. It includes Tableau Server, both on Linux and Windows; a new tool for data preparation, Tableau Prep; complex use cases with the Tableau REST API, and more. Moreover, this book goes beyond Tableau use cases and covers BI solutions in general and explains the concepts of integration between ETL based on Matillion and BI. Finally, you will learn about working with big data and modern data platforms such as Redshift and Snowflake.

Thank you to my beautiful wife, Svetlana, who supports me during my professional journey and always has a positive attitude. In addition, I want to hug my kids, Vasily, Anna, and Michael and hope one day they will be proud of their dad who planted trees in the backyard and wrote a couple of books. PS for sure, we will go on vacation soon and have some fun together!

—Dmitry Anoshin

To our baby, with love. We had a great time writing this book and waiting for you!
—Teodora and Slaven

Thank you Justin and Sydney for your support. I owe you some nice dinners and playground time! Appreciations to my fellow co-authors for giving me this opportunity.
—Tania Lincoln

Contributors

About the authors

Dmitry Anoshin is an expert in analytics with 10 years of experience. He started using Tableau as primary BI tool in 2011 as a BI consultant at Teradata. He is certified with both Tableau Desktop and Server. He leads probably the biggest Tableau user community, with more than 2,000 active users. This community has 2-3 Tableau talks every month led by top Tableau experts, Tableau Zen Masters, Viz Champions, and so on. In addition, Dmitry has previously written three books with Packt and reviewed more than seven books. Finally, he is an active speaker at data conferences and helps people to adopt cloud analytics.

Teodora Matic is a data analyst with a strong background in statistics and more than 5 years of experience in data analytics and reporting. She has been using Tableau since 2014. She has been working as a project manager and data analyst for leading market research companies, such as Ipsos and EyeSee Research, levering the power of Tableau to bring business insights to clients. She currently does data analysis and reporting at the International Committee of the Red Cross.

Slaven Bogdanovic has more than 10 years of experience in data analysis and reporting within both business and academia. His expertise covers complex statistical analysis and insight communication. He has been using Tableau since 2013. Currently, he works as a BI/big data developer at NCR Corporation. Previously, he was a senior research executive at Ipsos. Also, Slaven is a PhD candidate and a member of the Laboratory for Research of Individual Differences at the University of Belgrade. In addition, Slaven is the author of six articles published in academic and professional journals.

Tania Lincoln has over 12 years of development experience in BI and data analytics domain. She has a strong SQL, visualization, and analytics skill set, and has demonstrated the ability to mentor others on new technologies and process improvements. She is also experienced in taking a product from inception to launch and managing post-launch growth.

Dmitrii Shirokov has over 11 years of design and development of data-driven solutions. He has been using Tableau since 2011 in the majority of analytics projects. His expertise covers building data warehouses and sophisticated analytical solutions. Currently, he works as a solutions architect at Rock Your Data consulting company. Previously, he was a big data architect at Sberbank and also worked as a professional service consultant at Teradata.

About the reviewers

Shweta Savale is the cofounder and head of client engagements at Syvylyze (pronounced *civilize*) Analytics. Being one of the leading experts on Tableau, she has translated her expertise to successfully rendering analytics and data visualization services for numerous clients across a wide range of industry verticals. She has successfully trained over 2,200 participants across 150+ companies on Tableau, and is also an empaneled trainer for Tableau APAC and conducts public and private Tableau training across Singapore, Malaysia, Hong Kong, Thailand, Australia, and India.

In addition to being an entrepreneur and trainer, she has also authored *Tableau Cookbook – Recipes of Data Visualization*, published by Packt Publishing, UK.

Lana Anoshina is mom of three kids and she enjoys working with data and solving complex business issues with data visualization. She enjoys driving her Audi on West Coast and spending quality time with her family near the ocean.

Dave Dwyer has a BS in Information Systems from RIT (Rochester Institute of Technology), MBA from Drexel University, certified Six Sigma Black Belt and PMP. In his 20+ years as an IT professional, he has worked in a wide range of technical and leadership roles, in companies ranging from startups to Fortune 100 enterprises. A chance introduction to reporting and analytics 10 years ago hooked him and he never left. Dave feels the data science landscape of analytics, visualization, big data, and machine learning will drive more real changes in business over the next 10 years than any other area.

Manideep Bhattacharyya is a Tableau enthusiast and Tableau certified professional with more than 16 years of industry experience. He graduated from science college Calcutta in 2003. He started his career at IBM as a Siebel certified professional and worked for 7 years and contributed to many global multinational projects across the world. Later on, he joined an Indian conglomerate and implemented Tableau with a large-scale multi-billion row dataset, and set a new standard for data discovery and visualization for CXOs and top management.

Packt is searching for authors like you

If you're interested in becoming an author for Packt, please visit authors.packtpub.com and apply today. We have worked with thousands of developers and tech professionals, just like you, to help them share their insight with the global tech community. You can make a general application, apply for a specific hot topic that we are recruiting an author for, or submit your own idea.

Table of Contents

Preface

Tableau is one of the most popular **business intelligence (BI)** solutions in recent times, thanks to its powerful and interactive data visualization capabilities. This comprehensive book is full of useful recipes from industry experts that will help you master Tableau skills and learn each aspect of Tableau's 2018.x offerings.

This book is enriched with features such as extracts, Tableau advanced calculations, geospatial analysis, building dashboards, and much more. It will guide you to exciting techniques of data manipulation, storytelling, advanced filtering, expert visualization, and forecasting using real-world examples. It will help you on your learning journey from the basic functionalities of Tableau, all the way to complex deployment on Linux. Moreover, you will learn about the advanced features of Tableau by using R, Python, and various APIs. The complexity of tasks increases gradually, and you will be guided all the way to mastering advanced functionalities through bite-sized, detailed recipes. Furthermore, the book is packed with troubleshooting techniques to optimize your BI tasks.

You will learn how to prepare data for analysis using the latest Tableau Prep. By the end of the book, you will be all ready to tackle BI challenges using Tableau's features.

Who this book is for

This book is for data analysts, data visualization, and BI users who are looking for quick solutions to common and not-so-common problems faced while using Tableau.

What this book covers

Chapter 1, *Getting Started with Tableau Software*, will consist of theory and recipes with a focus on the learning foundation of Tableau and allowing you to get familiar with the Tableau interface and basic tasks such as creating simple charts, tables, and filtering. You will come to understand the semantic layer of Tableau. You will learn through examples made with real data collected through a large market research study.

Chapter 2, *Data Manipulation*, will guide you through the process of manipulating data in Tableau using census data. From connecting to data sources, through adding multiple sources, joining them, and blending them—after practicing the recipes in this chapter, you will feel confident manipulating data sources in Tableau. Additionally, you will learn how to use the Tableau Pivot functionality, and set the semantic layer of your workbook to suit the requirement of the task by practicing converting measures to dimensions, continuous to discrete, and editing aliases.

Chapter 3, *Tableau Extracts*, will cover how Tableau dashboard performance is boosted using extracts. You will be informed about the different types of Tableau file formats and types of extract. The chapter introduces you to Tableau's new in-memory, blazingly fast data engine technology called Hyper, which was released in October 2017. Step-by-step instructions will help users learn how extremely large datasets can be sliced and diced in seconds using Hyper and hence improve the speed of analysis. This chapter will enable you to optimize the performance of your Tableau dashboards using aggregated extracts, dimension reduction, extract filters, incremental extract refreshes, and cross-data joins.

Chapter 4, *Tableau Desktop Advanced Calculations*, will start to explore the rest of Tableau Desktop functionality, such as table calculations, calculated fields, parameters, sets, groups, and level of detail expressions. Steps by step, you will learn how to leverage the full power of Tableau. This chapter is full of useful recipes that help you to master Tableau Desktop skills, from simple table calculations to advanced level of detail expressions, helping you to become a more advanced Tableau developer. The chapter uses real-life marketing data and will cover population geospatial use cases.

Chapter 5, *Tableau Desktop Advanced Filtering*, covers filters from A to Z. After getting familiar with filtering in the first chapter, you will expand your skills. Through practical exercises that use data from the packaged food industry, you will have an opportunity to master all kinds of filters—you will learn about implementing date filters, measure filters, top N filters, table calculation filters, and action filters. This chapter will also teach you how to manage the relationship between multiple filters by adding them to context.

Chapter 6, *Building Dashboards*, will focus on dashboard design techniques. This chapter will introduce the concept of dashboards and go through the process of designing a dashboard. Using real-life data about internet usage, you will start by making a basic dashboard before building on it by adding custom formatting and advanced functionalities. Moreover, you will learn about the role of visualization and the importance of using the right design layout in order to use the full power of Tableau and create awesome dashboards. Finally, you will build a self-service dashboard.

Chapter 7, *Telling a Story with Tableau*, covers creating stories with data. Through practical examples made with real-life business data from the automotive industry, you will learn how to use Tableau functionality for making stories in a way that is engaging and accessible to the audience, while at the same time accurate in communicating the message.

Chapter 8, *Tableau Visualization*, introduces techniques for creating advanced visualizations with Tableau Desktop. Here we go beyond Tableau's Show Me feature and instead look at the exact technique for how to master advanced visualizations that can make your dashboard story stand out from the crowd. We cover multiple use cases and recommend the best practice for each visualization, along with detailed steps for creating each one of them. The use cases vary from identifying elements in the data to create the biggest impact, to creating ranks for different categories over a period of time to visually track goals for organizations, to comparing multiple measures for performance over time. This chapter uses multiple different datasets for each visualization, such as an American football dataset, an unsatisfactory customer service dataset from the hospitality industry, US state college rankings, a stock prices dataset, CO2 emissions from energy consumption, FY18 PMMR spending and budget data, and more.

Chapter 9, *Tableau Advanced Visualization*, builds on what was covered in the previous chapter. The use cases vary from comparing multiple categories with high values in the 80-90% range, identifying the dominant players in the flow, and creating part-to-whole relationships, to visually eliminating size Alaska Effect. This chapter uses multiple different datasets for each visualization, including football league data, Wikipedia clickstream data, ITA's market research data, retail sales marketing profit and cost data, and statewise US population distribution data.

Chapter 10, *Tableau for Big Data*, looks at how visualizing data is important—regardless of its volume, variety, and velocity! The approach to visualizing big data is especially vital, as the cost of storing, preparing, and querying data is much higher. Organizations must leverage well-architected data sources and rigorously apply best practices to allow workers to query big data directly. In this chapter, we address the challenges of visualizing big data; the best practices for leveraging Hadoop, S3, Athena, and Redshift Spectrum directly; and how you can deploy Tableau on big data at massive scale.

Chapter 11, *Forecasting with Tableau*, will cover Tableau's built-in functions for the forecasting and integration of R packages. Using real-life data from health behavior research, you will learn how to perform regression analysis on simple and more complex datasets, and how to correctly interpret the results of statistical tests. Also, you will learn how to implement time series models. Toward the end of the chapter, you will see a working example of regression that relies on machine learning.

Chapter 12, *Advanced Analytics with Tableau,* will cover advanced analytics with Tableau, using Tableau integration with R. Using real-life data from the telecommunication, automotive, banking, and fast-moving consumer goods industries, you will learn how to discover the underlying structure of data, how to identify market niches, how to classify similar cases in segments, and how to extrapolate results on larger data sets. Also, you will learn how to identify and interpret unusual cases and anomalies in data.

Chapter 13, *Deploy Tableau Server,* covers Tableau Server and its purpose. It contains the steps to download and deploy Tableau Server in Windows and Linux environments. You will also learn about how a Tableau Server backup is created, monitored, and scheduled. Further server usage monitoring is discussed along with Tableau Server automatization with tabcmd and tabadmin. Overall, this chapter aims to have you well versed with how to automatically update and publish Tableau dashboards on Tableau Server and create appropriate security for restricting access.

Chapter 14, *Tableau Troubleshooting,* covers troubleshooting Tableau Desktop and Tableau Server. This chapter aims to lay down the basic foundation for the steps to be followed whenever an issue is encountered during your Tableau journey. This chapter has been split into three sections: performance troubleshooting, technical troubleshooting, and logs.

Chapter 15, *Preparing Data for Analysis with Tableau Prep,* covers a new Tableau product: Tableau Prep. It is designed to help you quickly and confidently combine, shape, and clean your data for analysis. Prep allows end users to clean and organize data before creating a data source. You will learn about this product's use cases and best practices.

Chapter 16, *ETL Best Practices for Tableau,* introduces an integration between Tableau Server and modern ETL tool Matillion. The reader will learn how to install tabcmd for Linux and build integration between ETL pipeline and Tableau Server activities such as refreshing extracts and exporting PDFs. This approach could be used for any ETL tool.

Chapter 17, *Meet Tableau SDK and API,* is a detailed and practical step-by-step guide to installing the Tableau SDK and API. You will learn how to take any data and convert it into a Tableau extract file (.tde). This data can be from a database, added at defined intervals as new data comes in, or the result of a predictive model created using the powerful machine learning libraries of Python. Furthermore, this chapter elaborates on how the Tableau SDK can be utilized to read a Tableau extract file in Tableau Desktop and how it can be shared on Tableau Server for further visualization. This chapter shows how predictive models and visualizations can peacefully coexist as separate layers. For this chapter refer to: https:/ /www.packtpub.com/sites/default/files/downloads/Tableau_2019_x_Cookbook.pdf.

To get the most out of this book

You will need to download Tableau Desktop 2018. Some understanding of BI concepts and Tableau is required.

Download the example code files

You can download the example code files for this book from your account at www.packt.com. If you purchased this book elsewhere, you can visit www.packt.com/support and register to have the files emailed directly to you.

You can download the code files by following these steps:

1. Log in or register at www.packt.com.
2. Select the **SUPPORT** tab.
3. Click on **Code Downloads & Errata**.
4. Enter the name of the book in the **Search** box and follow the onscreen instructions.

Once the file is downloaded, please make sure that you unzip or extract the folder using the latest version of:

- WinRAR/7-Zip for Windows
- Zipeg/iZip/UnRarX for Mac
- 7-Zip/PeaZip for Linux

The code bundle for the book is also hosted on GitHub at https://github.com/PacktPublishing/Tableau-2019.x-Cookbook. In case there's an update to the code, it will be updated on the existing GitHub repository.

We also have other code bundles from our rich catalog of books and videos available at https://github.com/PacktPublishing/. Check them out!

Download the color images

We also provide a PDF file that has color images of the screenshots/diagrams used in this book. You can download it here: http://www.packtpub.com/sites/default/files/downloads/9781789533385_ColorImages.pdf.

Conventions used

There are a number of text conventions used throughout this book.

CodeInText: Indicates code words in text, database table names, folder names, filenames, file extensions, pathnames, dummy URLs, user input, and Twitter handles. Here is an example: "You will also need to save a local copy of the Baby_names.csv dataset to your device, as we will be using it in the recipes."

A block of code is set as follows:

```
install.packages('rpart',repos='http://cran.us.r-project.org')
library(rpart)
cars <- read.table("C:\\!Slaven\\6 KNJIGA\\4 Advanced analytics\\4 decision
tree\\new_or_used_car.csv", header=T, sep=",")
fit <- rpart(FuturePurchase ~ Age + Gender + Education + FamilyStatus +
CurrentCar + AgeOfCurrentCar + MunicipalityType, method="class", data=cars)
plot(fit, uniform=TRUE, main="Classification of new cars buyers")
text(fit, all=TRUE, cex=.8)
```

Any command-line input or output is written as follows:

```
set enable_result_cache_for_session to off;
```

Bold: Indicates a new term, an important word, or words that you see onscreen. For example, words in menus or dialog boxes appear in the text like this. Here is an example: "From the **Connect** pane on the left-hand side, choose the **Text file** option."

 Warnings or important notes appear like this.

 Tips and tricks appear like this.

Sections

In this book, you will find several headings that appear frequently (*Getting ready, How to do it..., How it works..., There's more...,* and *See also*).

To give clear instructions on how to complete a recipe, use these sections as follows:

Getting ready

This section tells you what to expect in the recipe and describes how to set up any software or any preliminary settings required for the recipe.

How to do it...

This section contains the steps required to follow the recipe.

How it works...

This section usually consists of a detailed explanation of what happened in the previous section.

There's more...

This section consists of additional information about the recipe in order to make you more knowledgeable about the recipe.

See also

This section provides helpful links to other useful information for the recipe.

Get in touch

Feedback from our readers is always welcome.

General feedback: If you have questions about any aspect of this book, mention the book title in the subject of your message and email us at customercare@packtpub.com.

Errata: Although we have taken every care to ensure the accuracy of our content, mistakes do happen. If you have found a mistake in this book, we would be grateful if you would report this to us. Please visit www.packt.com/submit-errata, selecting your book, clicking on the Errata Submission Form link, and entering the details.

Piracy: If you come across any illegal copies of our works in any form on the Internet, we would be grateful if you would provide us with the location address or website name. Please contact us at copyright@packt.com with a link to the material.

If you are interested in becoming an author: If there is a topic that you have expertise in and you are interested in either writing or contributing to a book, please visit authors.packtpub.com.

Reviews

Please leave a review. Once you have read and used this book, why not leave a review on the site that you purchased it from? Potential readers can then see and use your unbiased opinion to make purchase decisions, we at Packt can understand what you think about our products, and our authors can see your feedback on their book. Thank you!

For more information about Packt, please visit packt.com.

Getting Started with Tableau Software

1

In this chapter, we will cover the following recipes:

- Connecting to the data
- Building a bar chart using Show Me
- Building a text table
- Adding filters
- Adding color
- Building a tree map
- Building a map
- Customizing tooltips
- Building a dual axis map

Technical requirements

To follow the recipes in this chapter, you will need to have Tableau 2019.x installed. You will also need to save a local copy of the `Baby_names.csv` dataset to your device, as we will be using it in the recipes. You can download this dataset from the GitHub repository: `(https://github.com/PacktPublishing/Tableau-2018-Dot-1-Cookbook/blob/master/Baby_names.csv)`.

Introduction to Tableau

Tableau is one of the fastest-evolving **business intelligence** (**BI**) and data visualization tools at the moment. The user-friendly interface, combined with powerful capabilities, makes it one of the most widely used and popular BI tools around the globe. Tableau offers many functionalities, and getting started with the basic ones is surprisingly easy. This chapter will get you familiar with Tableau basics and, by the end of it, you will have learned how to connect to a data source, and how to make simple visualizations.

To complete the recipes in this chapter, we will be using data on baby names in the US, which have been collected by the US Federal **Social Security Administration** (**SSA**). The Baby_names.csv dataset contains the most popular baby names (that have 100 or more registered appearances) in the US, from 2010 through 2017. The dataset contains information about the state, gender of the name, name itself, year, and number of babies with said name.

Connecting to the data

In this recipe, we will go through the basics of connecting to a data source. The first step you must take when you open Tableau, before you create any visualizations, is to connect to a data source. You will then use that data source to create your views and dashboards.

Getting ready

In this recipe, we will be using the Baby_names.csv dataset. Make sure that you have a local copy of the dataset saved to your device.

How to do it...

1. Open Tableau.
2. From the **Connect** pane on the left-hand side, choose the **Text file** option:

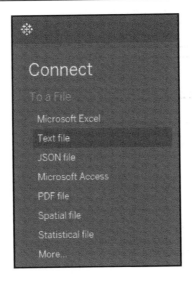

3. A new window will open. Navigate to your local copy of the `Baby_names.csv` dataset, select it, and click **Open**.

4. Tableau has now opened the **Data Source** page for you, where the file you loaded has been selected as the data source, and where you can also preview it.

5. To begin making your first visualization, just click on the **Sheet 1** tab in the bottom of the workbook.

You are all set!

How it works...

Tableau reads the file you connected to and recognizes fields and their respective data types. There are the following data types in Tableau:

- Number (decimal)
- Number (whole)
- Date and time
- Date
- String
- Boolean

After you have connected to the data source and you click on **Sheet 1**, you will see the **Data** pane on the left-hand side of the workspace, with all the fields from the data source listed, and their respective types marked by small symbols to the left of their names, as shown in the following screenshot:

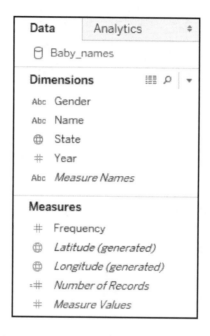

The globe symbols in front of **State**, **Longitude**, and **Latitude** denotes the geographical roles of these fields, which are important when building maps. On the other hand, the **Abc** symbol signifies strings, while the # symbol denotes numerical values.

There's more...

Tableau allows users to connect to a wide range of data. You can connect to different types of files that are stored locally on your device, or data stored on the cloud or in relational or multidimensional databases. You can connect to the list of data that is available on the **Start** page, which opens when you launch **Tableau Desktop**, under **Connect**.

See also

- For more on connecting to data, see the Tableau help resource on the topic at `https://onlinehelp.tableau.com/current/pro/desktop/en-us/basicconnectoverview.html`

Building a bar chart using Show Me

In this recipe, we will build a bar chart using **Show Me**. The **Show Me** option is a handy way to get started with building Tableau visualizations. To make a visualization, you don't need to know exactly how to do it, you just need to know what fields from your data source you would like to include in it. Tableau will suggest the appropriate visualizations.

Getting ready

To complete this recipe, you need to connect to the `Baby_names.csv` dataset and open a new blank worksheet.

How to do it...

We will now create the bar chart using the **Show Me** option, while referring to the given steps.

Creating a chart using Show Me

1. Hold the *Ctrl* key on your keyboard, then on **State** under **Dimensions**, and then choose **Frequency** under **Measures**.
2. Release the *Ctrl* key and click on **Show Me** in the top-right corner of the workbook:

3. A menu will open, offering various visualizations that are suitable for your data. Choose **horizontal bars**. You have just created your first visualization! Now, let's make it tidier and easier to read:

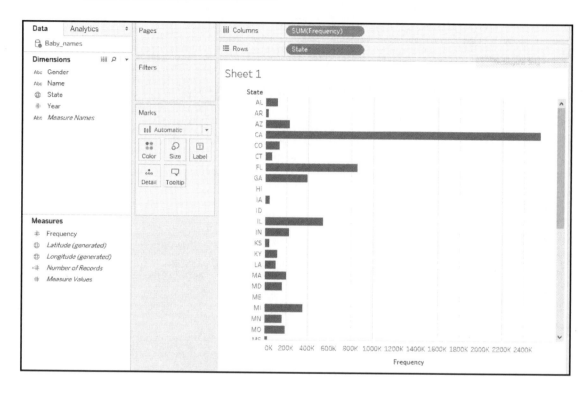

Sorting the chart

1. Hover over the **State** pill in the **Rows** shelf so that a white arrows appears on it. Click on the arrow and select **Sort...**:

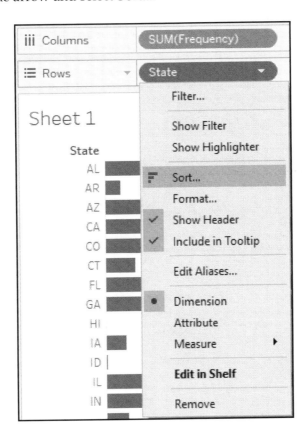

2. Under **Sort order**, choose **Descending**.

3. Under **Sort by**, select **Field**:

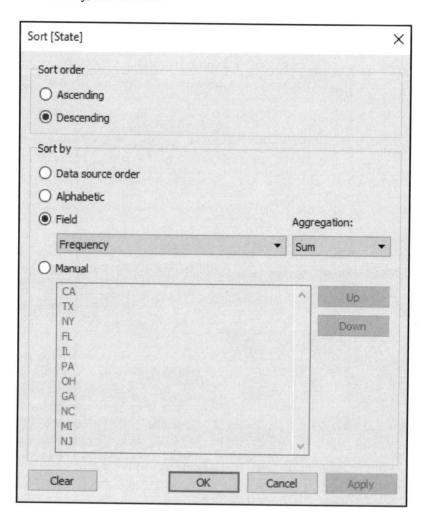

4. Click on **OK**. The states are now sorted in descending order, by the value of **Frequency**, as follows:

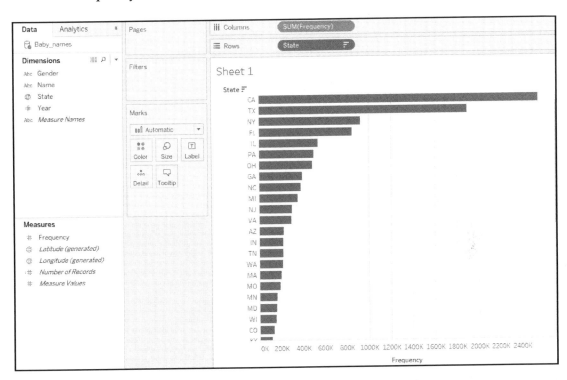

How it works...

Tableau classifies the fields from a data source you connect to into two main types:

- **Dimensions**: This section includes qualitative and categorical values, such as dates, strings, or geographical data
- **Measures**: This section includes quantitative and numerical values

Measures and **Dimensions** can be both continuous, which means that they add axes to a view, and discrete, meaning they add field headers to a view. Continuous fields are marked with a green color, and discrete are marked with blue. However, you will notice that **Measures** are mostly continuous, while **Dimensions** are discrete:

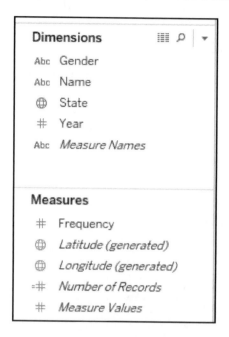

When you select some measures and dimensions and click on **Show Me**, Tableau presents you with a range of basic visualizations that require the particular combination of measures and dimensions you selected.

There's more…

When you connect to a data source, Tableau automatically assigns type (measure or dimension) to each field in your data source. However, you can always change them manually by right-clicking on the field name under **Measures/Dimensions** and selecting **Convert to Dimension / Convert to Measure**:

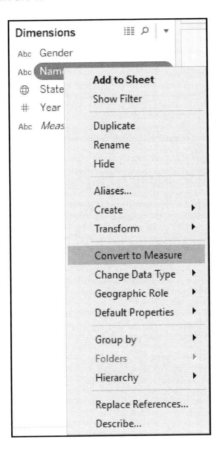

See also

- For more details on data types, check out the Tableau help resource on this topic at `https://onlinehelp.tableau.com/current/pro/desktop/en-us/datafields_ typesandroles.html`

Building a text table

In this recipe, we will build a simple table that includes two dimension, and one measure. Dimensions will define the column and row headers, while the measure will be aggregated.

Getting ready

Connect to the `Baby_names.csv` dataset and open a new worksheet.

How to do it...

1. Drag and drop **State** from **Dimensions** into the **Rows** shelf.
2. Drag and drop **Gender** from **Dimensions** into the **Columns** shelf.
3. Drag and drop **Frequency** from **Measures** onto **Text** in the **Marks** card:

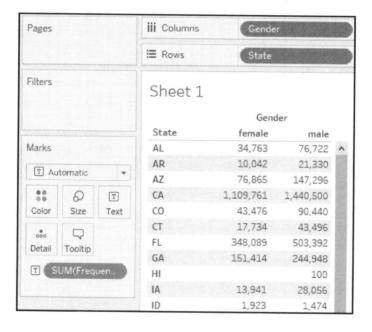

How it works...

We have placed **State** and **Gender**, two discrete dimensions, into the rows and columns of our table. However, this still leaves the table itself empty. We can only see the **Abc** placeholder text. When we place **Frequency**, a continuous measure, onto **Text**, Tableau fills our table with that measure, and automatically aggregates it along the dimensions we placed in rows and columns.

There's more...

When you place a continuous measure into a view, Tableau needs to aggregate it. It will use **SUM** as the default aggregation function. You can also see that if you look at the **Frequency** pill in **Text**, in the **Marks** card, it says **SUM(Frequency)**:

However, you can change the aggregation function. Hover over the **SUM(Frequency)** pill in the **Marks** card, so that a white arrow appears on it, and click on the arrow. If you hover over **Measure (Sum)** in the drop-down menu, it opens another drop-down menu. From it, you can choose from a range of aggregation functions, as shown in the following screenshot:

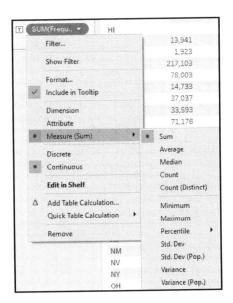

Keep in mind that this method of aggregation only affects the worksheet it is applied in. To change the default aggregation function for a particular measure across all worksheets, consider using the **Default Properties** function, which is available in the drop-down menu that will appear when we right-click a field under **Measures**.

See also

- For more on text tables, see the **Tableau Help** page on this topic at `https://onlinehelp.tableau.com/current/pro/desktop/en-us/buildexamples_text.html`

Adding filters

This chapter will get you familiar with basic filtering functionality in Tableau. We will create a chart that shows name frequency across years, but we will then filter one name to see how its popularity has been changing over the years, and also narrow our view down to one state.

Getting ready

Connect to the `Baby_names.csv` dataset, and open a new worksheet.

How to do it...

1. Drag and drop **Year** from **Dimensions** into the **Columns** shelf.
2. Drag and drop **Frequency** from **Measures** into the **Rows** shelf.
3. Drag and drop **Name** into the **Filters** shelf.
4. In the search bar at the top of the list, start typing `jac`.

5. Select **Jacob**, and click **OK**:

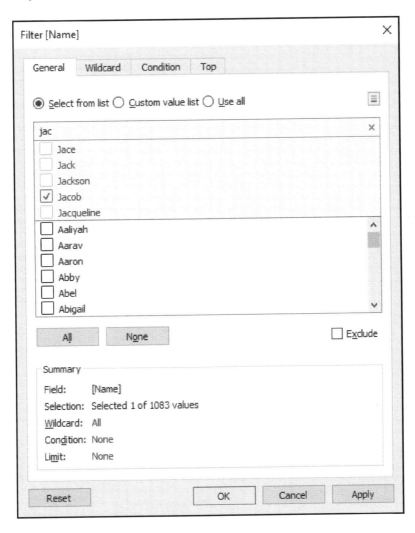

6. We can see that the name **Jacob** has been gradually decreasing in popularity since **2010**. Let's see how it has fared in Texas specifically. Drag and drop **State** from **Dimensions** into the **Filters** card.

7. In the search box in the **Filter [State]** window, type tx.

8. Select **TX**, click **OK**, and you will see the following results:

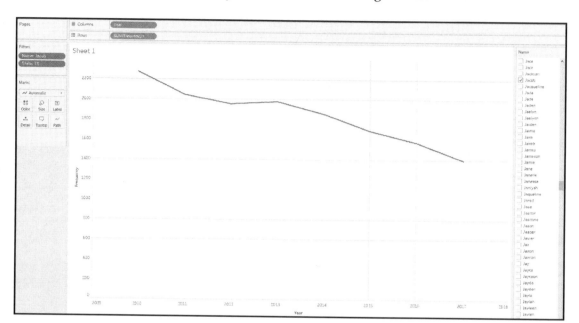

How it works...

Filters exclude rows from your dataset. When you select the name **Jacob** using a filter, only rows that contain the Jacob value from your dataset are analyzed, while all the other rows are excluded. You can also filter multiple values and select two, three, or 50 names to show in your view.

There's more...

One of the main advantages of Tableau filters is their interactivity. Let's execute the following steps to see how the **Filter** option works:

1. If you hover over the **Name: Jacob** pill in the **Filters** shelf, a small white arrow will appear on it.
2. Click on the arrow, and in the drop-down menu, click on **Show Filter**.

3. A list of all the names will appear in the top-right corner of the worksheet. Only **Jacob** is selected, because that's how we set our filter. However, you can select and deselect any name(s) to change your visualization:

4. If you hover over the filter control and click on the small black arrow that appears in the top-right corner, you can change the mode of the filter. You can choose whether you would like the filter to allow single or multiple values. You can also decide whether to implement the filter control as a drop-down list, checkboxes, or slider, as shown in the following screenshot:

See also

- For more information on filtering, see the **Tableau Help** page at `https://onlinehelp.tableau.com/current/pro/desktop/en-us/filtering.html`

Adding color

Colors are a very useful way to enrich your visualization. In this recipe, you will learn how to add information to your visualization by selecting **Dimension** and adding it to **Color**, which is present in the **Marks** card.

Getting ready

Connect to your local copy of `Baby_names.csv` and open a blank worksheet.

How to do it...

1. Drag and drop **State** from **Dimensions** into the **Columns** shelf.
2. Drag and drop **Frequency** from **Measures** into the **Rows** shelf.
3. Drag and drop **Name** into the **Filter** shelf.
4. In the **Filter[Name]** window, in the **General** tab, make sure **Select from list** is selected.
5. Click on **None** to deselect all values.
6. In the search bar at the top of the list, start typing `soph`.
7. Tableau will show the results that start with those letters, such as **Sophia** and **Sophie**. Select both values:

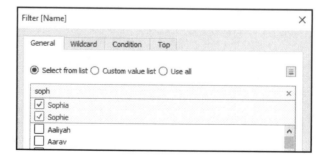

8. Click on **OK**.
9. Drag and drop **Frequency** to **Label** in the **Marks** card.
10. We have now created a chart with the summed total frequency of the names **Sophie** and **Sophia** per **State**. But, what if we wanted to know which of the two names is more popular in which state? We will achieve that by adding **Name** to **Color** in the **Marks** card.
11. Drag and drop **Name** from **Dimensions** onto **Color** in the **Marks** card:

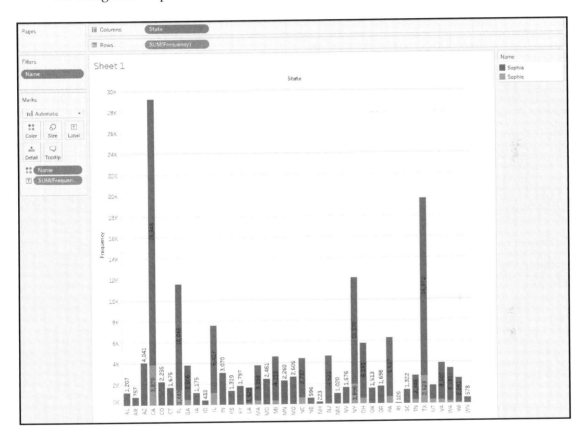

How it works...

When you add a discrete dimension (**Name**) to **Color**, Tableau disaggregates the measure you are using, **Frequency**, by the categories of **Name**, and assigns each category a different color. Since we filtered out all names except for **Sophia** and **Sophie**, only those two colors appeared in the chart. It's also possible, and often useful, to add a measure to **Color**. In that case, the value measure will be represented by a color gradient. For an example of adding a measure to **Color**, you can refer to the *Creating a map with a color gradient* recipe.

There's more...

It's possible to customize the colors in your view by performing the following steps:

1. Click on **Color** in the **Marks** card, and then click on **Edit Colors...**:

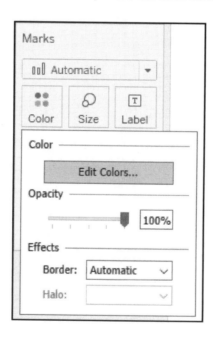

2. In the **Edit Colors[Name]** window that opens, you can select a color palette from the drop-down menu that appears and click on the **Assign Palette** button. This will assign colors from the palette that you chose to the categories of your dimension. You can also manually assign specific colors to a category by selecting it in the **Select Data Item** pane, and by clicking on the desired color on the right-hand side:

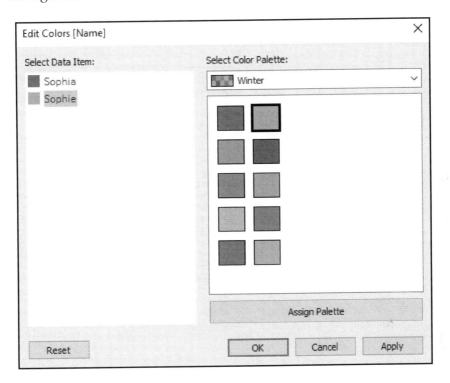

3. When you are satisfied with the colors, click **OK** to exit. Note that this will only affect the colors in the particular view you created.

4. You can also hardcode a color palette for a specific measure or dimension. Hover over the field pill under **Measures** or **Dimensions** and click on the white arrow that appears on it. In the drop-down menu, navigate to **Default Properties** | **Color...**:

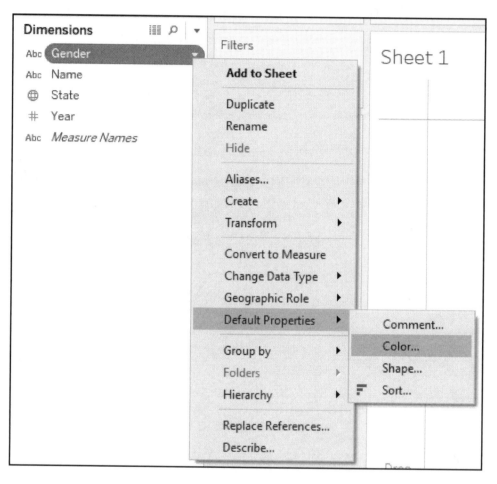

This will launch the **Edit Colors** window, where you can choose the color palette. However, once you assign your desired color palette to a field this way, it will be used by default every time you add this field to **Color** in a view.

If you plan to use a field in **Color** in more than one visualization, it's a good practice to hardcode the color palette for it. Using colors in your visualizations consistently makes them cleaner and easier to follow, especially as they get more complex.

See also

- For more information on color palettes, see the **Tableau Help** page at `https://onlinehelp.tableau.com/current/pro/desktop/en-us/viewparts_marks_markproperties_color.html`

Building a tree map

Tree maps are useful for showing relative proportions of many categories in a total. In this recipe, we will investigate the composition of our dataset to see which states are dominant, with the most records, and which are represented with fewer records.

Getting ready

Connect to the `Baby_names.csv` data source and open a new worksheet.

How to do it...

1. Drag and drop **Number of Records** from **Measures** onto **Size** in the **Marks** card.
2. Drag and drop **State** from **Dimensions** onto **Detail** in the **Marks** card.
3. Drag and drop **State** from **Dimensions** onto **Label** in the **Marks** card.

4. Drag and drop **Number of Records** from **Measures** onto **Label** in the **Marks** card:

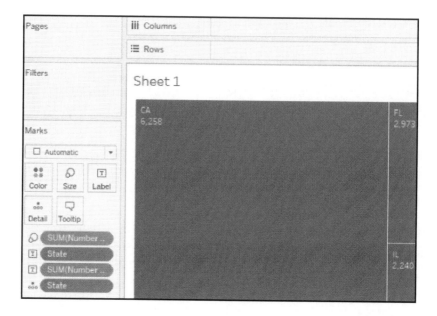

How it works...

The number of records is an automatically generated measure that simply represents the number of rows in the dataset. We are using it to see the relative representation of each state in our dataset.

There's more...

Placing a measure, in this case, **Number of Records**, on **Size** is necessary for creating a tree map. However, you can make your tree map even more intuitive by adding **Number of Records** to **Color** as well. You just need to drag and drop **Number of Records** from **Measures** onto **Color** in the **Marks** card button, and the value of **Number of Records** will also be reflected by a color gradient of the rectangles. You can also change and adjust the color palette by clicking on the **Color** button in the **Marks** card and choosing the settings you prefer:

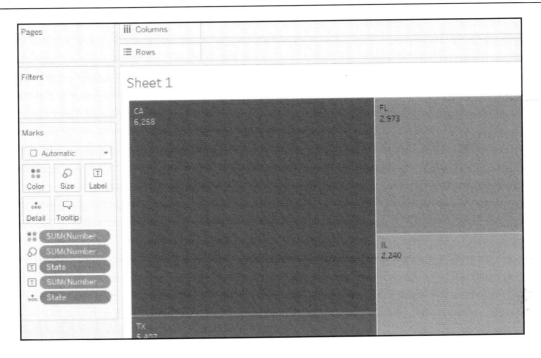

See also

- For more information, look at the following **Tableau Help** article on building tree maps: `https://onlinehelp.tableau.com/current/pro/desktop/en-us/buildexamples_treemap.html`

Building a map

Maps are a great way to present geographical data, as they are intuitive and easy to read. In this recipe, we will show name frequency by state, but this time using a map. This recipe will cover two frequently used ways to present data on a map: creating a map with circles of different sizes, and creating a filled map with a color gradient.

Getting ready

To complete this recipe, you will need to connect to the `Baby_names.csv` dataset and open a new blank worksheet.

How to do it...

First, we will make a map with circles.

Creating a map with circles

1. Drag and drop **State** into the worksheet workspace.
2. Drag and drop **Frequency** onto **Size** in the **Marks** card.
3. Click on **Size** in the **Marks** card, and move the slider to the center, through which we can increase and decrease the size of the circle in the following map:

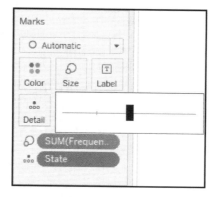

You can see the results in the following screenshot:

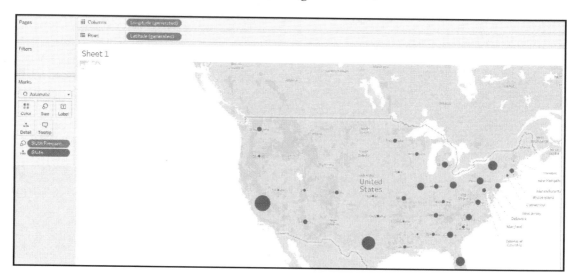

If the map is failing to display, navigate to **File|Workbook Locale** in the main menu toolbar and select **More....** When the **Set Workbook Locale** window opens, select **English (United States).**

Creating a map with a color gradient

1. Drag and drop **State** into the worksheet workspace.
2. Drag and drop **Frequency** onto **Color** in the **Marks** card:

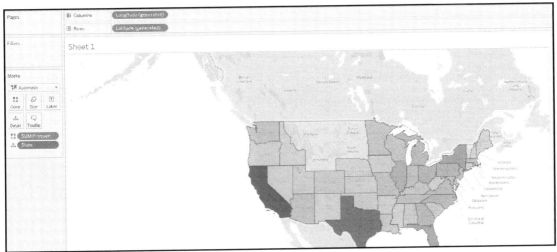

How it works...

Tableau has correctly recognized that the **State** dimension contains geographical information, and has assigned a geographical role to it. This is indicated by a small globe symbol (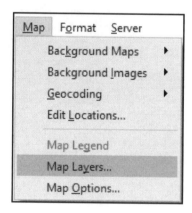) next to the dimension name in the **Dimensions** pane, as well as in the data preview on the **Data Source** page. Based on that, it has automatically generated two new measures, which are not in the dataset itself: **Longitude** and **Latitude**. When you drag and drop the **State** dimension into the worksheet workspace, the **Show Me** functionality is implemented. It places **State** in **Detail** in the **Marks** card, **Longitude** into the **Columns** shelf, and **Latitude** into the **Rows** shelf. Based on what we do with our measure, **Frequency**, Tableau automatically chooses the appropriate mark type, which is a circle or a map.

There's more...

It is possible to add and subtract layers from a map and change the map style by performing the following steps:

1. From the main menu toolbar, navigate to **Map | Map Layers...** to open the **Map Layers** pane:

2. In the **Map Layers** pane, you can add and remove map layers by checking and deselecting the boxes in front of them:

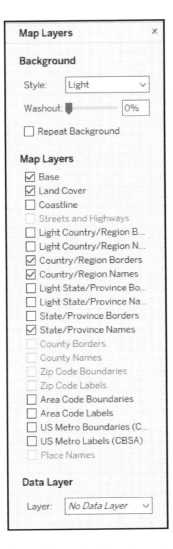

3. You can also add data layers by selecting them from the **Data Layer** drop-down menu. Depending on the data you are showing on your map, adding different data layers might add relevant information to your visualization.
4. It's also possible to adjust the background style under **Background**.

5. Set the map style and layers as default. This means that every time you create a new map, those settings will be applied.

See also

- For more on maps, see the **Tableau Help** page on this topic at `https:// onlinehelp.tableau.com/current/pro/desktop/en-us/maps_build.html`

Building a dual-axis map

In this recipe, you will learn how to create a dual-axis map. We will build on what we learned in the *Building a map* recipe and learn how to implement a dual axis.

Getting ready

Connect to the `Baby_names.csv` dataset and open a new worksheet.

How to do it...

1. Drag and drop **State** from **Dimensions** into the worksheet workspace so that a basic map appears.
2. Drag and drop **Latitude (generated)** from **Measures** into the **Rows** shelf to the right of the **Latitude (generated)** pill, which is already there:

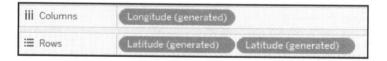

Now we have two maps, one beneath the other. Also, notice how new sections have appeared in the **Marks** card. There is the **All** section, followed by **Latitude (generated)**, which refers to the upper map, and **Latitude (generated) (2)**, which refers to the bottom map:

3. Click on the second section, **Latitude (generated)**, in the **Marks** card to expand it.
4. Drag and drop **Frequency** from **Measures** onto **Color**:

5. Click on the **Color** button and select **Edit Colors...**.

6. From the **Palette** drop-down menu, select **Gray**, and click on **OK**:

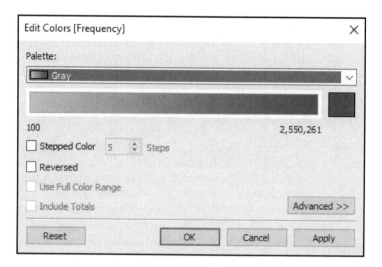

7. Click on the **Color** button again, and use the slider to decrease the opacity to around **51%**:

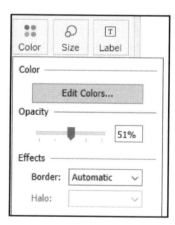

8. Click on the third section, **Latitude (generated) (2)**, to expand it. In it, drag and drop **Gender** from **Dimensions** onto **Color**.

9. Drag and drop **Frequency** from **Measures** onto **Size**.

10. Click on the **Automatic** drop-down menu and change the mark type to **Pie**:

11. Let's set the dual axis. In the **Rows** shelf, hover over the second **Latitude (generated)** pill so that a small white arrow appears on it:

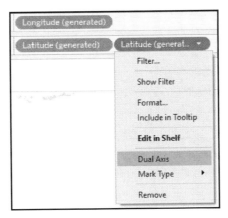

12. Click on the arrow, select **Dual Axis**, and you will get the following result:

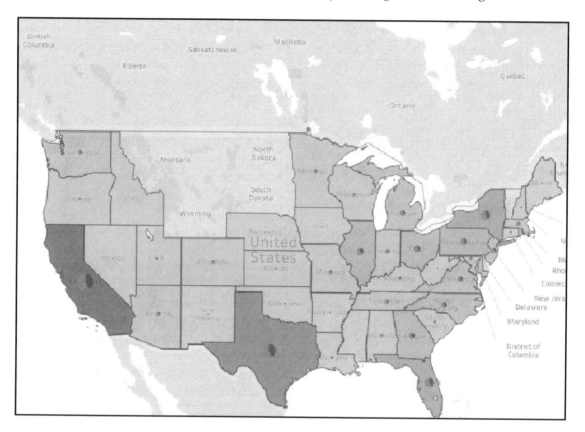

How it works...

Adding the **Latitude** measure to the **Rows** shelf twice duplicates our view, making two maps instead of one. The two maps initially have the same specifications in the **Marks** card and **State** in **Detail**. However, we then build them separately by adding different dimensions and measures on each of them, and they show different information. We have finally implemented the dual axis, and we have also made the maps overlap. We ended up with one map that has two layers.

There's more...

The dual axis can be implemented with different types of visualizations, not just maps. In the following example, we can see two different measures in the rows so that the upper bar chart shows **Frequency** and the lower chart shows **Number of Records**:

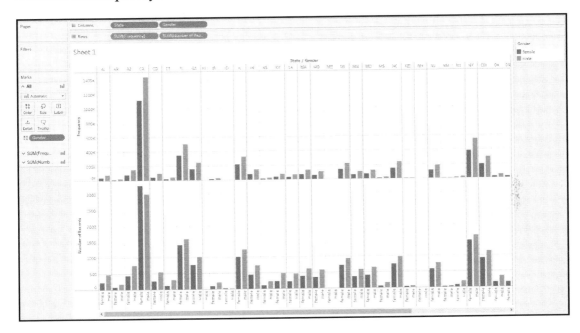

If we implement dual axis, both measures will be displayed in one chart:

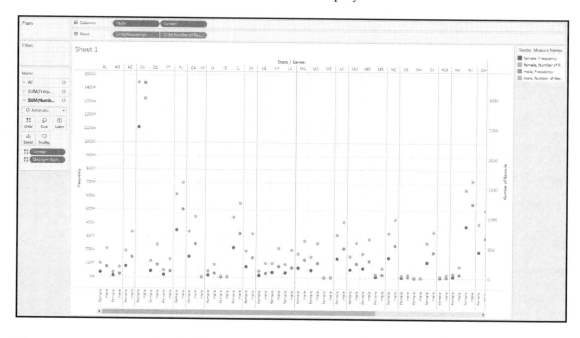

However, we must notice that the new chart has two y axes on each side—one showing **Frequency** and the other showing **Number of Records**. The axes are very different, as these two measures have different scales, thus showing that the same scale would make the measure with the narrower scale, in this case, **Number of Records**, look flat on the chart. However, Tableau does offer an option for synchronizing the axes, which is useful when the scales are similar.

To implement it, right-click on any of the two *y* axes and select **Synchronize Axis**:

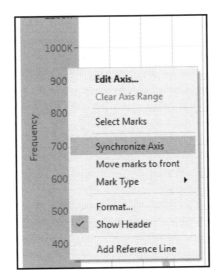

See also

- For more information, see the Tableau **Knowledge Base** article on dual axis: `https://kb.tableau.com/articles/howto/dual-axis-bar-chart-multiple-measures`

Customizing tooltips

When you hover over a point in your view, a tooltip will appear. Tooltips are small boxes, holding detailed information about a data point in the view, and are present by default. In this recipe, you will learn how to customize tooltips.

Getting ready

To follow this recipe, connect to the `Baby_names.csv` data source and open a new worksheet.

How to do it...

1. Drag and drop **Frequency** from **Measures** onto **Size** in the **Marks** card.
2. Drag and drop **State** from **Dimensions** onto **Detail** in the **Marks** card.
3. Drag and drop **State** from **Dimensions** onto **Label** in the **Marks** card.
4. Drag and drop **Frequency** from **Measures** to **Color** in the **Marks** card.
5. Click on the drop-down menu in the **Marks** card and select **Circle**:

6. Drag and drop **Name** from **Dimensions** into the **Filter** shelf.
7. In the **Filter [Name]** window, click **None** to deselect all values.
8. Start typing emma in the search bar at the top of the list, select **Emma**, and click on **OK**:

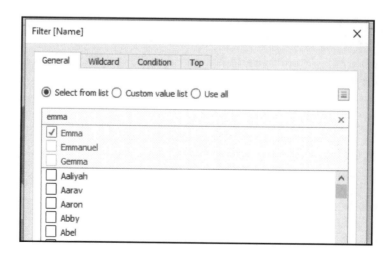

9. Drag and drop **Gender** from **Dimensions** onto **Detail** in the **Marks** card.

10. Drag and drop **Name** from **Dimensions** onto **Tooltip** in the **Marks** card.

11. Double-click on **Tooltip** in the **Marks** card.

12. In the **Edit Tooltip** window, hit *Enter* to add a row above the existing text and place your cursor in the new row.

13. Click on **Insert** and select **ATTR(Name)**:

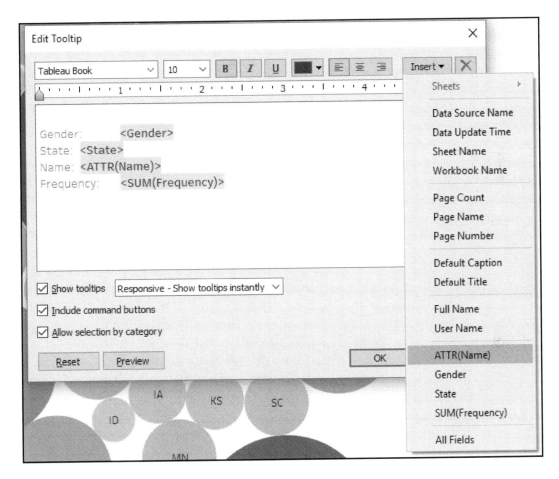

14. Click on **Insert** again and select **Gender**.

15. Between **<ATTR(Name)>** and **<Gender>**, type `is a beautiful`. After **<Gender>**, type `name`. The whole expression should be **<ATTR(Name)> is a beautiful <Gender> name**, as shown in the following screenshot:

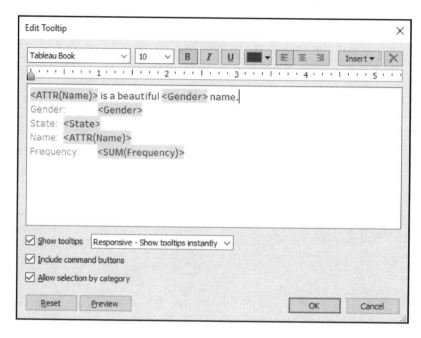

16. Click on **OK**. The expression we entered into the tooltip will now appear when you put your mouse over any of the circles:

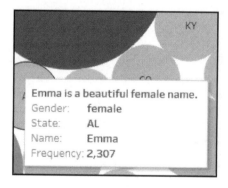

How it works...

Tooltips are, by default, set to hold information on the fields that are in the view and their current values. However, as we just saw, you can customize them by adding additional elements, or removing the ones that are there by default. We inserted fields such as **Name** and **Gender** into the **Tooltip** section; they will change automatically. If we change the **Name** filter from **Emma** to another name, it will change the value of the name in the sentence, as well as automatically update the gender.

There's more...

You can also insert another worksheet from the workbook into the tooltip. Let's say you want your user to be able to see where the particular state is on the map. We can do this by executing the following steps:

1. Create another sheet with the map, just by opening a blank worksheet and double-clicking on **State** in **Dimensions**.

2. On the original sheet, double-click on **Tooltip** to open the **Edit Tooltip** window and add an empty row:

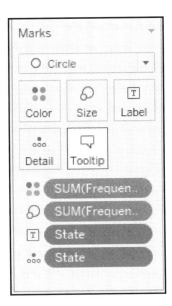

3. Click on **Insert** and navigate to **Sheets** | **Sheet 2**. Tableau will insert an expression referencing **Sheet 2** into the **Tooltip** section:

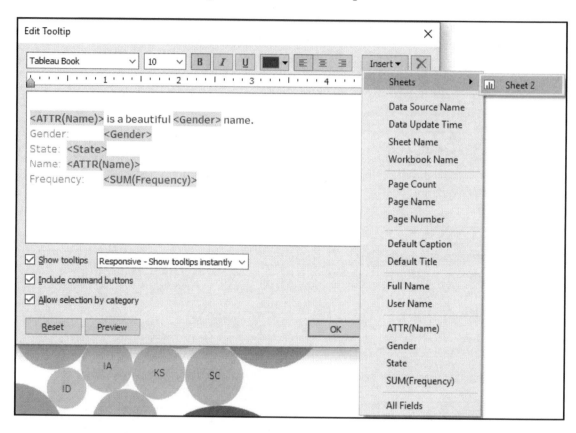

4. If you go to **Sheet 2**, you will notice that Tableau added **Tooltip (State)** as a filter. When your mouse cursor goes over any of the states in **Sheet 1**, a tooltip with a map marking that state will show up:

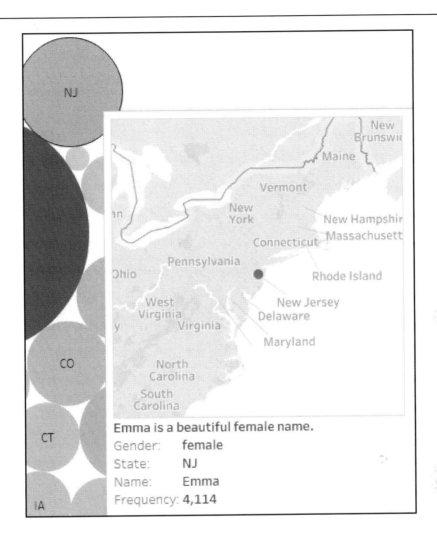

See also

- For more information on formatting tooltips, refer to the following **Tableau Help** page at `https://onlinehelp.tableau.com/current/pro/desktop/en-us/ formatting_specific_titlecaption.html`

2

Data Manipulation

In this chapter, we'll cover the following topics:

- Joining data sources
- Adding a secondary data source
- Data blending
- Data union
- Using Tableau Pivot
- Preparing data

Technical requirements

To follow the recipes outlined in this chapter, you'll need to have Tableau 2019.x installed. You'll also need to download and save the datasets associated with this chapter to your device:

- `Bread_basket_by_year.xlsx`, which can be found at: `https://github.com/PacktPublishing/Tableau-2018-Dot-1-Cookbook/blob/master/Bread_basket_by_year.xlsx`

- `Internet_satisfaction_by_region.csv`, which can be found at: `https://github.com/PacktPublishing/Tableau-2018-Dot-1-Cookbook/blob/master/Internet_satisfaction_by_region.csv`

- `Public_schools_1.csv`, which can be found at: `https://github.com/PacktPublishing/Tableau-2018-Dot-1-Cookbook/blob/master/Public_Schools_1.csv`

- `Public_schools_2.csv`, which can be found at: `https://github.com/PacktPublishing/Tableau-2018-Dot-1-Cookbook/blob/master/Public_Schools_2.csv`

- `Winery.csv`, which can be found at: `https://github.com/PacktPublishing/Tableau-2018-Dot-1-Cookbook/blob/master/Winery.zip`

- `Internet_satisfaction.csv`, which can be found at: `https://github.com/PacktPublishing/Tableau-2018-Dot-1-Cookbook/blob/master/Internet_satisfaction.csv`

- `Internet_usage.csv`, which can be found at: `https://github.com/PacktPublishing/Tableau-2018-Dot-1-Cookbook/blob/master/Internet_usage.csv`

Introduction

Before doing any work in Tableau, we must first connect to the data we'll be working on. In the first recipe in this book, *Connecting to data*, we learned how to connect to a data source. In this chapter, we'll build on that knowledge to become more skillful at manipulating, joining, unioning, and transforming data sources. In the last recipe of this chapter, *Preparing data*, we'll also address the topic of data preparation and getting our data ready for visualizing and further analysis.

In this chapter, we'll be using multiple datasets. In the first recipe, *Joining data sources*, we'll be using two datasets, `Public_Schools_1.csv` and `Public_Schools_2.csv`, which contain data on Boston public schools for the school year 2018/2019. The dataset originally comes from Kaggle's official site. In the *Adding a secondary data source* and *Data blending* recipes, we'll use the `Internet_satisfaction.csv` and `Internet_usage.csv` datasets, which describe the results of a consumer survey on internet usage in Serbia, as well as data on internet penetration per region of the country. In the *Data union* recipe, we'll be using `Bread_basket_by_year.xlsx` (originally found on `Kaggle.com`), which contains data about transactions in a bakery divided into two tables holding data for different years. In the *Using Tableau Pivot* recipe, we'll use `Internet_satisfaction_by_region.csv`, which holds some results of a customer satisfaction survey found in the `Internet_satisfaction.csv` file, but organized in a slightly different format. Finally, in the *Preparing data* recipe, we'll use the `Winery.csv` dataset (originally found on `Kaggle.com`), containing data on wines, their origin, pricing, and rating.

Joining data sources

The data we are working in is often contained in multiple tables. We can create a single, virtual table out of multiple original tables by joining them using common fields or keys. The result is a wider table that contains columns originating from different tables. The rows are matched by the values of the column, key, and fields.

Getting ready

In this recipe, we'll be using two
datasets, `Public_Schools_1.csv` and `Public_Schools_2.csv`. Make sure you have
both datasets saved to your device.

How to do it...

1. Upon opening Tableau, from the **Connect** pane on the left-hand side, choose **Text file** as shown in the following screenshot:

2. When the **Open** window opens, navigate to your local copy of
   `Public_Schools_1.csv`, select it, and click on **Open**.

3. Tableau will take you to the **Data Source** page, showing that you've successfully
   connected to the chosen data source. On the left-hand side of the page, under
   Files, all of the text files in the same folder are listed, and among them
   is `Public_Schools_2.csv`:

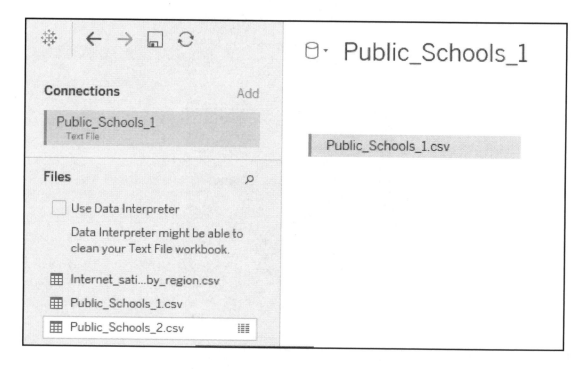

4. Drag and drop `Public_Schools_2.csv` from **Files** to the whitespace next to `Public_Schools_1.csv`:

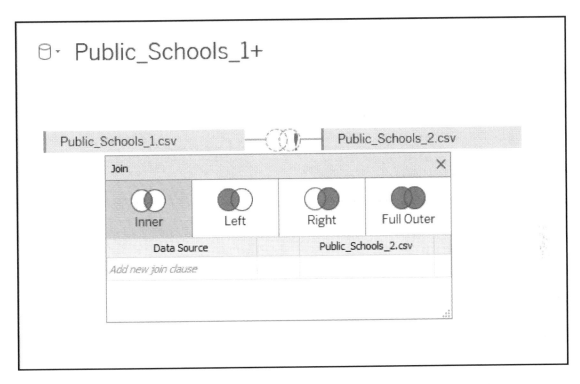

5. In the **Join** window that opens, click on the **Add new join clause** drop-down menu under **Data Source** and select **Objectid 1**.

6. Click on the white field on the right-hand side of the = sign, under **Public_Schools_2.csv**.
7. From the drop-down menu, select **School ID**:

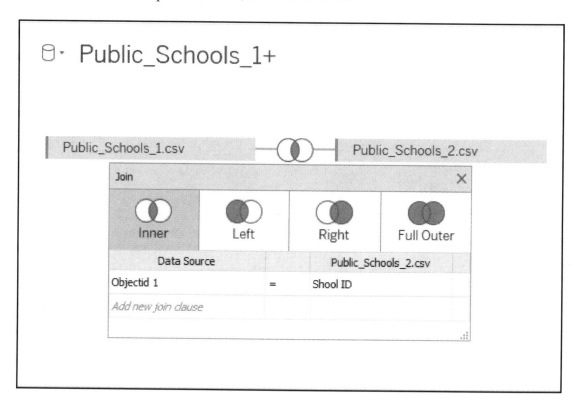

8. Click on **X** to close the **Join** window. You have successfully joined the data, and you can inspect the new joined table in the preview, which is shown in the following screenshot:

How it works...

In the preceding steps, we joined two tables, `Public_Schools_1` and `Public_Schools_2`. We matched the rows in the two tables using a unique key. In the **Join** window, we specified that the key fields in the two datasets are **Objectid 1** and **School ID**, respectively. These two fields contain exact same values, which allows Tableau to create one-on-one mapping between the tables. However, they have different names, which is why we need to specify them manually. If their names were the same, Tableau would automatically make the connection.

There's more...

What we performed is an **Inner** join of the two tables. There are also other joins, such as **Left**, **Right**, and **Full Outer**, offered in Tableau. They're generally available to switch between, in the **Join** window.

Using an inner join was appropriate in our case, because all of the rows in both tables could be matched—thanks to a unique key field. The inner joins produce tables with cases that have been matched in both tables.

The **Left** join keeps all of the values from the left tables, while using only the cases from the right table that have a match in the left table, as shown in the following screenshot:

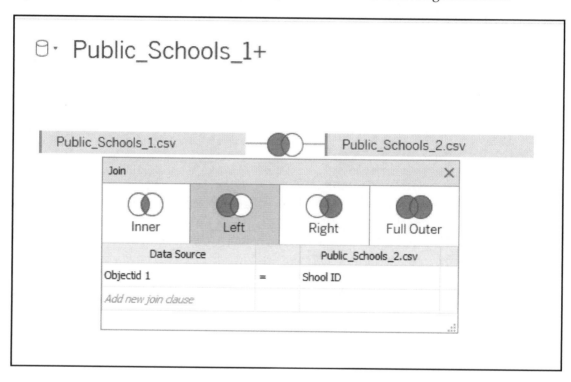

The **Right** join works on the same principle, but keeping all of the values from the right table, as shown in the following screenshot:

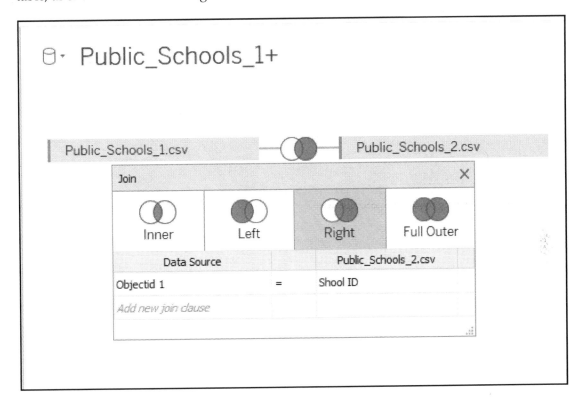

Finally, a **Full Outer** join keeps all of the cases from both tables, regardless of whether they have a match in the other table or not. Null values will be placed in cases where a match isn't found:

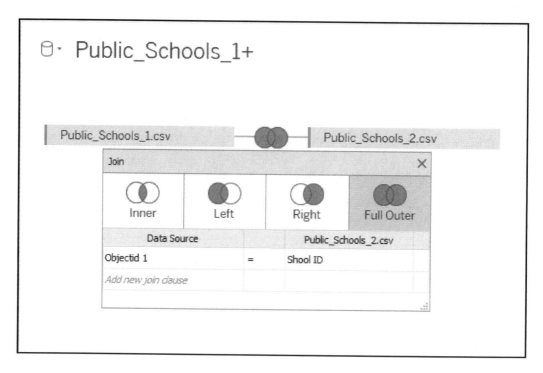

As of the 2018.2 release, Tableau also offers another kind of joins—**Spatial** joins. They allow you to join points and polygons from spatial tables on the basis of their location. This is achieved through a new joining predicate known as **intersect**, which matches the location of points from one table to polygons in another table, joining data when a point lies within a polygon.

See also

- For more detailed information on joining and troubleshooting your joins, you can refer to the **Tableau Help** page on the topic at `https://onlinehelp.tableau.com/current/pro/desktop/en-us/joining_tables.htm#About`.
- More information on spatial joins can be found at `https://www.tableau.com/about/blog/2018/8/perform-advanced-spatial-analysis-spatial-join-now-available-tableau-92166`.

Adding a secondary data source

When creating a workbook, or a dashboard, we often have multiple data sources that're relevant for the topic and want to include the data from all of them. However, we might not want to join them—we just want to include all of the visualizations that come from unrelated data sources in the same workbook or dashboard. We can easily do that by simply adding data sources to our workbook. Let's see how.

Getting ready

In this recipe, we'll be using two datasets, `Internet_satisfaction.csv` and `Internet_usage.csv`, as data sources. Make sure you have them both saved to your device.

How to do it...

1. Upon opening Tableau, from the **Connect** pane on the left-hand side, choose **Text file**.
2. When the **Open** window opens, navigate to your local copy of `Internet_satisfaction.csv`, select it, and click **Open**.

3. Tableau will take you to the **Data Source** page, where you can preview your file. Click on the **Sheet 1** tab to open a new blank worksheet.

4. In the new blank worksheet, at the top of the **Data** pane, notice that **Internet_satisfaction** is your data source. Now, let's add a secondary data source. In the main menu toolbar, click on **Data**.

5. From the drop-down menu, select **New Data Source**:

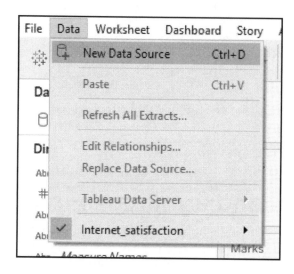

6. Alternatively, click on the new data source icon:

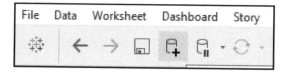

7. A **Connect** drop-down menu will open. From it, select **Text file**:

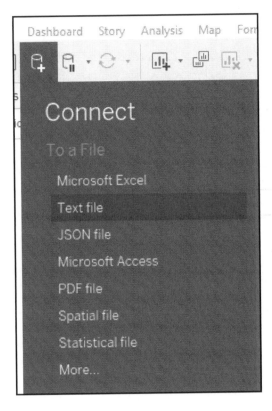

8. In the **Open** window that opens, navigate to your copy of `Internet_usage.csv`, select it, and click on **Open**.

9. Once again, the **Data Source** pane will open, this time previewing the `Internet_usage.csv` data source. Click on the **Sheet 1** tab again.

10. Notice that **Internet_usage** has now appeared in the top of the **Data** pane alongside **Internet_satisfaction**:

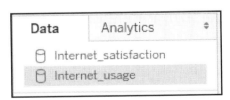

11. Try clicking on the data sources to switch between them. Notice how measures and dimensions change when you select a different data source.

How it works...

Once we've connected to two data sources, we can use them both to create views. Let's try it:

1. In the top of the **Data** pane, select **Internet_satisfaction** as the active data source by clicking on it.
2. Drag and drop **HH internet type** from **Dimensions** into the **Columns** shelf.
3. Drag and drop **Satisfaction overall** from **Measures** onto **Text** in the **Marks** card.
4. Right-click on the **SUM(Satisfaction overall)** pill in the **Marks** card, navigate to **Measure (Sum)**, and from the drop-down menu, select **Average**:

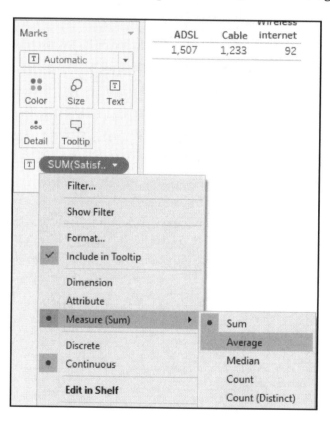

5. We've created a view using the `Internet_satisfaction` data source:

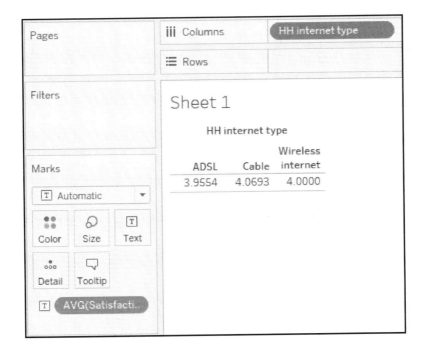

6. Now, open a new blank worksheet by clicking on the New Worksheet tab at the bottom of the workspace.
7. In the top of the **Data** pane, select **Internet_usage** as the active data source by clicking on it.
8. Drag and drop **Settlement type** from **Dimensions** into the **Columns** shelf.
9. Drag and drop **Internet penetration** from **Measures** onto **Text** in the **Marks** card.

10. Right-click on the **SUM(Internet penetration)** pill in the **Marks** card, navigate to **Measure (Sum)** and from the drop-down menu select **Average**:

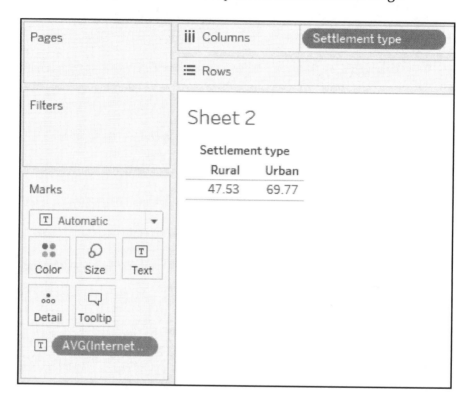

Here, we've created two tables that contain data and fields from two different data sources, as shown in the preceding screenshot.

There's more...

It's possible to connect to more than two data sources. However, be careful to use them in separate worksheets to prevent data blending. If you try using two data sources in the same worksheet, Tableau will automatically try to blend them. We will talk more about data blending in the next recipe, *Data blending*.

See also

- Feel free to refer to this page for more information: `https://kb.tableau.com/articles/howto/connecting-multiple-data-sources-without-joining-or-blending`

Data blending

Sometimes, our data sources might not be suitable for joining for multiple reasons. For example, they might be on different levels of aggregation, resulting in duplicates upon joining, or you might wish to use data source types that don't support cross-database joins, such as Google Analytics. But, we also want to make visualizations that contain fields from different data sources. That's when data blending comes in handy—it allows us to make a connection between data sources when joining isn't appropriate or possible.

Getting ready

Follow the steps from the previous recipe, *Adding a secondary data source*, to connect to the `Internet_satisfaction.csv` and `Internet_usage.csv` data sources.

How to do it...

1. We start off connected to two data sources: `Internet_satisfaction.csv` and `Internet_usage.csv` and a new open blank worksheet opened.
2. In the main menu toolbar, navigate to **Data**.

3. From the drop-down menu, select **Edit Relationships...**:

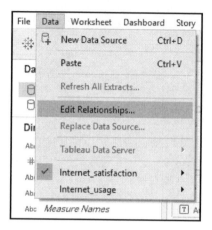

4. In the **Relationships** window, select **Custom**.
5. Click on **Add...**:

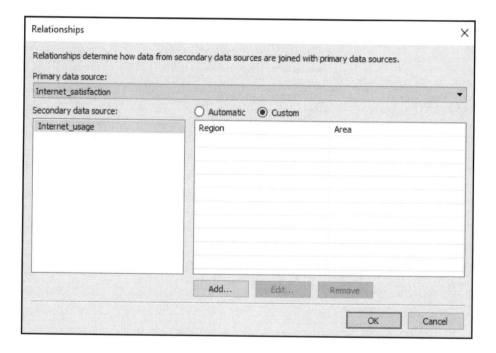

6. In the **Add/Edit Field Mapping** window, click on **Area** in one pane and **Region** in the other pane, so that they're highlighted in blue:

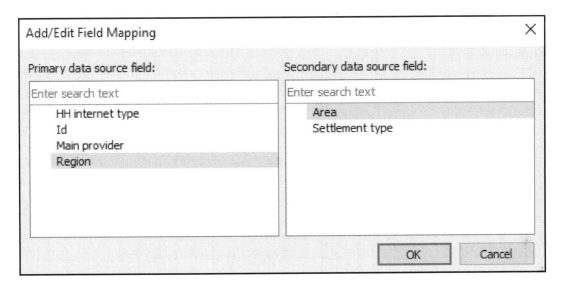

7. Click on **OK**.

8. Mapping of **Region** and **Area** will appear in the **Relationships** window now. Click on **OK** to exit it as well:

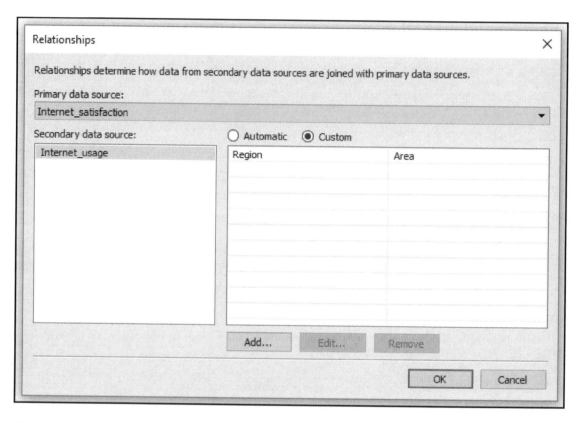

We've successfully blended our data sources!

How it works...

By blending the two data sources, we've instructed Tableau to treat **Area** from the Internet_usage data source and **Region** from the Internet_satisfaction data source as the same field. Now, we can create views that include fields from both data sources, despite them being on very different levels of detail and hence unsuitable for joining. To see how this works, let's create a new visualization that includes fields from both data sources:

1. On **Sheet 1**, in the **Data** pane, select **Internet_usage** as the active data source by clicking on it.

2. Drag and drop **Area** from **Dimensions** into the **Rows** shelf.
3. Drag and drop **Internet penetration** from **Measures** onto **Text** in the **Marks** card.
4. Right-click on the **Internet penetration** pill in the **Marks** card, navigate to **Measure (Sum)**, and from the drop-down menu, select **Average**.
5. In the **Data** pane, select **Internet_satisfaction** as the active data source by clicking on it.
6. Drag and drop **Satisfaction overall** from **Measures** onto **Text** in the **Marks** card.
7. Right-click on the **Satisfaction overall** pill in the **Marks** card, navigate to **Measure (Sum)**, and from the drop-down menu, select **Average**:

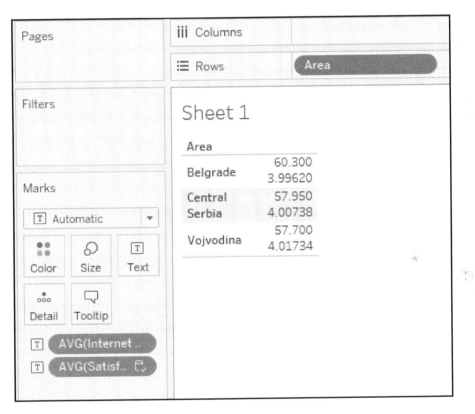

We've now created a single table showing internet penetration and overall satisfaction per region, with our measures coming from different data sources, as shown in the preceding screenshot.

There's more...

Note the orange link symbol ⧉ on the right-hand side of the **Region** field under **Dimensions**. It denotes that this is the linking field. You can easily stop using it as the linking field by clicking on the link symbol. It will change to a gray symbol ⧉ to signal that the link is broken.

If two fields in your data sources have the same name and the same values, Tableau will automatically blend your data sources using them. For example, if we renamed **Area** to **Region**, we wouldn't need to manually match these two fields—Tableau would automatically do it for us.

Even if Tableau performed the data blending automatically, it's always a good idea to check whether the fields have been matched correctly by opening the **Relationship** window and inspecting existing relationships.

See also

- You can find more information on data blending on the **Tableau Help** page on the topic at https://onlinehelp.tableau.com/current/pro/desktop/en-us/multiple_connections.htm

Data union

Tableau data union functionality allows us to merge multiple tables by appending the rows of one table to another.

Getting ready

In this recipe, we'll be using the Bread_basket_by_year.xlsx file, so make sure you have saved it to you device.

How to do it...

1. Upon opening Tableau, from the **Connect** pane on the left-hand side, choose **Microsoft Excel**:

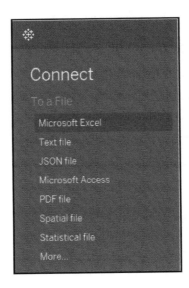

2. When the **Open** window opens, navigate to your local copy of `Bread_basket_by_year.xlsx`, select it, and click **Open**.

3. On the **Data Source** page, two tables contained within our data source, **2017** and **2018**, appear. Beneath them, we see the **New Union** option:

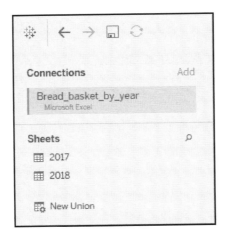

4. Drag and drop **New Union** onto the canvas.

5. A new **Union** window will open. Drag and drop **2017** from **Sheets** into the **Union** window as well, as shown in the following screenshot:

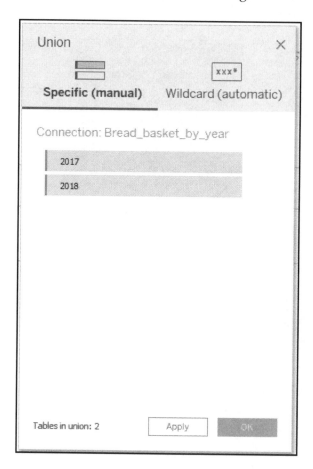

6. Click on **Apply** and then on **OK** to exit the **Union** window.

How it works...

We have successfully unioned the two tables. In the **Data Source** page, they're now previewed as a single table, with two new columns that don't exist in either of the datasets—**Sheet** and **Table Name**. These two columns provide the metadata about the union, by denoting the source of the rows as shown in the following screenshot:

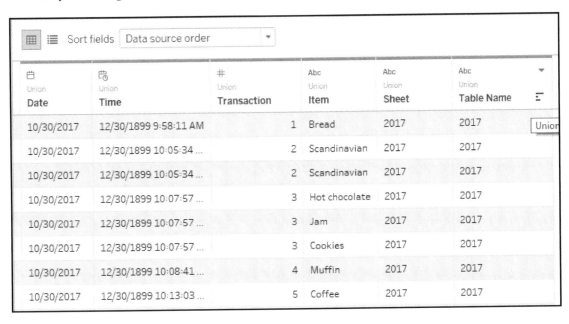

What actually happened is that the rows from both datasets were merged into one table. We can see that if we open a new blank worksheet and drag and drop **Date** from **Dimensions** into the **Rows** shelf, the new unioned data source contains years coming from both datasets. Our union was successful because the tables had the same number of columns and the same column names. This allowed Tableau to match columns correctly.

There's more...

It's also possible to union tables in Tableau using wildcard search. This means setting up search criteria to search for a string in tables' names, and letting Tableau automatically union the tables the names of which satisfy the specified criteria.

See also

- For more information on data unions, see the **Tableau Help** page at https://onlinehelp.tableau.com/current/pro/desktop/en-us/union.htm

Using Tableau Pivot

Sometimes, our data isn't organized in a format that's suitable for creating views we would like to produce. Tableau Pivot functionality offers an easy way to restructure our data into a format that might be more suited to our needs.

Getting ready

To perform the steps in this recipe, we'll be using the `Internet_satisfaction_by_region.csv` file as the data source. Make sure you have it saved to your device and connect to it.

How to do it...

1. In the **Data Source** page, hold the *Ctrl* key and click on the header of all three fields in the data source preview to select them all.
2. Release the *Ctrl* key and right-click on any of the headers.

3. In the drop-drown menu, select **Pivot,** as shown in the following screenshot:

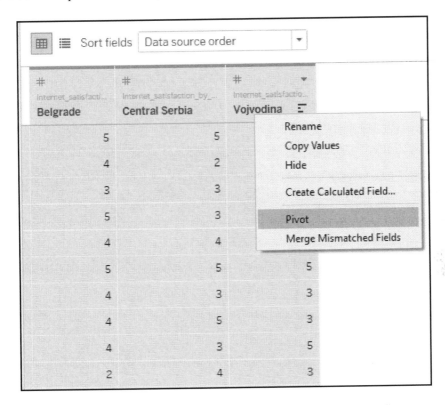

How it works...

In the preview on the **Data Source** page, we see that the format of the data has changed. The original column names—**Belgrade**, **Central Serbia**, and **Vojvodina**—have now become labels in a new column—**Pivot Field Names**.

On the other hand, the values from the three original columns have all been merged into one new column—**Pivot Field Values**:

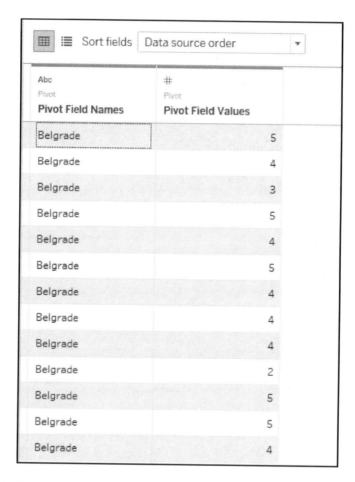

What happened is that we've simply transposed the table, so that we have values from all three columns placed into one column (one beneath the other), while the labels in the **Pivot Field Names** column denote the original column each value (row) originates from.

If we navigate to **Sheet 1,** we'll see that we now have **Pivot Field Names** as a dimension, and **Pivot Field Values** as a measure. For ease of use, we can rename them into something more intuitive. We can do this by right-clicking on the field and selecting **Rename** from the drop-down menu. We can then type in the desired name. For example, we can rename **Pivot Field Names** to **Region** and **Pivot Field Values** to **Satisfaction with internet**:

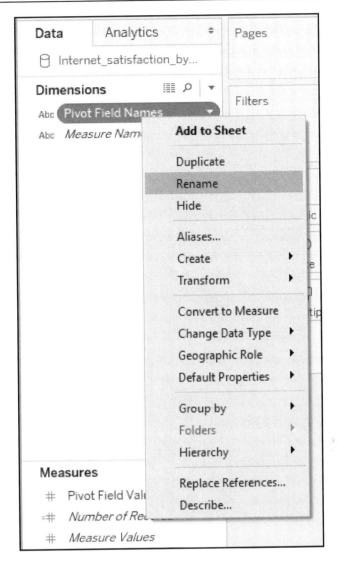

This new structure of the data source is much handier than the original one, because it allows us to make visualizations containing all three regions. Let's see how:

1. Drag and drop **Region** from **Dimensions** into the **Columns** shelf.

2. Drag and drop **Satisfaction with** internet from **Measures** into the **Rows** shelf:

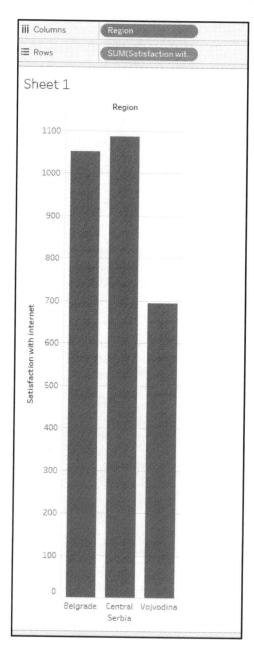

We've created a chart with a single measure and single dimensions that we'd previously created by pivoting our data source.

 Keep in mind that other sheets using a data source might be affected by pivoting. If any of the original columns that're being pivoting have already been used in a view, they won't be available anymore after pivoting.

There's more…

You can also pivot your data by using a custom SQL query, by simply adding the UNION ALL operator to it.

See also

- Check out the **Tableau Help** page on data pivoting, including pivoting with SQL queries at https://onlinehelp.tableau.com/current/pro/desktop/en-us/pivot.htm

Preparing data

Once we have connected to our data, we want to start making visualizations. However, our data might need some more touch-ups before it's ready to produce some stunning charts. This recipe will cover some common steps we need to take upon importing a data source in order to prepare it for further analysis.

Getting ready

Throughout this recipe, we'll be using the Winery.csv dataset. Make sure you have it saved to your device and are connected to it.

How to do it…

The following short recipes will guide you through several steps you'll often need to take when preparing your data for visualizing.

Splitting fields

In this recipe, we'll learn how to split a field into multiple fields:

1. In the **Data Source** page, right-click on the header of the **Taster Name** field.
2. Alternatively, navigate to **Sheet 1**, and right-click on the **Taster Name** field under **Dimensions**. In the drop-down menu, navigate to **Transform**:

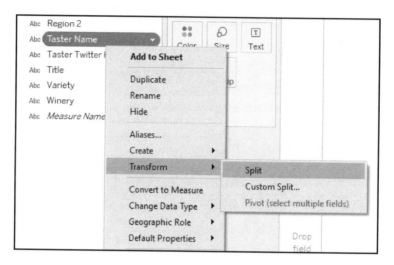

3. From the drop-down menu, select **Split**:

We've now created two new fields—**Taster Name - Split 1** and **Taster Name - Split 2**:

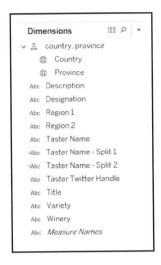

Converting measures into dimensions

Now, let's see how to convert measures into dimensions:

1. Right-click on the **F1** field under **Measures**.
2. From the drop-down menu, select **Convert to Dimension**:

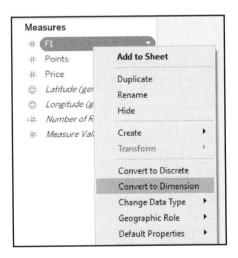

Renaming fields

Let's rename some of our fields to make them easier to use:

1. In the **Data Source** page, double-click on the **Taster Name – Split 1** text in the column header:

2. Alternatively, navigate to **Sheet 1**, right-click on the **Taster Name - Split 1** field under **Dimensions** in the **Data** pane, and select **Rename**:

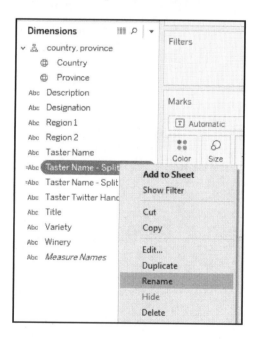

3. Type in the new name of the field as `Taster First Name`:

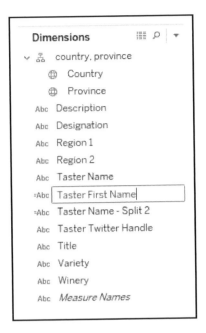

4. Double-click on **Taster Name – Split 2** in the **Data Source** page:

5. Rename the field to `Taster Last Name`:

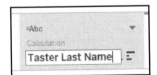

Adding aliases

Finally, let's add an alias to one of our fields:

1. Navigate to **Sheet 1**.
2. Drag and drop **Taster Name** from **Dimensions** into the **Rows** shelf.
3. Drag and drop **Taster Last Name** from **Dimensions** into the **Rows** shelf. We see that the taster named **Sean P. Sullivan** had his name incorrectly parsed due to having a middle initial—his actual last name was cut off and his middle initial is saved as his last name, as shown in the following screenshot:

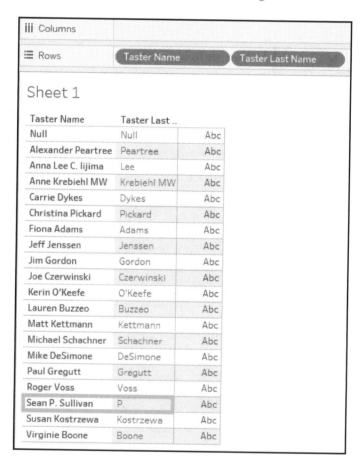

Let's correct that by adding an alias.

4. Right-click on the **Taster Last Name** field under **Dimensions**.
5. From the drop-down menu, select **Aliases**:

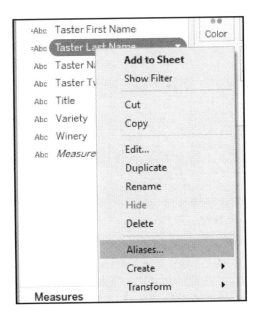

6. Alternatively, right-click on the **Taster Last Name** pill in the **Rows** shelf, and select **Edit Aliases...**.
7. In the **Edit Aliases [Taster Last Name]** window, scroll down to find the value **P**.
8. Click on the text **P.** in the right column, under **Value (Alias)**.

9. Instead of **P.**, type in the actual last name of the wine taster—Sullivan:

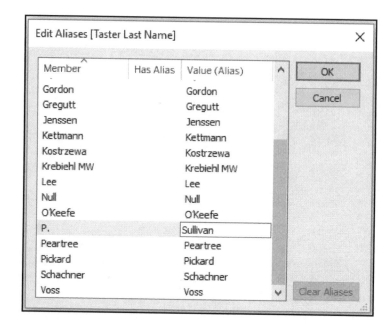

10. Click on **OK** to exit the window.

How it works...

In this recipe, we've performed some basic data preparation.

In the first step, we split the field **Taster Name** into two fields—one containing the first and one the last name of the wine taster. Of course, this step wasn't necessary, but it's a step that often needs to be performed when dealing with string fields. It allows for more detail and flexibility in data analysis—instead of having the first and the last name concatenated, we now have them in separate columns, and we have used them separately to analyze data only by first name, last name, or both.

The next step we performed was converting a field, **F1**, from a measure into a dimension. We performed this step because **F1** is actually an index field. It isn't really a continuous measure, although Tableau automatically designated it as one due to its numerical content. But we know its values are actually discrete, because they don't represent a quantity—they serve merely as a unique identifier of the cases (rows). When to convert a measure into a dimension, and vice versa, depends exclusively on our judgement and familiarity with the dataset. We should have a good understanding of what the fields in our dataset actually represent and adjust them to a measure/dimension according to our knowledge.

In the third step, we renamed the fields we produced when splitting the **Taster Name** field. The names automatically assigned by Tableau weren't very informative. When creating views, we always want to make sure both we ourselves and the end users of our workbook or dashboard know exactly what's being presented. We should always strive to make fieldnames clear, unambiguous, and informative.

Finally, we assigned an alias to the **Taster Last Name** field member. Aliases are alternative names we can assign to members of discrete dimensions. In this case, we used an alias to correct a case of inappropriately parsed text resulting from a split. But you can use aliases whenever you would like to change a dimension member's name. As we saw, it isn't necessary to assign aliases to all of the members of a dimension—you can assign an alias to only one member, to all of them, or to any number in between.

There's more...

When splitting string fields, it's important to carefully inspect your data before and after splitting. As we saw in this example, it can easily happen that some instances don't follow the same format as the majority, and they won't be properly split.

Sometimes, the splits we need to make are quite complex—the fields might not contain the same number of separators (as was the case our example) or they might contain different separators. More frequently than not, the dataset you're using will also be too large to manually correct the fields that aren't properly split. For those and similar cases, Tableau offers custom splits, as well as splitting the fields through regular expressions.

See also

- See the **Tableau Help** page on splitting data at `https://onlinehelp.tableau.com/current/pro/desktop/en-us/split.htm`.

- Also, you can refer to: `https://onlinehelp.tableau.com/current/pro/desktop/en-us/datafields_fieldproperties_aliases_ex1editing.htm` for more information on creating and editing aliases.

- You can also refer to `Chapter 1`, *Getting Started with Tableau Software*, to learn more about data types, measures, and dimensions.

3
Tableau Extracts

In this chapter, we will cover the following topics:

- Overview of different file formats in Tableau
- Creating a data source extract
- Configuring an incremental extract
- Upgrading to Hyper
- Creating extracts using cross-database joins
- Troubleshooting extracts with Tableau Server

Introduction

This chapter will cover how the Tableau dashboard performance is boosted by using extracts. We'll look at different types of Tableau file formats and types of extracts. The chapter introduces us to Tableau's in-memory fast-data-engine technology, called Hyper, that was released in October 2017, and we'll discuss what updates to expect with version 2018.3. This chapter will enable us to optimize performance of their Tableau dashboards using aggregated extracts, dimension reduction, extract filters, incremental extract refreshes, and cross-data joins. The principles we use to connect to text files, although very simple examples, can apply to more sophisticated data sources.

Overview of different file formats in Tableau

We'll look at the different file formats used in Tableau: **Tableau Workbooks (*.twb)**, **Tableau Bookmarks (*.tbm)**, **Tableau Packaged Workbooks (.twbx)**, and **Tableau Extracts (*.hyper or .tde)**.

How to do it...

In this recipe, we'll learn about the different file formats in Tableau. Tableau Extracts will be introduced in this recipe and covered in more detail in the *Creating a data source extract* recipe.

Tableau Workbook (TWB)

A **Tableau Workbook (TWB)** is created by the Tableau Desktop. They hold the analytics you create as a collection of one or more of the following: worksheets, dashboards, or stories. Workbooks help to organize your insights. Users can view workbooks on a desktop or server. If sharing these workbooks, the recipient must have access to the data source being used. Workbooks are saved with the `.twb` extension.

To save a workbook, go to **File | Save As**. Provide a name for the **File name** field and select **Tableau Workbook (*.twb),** as shown in the following screenshot:

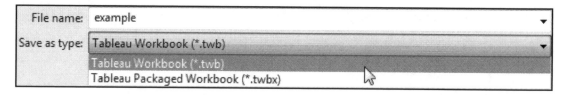

Tableau Packaged Workbook

Workbooks often reference external resources, such as data sources, images, data files, or extract files. When you save a workbook to share with others, it's best to save a packaged workbook instead. Packaged workbooks are made of the workbook and the external resources. They are saved with the `.twbx` extension. Packaged workbooks can be viewed using a desktop, server, or reader.

To save a **Tableau Packaged Workbook (TWBX)**, go to **File | Save As**. Provide a name for the the **File name** field and select **Tableau Packaged Workbook**:

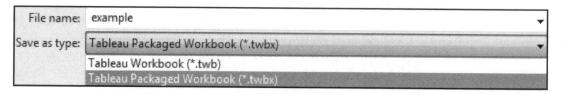

Tableau Bookmark

Tableau Bookmark (TBM) can be used to save the individual worksheet of a workbook. It can include data connections and formatting. The major benefit of bookmarks is that they allow two or more developers to work on the same data, where they can then collate their worksheets to a single workbook. Bookmarks can be accessed from any workbook using the **Bookmark** menu if they are saved in the Tableau repository:

1. To save a bookmark, go to **Window** | **Bookmark** | **Create Bookmark**:

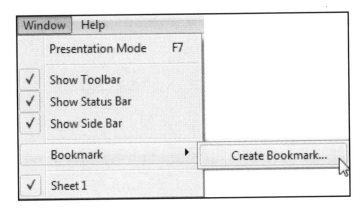

2. To access a bookmark, go to **Window** | **Bookmark** and find them listed under the **Create Bookmark...** option:

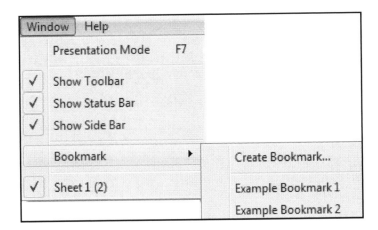

Tableau Data Extract

Tableau Data Extract (**TDE**) contains a compressed local snapshot of the data pulled from any data source based on the join and extract filter conditions specified. Under the hood, it's a columnar store, which makes aggregation and column access very quick. Generally, this will be easier to work with than live-querying the database for every change. Data extracts can be published to the server so they can be used by others and scheduled to update on a regular cadence. We'll go into detail of how to create an extract in the *Creating a data source extract* recipe.

Hyper

Hyper is a new the technology used in Tableau's data engine since 10.5. It allows users to build bigger extracts more quickly than traditional data extracts. Users dealing with large volumes of data can benefit from upgrading. In 2018.3, we see a new feature that allows users to choose how their data is stored, via a single-table or multiple-table extract option. Multiple-table extracts can potentially improve performance and reduce the extract size. There are conditions on when multiple-table extracts can be used, detailed in the *Creating a data source extract* recipe.

How it works...

In this section, we will look briefly at the TWB, TWBX, and TBM file formats.

Tableau Workbook

We saved a workbook by using **File** and **Save As**. We provided a filename for the **File name** field and selected **Tableau Workbook**.

Tableau Packaged Workbook (TWBX)

We saved a **Tableau Packaged Workbook** (**TWBX**) by using **File** and **Save As**. We provided a a filename for the **File name** field and selected **Tableau Packaged Workbook**.

Tableau Bookmark (TBM)

We saved a **Tableau Bookmark** (**TBM**) bookmark by going to the **Window** menu. We chose **Bookmark** and then selected **Create Bookmark....**

We accessed the bookmark by going to the **Window** menu. We chose **Bookmark** and **Create Bookmark...**, and then we selected the bookmarks listed within the menu.

Creating a data source extract

In this recipe, we'll learn how to create a data source extract.

Getting ready

Use Tableau 2019.x. Make sure you know how to connect to your data. We can also refer to the *Connecting to Data* recipe in `Chapter 1`, *Getting Started with Tableau Software*.

How to do it...

We'll quickly go through an example of connecting to data in text files in order to create the extract.

Connecting to data

To follow along in this example, connect to `books_tags.csv` and `books.csv`, and then perform the following steps:

1. Use **Text file** to connect to `books_tags.csv`:

2. Add another text file connection to `books.csv`:

3. Join on **Goodreads Book Id** and **Book Id**:

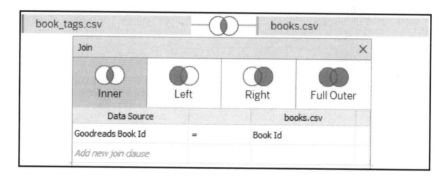

Creating an extract

After we've successfully connected to the data, we can create an extract, which can be accomplished in multiple places within Tableau. Here, we'll describe a method from the **Data Source** tab:

1. On the **Data Source** tab, select the **Extract** radial button:

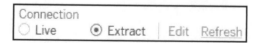

2. Click on the **Sheet 1** tab to initiate the extract:

3. Choose a name for the file and click on **Save**. Here, we have chosen the defaults:

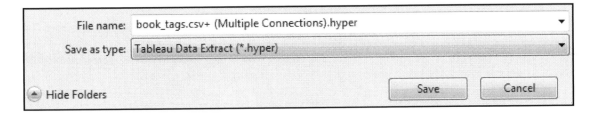

Optional settings for extracts

1. There are several options to optimize how the data should be stored, which can help with extract sizes and refresh times. Use the **Edit** link for the menu:

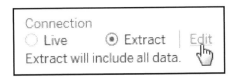

2. We can configure how the data should be stored by considering the following two available options:

   - **Single table**: This option is the default structure used by Tableau. Select the **Single table** option if the amount of data should be limited with extract filters, aggregations, limiting rows, or when using pass-through functions.
   - **Multiple tables**: Select **Multiple tables** if your extract has one or more equality joins and the data types of these columns are identical. The options to specify how much data to extract are not valid with **Multiple tables** and will be grayed out:

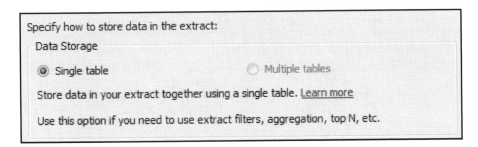

When choosing the **Single table** storage, go to *step 2*. When choosing **Multiple tables** storage, go to *step 5*.

3. For **Single table** storage, it is optional to add filters, select **Add...** to limit the data based on a column and value:

4. Select **Aggregate data for visible dimensions** to aggregate the data, which consolidates the number of rows that can have a positive impact on performance:

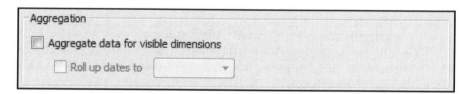

5. Select the **Number of Rows** option specify how many rows are returned in the extract. Tableau will first apply filters and aggregations, and then extract the number of rows specified. Some data sources don't support sampling, so this option may not be available:

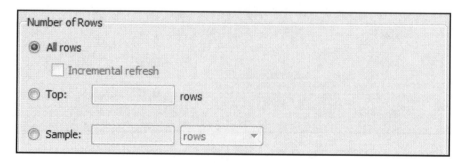

6. The **Hide All Unused Fields** option is optional. Select this option to exclude the hidden fields on the sheets or the **Data Source** tab from the extract:

7. Save the extract by following the directions within the *Creating an extract* section.

The workbook will automatically use the extract once it's created. The connection to the data extract will not persist when it's opened again unless the workbook is saved.

How it works...

We created a local extract by navigating to the **Data Source** tab and selecting **Extract**. To initiate the **Extract**, we click on **Sheet 1** and **Save**.

Edit provides options for data storage since version 2018.3, and limits data by filtering, aggregating, limiting rows, or hiding fields. These options help optimize the extracts by limiting their size and refresh times.

There's more...

Locally, once the data source is extracted, we can update it by selecting **Refresh**, as shown in the following screenshot:

With Tableau Server, as long as the server has rights and access to the data source, we can publish the extract and assign it to a refresh schedule. Updating the workbook to reference the published extract will refresh the data per a defined schedule instead of manually.

In situations where data needs to be accessed offline, using a local extract is better than using a published version.

See also

Refer to Tableau's online help section, **Extract Your Data**: `https://onlinehelp.tableau.com/v2018.3/pro/desktop/en-us/extracting_data.htm`.

Extract encryption at rest is a new data feature that allows users to encrypt their extracts on Tableau Server. Admins can enforce this policy on all extracts or allow users to choose. Other Tableau tools like Desktop or Prep will not have encryption features.

Configuring an incremental extract

By default, extracts will update using a full refresh, meaning all of the rows are replaced during a build. Depending on the size of the extract and whether there is a mechanism to identify new rows, incremental extracts can help provide users with new data more quickly. Rather than rebuilding the entire extract, for example, each day we can add the new rows based on date instead.

Getting ready

Use Tableau 2019.x, make sure you have a data source ready.

How to do it...

Rather than refreshing the entire extract each time, we can configure a refresh to add only the rows that are new since the previous refresh:

1. Create a data source using a **Text file** connection to `madrid_2017.csv`.
2. Select the **Extract** radio button and click on **Edit**:

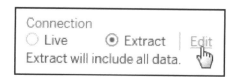

3. Select **All rows** under **Number of Rows** to extract:

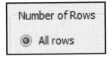

 Incremental refresh can only be defined when you are extracting as **Single table** with the **All rows** in database.

4. Select **Incremental refresh** and then specify a column that identifies new rows:

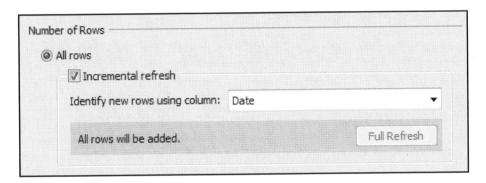

5. Click on **OK** and save the .hyper file:

6. Click on **Sheet 1** and give the extract a name:

 These steps can be used for new or existing extracts. When editing an existing extract, the last refresh is shown.

7. To verify the latest date loaded, add **Date** to the **Columns** shelf.

8. Show the maximum value by right-clicking on **Date**, choosing **Measure**, and then selecting **Maximum**:

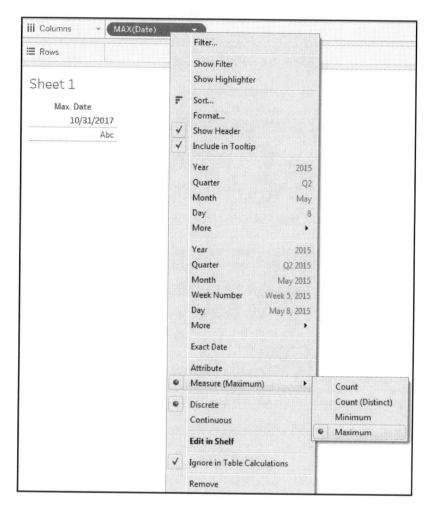

9. Save the workbook and close Tableau.
10. To simulate the incremental load, copy all the data from `Nov.csv` and paste it at the end of `madrid_2017.csv`. Save the file.
11. Open the workbook and click on **Refresh**:

12. Go back to **Sheet 1**, we now see November 30 as the **Max. Date**:

Max. Date
11/30/2017
Abc

How it works...

We selected the **Incremental refresh** checkbox and identified **Date** as the column Tableau would use to check for the presence of new rows.

There's more...

View the refresh history for an extract by selecting a data source on the **Data** menu and then select **Extract** and **History...**:

The **Extract History** window shows the date and time of each refresh, whether it was full or incremental, and the number of rows processed. If the refresh was from a file, it also shows the source filename.

We can see all these details in the following screenshot:

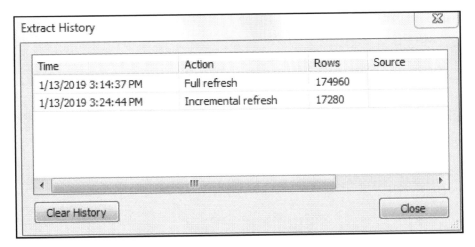

Extract History

Time	Action	Rows	Source
1/13/2019 3:14:37 PM	Full refresh	174960	
1/13/2019 3:24:44 PM	Incremental refresh	17280	

Clear History   Close

See also

- See Tableau's online help section, **Extract Your Data** under **Refresh Extracts**: `https://onlinehelp.tableau.com/current/pro/desktop/en-us/extracting_refresh.htm`

Upgrading to Hyper

Since 10.5, extracts use the `.hyper` format instead of `.tde`. Hyper is an improved data engine that allows for bigger extracts in the billions of rows, faster extract creation, and better performance. This section describes the steps to upgrade the `.tde` extract to the `.hyper` extract. It also details the compatibility considerations since Tableau Desktop, Online, and Server do not upgrade simultaneously.

Getting ready

In this recipe, we'll learn how to upgrade the `.tde` extracts to `.hyper`.

How to do it...

If using local extracts, use Tableau Desktop to manually upgrade a `.tde` extract to a `.hyper` extract.

1. Open a workbook that uses a `.tde` extract.
2. From the **Data** menu, select **Extract | Upgrade**:

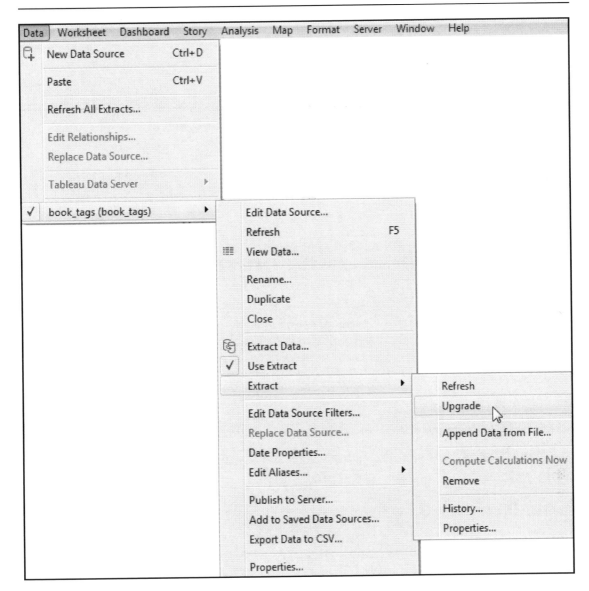

3. Select **File** | **Save** to complete the extract upgrade.

Outside of Tableau Desktop, extracts can be upgraded in the following way from Tableau Server or Tableau Online:

- Manual refresh
- Scheduled full or incremental extract refresh

How it works...

We opened a workbook using a `.tde` extract in the latest version. We upgraded the extract and saved the file.

See also

- To further understand what to expect after an extract upgrade, please see Tableau's help pages `https://onlinehelp.tableau.com/current/pro/desktop/en-us/extracting_upgrade.htm#user_after`

Creating extracts using cross-database joins

This section details the steps involved in creating table joins from separate data sources and extracts. Cross-database joins are helpful when you need to analyze data from two or more different databases as if they were one. Typically, a technology team resource would be needed to stage and integrate this data in a single place.

Getting ready

In this recipe, we'll learn how to perform a cross-database join.

How to do it...

Cross-database joins allow users to engage with the data in Tableau as if it lives in a single source.

To follow along, use `book_tags.xlsx` and `books.csv`, and then perform the following steps:

1. Open Tableau and create a **Microsoft Excel** data source connection to `book_tags.xlsx`:

2. Use **Add** to bring in another data source:

3. Connect to the `books.csv` text file, which is a different data source:

4. Join on the key fields, **Goodreads Book Id** and **Book Id**:

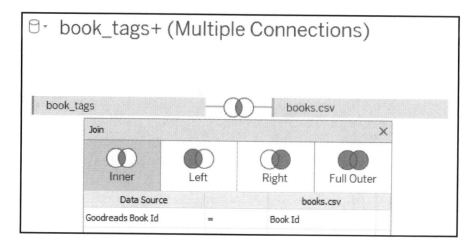

 The fields used in a cross-database join should be the same data type. We can use any of the join types.

Notice each connection is in a different color:

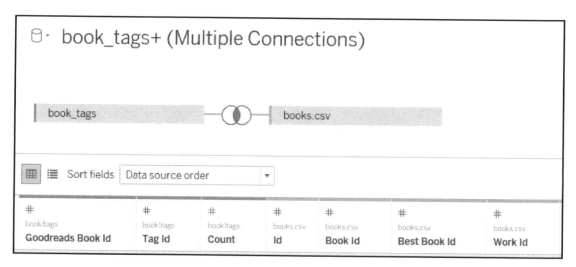

How it works...

We connected to two data sources of different types: Excel and text. The field used in the cross-database join are of the same data type. We were able to identify columns from each data source by the color assigned to each column and table. We saw blue for the Excel sheet and orange for the text file.

See also

Cross-database joins are very powerful and put more ability into the hands of users to quickly address reporting needs. For an additional tool, investigate Tableau Prep and see Chapter 15, *Preparing Data for Analysis with Tableau Prep*.

Troubleshooting extracts with Tableau Server

After a .tde extract has been upgraded, it can't be opened using an earlier version of Tableau Desktop. If you can't upgrade, you'll need to keep your extract in the .tde format.

Getting ready

You'll need an older version of Tableau Desktop installed on your machine and/or the original data source connection.

How to do it...

If you've upgraded by mistake or wish to retain a previous version, consider the following two options:

- Recreate an extract using an earlier version of Tableau Desktop by connecting to the original data source using an earlier version of Tableau Desktop
- Roll back an extract to a previous version, if revision history is turned on for Server or Tableau Online, by downloading the earlier version

How it works...

When we've mistakenly upgraded to a later version, we must roll back to a previous version. You do this rollback by either recreating the work in an older version of Tableau or by getting an older version from the server.

There's more...

If you need to keep an extract in the `.tde` format, don't upgrade the extract; keep an earlier version of Tableau Desktop for extracts, refreshes, or appending data. Also disable extract refreshes on the server for any that should remain in the legacy format. See the *Hyper* section to understand which actions can cause an extract to upgrade.

See also

Consider upgrading to 2018.x or later so the benefits of Hyper extracts can be utilized across all platforms.

When upgrading, we should understand the following backward-compatibility limitations:

- The `.hyper` files can't be downgraded to the `.tde` extracts
- Older versions of Tableau Desktop can't be published to an upgraded server environment
- Upgraded extracts can't be opened in an earlier version of Tableau, which could limit how they're shared with others who are using older versions
- **Export as a Version** can't be used to downgrade a workbook with the `.hyper` extracts

4
Tableau Desktop Advanced Calculations

In this chapter, we will cover the following topics:

- Creating calculated fields
- Implementing quick table calculations
- Creating and using groups
- Creating and using sets
- Creating and using parameters
- Implementing the basics of level of detail expressions
- Using custom geocoding
- Using polygons for analytics

Technical requirements

To follow the recipes outlined in this chapter, you will need to have Tableau 2019.x installed. You will also need to download and save the following datasets associated with this chapter to your device:

- `Unemployment_rates_1990-2016.csv` (available at `https://github.com/ PacktPublishing/Tableau-2018-Dot-1-Cookbook/blob/master/Unemployment_ rates_1990-2016.csv`)
- `Province_geocoding.csv` (available at `https://github.com/ PacktPublishing/Tableau-2018-Dot-1-Cookbook/blob/master/Province_ geocoding.csv`)

- `Serbian_provinces_population_size.csv` (available at https://github.com/PacktPublishing/Tableau-2018-Dot-1-Cookbook/blob/master/Serbian_provinces_population_size.csv)

- `Serbia_Provinces_Features.csv` (available at https://github.com/PacktPublishing/Tableau-2018-Dot-1-Cookbook/blob/master/Serbia_Provinces_Features.csv)

- `Serbia_Provinces_Points.csv` (available at https://github.com/PacktPublishing/Tableau-2018-Dot-1-Cookbook/blob/master/Serbia_Provinces_Points.csv)

Introduction

Although Tableau is very versatile even when just it's basic features are used, it is the wide range of advanced functionalities that make it very powerful. This chapter will gently introduce you to more advanced Tableau features. Through easy-to-understand, step-by-step recipes, you will get comfortable with calculated fields, quick table calculations, groups and sets, parameters, and level of detail expressions. To become a true Tableau master, you are encouraged to keep expanding your knowledge and practicing those concepts beyond this chapter. In the first six recipes, we will be dealing with the topics of table calculations and calculated fields, groups and sets, parameters, and LOD expressions, and we will use the `Unemployment_rates_1990-2016.csv` dataset, provided by United States Department of Labor, Bureau of Labor Statistics. The dataset contains data on the size of the civilian labor force—the number of employed and unemployed people by metropolitan statistical area of the United States, between 1990 and 2016.

Also, after becoming familiar with maps in Chapter 1, *Getting Started with Tableau Software*, you will also learn how to take Tableau geospatial analytics a step further and use custom geocoding and polygon maps. In the last two recipes covering geospatial analytics, we will be using the `Province_geocoding.csv`, `Serbian_provinces_population_size.csv`, `Serbia_Provinces_Features.csv`, and `Serbia_Provinces_Points.csv` datasets. These datasets contain different combinations of geocoding data (longitude and latitude) of Serbian provincial centers and borders, as well as data on their population sizes. Let's dive in!

Creating calculated fields

Calculated fields are custom fields you can add to your data source. Their values are determined by the custom formula you yourself write. In this recipe, we will create a simple calculated field that contains the difference in value of **Civilian Labor Force** between each data point and the data point preceding it.

Getting ready

Connect to the `Unemployment_rates_1990-2016.csv` dataset, and open a blank worksheet.

How to do it...

1. Click on the black drop-down arrow in the **Data** pane, to the right of **Dimensions**.
2. Select **Create Calculated Field...**. Alternatively, from the main menu toolbar select **Analysis**, and choose **Create Calculated Field**:

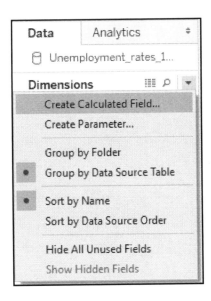

3. Rename the field from **Calculation 1** to `Difference from Previous`. Click on the **Apply** button and then click on **OK**.

4. In the formula pane, type the following expression and click on the **Apply** button and then click on **OK**:

```
SUM([Civilian Labor Force])-LOOKUP(SUM([Civilian Labor Force]),-1)
```

Let's see how it looks in the following screenshot:

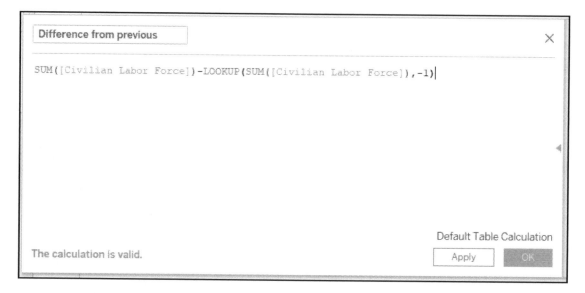

5. The new calculated field, **Difference from Previous**, has appeared under **Measures**.

6. Drag and drop the new calculated field into **Text** in the **Marks** cards.

7. Drag and drop the new calculated field into the **Rows** shelf.

8. Drag and drop **Year** from **Dimensions** into the **Columns** shelf:

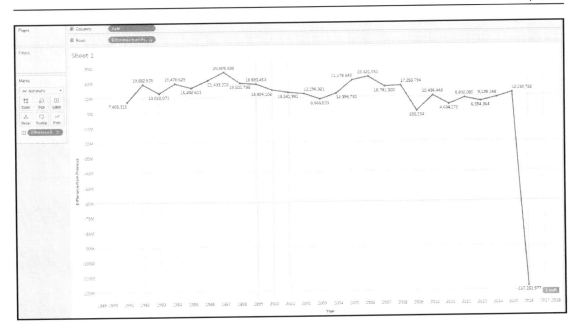

How it works...

We created a calculated field that contains the difference between the current and the previous data point. We used the LOOKUP function to return the aggregated value of Civilian Labor Force for the previous data point, and then subtracted it from the aggregated value of Civilian Labor Force in the current data point. This resulted in a new field that contains this difference, and which we can now use in our visualizations. Keep in mind that all table calculation functions, including the LOOKUP function, require an aggregated value to work with. That means that, when we use fields without an aggregation function – for example, just Civilian Labor Force instead of SUM([Civilian Labor Force])—we may get an error in the calculated field.

However, it is important to note that our original dataset has remained unchanged—the calculated field we created has not been written to it and, if we were to open a new Tableau workbook and connect to the Unemployment_rates_1990-2016.csv dataset, we would not find our calculated field among the fields in the data source.

There's more...

The type of calculation we created in this recipe is called table calculation, which simply means that the value of the calculated field we created is dependent on the dimension we use with it in our visualization. If we were, for example, to choose **Month** instead of **Year**, we would get the difference from the previous month. If we look at the **Data Source** sheet, we will see that the value of this calculated field in each row is **Undefined**, as shown in the following screenshot:

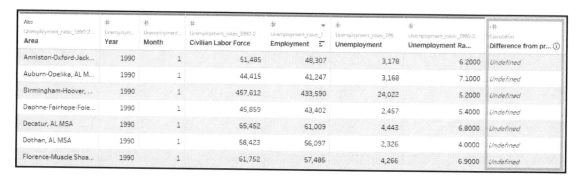

However, calculated fields can also have other types of output. We could, for example, sum up **Employment** and **Unemployment** to get **Civilian Labor Force**, using the `[Employment]+[Unemployment]` expression. If we look at the **Data Source** preview now, we can see the value of the new calculated field for each row in our data source:

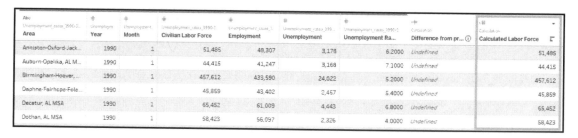

Tableau offers a multitude of functions that can be used to perform a very versatile and wide range of tasks. To truly master Tableau calculated fields, one must understand and get comfortable with using functions. Every function in Tableau has certain arguments it requires. To view functions, their descriptions, and the arguments they take, open a new calculated field and click on the arrow on the right-hand side of the editor window. This will expand the window to display a list of functions with their associated details:

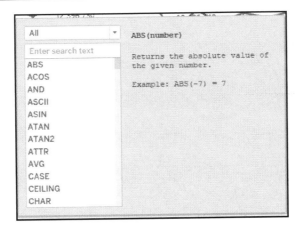

You should also always be mindful of the fact that not all functions can be applied to all data types. For example, the **SUM** function cannot be applied to strings, but can be applied to numerical values. In the drop-down menu on top of the list of functions, you can select functions suited for different data types.

See also

- For more detailed input on calculated fields, see the **Tableau Help** page at https://onlinehelp.tableau.com/current/pro/desktop/en-us/functions_operators.html.

Implementing quick table calculations

Table calculations are a type of calculated fields. They allow you to transform the values in your view, taking into account only the values that are currently in the view (and not considering the ones that are filtered out). In the previous recipe, we have created a table calculation through a calculated field. Quick table calculations are a handy way to implement common table calculations into your view, without setting them up manually.

Getting ready

In order to follow this recipe, you will need to connect to the Unemployment_rates_1990-2016.csv dataset, and open a blank worksheet.

How to do it...

1. Drag and drop **Year** from **Dimensions** into the **Columns** shelf.
2. Drag and drop **Civilian Labor Force** from **Measures** into the **Rows** shelf.
3. Again, drag and drop **Civilian Labor Force** from **Measures** onto **Label** in the **Marks** card.
4. Hover over the **Civilian Labor Force** pill in **Text** and click on the white arrow that appears on it.
5. In the drop-down menu, navigate to **Quick Table Calculation** | **Percent Difference** as shown in the following screenshot:

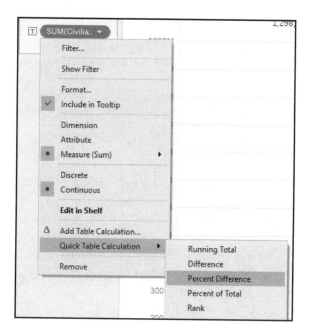

6. Hover over the **Civilian Labor Force** pill again, and click on the white arrow that appears on it.
7. From the drop-down menu, select **Edit Table Calculation...** as shown in the following screenshot:

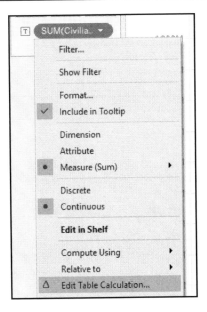

8. In the **Table Calculation** window that appears, click on the **Relative to** drop-down menu in the bottom, and select **First**:

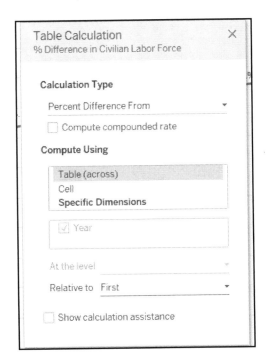

9. When you are done, close the window:

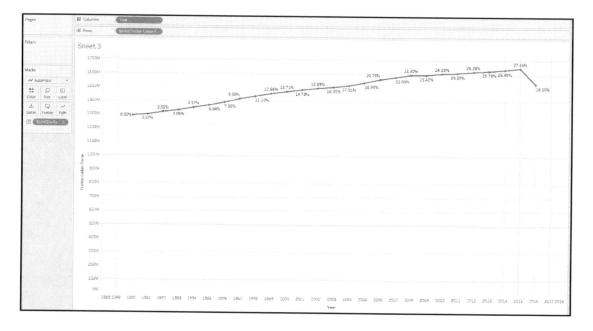

How it works...

Quick table calculations allow for quick implementation of common transformations, with the default setting. In this case, we implemented the **Percent Difference** calculation. By default, it sets the difference to be relative to the previous data point (**Year**). Then, we edited the default settings a bit by changing the calculation to be relative to the first data point in the view, not the previous one. Because of that, all of the percentages in our view are set to be relative to the year 1990. However, it is important to note that table calculations only take into account the data that is in the view. So, for example, if we filtered the year 1990 out from our view, all our calculations would then be relative to the year 1991, which would become the first data point in the view.

There's more...

Quick table calculations are just shortcuts to implementing common table calculations. Table calculations can also be implemented manually. To implement a table calculation from scratch, click on the pill of the measure you would like to transform (in this recipe, **Civilian Labor Force**), and select **Add Table Calculation** from the drop-down menu. In the **Table Calculation** window that opens, you can adjust all the relevant parameters based on the calculation type you select.

See also

- See the detailed **Tableau Help** page for an in-depth overview of table calculations, including quick table calculations, at `https://onlinehelp.tableau.com/current/pro/desktop/en-us/calculations_tablecalculations.html`.

Creating and using groups

Groups are a handy way to combine multiple members of a field into a new member. In the example we will be working on in this recipe, we will group individual years into decades, so that we are able to see the data on the level of decade.

Getting ready

Connect to your local copy of the `Unemployment_rates_1990-2016.csv` dataset, and open a new blank worksheet.

How to do it...

1. Right-click on the **Year** field under **Dimensions**.

2. In the drop-down menu, navigate to **Create | Group...**:

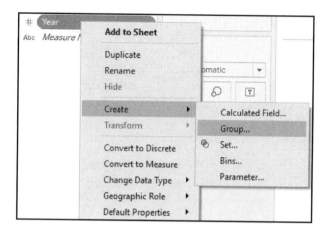

3. In the **Field Name** field, change the name of the group to Decade.

4. In the **Create Group [Year]** window, select years **1990** through **1999** by clicking on the first and the last year while holding the *Shift* button on the keyboard.

5. When the years are selected, click on **Group** at the bottom of the list or, alternatively, right-click on the selection and select **Group**:

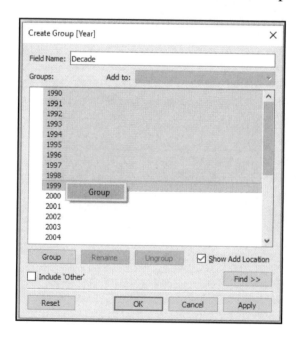

6. A new group will appear, called **1990, 1991, 1992 and 7 more**. The name of the group will be enabled for editing by default. Rename the group to 1990s as shown in the following screenshot:

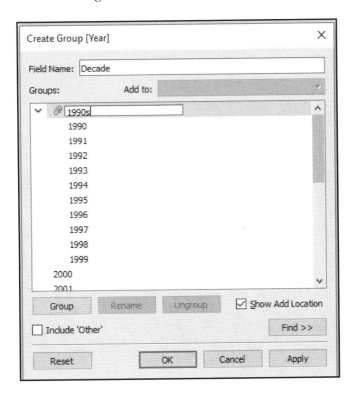

7. Now, select years 2000 through 2009 and click the **Group** button.
8. Rename the group to 2000s.
9. Finally, select the remaining years—**2010** through **2019** and click on the **Group** button to group them.
10. Rename the group to 2010s.
11. When all three groups are created and renamed, click **OK**.
12. The new group has now appeared under **Dimensions** in the **Data** pane, denoted by a paperclip symbol: ⌀ . Drag and drop **Decade** into the **Rows** shelf.
13. Drag and drop **Employment** from **Measures** onto **Text** in the **Marks** card.
14. Hover over the **AVG(Employment)** pill in the **Marks** card and click on the white arrow that appears on it.

15. Navigate to **Measure (Sum)** and select **Average**:

How it works...

Groups allow us to analyze our data on an aggregated level that is not available in the raw dataset we are using. By grouping, we have created a new group and field. When we insert it into a view and a measure (in this case, **Employment**), the measure is aggregated on the level of group. This means that, if we use the **Average** function, Tableau returns a single average value calculated across all the rows that belong to the same group member (in our case, **Decade**).

There's more...

When we do not want to classify all the field members into groups, Tableau allows us to group all remaining members into a single, **Other**, category. When you are done creating the groups you want to have in your new group field, tick the box in front of **Include 'Other'** in the bottom of the **Create Group** window. Tableau will group all the ungrouped members into a single group, named **Other**:

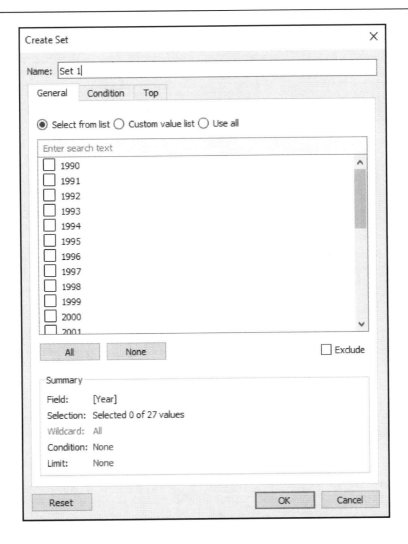

See also

- For more on grouping, see the **Tableau Help** page on the topic at `https://onlinehelp.tableau.com/current/pro/desktop/en-us/sortgroup_groups_creating.html#Include`.

Creating and using sets

Sets are, in a sense, the opposite of groups. We use them to slice our data: subset our data based on a condition, and explore it on a more granular level. In the following recipe, we will create a set that makes a distinction between years that had above average employment, and years that had below average employment.

Getting ready

Connect to the `Unemployment_rates_1990-2016.csv` dataset, and open a blank worksheet.

How to do it...

1. Right-click on the **Year** field under **Dimensions**.
2. In the drop-down menu, navigate to **Create | Set...** as shown in the following screenshot:

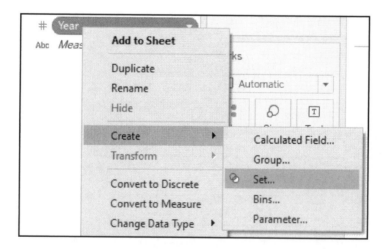

3. In the **Name** field, change the name of the set from **Set 1** to `Above average employment years`:

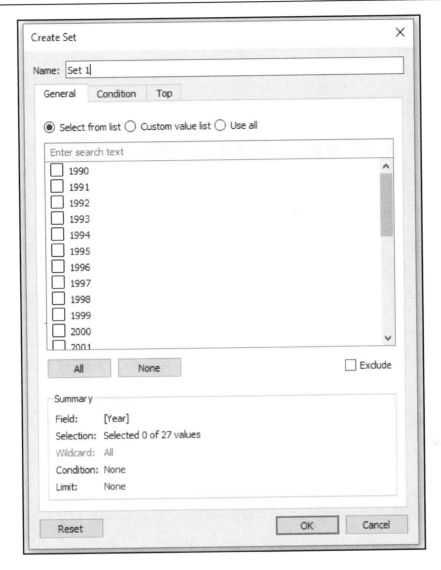

4. Click on the **Condition** tab and select **By field**.

5. From the first drop-down menu, choose **Employment**.

6. From the second drop-down menu, select **Average**.

7. From the third drop-down menu, select the >= (greater or equal to) sign.

8. In the number field, type 297027. This is the overall average of employment for all years.

9. Click **OK** to exit the window:

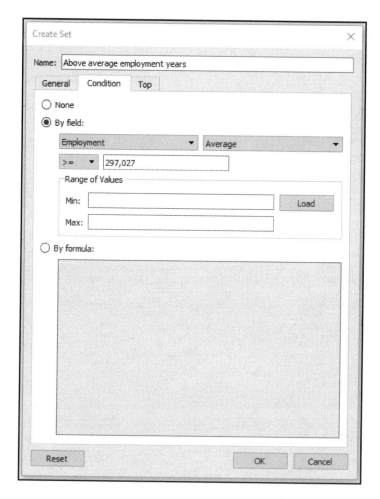

10. A new section, **Sets**, has appeared in the **Data** pane, below **Measures**. It contains our new set, denoted by the set symbol ⊚ . Drag and drop the set we created onto **Color** in the **Marks** label.

11. Drag and drop **Year** from **Dimensions** into the **Columns** shelf.

12. Right-click on the **Year** pill in the **Columns** shelf, and in the drop-down menu switch to **Discrete**.

13. Drag and drop **Employment** from **Measures** into the **Rows** shelf.

14. Hover over the **Employment** pill in the **Rows** shelf and click on the white arrow that appears on it.

15. In the drop-down menu, navigate to **Measure (Sum)** and select **Average**. This
    will provide the following output:

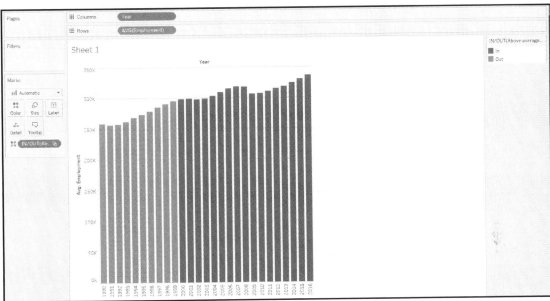

How it works...

In this recipe, we have created a set based on a condition: the value of **Employment**. We
have set the condition so that all the data points that have the value of **Employment** equal
to or higher than **297027** (which is the average value of **Employment** across the entire
dataset) are included in the set, and all the other data points are excluded from it. This
created a new field—our set, which we then used in the visualization. The set field now
works as a discrete dimension with two values: **In** and **Out** that denote the data points that
are in/out of the set. We used these values in our visualization to color the year with
average or above average employment.

If you want the set members to appear in your visualization, right-click on
the **Set** pill that you have included in your view, and in the drop-down
menu switch from **Show In/Out of Set** to **Show Members in Set**.

There's more...

Tableau offers two types of sets: fixed and dynamic. The set we made in this recipe is a dynamic set. It means the members of the set will change with the underlying data. However, there is a constraint related to dynamic sets: they can only be based on one dimension.

On the other hand, fixed sets do not change: their members always remain the same. We can create a fixed set by simply selecting data point as our view, right-clicking on the selection, and choosing the **Create Set...** option from the drop-down menu, as shown in the following screenshot:

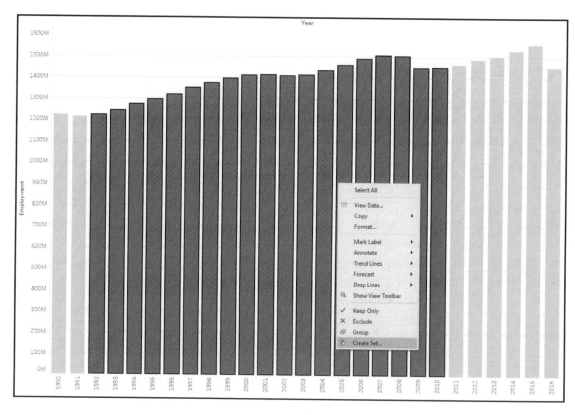

See also

- See the **Tableau Help** page on sets for more information at `https://onlinehelp.tableau.com/current/pro/desktop/en-us/sortgroup_sets_create.html`.

Creating and using parameters

In the previous recipe, *Creating and using sets*, we created a set to divide years into the ones with above average and the ones with below average employment. We did this by hardcoding the average value in the definition of our set. But, what if we wanted to make visualizations where we can input different values ourselves, so our visualization changes dynamically when we change the value? We can easily achieve this using parameters. Let's create a set where we can dynamically change the value that defines the set.

Getting ready

We will use the `Unemployment_rates_1990-2016.csv` dataset, so make sure you are connected to it, and open a new blank worksheet.

How to do it...

1. In the **Data** pane, click on the black arrow to the right of the **Dimensions** tab and select **Create Parameter...**:

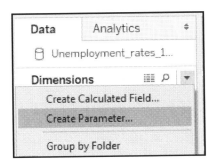

2. In the **Create Parameter** window, change the name of the parameter from **Parameter 1** to `Average employment cut-off`:

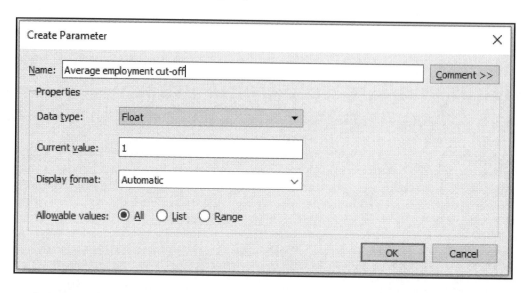

3. Leave all the other settings as they are, and click **OK** to exit the window. A new section, **Parameters**, will appear in the **Data** pane, beneath **Measures**. It will contain our new parameter, **Average employment cut-off**:

4. Right-click on the **Average Employment cut-off** parameter under **Parameters** and select **Show Parameter Control**:

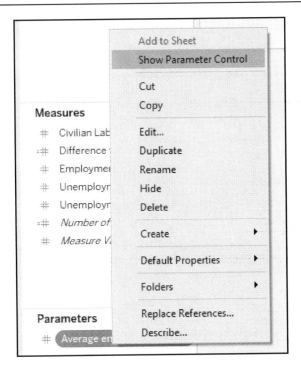

The parameter control card will appear in the top-right corner of the workspace. Notice that it shows the value we have set as the current value when creating it, which is 1:

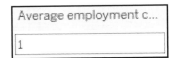

5. We have created the parameter. Now, let's create the set we will use it with. Right-click on the **Year** pill under **Dimensions**, and navigate to **Create** | **Set....**

6. In the **Create Set** window, change the name of the set from **Set 1** to Above cut-off employment.

7. Switch from the **General** tab to the **Condition** tab, and select **By formula**.

8. In the formula space, type the `AVG([Employment])>[Average employment cut-off]` expression as shown in the following screenshot:

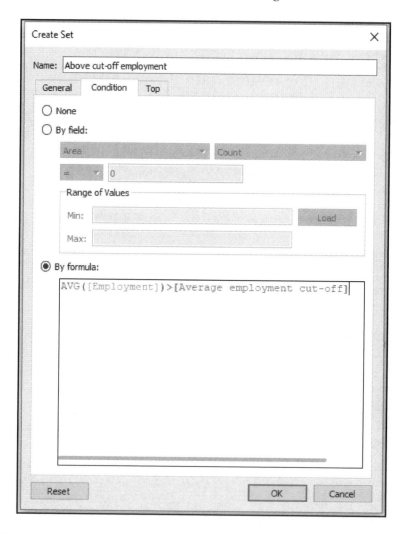

9. When you are done, click **OK** to close the window. Our set, **Above cut-off employment**, has now appeared together with a new **Set** section in the **Data** pane.

10. Finally, let's make a visualization using the new set. Drag and drop **Year** from **Dimensions** into the **Columns** shelf.

11. Right-click on the **Year** pill in the **Columns** shelf, and in the drop-down menu switch to **Discrete**.

12. Drag and drop **Employment** from **Measures** into the **Rows** shelf.

Although we have used average employment as the aggregation function when creating our set, we can leave the **SUM** aggregation function in our view. The two are unrelated, since the function in the set is used to define the set, and is not related to the measures we might use in our view.

13. Drag and drop the **Above cut-off employment** set from **Sets** onto **Color** in the **Marks** card.

14. All our bars are colored as **In** set, because the **Average employment cut-off** parameter's value is set to 1. In the parameter control card, try changing the value to 300000.

15. Try changing the value a couple of more times, to see how the years that are in/out of the set change with the parameter value:

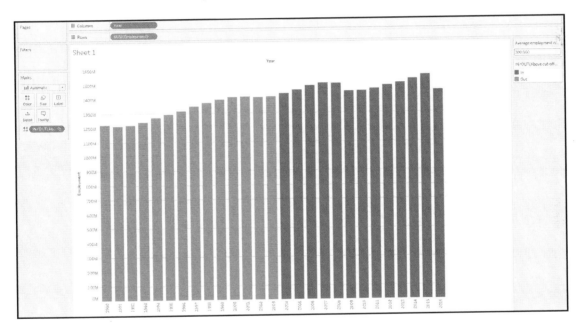

How it works...

Parameters are values that can change dynamically based on user input. They can replace constant values, in a range of different cases.

In the preceding example, we created a parameter that takes a number as an input from the user. We then used the value of the user input as the threshold score for membership in the set, by setting a condition. So, instead of the constant (average) value we inserted as the threshold value for set membership in the previous recipe, now we have a dynamic value, which changes our set every time a user inputs a new number. So, every time we change the user input, different years are included in or excluded from the set.

There's more...

There are many ways in which we can use parameters to make our visualizations interactive. For example, we can use parameters to switch between different fields (measures or dimensions in our view) or create dynamic reference lines. Generally, when using parameters, you will mostly be using them together with calculated fields. Parameters themselves cannot be included in the view. They are included by creating a calculated field that takes advantage of the parameter, and then including the calculated field in the view.

See also

- Tableau help has some useful resources on parameters. Make sure you check out the following page: https://onlinehelp.tableau.com/current/pro/desktop/en-us/changing-views-using-parameters.html.

Implementing the basics of level of detail expressions

Level of detail (LOD) expressions are a very useful feature of Tableau. In order to understand what LOD expressions do, we must first understand what LOD is. When we use one dimension in our view, Tableau aggregates the measures along this dimension; so, we say that this dimension provides the LOD. If we add another dimension to the view, measures will be additionally disaggregated along this dimension as well, leading to an even more granular LOD. LOD expressions allow us to control the LOD that will be used in our view independently of the fields that are included in the view itself. We can make it either more or less granular than the LOD provided by the fields included in the visualization itself, which provides for flexibility in creating our views.

Getting ready

To follow the steps in this recipe, connect to the `Unemployment_rates_1990-2016.csv` dataset, and open a new blank worksheet.

How to do it...

1. In the **Data** pane, click on the black arrow to the right of **Dimensions** and select **Create Calculated Field....**

2. Rename the new calculated field from **Calculation 1** to `Difference from average`.

3. In the formula space, type `AVG(([Employment])-{FIXED: AVG([Employment])})`, as shown in the following screenshot:

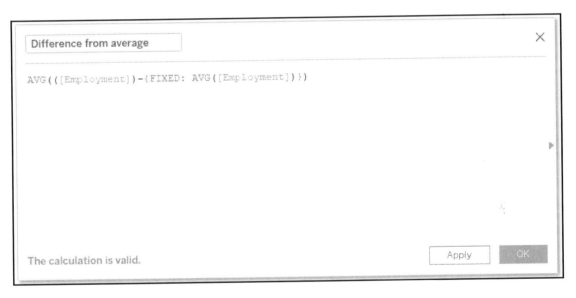

4. Click on **Apply** and then click on **OK** to exit the window. The new calculated field, **Difference from average**, has now appeared under **Measures** in the **Data** pane.

5. Drag and drop **Difference from average** from **Measures** into the **Rows** shelf.

6. Drag and drop **Year** from **Dimensions** into the **Columns** shelf.

7. Right-click on the **Year** pill in the **Columns** shelf, and in the drop-down menu switch to **Discrete**.

8. Drag and drop **Employment** from **Measures** onto **Label** in the **Marks** card as shown in the following screenshot:

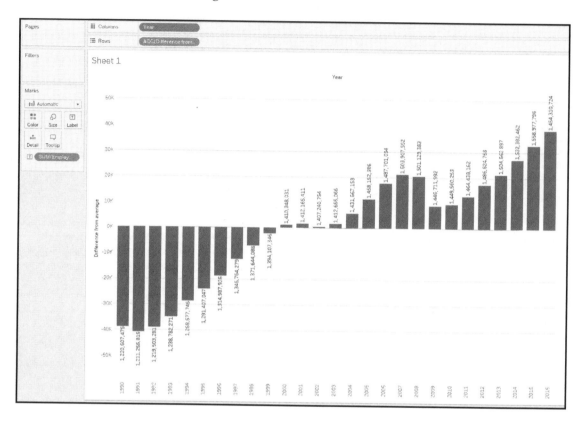

How it works...

In this recipe, we created a visualization where difference from the overall average of employment is calculated, but in such a way that the overall average is used as a reference point regardless of what is included in the visualization. So, when we include **Year**, our visualization shows the average difference in **Employment** per year (when we say average, we mean average across all the rows in the data source that belong to the particular year) from the overall average of **Employment**.

If we, for example, included **Month** in our visualization as well, the average difference would be computed for each month of each year, but would still be calculated relative to the overall average of **Employment**. That's because we told Tableau to keep the overall average fixed, regardless of what is in our visualization.

There's more...

In this recipe, we used a FIXED LOD expression. With the FIXED LOD expression, we specify the exact LOD we want to have in our visualization, and it is completely unaffected by the LOD we include in our view. Because of this, we kept the overall average of **Employment** in our calculation, despite introducing other dimensions into the view that would normally disaggregate our measure.

Tableau also offers the following two other types of LOD expressions. Let's take a quick look at what they do:

- INCLUDE: These expressions allow us to introduce an additional LOD into the view that is more granular than the one determined by the visualization itself. The INCLUDE expressions take into account the LOD that is included in the visualization, but always disaggregates data additionally by the dimension we specified in the INCLUDE expression itself.
- EXCLUDE: These expressions do the opposite of the INCLUDE expressions—they keep the data at the certain level of granularity that is higher than the one introduced by the view itself. This means that, when we create our visualization, Tableau will aggregate the measure according to the view, with the exception of the dimension that is specified in the EXCLUDE expression. This will result in the values repeating across multiple data points in our view because, instead of aggregating them across these data points, they are aggregated at a higher level.

See also

- For an excellent explanation of LOD expressions, read the Tableau white paper about them at https://www.tableau.com/learn/whitepapers/understanding-lod-expressions

Using custom geocoding

Tableau can recognize many locations as geographical values and assign geographical coordinates to them, allowing us to map them without actually knowing their exact coordinates. But, sometimes, we would like to use map locations that Tableau does not recognize as geographical data and can't generate longitude and latitude for.

In those cases, we can provide Tableau with the geographical coordinates ourselves using custom geocoding.

Getting ready

In this recipe, we will use two datasets: one we want to create our views from, and one that contains custom geocoding data. Make sure you have both the `Serbian_provinces_population_size.csv` and `Province_geocoding.csv` datasets saved to your device. Also, make sure the `Province_geocoding.csv` dataset is saved to a separate folder. Connect to the `Serbian_provinces_population_size.csv` dataset, and open a new blank worksheet.

The dataset containing custom geocoding data (the longitude and latitude of the locations we would like to map) has to be stored in a text file, and in a separate folder.

How to do it...

1. In the main menu toolbar, navigate to **Map**.
2. From the drop-down menu, navigate to **Geocoding | Import Custom Geocoding...** as shown in the following screenshot:

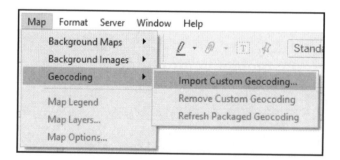

3. In the **Import Custom Geocoding** window, click on three dots (**...**) to open the directory where you saved `Province_geocoding.csv`:

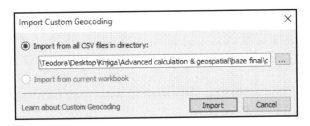

4. In the **Choose Source Folder** window that opens, navigate to the folder in which you have saved the `Province_geocoding.csv` file with custom geocoding data, select it, and click **Select Folder**.

5. The path to the folder will now appear in the **Import Custom Geocoding** window. Click on **Import**, and wait while Tableau processes your request.

6. When the custom geocoding is imported, right-click on the **Province** pill under **Dimensions**, and in the drop-down menu navigate to **Geographical Role** and choose **Province-Serbia**:

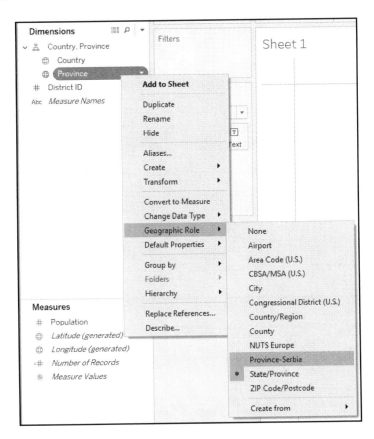

7. We have now set up our custom geocoding for **Province-Serbia**, which is also indicated by a small globe with a paper symbol (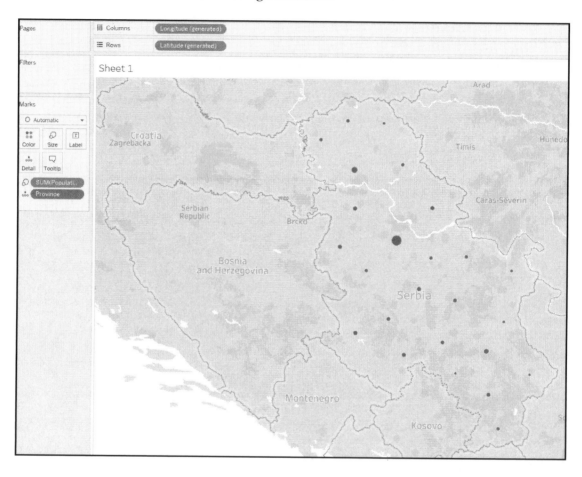) that has appeared next to it. To use it in a map, just drag and drop **Province** from **Dimensions** into the workspace.

8. Finally, add **Population**, by dropping it from **Measures** onto **Size** in the **Marks** card as shown in the following screenshot:

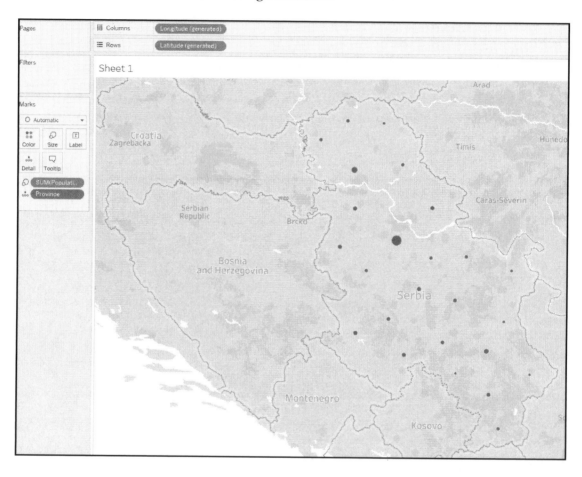

How it works...

We used the `Province_geocoding.csv` dataset to set up custom geocoding for **Province**. The `Province_geocoding.csv` dataset contains longitudes and latitudes of each province. Once we have imported that data as geographical coordinates, we assign that geocoding to the dimension from the `Serbian_provinces_population_size.csv` dataset, **Province**. Since the names of the provinces are the same in both files, Tableau is able to make a connection between the **Province** dimension in the `Serbian_provinces_population_size.csv` file, and longitude and latitude from the `Province_geocoding.csv` file. Thanks to this, we can now map **Province** correctly.

There's more...

The same outcome could also be achieved with data blending. We could connect to both datasets, `Province_geocoding.csv` and `Serbian_provinces_population_size.csv`, and blend them by **Province** and **Province-Serbia**. This would allow us to use **Longitude** and **Latitude** from `Province_geocoding.csv` and combine it with **Province** from the `Serbian_provinces_population_size.csv` data source in our view. However, custom geocoding does have some advantages over this method. For example, once we import it, we can reuse it in other workbooks as well.

See also

- See this Tableau help resource for more details on custom geocoding at `https://onlinehelp.tableau.com/current/pro/desktop/en-us/custom_geocoding.html`

Using polygons for analytics

In the previous recipe, *Using custom geocoding*, we have imported and used custom geocoding to map Serbian provincial centers. In this recipe, we will go a step further and map the region's borders in order to create a filled map. We will achieve this by using polygon mapping.

Getting ready

In this recipe, we will use two datasets: `Serbia_Provinces_Features.csv` and `Serbia_Provinces_Points.csv`. The `Serbia_Provinces_Features.csv` dataset contains data on Serbian provinces' populations, while `Serbia_Provinces_Points.csv` contains coordinates for mapping. Open them both, and make sure they are joined by **ID**. Double-click on the set intersection symbol to make sure the datasets are joined by **ID**:

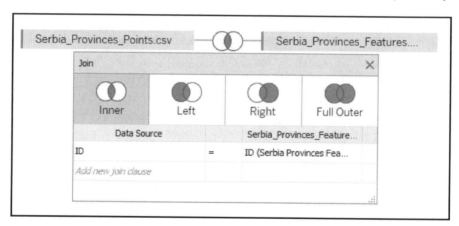

How to do it...

1. Drag and drop **Longitude** from **Measures**, the `Serbia_Provinces_Points.csv` table, into the **Columns** shelf.

2. Right-click on the **Longitude** pill in the **Columns** shelf, and select **Dimension**.

3. Drag and drop **Latitude** from **Measures**, the `Serbia_Provinces_Points.csv` table, into the **Rows** shelf.

4. Right-click on the **Latitude** pill in the **Rows** shelf, and select **Dimension**.

5. In the **Marks** card, use the drop-down menu to change mark type from **Automatic** to **Polygon**. You will notice a new button, **Path**, appearing in the **Marks** card, as shown in the following screenshot:

6. Right-click on the **Point order** field under **Measures** and select **Convert to Dimension**.

7. Drag and drop **Point order** from **Dimensions** onto **Path** in the **Marks** card.

8. Drag and drop **Province** from **Dimensions** onto **Detail** in the **Marks** card.

9. Finally, drag and drop **Population** from **Dimensions** to **Color**:

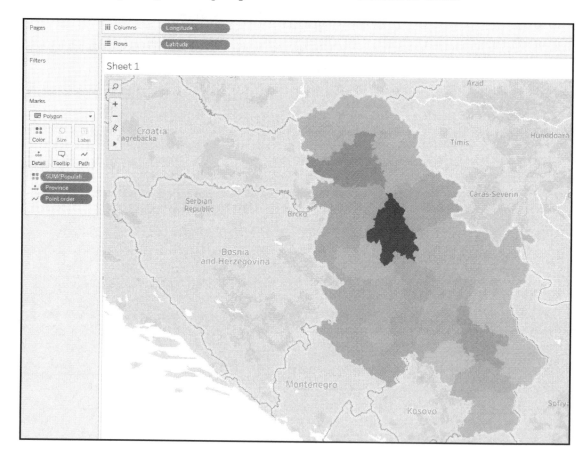

How it works...

Polygon maps are created by giving Tableau the coordinates of the shape we want to draw, and then connecting the dots by drawing a path between them. We have created a map with custom territories – provinces—by giving Tableau the exact coordinates (longitude and latitude) of their borders, which were contained in the `Serbia_Provinces_Points.csv` dataset. The **Point order** dimension notifies Tableau in which order to connect the dots (coordinate points). Finally, placing **Province** in **Detail** completed our map.

There's more...

Polygon mapping allows us to draw any shape, not just geographical maps. As long as we know the *x* and *y* axis coordinates of the shape (for example, in pixels), and have them recorded in a file, we can draw any shape we like and use it in our visualizations. Mapping an image does require some patience, but getting a visualization of a customized shape that can be reused can be well worth it!

See also

- For more information, check out this Tableau resource on polygon maps at `https://www.tableau.com/learn/tutorials/on-demand/polygon-maps-8`.

5
Tableau Desktop Advanced Filtering

In this chapter, we will cover the following topics:

- Implementing a top N filter
- Adding filters to context
- Creating a measure filter
- Creating date range filters
- Creating relative date filters
- Implementing table calculation filters
- Implementing action filters

Technical requirements

To follow the recipes outlined in this chapter, you will need to have Tableau 2019.x installed. You will also need to download and save the following datasets associated with this chapter to your device:

- `Winery.csv` (available at `https://github.com/PacktPublishing/Tableau-2018-Dot-1-Cookbook/blob/master/Winery.zip`)
- `Bread_basket.csv` (available at `https://github.com/PacktPublishing/Tableau-2018-Dot-1-Cookbook/blob/master/Bread_basket.csv`)

Introduction

In Chapter 1, *Getting Started with Tableau,* we encountered filters and learned how to implement basic ones. Filters allow us to use just part of the rows in a dataset, and this basic principle is common to all the filters we will be working with.

However, Tableau's filtering capabilities extend far beyond the basic filtering you have learned so far. In this chapter, you will become comfortable with implementing top N filters, measure filters, different kinds of date filters, table calculation filters, and action filters.

In this chapter, we will mostly be using the Winery.csv dataset, originally found on Kaggle.com. It contains data on wines—which winery they belong to, which province they originate from, number of points, price of the wine, and the name of the wine taster who rated them, among other details.

In the two recipes dealing with date filters, *Creating date range filters* and *Creating relative date filters,* we will be using the Bread_basket.csv dataset, which contains transactions from a bakery with their dates. This dataset was also originally found on Kaggle.com.

Implementing a top N filter

Top N filtering allows you to filter only the top N members of a dimension, which is determined by their value in another field you select.

Getting ready

To follow the steps in this recipe, you will need to connect to the Winery.csv dataset, and open a new blank worksheet.

How to do it...

1. Drag and drop **Winery** from **Dimensions** into the **Rows** shelf.
2. Drag and drop **Price** from **Measures** into the **Columns** shelf.

3. Right-click on the **SUM (Price)** pill in the **Columns** shelf, navigate to **Measure (Sum)**, and select **Average**.
4. Drag and drop **Winery** from **Dimensions** into the **Filters** shelf.
5. In the **Filter [Winery]** window, navigate to the **Top** tab.
6. Select **By field**, and change top **10** to top **5** by entering the value 5 in the box, as follows:

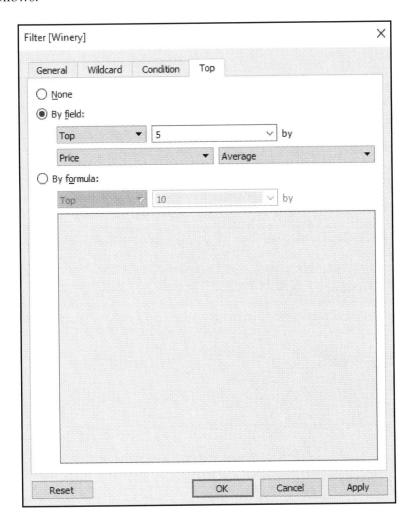

7. Click **OK** to exit the window.

8. Finally, let's sort our view by price. Right-click on the **Winery** pill in the **Rows** shelf and select **Sort...**, as follows:

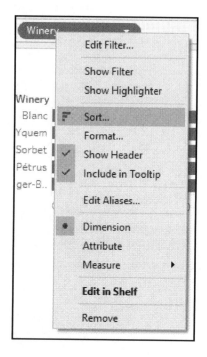

9. In the **Sort [Winery]** window, under **Sort Order**, select **Descending**.

10. Under **Sort By**, select **Field**, and make sure it is set to **Price** under **Field Name** and to **Average** under **Aggregation**, as follows:

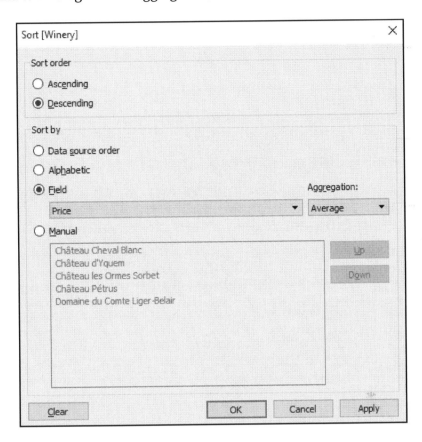

11. Click **OK** to exit the window. Our view now shows only the top five wineries by the average price of their wines, as shown in the following screenshot:

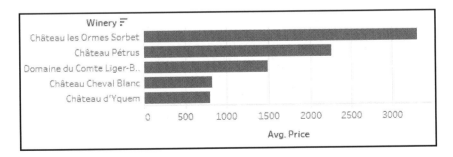

How it works...

We have selected the top five wineries by the average price of their wines. Although the filter is by a dimension—in this case, **Winery**—we also needed to include a measure (in this case, **Price**) by which to select the top five wineries.

There's more...

Besides choosing the top N members of a dimension, Tableau also allows us to choose the bottom N. In the **Filter [Winery]** window, click on the **Top** drop-down menu and select **Bottom**, as shown in the following screenshot:

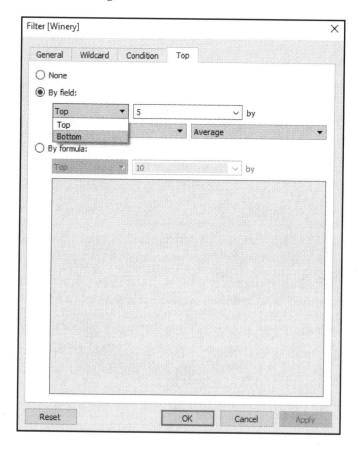

It is also possible to filter the top/bottom N members by custom formula. In the **Filter [Winery]** window, select **By formula**, and Tableau will allow you to type in your custom expression to filter by.

See also

- For more information on top N filtering, read the Tableau resource at `https://kb.tableau.com/articles/howto/using-a-top-n-parameter-to-filter-a-table`

Adding filters to context

In the previous recipe, *Implementing a top N filter*, we learned how to create a top N filter. In this recipe, we will expand that knowledge to situations where we have multiple filters, a top N filter being one of them.

In these situations, we can get a different output to what we expect. We will learn how to properly set up our filters so that the output is what we want it to be.

Getting ready

Follow the previous recipe, *Implementing a top N filter*, to create the worksheet we will be working on in this recipe.

How to do it...

1. Let's add a filter by **Province** to filters. Drag and drop **Province** from **Dimensions** to the **Filters** shelf.
2. In the **Filter [Province]** window, click **All** beneath the list of regions to select all regions.
3. Click **OK** to exit the window.
4. Right-click on the **Province** pill in the **Filters** shelf and, from the drop-down menu, select **Show Filter**.
5. Let's say we want to see the top five wineries by price in the province of Burgundy. From the **Province** filter, select **Burgundy**.

You can start typing `Burgundy` to narrow your choices.

6. However, this selection doesn't give us the expected result—our view is only displaying one winery now, instead of five:

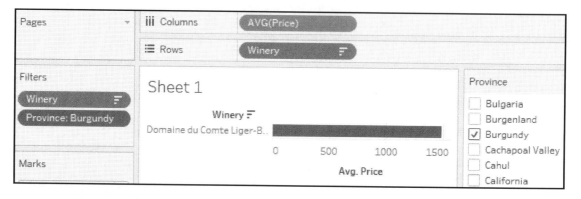

7. To correct that, right-click on the **Province: Burgundy** pill in the **Filters** shelf and, from the drop-down menu, select **Add to Context**:

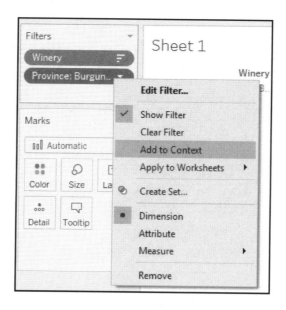

In the following screenshot, the chart is now showing the top five wineries in the province of **Burgundy**:

How it works...

We started from a view showing the top five wineries by the average price of their wines. Then, we added the filter by **Province**, in order to see the top five wineries per province. However, the result we got was not what we wanted—when we selected the region of Burgundy, we got the winery that is in the top five wineries at the level of the total sample, which is also in the province of Burgundy.

We achieved the output we desired when we added the **Province** filter to context—now, our view shows the top five wineries within each region. What changed when we added the **Province** filter to context?

By adding the **Province** filter to context, we gave it priority over the top N filter. Context filters are filters that set the context in which other filters are applied. They take priority over the other filter(s) in the view, which are applied only on rows that have been filtered by the context filters.

There's more...

Context filters can also be used to boost performance of the view in cases of multiple filters or very large data sources, which would normally be slowed down by an additional filter.

See also

- For more on context filters, see the **Tableau Help** article on the topic at `https://onlinehelp.tableau.com/current/pro/desktop/en-us/filtering_context.html`

Creating a measure filter

So far, we have been filtering our views using dimensions as filter fields. However, Tableau also allows us to filter views by measures. In this recipe, we will be exploring the possibilities of this feature.

Getting ready

Connect to the `Winery.csv` dataset, and open a new blank worksheet.

How to do it...

1. Drag and drop **Country** from **Dimensions** into the canvas.
2. Drag and drop **Price** from **Measures** onto **Color** in the **Marks** bar.
3. Right-click on the **SUM (Price)** pill in **Color**, navigate to **Measure (Sum)** and, from the drop-down menu, select **Average**.
4. Drag and drop **Points** from **Measures** into the **Filters** shelf.

5. In the **Filter Field [Points]** window, select **All values** and click **Next >**:

6. In the **Filter [Points]** window, leave the **Range of values** option as its default (**80** to **100**), and click **OK**:

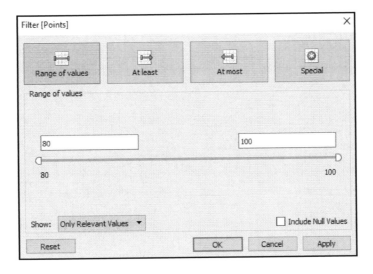

7. Right-click on the **Points** pill in the **Filters** shelf, and select **Show Filter**. When the filter control slider appears in the top-right corner of the worksheet, try moving the slider to select a different range of values. Different countries will be highlighted based on the selected range, as shown in the following screenshot:

How it works...

We have chosen to filter our view by the number of **Points**. We have turned on filter control so that we can select the range of **Points** we want to include in the view. When we change the number of **Points**, countries that are displayed stay the same, but the color changes. That's because different rows get included in the view.

For example, when we set the range of **Points** to 85-90, the **Price** is only calculated on the rows that satisfy the condition specified by the filter—that is, where **Points** are between 85 and 90. So, the average price that is presented in the changes as different rows are being excluded and included in the view by the filter.

There's more...

When filtering a view by measures, we can also select the **At least** and **At most** options.

The **At least** option keeps the maximum value at the maximum value in our dataset, while we can adjust the lowest value. The **At most** option provides the opposite—the minimum value is kept at the minimum value available in the dataset, while we can adjust the highest value.

See also

- For more information on filtering by measures, read the comprehensive **Tableau Help** guide to filtering at `https://onlinehelp.tableau.com/current/pro/desktop/en-us/filtering.html`

Creating date range filters

Tableau recognizes dates as a special data type, and has specific filtering functionalities related to dates. This recipe will go through the steps of filtering data by date range.

Getting ready

To perform the steps in this recipe, connect to the `Bread_basket.csv` dataset and open a new blank worksheet.

How to do it...

1. Drag and drop **Item** from **Dimensions** into the **Rows** shelf.
2. Drag and drop **Number of Records** from **Measures** onto **Text** in the **Marks** card.
3. Now, let's filter our view by date range. Drag and drop **Date** from **Dimensions** into the **Filter** shelf.
4. In the **Filter Field [Date]** window, select **Range of Dates**, and click **Next >**:

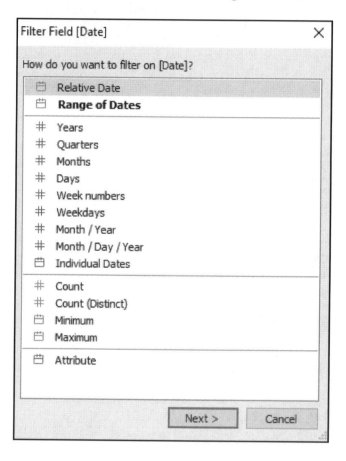

5. In the **Filter [Date]** window that opens, select the desired date range. For this example, let's select data from 12/1/2017 through 2/1/2018. Click on the date field on the left-hand side, and select **12/1/2017** from the drop-down calendar. Repeat the same steps in the right-hand field to select the end date—**2/1/2018**, as shown in the following screenshot:

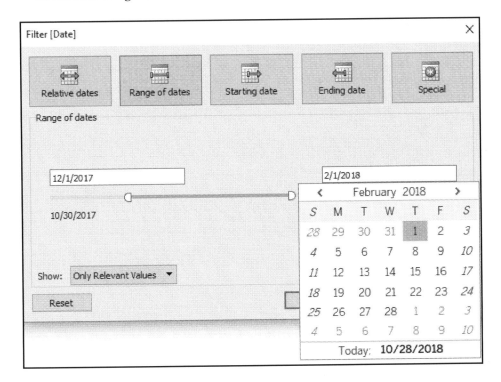

6. Click **OK** to exit the window. Our view is now showing only the data for the time period we selected:

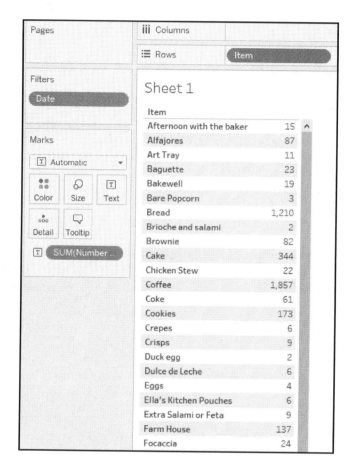

How it works...

In this recipe, we chose to select all of the records in our dataset that fall within a certain date range. We specified the start date and the end date, and Tableau filtered out all dates that fall out of this range.

Although date filters are specific for the data field type, they work just like any other filter. When we specified the range of dates, Tableau filtered out all of the rows in our data source that contain date values that are outside the specified range, and included only the rows with the date values that fall within the specified range in our view.

There's more...

When filtering by date range, Tableau also offers the options **Starting date** and **Ending date**.

When we choose **Starting date**, we set the earliest date in our date range, while the end date is set to the latest date available in the data source.

Let's view what we have selected in the following screenshot:

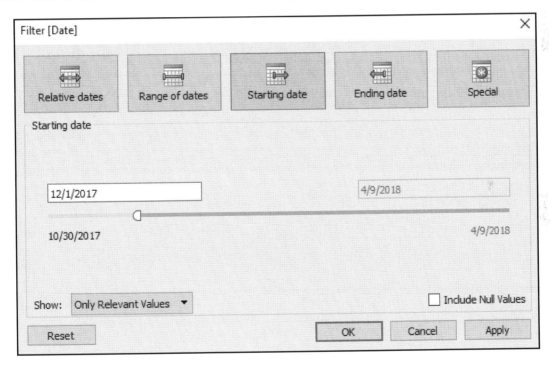

On the other hand, with the **Ending date** option, we set the latest date in the date range that we would like to filter by, while the starting date is set to the earliest available date in our data source.

See also

- For more information on filtering by dates, read the comprehensive **Tableau Help** guide to filtering at `https://onlinehelp.tableau.com/current/pro/desktop/en-us/filtering.html`

Creating relative dates filters

In the previous recipe, *Creating date range filters*, we created a date range filter. In this recipe, we will explore another kind of date filter—a relative date filter. Relative date filters allow us to filter dates that are relative to a selected date.

Getting ready

To follow the steps outlined in this recipe, connect to the `Bread_basket.csv` dataset, and open a new blank worksheet.

How to do it...

1. Right-click on the previously created **Date** filter and select **Edit...**.
2. In the **Filter [Date]** window, select the **Relative dates** option.

3. Select the period you would like to see. Let's set the last five days. Select the radio button in front of **Last**, and type 5 in the associated box.

4. In the bottom-left corner, check the box in front of **Anchor relative to** and choose a date, being careful that it's actually included in our dataset. For example, let's select **2/1/2018** by clicking on the date field and selecting the date from the drop-down calendar. We can view our selection in the following screenshot:

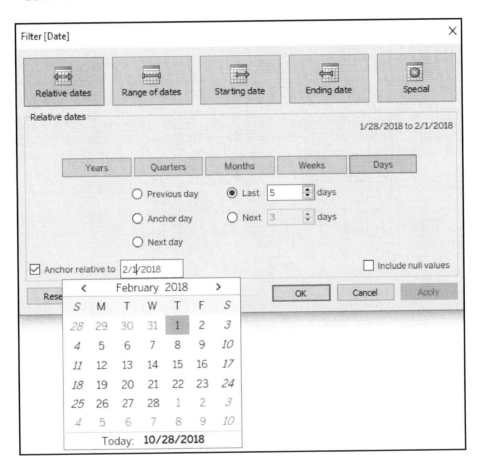

5. Click **OK** to exit the window. You can see the generated output in the following screenshot:

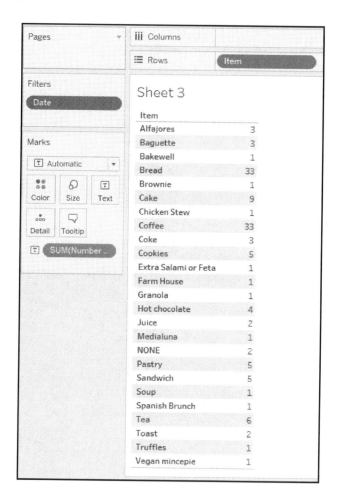

How it works...

In this recipe, we explored relative date filters, by creating a filter relative to a random date we chose, that is, **2/1/2018**. We chose the date, and we chose to see the last five days relative to the chosen date. Our view is now showing the selected number of days relative to the chosen date.

There's more...

When working with relative date filters, Tableau allows a multitude of options. As well as specifying the number of days, we can also choose to show the selected number of years, quarters, months, or weeks relative to the selected date. Besides this, we can show not only a time period preceding the selected date, but also the one following it, by choosing **Next** instead of **Last**.

Finally, besides setting a fixed date as we did in this recipe, we can also choose **Today**, **Yesterday**, or **Tomorrow** as the anchor dates, which is very useful when we want to have a view that is updated with fresh data relative to the current date.

See also

- For more information on filtering by dates, read the comprehensive **Tableau Help** guide to filtering at `https://onlinehelp.tableau.com/current/pro/desktop/en-us/filtering.html`

Implementing table calculation filters

When table calculations are included in the view, filtering can be tricky as it changes table calculations and can give us undesired results.

In this recipe, we will go through an example of what can happen when we filter a view that includes table calculation, and an easy way to include a table calculation filter that will give us the desired result.

Getting ready

Connect to the `Winery.csv` dataset, and open a new blank worksheet.

How to do it...

1. Drag and drop **Country** from **Dimensions** into the **Rows** shelf.
2. Drag and drop **Number of Records** from **Measures** into the **Columns** shelf.
3. Drag and drop **Taster Name** from **Dimensions** onto **Color** in the **Marks** card.
4. Right-click on the **Number of Records** pill in the **Columns** shelf and in the drop-down menu navigate to **Quick Table Calculation** | **Percent of Total**:

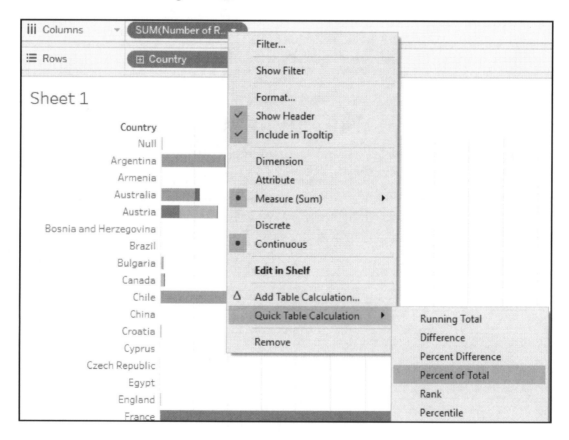

5. Once again, right-click on the **Number of Records** pill in the **Columns** shelf and in the drop-down menu navigate to **Compute Using** | **Taster Name**:

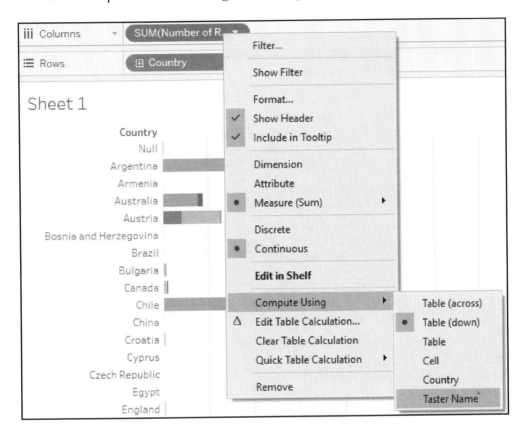

6. We can now see the percentage of reviews done by each of the tasters in each of the countries. However, the view looks pretty messy, and it's difficult to identify individual wine tasters, as shown in the following screenshot:

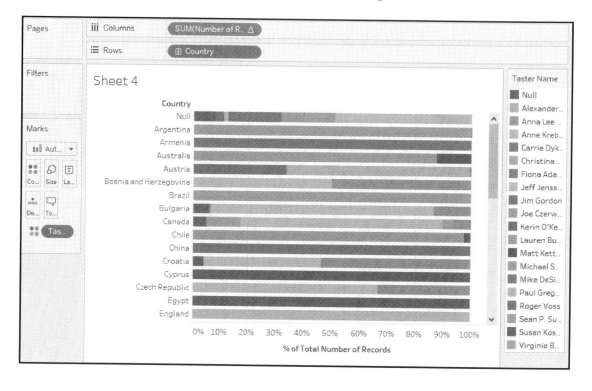

7. Let's say we want to filter out a single taster, and see their share of reviews in each country. Drag and drop **Taster Name** from **Dimensions** into the **Filters** shelf.

8. In the **Filter [Taster Name]** window, click on **None** to deselect all names. Then, select **Anna Lee C. Iijima** and click **OK**:

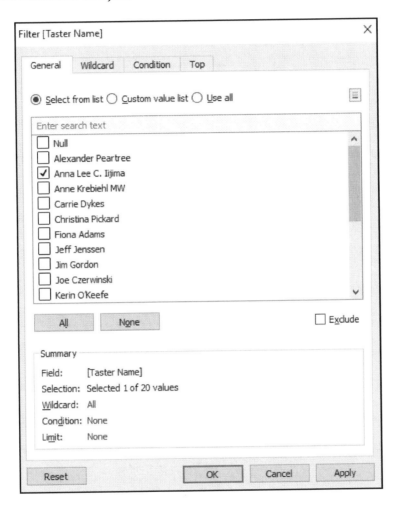

The view we got is not what we needed! See the following screenshot:

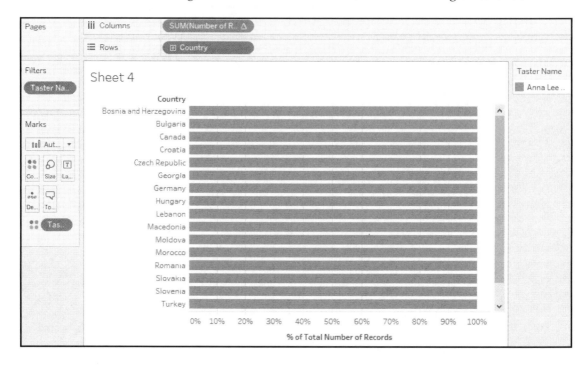

9. Let's correct that. In the main menu toolbar, click on **Analysis** and select **Create Calculated Field...**.

10. In the calculated field editor window, rename the calculated field from **Calculation1** to `Filter by Wine Taster`.

11. In the formula space, write the following expression:

    ```
    LOOKUP(ATTR([Taster Name]),0)
    ```

    The preceding expression is shown in the following screenshot:

12. Click **OK** to exit the window.

13. Remove **Taster Name** from the **Filter** shelf and drag and drop the new calculated field, **Filter by Wine Taster**, into the **Filter** shelf instead.

14. In the **Filter [Filter by Wine Taster]** window, select **Anna Lee C. Iijima** and click **OK**. The view now shows the percentage of records by this wine taster in each country:

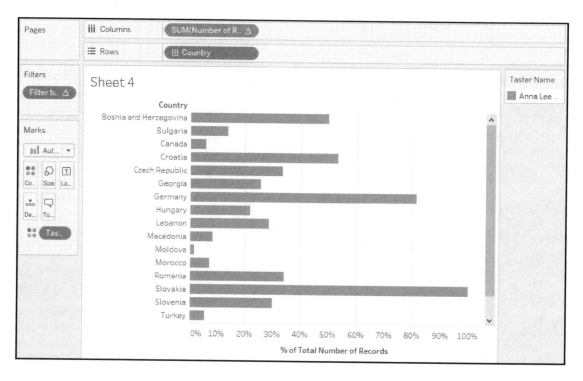

How it works...

Table calculations only take into account data that is in the view. We have created a table calculation to show the proportion of records by each wine taster. However, when we exclude all wine taster names but one, Tableau recalculates the table calculation using only data that is in the view, which means that all records in each country now belong to a single **Taster Name**.

This results in a completely uninformative view, which tells us that 100% of records belong to this particular taster.

By implementing the table calculation filter, we allow the original table calculation (that computes the percentages) to take place before the view is actually filtered, and not the other way around, which is the case when we just implement the filter by **Wine Taster**.

Because of this, our view is filtered after the table calculation is performed, and the table calculation is unaffected by some of the rows being filtered out of the view.

There's more...

We could achieve the same result by simply hiding all wine taster names except the one we want to see from the view. This can be a good, quick solution for creating a one-time, static view.

However, this is generally not recommended because it's not interactive (it's not that easy to switch between different values of the filters), and can also be confusing to someone who is looking at the view for the first time—they could not really tell what the view has been filtered by.

See also

- To gain a deeper understanding of how Tableau performs operations, read the useful **Tableau Help** page on the order of operations at `https://onlinehelp.tableau.com/current/pro/desktop/en-us/order_of_operations.html`

Implementing action filters

Action filters allow us to filter values across multiple worksheets in a simple, intuitive way—just by clicking on the data point in our view that we would like to filter by.

Getting ready

In this recipe, we will be using the `Winery.csv` dataset. Make sure you are connected to it, and open a new blank worksheet.

How to do it...

1. Drag and drop **Country** from **Dimension** onto **Detail** in the **Marks** card.
2. Drag and drop **Points** from **Measures** onto **Color** in the **Marks** card.
3. Right-click on the **SUM (Points)** pill in **Color**, navigate to **Measure (Sum)**, and from the drop-down menu, select **Average**.
4. Create a new blank worksheet by clicking on the New Worksheet tab at the bottom of the workspace. Alternatively, in the main menu toolbar, navigate to **Worksheet | New Worksheet** from the drop-down menu.

5. In the new worksheet, drag and drop **Country** from **Dimensions** onto **Color** in the **Marks** card. A dialog window may pop up, asking you if you would like to filter out some of the countries. Select **Add all members**:

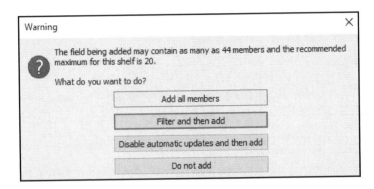

6. Drag and drop **Province** from **Dimensions** onto **Detail** in the **Marks** card.
7. Drag and drop **Price** from **Measures** onto **Size** in the **Marks** card.
8. Right-click on the **SUM (Price)** pill in **Size**, navigate to **Measure (Sum)**, and from the drop-down menu, select **Average**.
9. In the **Marks** card, click on the drop-down menu and change the mark type from **Automatic** to **Circle**:

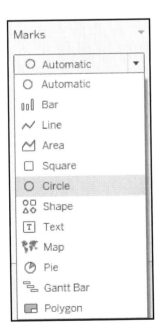

10. Navigate to **Sheet 1**. In the main menu toolbar, select **Worksheet** and in the drop-down menu, navigate to **Actions...**:

11. In the **Actions** window that opens, click on the **Add Action >** button and select **Filter...**:

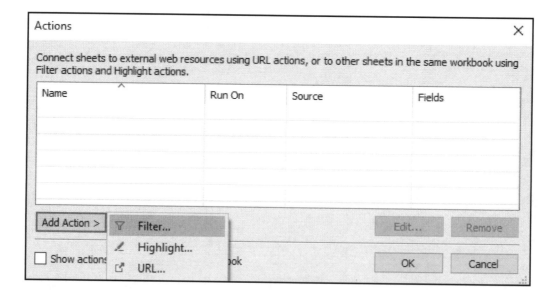

12. In the **Add Filter Action** window, use the **Name** field to change the name of the filter from **Filter1** to `Filter per Country`.

13. Under **Run action on,** select **Select**.

14. Set **Target Sheets** to **Sheet 2**.

15. Click **OK** to exit the window:

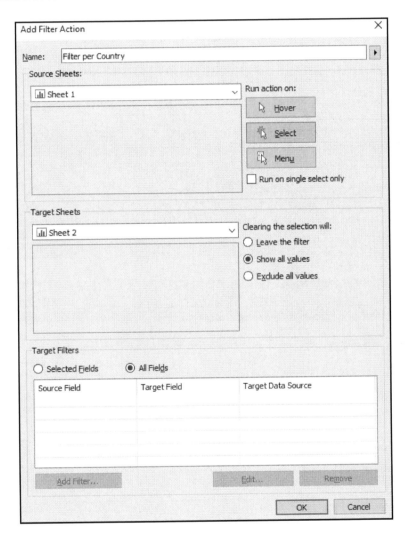

16. You will notice that our filter, **Filter per Country**, has now appeared in the list in the **Actions** window. Click **OK** to exit the **Actions** window.

17. We have now set up the action filter. Click on any country in the map on **Sheet 1** and observe the result on **Sheet 2**. Notice that the action filter has now also appeared in the **Filters** shelf. For example, if we click on Australia in **Sheet 1**, Australia will automatically be filtered in **Sheet 2**, as follows:

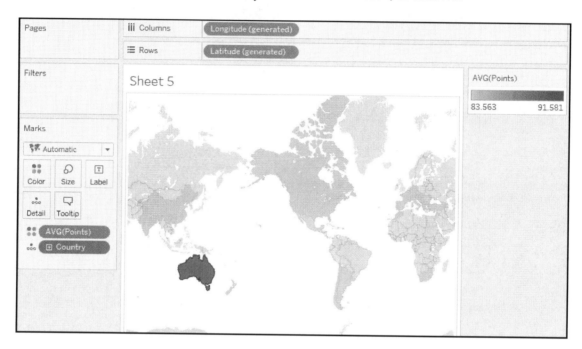

Let's look at the result in the following screenshot:

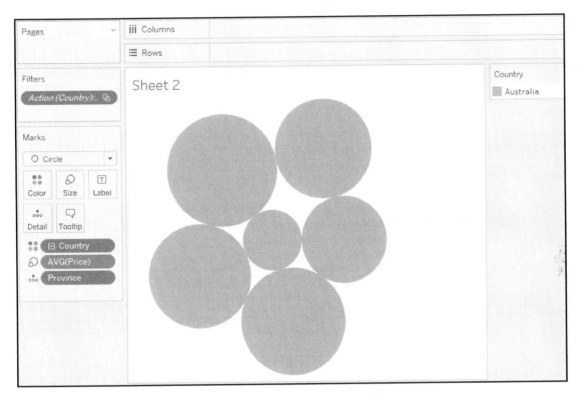

How it works...

In this recipe, we have set up a filter action. Filter actions send information between worksheets. When we click on a mark in **Sheet 1**, it sends information to **Sheet 2**, and automatically sets the selected mark in **Sheet 1** as a filter in **Sheet 2**.

Note that the view in **Sheet 1** is aggregated per **Country** and **Province**, while the view in **Sheet 2** does not contain information on **Province**. Regardless of the different level of detail in the two views, Tableau filters out the common element—the selected **Country**—from **Sheet 2**.

There's more...

When implementing action filters, Tableau offers various options.

Apart from setting the action on selection, as we have done this time, it is also possible to run the action on hover, or by using a menu.

Also, we can choose what happens once the selection is cleared. Upon clearing the selection, we can choose to leave the filter, show all values, or exclude all values.

See also

- For more information on filter actions, see the **Tableau Help** page on the topic at https://onlinehelp.tableau.com/current/pro/desktop/en-us/actions_filter.html

6
Building Dashboards

In this chapter, we will cover the following recipes:

- Creating a dashboard
- Formatting a dashboard
- Setting filters
- Setting filters across various data sources
- Navigating through actions
- Adding highlight actions
- Setting layouts
- Building a self-service dashboard

Technical requirements

To follow the recipes from this chapter, you will need to download the `Internet_usage.csv` file (which can be downloaded from `https://github.com/PacktPublishing/Tableau-2018-Dot-1-Cookbook/blob/master/Internet_usage.csv`) and `Internet_satisfaction.csv` (which can be downloaded from `https://github.com/PacktPublishing/Tableau-2018-Dot-1-Cookbook/blob/master/Internet_satisfaction.csv`) datasets and save them to your device.

Introduction

By now, you have learned how to create individual tables and charts from your data. In this chapter, we will learn how to bring them all together in a dashboard. Dashboards are a powerful way to present visualizations that come from multiple worksheets, and even multiple data sources, in one view. We will learn how to create a dashboard, customize its visual style and layout, and implement advanced functionalities, such as actions and parameter filters. After completing the recipes in this chapter, we will be well equipped to start creating our own dashboards.

We will be using two datasets that describe the results of a consumer survey, on internet use in Serbia, and we will view the satisfaction of users with various aspects of service from various internet providers. The `Internet_satisfaction.csv` dataset contains only internet users, and holds information on the regions of Serbia. It also tells us where they live; their main internet provider; what type of Internet is used in the household; and their satisfaction with the overall service, connection speed, and connection stability. The satisfaction was rated on a 5-point scale, where 1 means "completely dissatisfied" and 5 means "completely satisfied." The other dataset, `Internet_usage.csv`, contains information on household Internet penetration by region of Serbia, and settlement type (urban or rural). Notice that the field that holds information on region has the same values, but different names, across the two datasets.

Creating a dashboard

In this recipe, you will be guided through an explanation and overview of the basics of creating a dashboard. We will create a simple dashboard containing three worksheets, and we will build on it in the upcoming recipes.

Getting ready

To create the dashboard, we will use the `Internet_satisfaction.csv` dataset. Make sure you have a local copy of the dataset saved and that you are connected to the dataset.

How to do it...

1. In a blank worksheet, drag and drop **Main provider** from **Dimensions** into the **Columns** shelf.
2. Then, drag and drop **Satisfaction overall** from **Measures** into the **Rows** shelf.
3. Hover over the **SUM(Satisfaction overall)** pill so that a small downward arrow appears on it and click on it.
4. Navigate to **Measure (Sum)**, and in the drop-down menu, select **Average**:

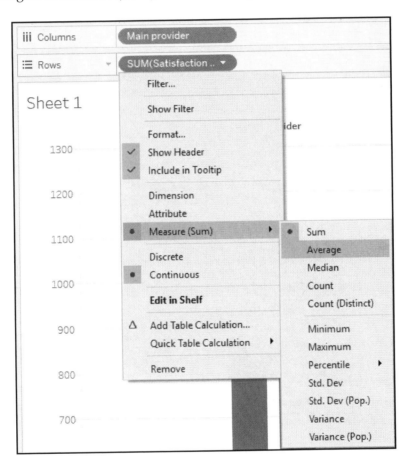

5. In the **Marks** card, change the mark type from **Automatic** to **Circle**.
6. Double-click on the title at the top of the workspace, and in the **Edit Title** window, change it from **Sheet 1** to Overall Satisfaction per Provider and click on **Apply**. You will see the title name is changed to **Overall Satisfaction per Provider**; then, click on the **OK** button:

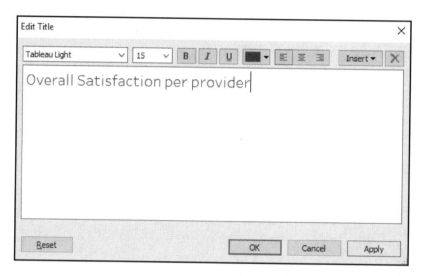

7. In the main menu toolbar, click on **Worksheet**, and then select **New Worksheet**.
8. Drag and drop **HH internet type** into the **Columns** shelf.
9. Drag and drop **Satisfaction speed** into the **Rows** shelf.
10. Hover over the **SUM(Satisfaction speed)** pill so that a small downward arrow appears on it and click on it.
11. Navigate to **Measure (Sum)**, and in the drop-down menu, select **Average**.
12. Double-click on the worksheet title and change the title from **Sheet 2** to Satisfaction with speed. Click on **Apply** and then click on the **OK** button.
13. In the main menu toolbar, click on **Worksheet**, and then select **New Worksheet**.
14. Drag and drop **HH internet type** into the **Columns** shelf.
15. Drag and drop **Satisfaction stability** into the **Rows** shelf.
16. Hover over the **Satisfaction stability** pill so that a small downward arrow appears on it and click on it.
17. Navigate to **Measure (Sum)**, and in the drop-down menu, select **Average**.
18. Double-click on the worksheet title and change the title from **Sheet 3** to Satisfaction with stability.

19. From the main menu toolbar, select **New Dashboard** under **Dashboard**:

A blank dashboard will appear, looking like this:

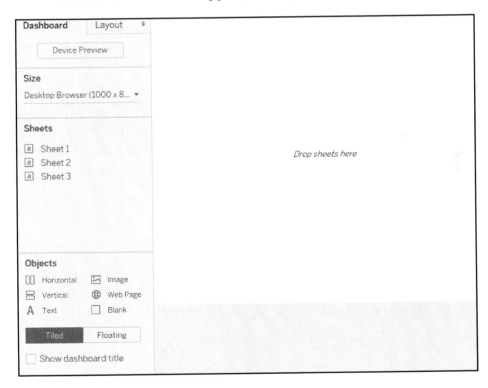

20. Drag and drop **Sheet 1** from the **Dashboard** pane (on the left side of the screen) into the dashboard view:

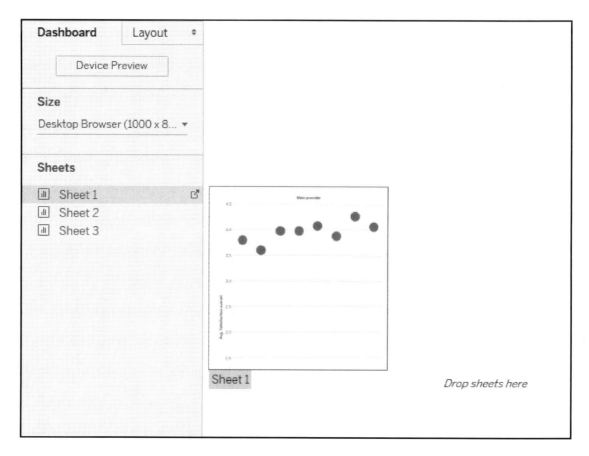

21. Drag and drop **Sheet 2** from the **Dashboard** pane into the dashboard view, below **Sheet 1**.

22. Drag and drop **Sheet 3** from the **Dashboard** pane into the dashboard view, to the right of **Sheet 2**. In the following screenshot, we can see the various elements that are present in the dashboard:

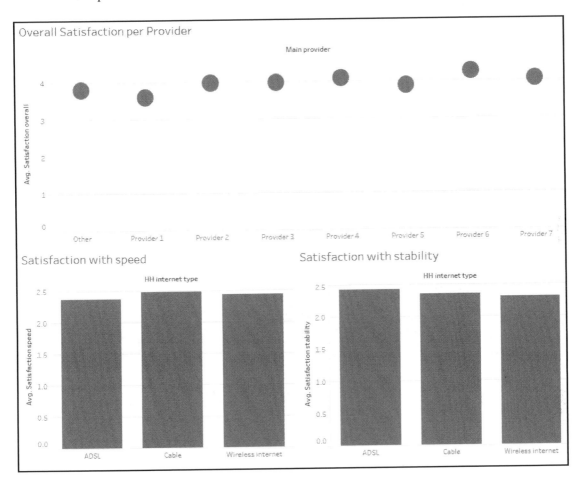

How it works...

In this recipe, we have created a basic dashboard. First, we have created a couple of worksheets. Then, we have placed them all in one dashboard.

Dashboards can hold multiple worksheets. Apart from worksheets, they can also contain images, links, text boxes, and web pages. Although dashboards can contain many elements, they are meant to present data in an easy-to-read manner, so you should always strive to maintain a clean look and not make your dashboard overcrowded.

There's more...

Dashboards can be linked with one another and filtered across. We will cover this in detail in the upcoming recipes.

See also

- You can explore creating dashboards some more using the Tableau help resources at `https://onlinehelp.tableau.com/current/pro/desktop/en-us/dashboards_create.html`.

Formatting a dashboard

Dashboards can be formatted and customized, beyond the formatting of the charts themselves. By using colors and fonts, you can create a visual identity you like and make the dashboard cleaner and easier to read.

Getting ready

In this recipe, we will follow the *Creating a dashboard* recipe from this chapter to create a basic dashboard. We will build on it.

How to do it...

Let's now set and format the dashboard title, referring to the given steps.

Setting and formatting dashboard title

1. In the **Objects** pane, check the box in front of **Show dashboard title**:

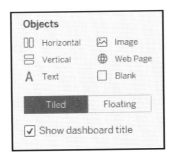

2. Double-click on the title and, in the **Edit Title** window, change it from **Dashboard 1** to Satisfaction. Select the title text and change the font size to **24**, change the color to orange, and apply bold font:

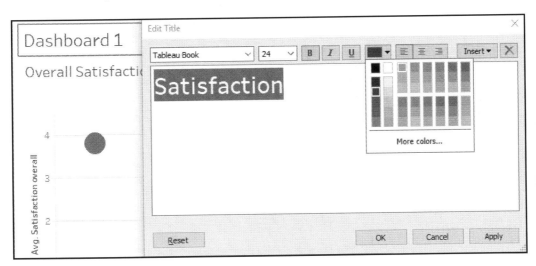

3. Alternatively, navigate to the main menu toolbar, click on **Dashboard**, and select **Format.**

4. The **Format Dashboard** pane will appear on the left-hand side. Under **Dashboard Title**, you can adjust the text, font, color, and size under **Font**; text alignment under **Alignment**; text background color under **Shading**; and border of the title under **Border**:

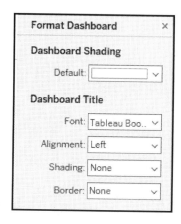

Formatting worksheet titles

1. From the main menu toolbar, navigate to **Dashboard** and select **Format**.
2. Under **Worksheet Titles**, click on the **Font** drop-down arrow, change the text color to orange, and apply bold font.
3. Click on **Shading** to change the background color to light gray, and move the slider under the palette to the left to make the shade even lighter:

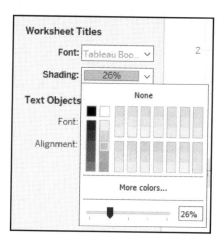

4. Alternatively, you can format the titles individually by double-clicking on them, selecting the title text in the **Edit Titl**e window, and adjusting font size, color, alignment, and so on.

Formatting text objects

1. From the **Objects** pane, drag and drop **Text** into your dashboard view, below the **Sheet 1** chart. If you still have the **Format** pane open, you will need to close it in order for the **Objects** pane to appear:

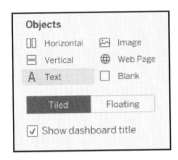

2. In the **Edit Text** window, type `*Brand names have been removed`. Then, click **OK**.
3. Hover over the top border of the **Text** object until an arrow appears, hold it, and drag it down to decrease the **Text** object's height, while simultaneously increasing the **Sheet 1** area.
4. In the main menu toolbar, navigate to **Dashboard | Format**.
5. Under **Text Objects**, click on **Font** and apply italic font:

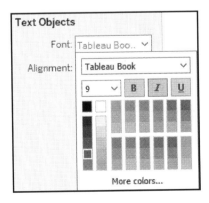

6. Alternatively, you can double-click on the text object and set the font size, shading, alignment, and more by selecting the text in the **Edit Text** window and choose the desired settings.

Formatting the dashboard background

1. In the main menu toolbar, navigate to **Dashboard | Format**.
2. Under **Dashboard Shading,** you can select the desired color of the background. This time, let's leave it white:

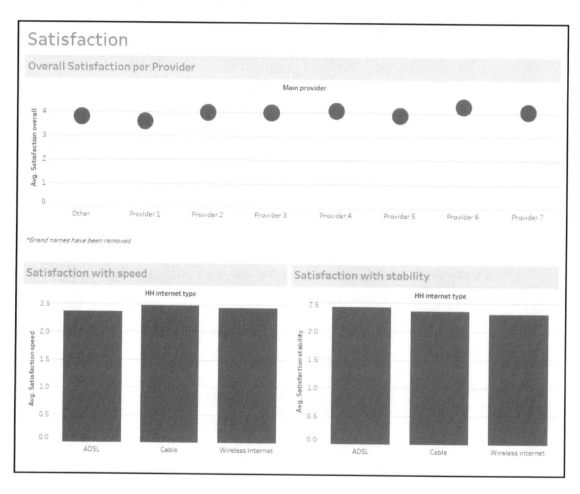

How it works...

Tableau offers a multitude of formatting options. We have formatted our dashboard title, individual sheet titles, and a background. It also offers an option for formatting the dashboard title, which we've left as white this time, in order to not take attention away from the dashboard content due to too many colors.

Although Tableau allows us to apply formatting to virtually every element in our dashboard, when formatting a dashboard, you should always keep in mind that less is more! For the best effect, keep the color palette simple, the background neutral, and the text colors and fonts simple and uniform.

There's more...

The majority of the work that will make your dashboard look great is done when creating and designing visualizations themselves. Make sure your visualizations are formatted well, and use the dashboard formatting options to bring it all together and add some final touches.

See also

- For some more tips on dashboard design, you can refer to the Tableau help resources at `https://onlinehelp.tableau.com/current/pro/desktop/en-us/dashboards_best_practices.html`
- You may also check out the Tableau public gallery for some inspirational designs: `https://public.tableau.com/en-us/s/gallery`

Setting filters

When creating a dashboard, it is possible to allow the end user to filter across multiple dashboard elements, so they all reflect the same selection. Filters can be applied directly from the dashboard, or through a worksheet—we will cover both ways. We will also cover filtering by worksheets in the dashboard, meaning we will use a visualization in the dashboard as a filter. Finally, we will briefly go through implementing action filters.

Getting ready

Follow the *Creating a dashboard* recipe from this chapter to create a basic dashboard. We will build on it.

How to do it...

We will begin with *Setting filters* through the dashboard itself.

Setting filters through the dashboard

1. Click on the **Sheet 3** bar chart in the dashboard.
2. Click on the white arrow (More Options) that appears next to the chart area and navigate to **Filters | HH internet type**:

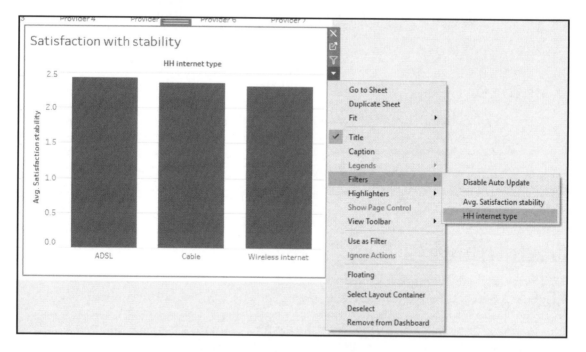

3. After the filter by **HH internet type** has appeared in the top-right corner of the dashboard, click on it, and then click on the white arrow (More Options) that appears alongside the filter area.
4. Navigate to **Apply to Worksheets**, and from it, select **Selected Worksheets...**:

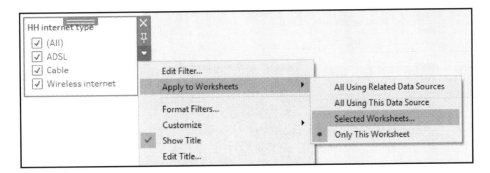

5. Click on the **All on dashboard** button and then click on **OK**:

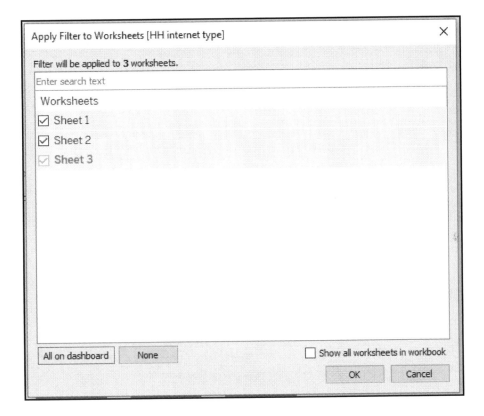

6. Click on the filter by **HH internet type**, and then click on the white arrow (More Options) that appears along the filter area.

7. From the drop-down menu, select **Single Value (dropdown)**.

8. Try it by selecting different Internet types:

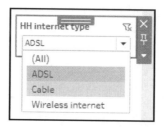

Setting filters through the worksheet

Now, let's try another way of setting up filters. Before starting this recipe, undo the work you did in following the *Setting filters through the dashboard* recipe, so we start from scratch. We will now set the same filter, but through the worksheet. We will start from the dashboard without any filters applied:

1. Navigate to **Sheet 1** by clicking on the **Sheet 1** tab at the bottom of the workspace.

2. Drag and drop **HH internet type** from **Dimensions** into the **Filters** shelf.

3. In the **Filter [HH internet type]** window, select **All** and then click **OK**.

4. Hover over the **HH internet type** pill in the **Filters** shelf so that a white arrow appears on the right.

5. Click on the arrow and from the drop-down menu, select **Show filter**:

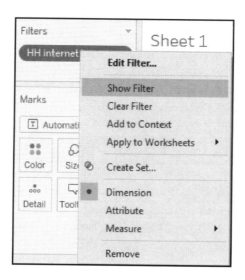

6. Hover over the **HH internet type** card that has appeared and click on the small arrow in the top-right corner.

7. Select **Single Value (dropdown)**.

8. Once again, hover over the **HH internet type** pill in the **Filters** shelf so that a white arrow appears on the right, and click on it.

9. Select **Apply to Worksheets**, and from it, select **Selected Worksheets…**.

10. Click **All**, and then click **OK**.

11. Navigate back to the dashboard by clicking on the **Dashboard 1** card in the bottom of the workbook.

12. If the filter you just added to **Sheet 1** is not visible in the dashboard, click on the **Sheet 1** chart and then click on the white-on-gray **X** that appears along the outer border of the filter area:

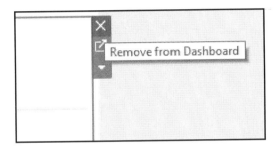

The alternative method would be to click on the sheet in the dashboard, and navigate to **Filter | HH internet type** from the drop-down menu.

13. After the chart has disappeared from the dashboard, drag and drop **Sheet 1** from the **Dashboard** pane into the dashboard view again, in the same spot, and the filter will appear in the dashboard.

Adding filters through a worksheet works best before your worksheet has been added to the dashboard. If the filter card is visible before the worksheet is added to the dashboard, it will automatically appear in the dashboard as well when you add your worksheet to it.

Filtering by worksheets in the dashboard – action filters

We will now set a filter using one dashboard element to filter out other dashboard elements. We will also introduce action filters. We will start with the dashboard and avoid applying any filters:

1. Click on the **Sheet 1** chart in the dashboard.
2. Click on the white arrow (More Options) that appears alongside the chart area.
3. From the drop-down menu, select **Use as Filter**:

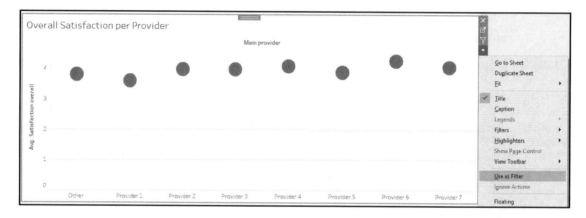

4. Try it by clicking on any column header or any circle in the **Sheet 1** chart.
5. You have now created an action filter, which you can see if you navigate to **Dashboard** in the main menu toolbar and click on **Actions...**:

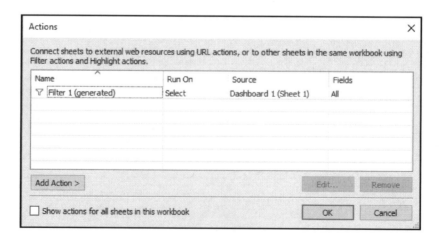

6. Alternatively, you can create an action filter from scratch. Navigate to **Dashboard** in the main menu toolbar and click on **Actions....**

7. In the **Actions** window, click on the **Add Action >** button and select **Filter...**:

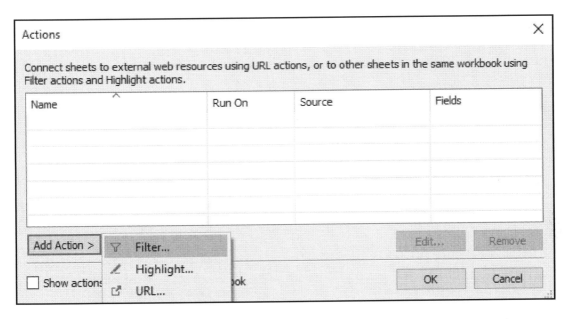

8. In the **Add Filter Action** window, under **Source Sheets**, leave all three sheets checked.

9. Under **Run action on**, click on **Select**.

10. Under **Target Sheets**, leave all three sheets checked.

11. Under **Clearing the selection will**, select the **Show all values** option:

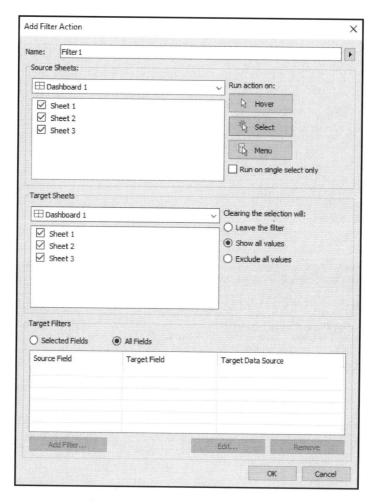

12. Click on **OK.**
13. In the **Actions** window, click on **OK**.
14. All three sheets in the dashboard are acting as filters. Try it out by clicking on any bar/circle, or a column header, in any of the charts.

How it works...

Actions work by passing commands between worksheets. So, when you assign a filter action to one sheet, and perform the action that triggers it, it affects the other sheet(s) by filtering them. Filtering is a great way to make your dashboard more interactive, engaging, and easier to read. Do not hesitate to include multiple filters in your dashboard, as it can help your end users narrow down to the data they need.

There's more...

There are many more ways to filter your views in Tableau. They are covered in great detail in Chapter 5, *Tableau Desktop Advanced Filtering*. All those types of filters can be applied to dashboards as well.

See also

- For more information on filtering, check out **Tableau Help** at https://onlinehelp.tableau.com/current/pro/desktop/en-us/filtering.html.

Setting filters across various data sources

So far, we have discovered how to apply a filter to multiple dashboard elements when they are all coming from the same data source. However, Tableau also allows us to filter across elements that come from different data sources.

Getting ready

In this recipe, we will create a dashboard from scratch, so we can go through every step of connecting to the data sources. We will use both the Internet_usage.csv and Internet_satisfaction.csv datasets, so before we begin, you need to make sure you have them both saved on your device.

How to do it...

1. Connect to the `Internet_satisfaction.csv` dataset.
2. From the main menu toolbar, click on **Data** and select **New Data Source**.
3. Navigate to your local copy of the `Internet_usage.csv` dataset and add it as a data source.
4. Click on the **Sheet 1** tab.
5. In the **Data** pane, two data sources will now appear. Make sure `Internet_usage` is selected.
6. Drag and drop **Area** from **Dimensions** into the **Columns** shelf.
7. Drag and drop **Internet penetration** from **Measures** into the **Rows** shelf.
8. Hover over the **Internet penetration** pill so that a small white arrow appears, and click on it.
9. Navigate to **Measure (Sum)**, and select **Average** from the drop-down menu.
10. Right-click on the **Sheet 1** tab in the bottom of the workbook, select **Rename sheet**, and rename the sheet to **Internet penetration**.
11. Create another new sheet by clicking on the New Worksheet tab from the bottom of the workbook.
12. Make sure the `Internet_satisfaction` data source is selected in the **Data** pane.
13. Drag and drop **Region** from **Dimensions** into the **Columns** shelf.
14. Drag and drop **HH internet type** from **Dimensions** onto **Color** in the **Marks card**.
15. Drag and drop **Number of Records** from **Measures** into the **Rows** shelf.
16. Hover over the **Number of Records** pill so that a white arrow appears:

17. Click on it and navigate to **Quick Table Calculation | Percent of Total**.
18. Click on the white arrow again and select **Edit Table Calculation...**.
19. In the **Table Calculation** window, choose **Table (down)**, deselect the **Show calculation assistance** box, and close the window:

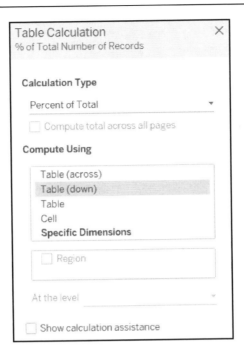

20. Rename the sheet to **HH internet type**.
21. From the main menu toolbar, navigate to **Data** | **Edit Relationships...**, as shown in the following screenshot:

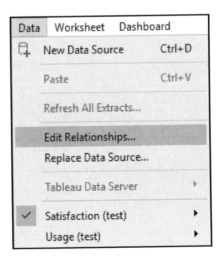

22. In the **Relationships** window, select **Custom** and click on **Add...**:

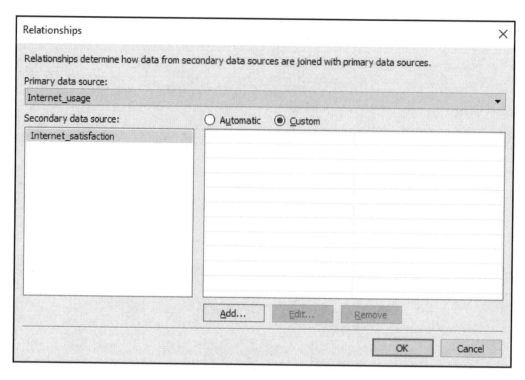

23. In the **Add/Edit Field Mapping** window, highlight **Area** and **Region** by clicking on them, and click on **OK**:

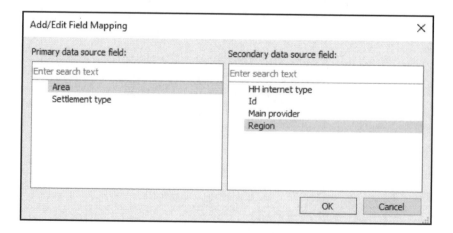

24. Click **OK** in the **Relationships** window.
25. Let's create the filter. In the **Internet penetration** sheet, drag and drop **Area** from **Dimensions** into the **Filters** shelf.
26. When the **Filter [Area]** window opens, click on **OK**.
27. Hover over the **Area** pill in the **Filters** shelf and click on the white arrow that appears.
28. Select **Show Filter**.
29. Hover over the **Area** pill in the **Filters** shelf and click on the white arrow that appears.
30. Navigate to **Apply to Worksheets | Selected Worksheets....**
31. In the **Apply Filter to Worksheets [Area]** window that opens, select the box in front of the second sheet, **HH internet type,** and click on **OK**. We notice that a small symbol appears next to **Area** in the **Filters** shelf. If you hover over it, it will inform you that the filter applies to selected worksheets with a related data source:

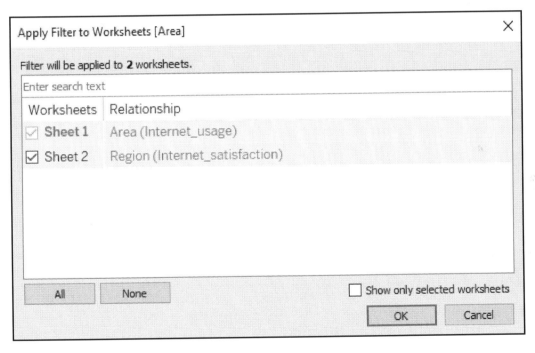

32. Create a new dashboard by clicking on the New Dashboard tab in the bottom of the worksheet.

33. Drag and drop the **Internet penetration** sheet from the **Dashboard** pane into the workspace.
34. Drag and drop the **HH internet type** sheet from the **Dashboard** pane into the workspace, under the **Internet penetration** sheet.
35. The **Area** filter will appear in the dashboard as well.
36. Try it by selecting and deselecting different areas.

How it works...

This recipe relies on data blending. By editing the relationship between the **Region** and **Area** dimensions in the two data sources, we make a link between the two, and tell Tableau to treat them as the same dimension. This allows us to filter across the sheets using this dimension, just as if it was coming from one data source. Refer to `Chapter 2`, *Data Manipulation*, and go through the *Data blending* recipe for more details.

There's more...

Multiple dimensions can be linked and filtered in Tableau. Also, more than two data sources can be used in a single dashboard and, if all conditions for data blending are satisfied, they can all be used to filter across the worksheet from other dashboards.

See also

- For more on data blending, see the **Tableau Help** page at `https://onlinehelp.tableau.com/current/pro/desktop/en-us/multiple_connections.html`

Adding highlight actions

So far, we have experienced using filter actions. Now, we will use another kind of action: highlight actions. Highlight actions let us highlight the same category in other visualizations in the dashboard on a click or hover. They can be very useful in boosting the readability of the dashboard.

Getting ready

For this recipe, we will make a dashboard from scratch using the `Internet_satisfaction.csv` dataset, so before we begin, make sure you download it to your device and connect to it.

How to do it...

1. Create a new worksheet by clicking on the New Worksheet tab in the bottom of the workbook.
2. Drag and drop **Region** from **Dimensions** into the **Rows** shelf.
3. Drag and drop **Satisfaction overall** from **Measures** into the **Columns** shelf.
4. Hover over the **Satisfaction overall** pill so that a small downward arrow appears on it and click on it.
5. Navigate to **Measure (Sum)**, and in the drop-down menu, select **Average**:

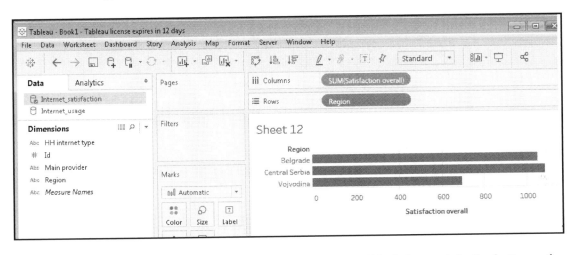

6. Create a new worksheet by clicking on the New Worksheet tab in the bottom of the workbook.
7. Drag and drop **Region** from **Dimensions** into the **Rows** shelf.
8. Drag and drop **Satisfaction speed** from **Measures** into the **Columns** shelf.
9. Hover over the **Satisfaction speed** pill so that a small downward arrow appears on it and click on it.

10. Navigate to **Measure (Sum)**, and in the drop-down menu, select **Average**:

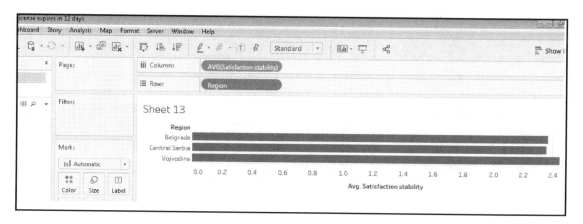

11. Create a new worksheet by clicking on the New Worksheet tab in the bottom of the workbook.
12. Drag and drop **Region** from **Dimensions** into the **Rows** shelf.
13. Drag and drop **Satisfaction stability** from **Measures** into the **Columns** shelf.
14. Hover over the **Satisfaction stability** pill so that a small downward arrow appears on it and click on it.
15. Navigate to **Measure (Sum)**, and in the drop-down menu, select **Average**:

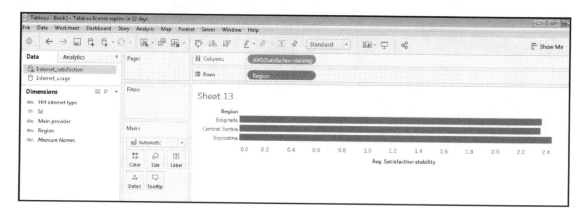

16. Create a new dashboard by clicking on the New Dashboard option in the bottom of the workbook.

17. Drag and drop **Sheet 1** from the **Dashboard** pane to the dashboard view.

18. Drag and drop **Sheet 2** under **Sheet 1**, and **Sheet 3** under **Sheet 2**:

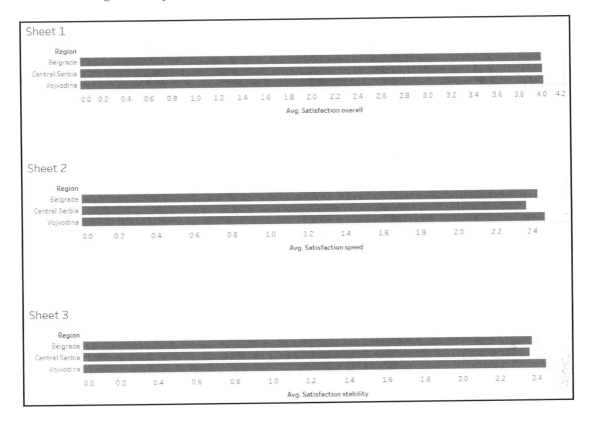

19. From the main menu toolbar, navigate to **Dashboard** | **Actions....**

20. In the **Actions** window, click on the **Add Action >** option and select **Highlight...**:

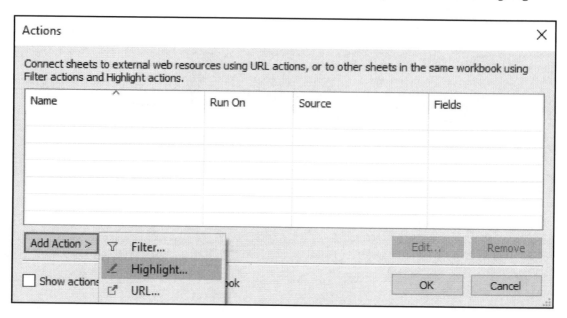

21. Under the **Source Sheets** and **Target sheets** options, leave all sheets selected. Keep in mind that **Dashboard 1** needs to be selected under both **Source Sheets** and **Target Sheets**.

22. Under the **Run action on** option, select **Hover**:

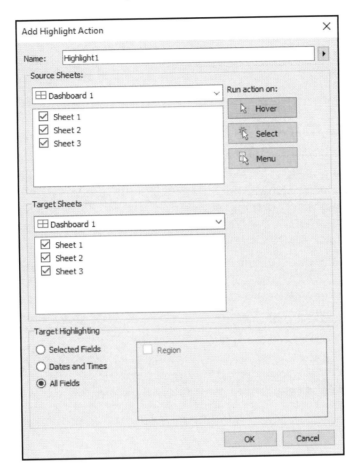

23. Click on **OK**.
24. Click **OK** in the **Actions** window.
25. Test it by hovering over any of the bars or column headers in any of the charts.

How it works...

Actions send information across different worksheets, allowing a selection or hover that you can perform on one worksheet in the dashboard to trigger the action across other sheets. In this case, hovering over a chart from one sheet highlights the corresponding data points in other sheets.

There's more...

We chose to run the highlight action on hover. However, Tableau offers other options as well, such as activating actions on selection, or through a menu. Depending on the kind of action you are implementing and what kind of effect you would like to achieve, other ways to run your action might be more appropriate.

See also

- For some more information on highlight actions, see the Tableau help resource on highlight actions at `https://onlinehelp.tableau.com/current/pro/desktop/en-us/actions_highlight.html`.

Setting layouts

Tableau lets users control the overall dashboard size. It offers the following three size options:

- **Fixed**: This option helps in keeping the size of the dashboard fixed, regardless of the window used to display it.
- **Range**: Where the dashboard scales between two sizes that you specify.
- **Automatic**: Where the dashboard automatically resizes to fit the window.

Additionally, Tableau offers different dashboard layouts, adjusted for different types of devices. This allows you to make only one dashboard, but still control the way it appears to your end users when they view it on a range of different devices.

Getting ready

Follow the *Creating a dashboard* recipe to create the dashboard that you will be working with in this recipe.

How to do it...

We will begin by setting the screen size.

Setting a fixed size

1. Navigate to the **Dashboard** pane on the left-hand side, and click on the drop-down menu under **Size**. **Fixed size** is selected by default.
2. From the drop-down menu, select the preferred screen resolution. You can also manually adjust **Width** and **Height** by typing the figures in the appropriate boxes, or increase/decrease them by clicking the up/down arrows adjacent to the boxes:

Setting the automatic size

1. In the **Dashboard** pane on the left-hand side, under **Size**, click on the drop-down menu.

2. In the first drop-down menu that appears, switch from **Fixed size** to **Automatic**:

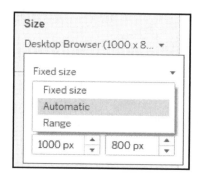

Setting the range size

1. In the **Dashboard** pane on the left-hand side, under **Size**, click on the drop-down menu.
2. In the first drop-down menu that appears, switch from **Fixed size** to **Range**.
3. Set the minimum screen size either by typing in the desired **Width** and **Height** in the appropriate boxes, or using the up and down arrows adjacent to the boxes.
4. Set the maximum screen size using the same procedure.
5. You can also disable the minimum or maximum screen size by deselecting the box next to it:

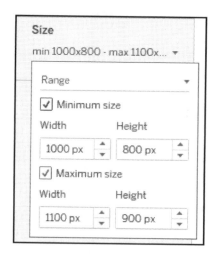

Adding a device layout

1. In the **Dashboard** pane on the left-hand side, click on **Device Preview**:

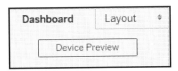

2. A **Device Preview** ribbon with options will appear at the top of the dashboard view:

3. Shuffle through **Device type** using the left and right arrows to choose a device type.
4. Alternatively, click on the **Device type** box to open a drop-down menu and choose a device type.
5. When a device type is selected, the **Model** box appears to the right of the **Device type** box, as shown in the preceding screenshot.
6. You can use the **Model** box to choose a specific model of the device. If you are not sure what device model your end users will be viewing the dashboard on, or whether that device model is offered, leave the default option, **Generic Desktop Monitor/Tablet/Phone**, selected.
7. Use the button to the right of the **Model** box to switch between **Portrait** and **Landscape** modes.
8. If the **Device type** box selected is **Phone**, you can check the **Tableau Mobile** checkbox. It allows you to see what the dashboard will look like in the **Tableau Mobile app**. To see what it will look like in the browser, deselect the box.
9. Click on the **Add Desktop/Tablet/Phone Layout** checkbox to add a layout for a particular device.

Customizing the device layout

1. Once you click the **Add Desktop/Tablet/Phone Layout** button, the new layout you added will appear in the **Dashboard** pane, alongside the default layout:

2. Click on different layouts that you have added to the **Dashboard** pane to preview them.
3. When you click on a device, such as the **Tablet** layout, you can set the size of the dashboard on the **Tablet** screen in the **Dashboard** pane, under **Size – Tablet**. Check the radio button in front of **Fit all** to fit the entire dashboard onto a tablet screen, or check **Fit width** to fit the dashboard by width, while setting the height manually in the **Height** box.

4. Under **Layout – Tablet**, you can leave the default option selected, and you can also check **Custom**. If you check **Custom**, a menu that allows you to manipulate dashboard elements will appear:

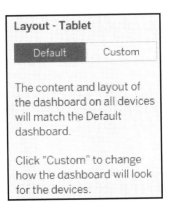

How it works...

When customizing the device layout, you can choose to have the same layout on all devices, or choose a custom layout for different devices. If you choose the latter, you can pick and choose which sheets to display on a specific device type and how to arrange them, without your default layout or layouts for other device types being affected by it.

There's more...

Each worksheet in the dashboard can have its position tiled or floating. The tiled layout snaps elements into positions, so that they fit next to each other, while floating allows you to move elements around freely, even overlapping them. Strive to use the tiled layout when possible, and save floating for filters, legends, images, and other small elements that can overlap with worksheets to save space.

If you have floating elements in your dashboard, you should use the fixed display size! Otherwise, the tiled elements will resize with the screen size, while the floating elements will keep their position, leading to a messy look.

See also

- Check out the Tableau help resources on setting dashboard layouts at `https://onlinehelp.tableau.com/current/pro/desktop/en-us/dashboards_organize_floatingandtiled.html#Control`.

Building a self-service dashboard

Setting up a self-service dashboard is a great way to allow your end users to explore their data at their own pace. In this recipe, we will bring together the things that we've learned throughout this chapter, and some more, to create a dashboard with rich functionality. We will implement parameters and action filters to demonstrate an interactive experience, and also embed a web page and an active link into our dashboard.

Getting ready

For this recipe, we will make a dashboard from scratch using both the `Internet_usage.csv` and `Internet_ satisfaction.csv` datasets, so before we begin, make sure you download them to your device and connect to them. Also, save the image file associated with this chapter (it can be downloaded from `https://github.com/PacktPublishing/Tableau-2018-Dot-1-Cookbook/blob/master/Chapter%206.PNG`) to your device, as we will be using it in our dashboard.

How to do it...

We will now switch between dimensions using parameters.

Switching between dimensions with parameters

1. Connect to the data sources.
2. Click on the **Sheet 1** tab in the bottom of the workbook.
3. In the **Data** pane, make sure the `Internet_usage` data source is active.
4. Click on the black downward-pointing arrow to the right of **Dimensions** and select **Create Parameter...**:

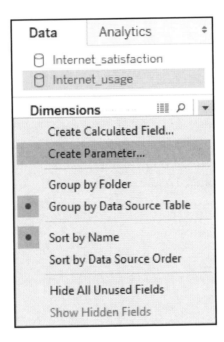

5. In the **Create Parameter** window, change the name of the parameter from **Parameter 1** to `Region or Settlement Type`.
6. In the **Data type** drop-down menu, choose **String**.
7. Under **Allowable values**, change the selection from the default of **All** to **List**.
8. In the **List of values** pane that appears, click on the **Click to add new value** placeholder and type `Region`.

9. In the row under add another value, `Settlement Type`, as shown in the following screenshot:

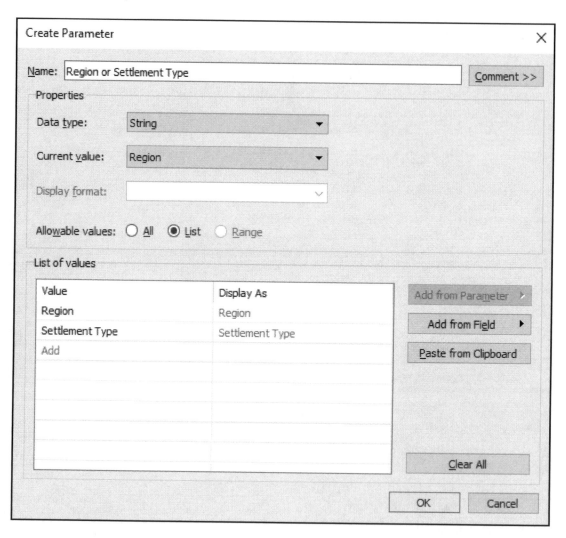

10. Click on **OK**.
11. A new section, **Parameters**, will appear under **Measures**, showing the parameter you just made (**Region or Settlement Type**). Hover over the **Region or Settlement Type** pill until a white arrow appears, click on it, and choose **Show Parameter Control**:

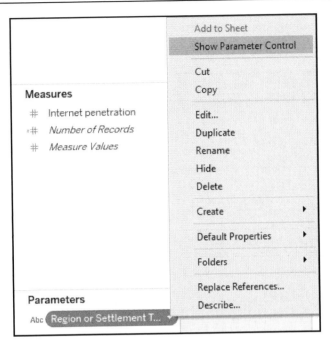

12. Let's create a calculated field that we will use in our visualization to switch between dimensions. Click on the black downward-pointing arrow to the right of **Dimensions** and select **Create Calculated Field...**:

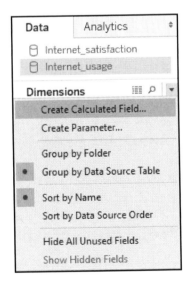

13. When the calculated field window opens, change the name from **Calculation1** to `Switching`, click on **Apply**, and type the following expression:

```
CASE [Region or Settlement Type]
when "Region" then [Area]
when "Settlement Type" then [Settlement type]
END
```

Let's see how it looks:

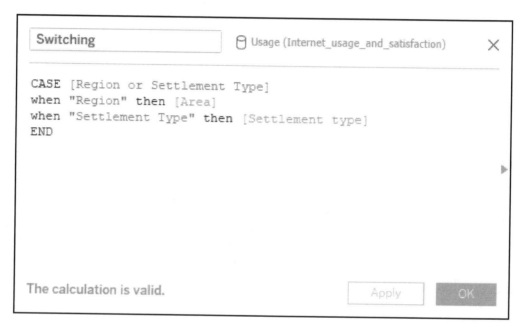

14. Click on **Apply** and click on **OK**.
15. Let's create the visualization. Drag and drop the new dimension you created, **Switching**, into the **Columns** shelf.
16. Drag and drop **Area** from **Dimensions** to the **Columns** shelf as well, to the right of the **Switching** pill.
17. Drag and drop **Internet penetration** from **Measures** into the **Rows** shelf.
18. Hover over the **Internet penetration** pill so that a small downward arrow appears and click on it.
19. Navigate to **Measure (Sum)**, and in the drop-down menu, select **Average**:

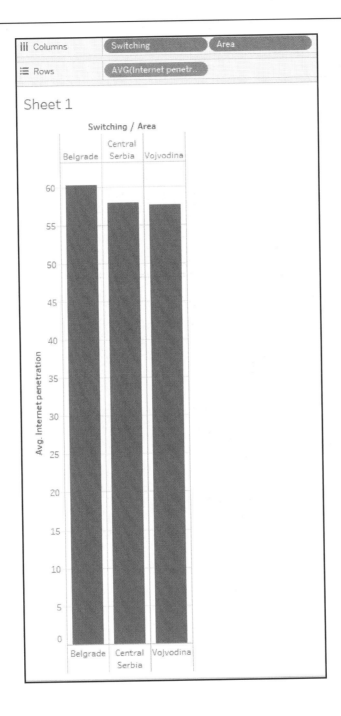

20. Drag and drop **Area** from **Dimensions** to **Color** in the **Marks** card.
21. Change the mark type in the drop-down menu in the **Marks** card from **Automatic** to **Shape**.
22. Right-click on the column field label in the chart, **Switching/Area**, and select **Hide Field Labels for Columns**:

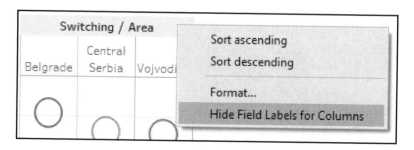

23. Hover over the **Area** pill in the **Columns** shelf until a white arrow appears; click on it and deselect **Show Header**:

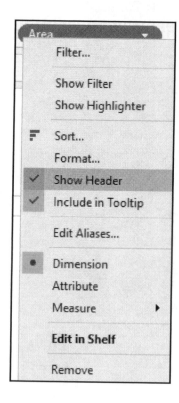

24. Double-click on **Tooltip** in the **Marks** card, and, in the **Edit Tooltip** window, remove **Switching**: <**Switching**>. When you are done, click **OK**.

25. Try it by switching from **Region or Settlement Type** and back in the parameter-control drop-down menu.

26. Click on the New Dashboard option in the bottom of the worksheet to create a new dashboard.

27. Drag and drop **Sheet 1**, which you just made, into the dashboard view:

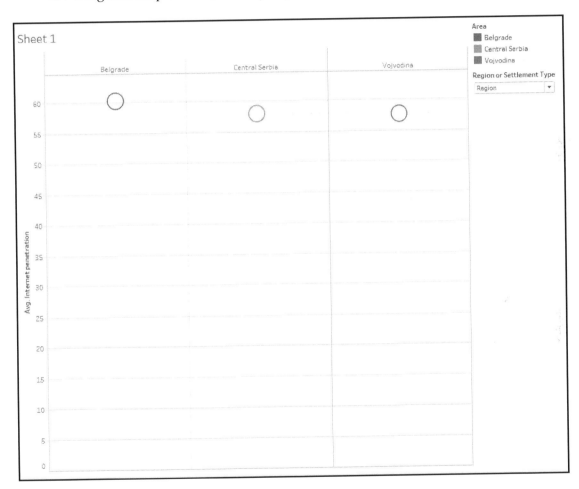

Adding a hyperlink to an image object

1. In the dashboard, from the **Objects** pane, drag and drop **Image** into the dashboard view, to the right of the **Sheet 1** visualization.
2. Navigate to the `Chapter 6` image you saved on your device, select it, and click on **Open**.
3. Right-click on the **Image** object in the dashboard, and click on **Fit image**.
4. Right-click on the image again, and select **Set URL...**:

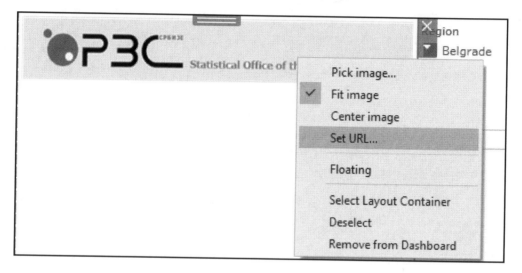

5. In the **Set URL** window, paste the `http://www.stat.gov.rs/en-US` link and click on **OK**:

6. Test it by clicking on the image element. It will launch your browser and take you to the home page of the **Statistical Office of the Republic of Serbia**.

Adding a web page to the dashboard

1. From the **Objects** card, drag and drop **Web Page** under the **Sheet 1** chart in the dashboard view:

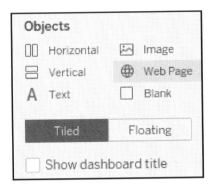

2. In the **Edit URL** window, paste the following Wikipedia link on internet use:
   `https://en.wikipedia.org/wiki/Global_Internet_usage`.

Adding an action filter

Let's finish the dashboard by adding another worksheet to it. We will then apply the action filter to both the worksheets in the dashboard:

1. Create a new worksheet by clicking on the New Worksheet tab in the bottom of the workbook.
2. Make sure **Internet_satisfaction** is selected as the data source.
3. Drag and drop **Satisfaction stability** from **Measures** into the **Columns** shelf.
4. Hover over the **Satisfaction stability** pill so that a small arrow appears on it and click on it.
5. Navigate to **Measure (Sum)**, and in the drop-down menu, select **Average**.
6. Drag and drop **Region** from **Dimensions** into the **Rows** shelf.
7. Drag and drop **Satisfaction speed** from **Measures** into the **Rows** shelf, to the right of the **Region** pill.
8. Hover over the **Satisfaction speed** pill so that a small arrow appears on it and click on it.
9. Navigate to **Measure (Sum)**, and in the drop-down menu, select **Average**.
10. In the **Marks** card, change the mark type to **Circle** using the drop-down menu.
11. Drag and drop **Main provider** from **Dimensions** to **Color** in the **Marks** card.

12. Click on **Dashboard**, and drag and drop **Sheet 2** into the dashboard view, under the **Image** object.

13. Increase the height of the **Sheet 2** chart while decreasing the **Image** object by hovering over the **Sheet 2** chart top border, holding it with your mouse, and moving it up.

14. In the dashboard view, click on the **Sheet 1** chart and then click on the white pointing arrow (More Options) that appears alongside the chart area.

15. Select **Use as Filter**:

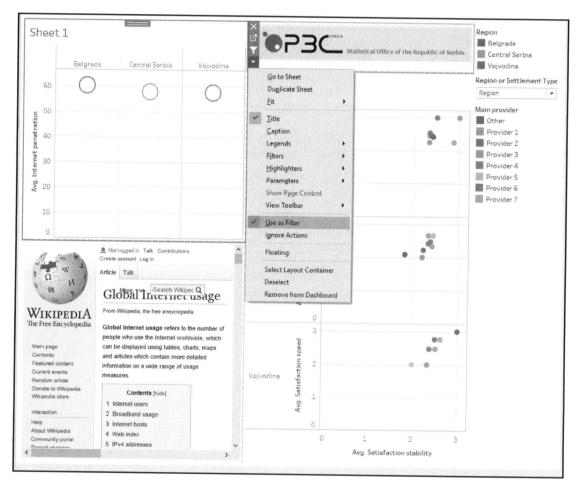

16. Try it out by choosing different parameter values from the **Region or Settlement type** drop-down menu and selecting and deselecting different regions in the **Sheet 1** visualization.

How it works...

In this recipe, we created a parameter to allow our users to choose an input value; in this case, it is which dimension to use. Then, we created a calculated field that utilizes parameter to switch between dimensions, and we used that calculated field in the visualization. When the user changes the parameter value, it also changes the value of the calculated field, and our visualization changes accordingly.

There's more...

Parameters can also be used to switch measures in your view, using the same principle we employed with dimensions in this recipe. It is also possible to switch between visualizations, such as a bar chart and a scatter plot, by creating them on separate sheets and then using a parameter to switch between the sheets.

From the 2018.2 version, Tableau also offers a new functionality: dashboard extensions. Extensions enable integration with other applications and new functionalities via special areas on the dashboard. You can find out more about dashboard extensions at https://www.tableau.com/about/blog/2018/6/announcing-dashboard-extensions-20182-beta-89581.

See also

- For more information on filtering with parameters, see the **Tableau Help** page on the topic at https://www.tableau.com/about/blog/2012/7/filtering-parameters-18326.

Telling a Story with Tableau 7

In this chapter, we will cover the following recipes:

- Creating a Tableau Story
- Setting the narrative of the Story
- Choosing the right charts
- Writing effective headlines
- Recommendation and executive summary
- Formatting the Story

Technical requirements

To follow the recipes in this chapter, you will need to download the `Recycling_campaign_effects.csv` dataset from `https://github.com/SlavenRB/Storytelling_with_Tableau/blob/master/Recycling_campaign_effects.csv` and save it to your device.

Introduction

So far, you have learned how to create individual charts and dashboards. In this chapter, you will go a step further and learn how to connect them in a meaningful Story. The Tableau Story functionality enables you to order visualizations in a logical and simple manner that helps your audience understand your insights better. Data that is presented within a Story is much easier to remember. Also, telling data stories gives you an opportunity to present your results in a broader context. Making stories in a Tableau is a lot like playing a game of "connect the dots". You just need to make the right links between your points and a picture will appear.

Creating a Tableau story

In this recipe, you will be given an explanation and overview of the technical basics of creating a Tableau story. In the following recipes, you will learn how to elaborate on the story, by picking adequate charts, putting them in the right order, writing insights, and formatting them in an appealing way. First, we will create a simple Story containing two worksheets, and we will build on it in the following recipes.

Getting ready

To create the Story, we will use the `Recycling_campaign_effects.csv` dataset. This dataset comes from a survey that is aimed at measuring the effectiveness of a campaign that is promoting recycling milk cartons. To promote recycling the carton packaging, a milk manufacturer placed specialized recycling bins around major cities and advertised the campaign on the labels of the milk packaging. Three months later, they wanted to know how many people knew about the recycling possibilities and how many people are actually recycling their milk cartons. They also conducted a survey asking milk buyers about their habits related to carton disposal. The variables that we are going to use are as follows:

- **Aware of recycling possibility**: This variable describes whether a person knows that milk carton packaging can be recycled in Serbia. The values of the variable are yes and no.
- **Milk carton disposal**: This variable concerns a person's typical place of milk carton disposal. The values of the variable are recycling garbage can and standard garbage can.
- **Read labels**: This describes the respondent's habit of reading labels on products that they purchase. The variable values are yes and no.

First, save `Recycling_campaign_effects.csv` on your computer, open Tableau, and connect it to your local copy of the data.

How to do it...

1. Open a blank worksheet and drag and drop **Milk cartons disposal** from **Dimensions** into the **Columns** shelf.
2. Drag and drop **Number of Records** from **Measures** to the **Rows** shelf.
3. Drag and drop **Number of Records** from **Measures** to **Label** in the **Marks** card.
4. Hover over the **Milk carton disposal** pill in the **Marks** card so that a small downward arrow appears and click on it.
5. Navigate to **Quick Table Calculation** | **Percent of Total**:

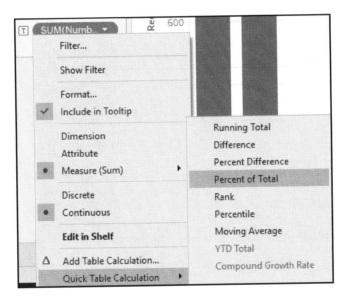

6. Change the label of the sheet from **Sheet 1** to `Recycling`:

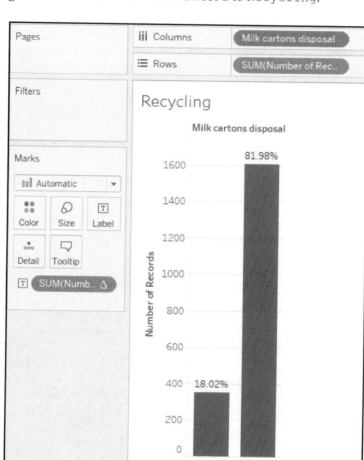

7. Open a blank worksheet and drag and drop **Aware of recycling possibility** from **Dimensions** into the **Columns** shelf.

8. Drag and drop **Number of Records** from **Measures** to the **Rows** shelf.

9. Drag and drop **Number of Records** from **Measures** to Label in the **Marks** card.

10. Hover over the **Number of Records** pill in **Marks** card so that a small downward arrow appears and click on it.

11. Navigate to **Quick Table Calculation | Percent of Total**.

12. Change the label of the sheet from **Sheet 2** to `Awareness`:

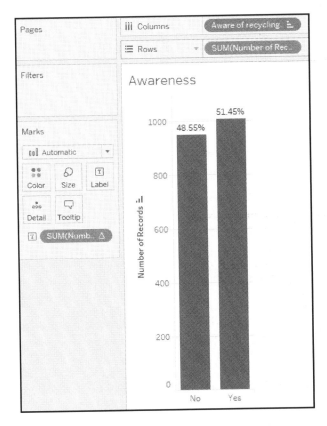

13. In the main menu, go to **Story** and click on **New Story**:

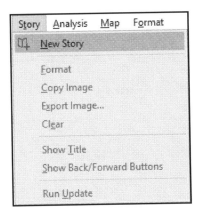

14. Alternatively, click on the icon at the bottom (circled in the following screenshot) of the screen to create a new story:

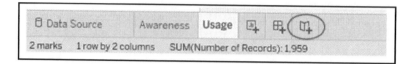

15. Drag and drop **Recycling** from the **Story** sidebar at the left-hand side to the **Drag a sheet here** placeholder in the canvas.

16. Double-click on the gray box at the top of the canvas to make the text editable and then type Recycling:

 The caption in the box has to be more descriptive, but for the sake of simplicity at this point, we will just put the title. In the following recipes, we will learn how to write effective captions.

17. In the **Story** tab on the left-hand side, under the **New Story** section, click on the **Blank** button:

18. Drag and drop **Awareness** from the **Story** sidebar to the **Drag a sheet here** placeholder in the canvas.
19. In the gray box at the top of the canvas, type Awareness.
20. Double-click on **Story 1** and in the **Edit title** box, type Effectiveness of Recycling Promotion:

How it works...

Basically, the Tableau Story is a collection of multiple worksheets or dashboards that are organized in a planned order. It helps us walk the audience through our data in the right way. Using Tableau Story enables us to suggest the path, to guide our viewer through the data in a way that will help them see a meaningful Story behind it.

There's more...

Tableau also offers two additional formatting styles, numbers and dots.

1. Open the **Layout** tab in the **Story** pane.
2. Under **Navigator Style**, choose **Numbers**:

In your **Story**, it will look as follows:

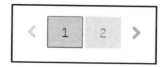

3. In the same menu, you can also select only dots to be displayed:

If you want to get rid of left/right arrows, just deselect the **Show arrows** checkbox.

 When you are dealing with busy charts or dashboards, both of these options can save you some space. As we said before, strive to keep it simple and remember that less is more!

See also

You can learn more about creating stories by using the following resources:

- https://onlinehelp.tableau.com/current/pro/desktop/en-us/Story_create.html
- https://www.encorebusiness.com/blog/tableau-tips-tricks-tableau-Story-telling/
- https://www.coursera.org/learn/dataviz-dashboards

Setting the narrative of the Story

To present an effective Story, you need to discover it in your data first. This sounds demanding, but actually it's not. If you have data to analyze, you also have a Story to tell. We don't have to be talented novelists to write a good Story. However, we can borrow some tips from them. First, let's take a look at what every Story contains. In every Story, we can find the following elements:

- **Introduction**: In the introduction, we need to describe the setup of the situation and introduce the main characters. For example, in business, the situation often denotes the market context, while characters are brands that we are interested in.
- **Conflict**: The conflict phase is where we present the main problem. In this phase, we are usually faced with dilemmas where we need to choose the direction of the following steps in the analysis. The conflict phase is resolved when we decide on the specific route to take while investigating our data.
- **Development**: The development phase is usually devoted to a description of different approaches to the problem and our process of searching for the solution. The main purpose of this phase is to inform our audience about what we have done with our data and which hypotheses are already tested.
- **Climax**: The climax is the moment when all the pieces of the puzzle come together. At that point, the key insight of our analysis should have been clarified.
- **Resolution**: In the resolution phase, we are presenting the final result. In this phase, we are suggesting a solution to the problem, along with the arguments that support it.

Getting ready

Let's get back to recycling data. Follow the previous recipe, *Creating a Tableau Story*, and make the **Recycling and Awareness** sheet. So far, we have found that more than 50% of the milk buyers know that carton packaging can be recycled in Serbia, but only 18% dispose of their packaging in specialized recycling bins. In terms of storytelling, this phase can be considered an introduction or setup phase. The following phase is Conflict.

Conflict

In the Conflict phase, we should identify possible approaches in dealing with our data and select the most relevant. We have just arrived at the crime scene, and we are observing the pieces of evidence. Our investigation is about to start.

How to do it...

1. Open a blank worksheet and drag and drop **Aware of recycling possibility** from **Dimensions** into the **Column** shelf.
2. Drag and drop **Number of Records** from **Measures** into the **Rows** shelf.
3. Drag and drop **Milk carton disposal** from **Dimensions** into the **Column** shelf to the right-hand side of the **Aware of recycling possibility** story.
4. Drag and drop **Milk carton disposal** from **Measures** to **Color** in the **Marks** card.
5. Drag and drop **Number of Records** from **Measures** to **Label** in the **Marks** card.
6. Hover over the **Number of Records** green pill in the **Marks** card so that a small downward arrow appears and click on it.
7. Navigate to **Quick Table Calculation** | **Percent of Total**.
8. Click on the **Sheet 3** tab at the bottom of the page and type `Aware but not recycling`:

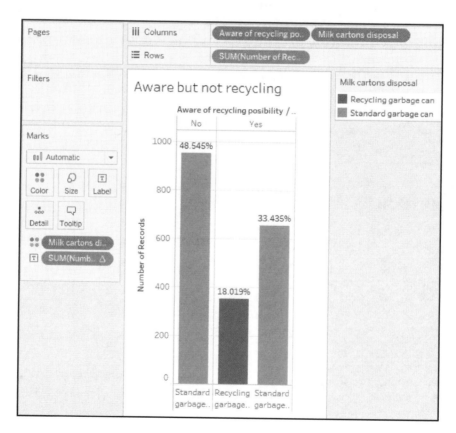

How it works...

In the *Creating a Tableau Story* recipe, we discovered that a third of milk carton buyers know about the possibility of recycling, but still dispose of the packaging in the standard garbage bins. Also, we know that almost half of the milk buyers don't even know about the possibility of recycling the milk cartons. At this point, we are in the conflict phase as we should decide on where to focus our efforts. Should we investigate those who do not know about the recycling potential or those who are aware but are not willing to support it?

When we are making decisions such as this, it is always important to keep our audience in mind. Telling a Story always requires taking the perspective of your listener. In this case, our listener is a **public relations** (PR) manager of a milk manufacturing company. We need to step into their shoes and put their glasses on. Let's try to figure out what our PR manager can do about the fact that every third person that knows about recycling is possibly not motivated to practice it. As a PR manager, we can try to think of ways to motivate those people. For example, we could organize a lottery game or give a discount to those who dispose of their garbage in specialized garbage bins. However, it is much more likely that we would focus on people who don't know about the recycling possibility yet.

Considering the tools that we have at our disposal, raising awareness seems to be a more achievable goal than a direct change of behavior. Furthermore, as a PR manager, we would want to know the reasons for the relative failure of our current campaign. Maybe we still can fix something and turn it into a success, or at least avoid the trap in the future. It is important to remember that another stakeholder in the same situation would probably have a different perspective, plan a different strategy, and take different steps in solving the problem. Let's go back to our PR manager and see what we can do about our data to help them out.

Development

In the Development phase, we are going to test our hypothesis. It's time to work around our business problem.

How to do it...

1. Open a blank worksheet and drag and drop **Gender** from **Dimensions** into the **Columns** shelf.
2. Drag and drop **Number of Records** from **Measures** to the **Rows** shelf.

3. Drag and drop **Aware of recycling possibility** from **Dimensions** to **Color** in the **Marks** card.

4. Hover over the **Number of Records** pill in the **Rows** shelf so that a small downward arrow appears and click on it.

5. Navigate to **Quick Table Calculation | Percent of Total**. Choose the **Edit Table Calculation...** option and select **Table (down)**.

6. Press *Ctrl* and drag and drop **Number of Records** from **Rows** to **Label** in the **Marks** card.

7. Click on the **Sheet 4** tab at the bottom of the page and enter Awareness by Gender:

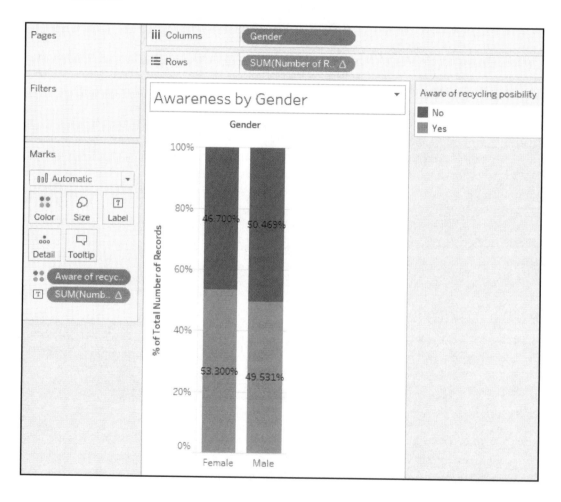

As we can see in the preceding screenshot, among females there are more buyers who are aware of recycling possibilities. The difference is not so striking, but it provides us with some insight. However, we should continue digging.

8. Open a blank worksheet, drag and drop **Age** from **Dimensions** into the **Column** shelf.

9. Drag and drop **Number of Records** from **Measures** into the **Rows** shelf.

10. Drag and drop **Aware of recycling possibility** from **Dimensions** to **Color** in the **Marks** card.

11. Hover over the **Number of Records** pill in the **Rows** shelf so that a small downward arrow appears and click on it.

12. Navigate to **Quick Table Calculation** | **Percent of Total**. Choose **Edit Table Calculation...** and then select **Table (down)**.

13. Press *Ctrl* and drag and drop **Number of Records** from **Rows** to **Label** in the **Marks** card.

14. Click on the **Sheet 5** tab at the bottom of the page and enter `Awareness by Age`:

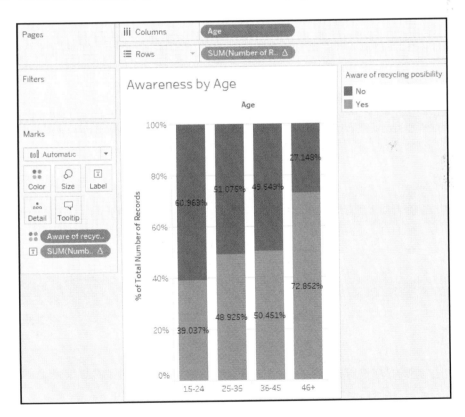

Analyzing the results by age groups reveals some interesting differences in the level of awareness. Almost 75% of people aged 45 or older know that milk cartons can be recycled in Serbia. On the other hand, more than 60% buyers in the 15-24 age group do not know about this possibility. Based on that, we can conclude that the 15-24 group is the least informed and that we need to make a concerted effort to raise their awareness. That is our first clue. Let's investigate some more.

15. Open a blank worksheet, drag and drop **Read labels** from **Dimensions** into the **Column** shelf.

16. Drag and drop **Number of Records** from **Measures** into the **Rows** shelf.

17. Drag and drop the **Aware of recycling possibility** from **Dimensions** to **Color** in the **Marks** card.

18. Hover over the **Number of Records** pill in the **Rows** shelf so that a small downward arrow appears and click on it.

19. Navigate to **Quick Table Calculation | Percent of Total**. Choose **Edit Table Calculation...** and select **Table (down)**.

20. Drag and drop **Number of Records** from **Measures** to **Label** in the **Marks** card.

21. Hover over the **Number of Records** pill in the **Marks** card so that a small downward arrow appears and click on it.

22. Go to the **Quick Table Calculation** option and choose **Percent of Total**. Then, pick **Edit Table Calculation...** and select **Table (down)**.

23. Click on the **Sheet 6** tab at the bottom of the page and enter `Awareness by Reading labels`:

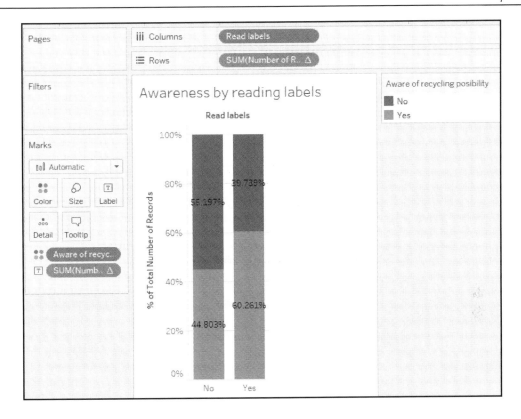

How it works...

We have discovered that the level of awareness of recycling possibilities is much higher among those who regularly read labels on food packaging.

Let's consolidate what we have found up to this point. We learned that men and women do not differ in their awareness about recycling significantly. We know that among the 15-24 age group of milk buyers, we have the highest percentage of those who are not aware that the milk carton can be recycled in Serbia. We also know that the level of awareness is lower among those who do not regularly read labels on packaging.

Climax

The Climax phase is the turning point where we arrived at the answer to our key question.

How to do it...

1. Open a blank worksheet and drag and drop **Age** from **Dimensions** into the **Column** shelf.
2. Drag and drop **Number of Records** from **Measures** into the **Rows** shelf.
3. Drag and drop **Read labels** from **Dimensions** into **Color** in the **Marks** card.
4. Hover over the **Number of Records** pill in the **Rows** shelf so that a small downward arrow appears and click on it.
5. Navigate to **Quick Table Calculation** | **Percent of Total**. Choose **Edit Table Calculation** and then click on **Table (down)**.
6. Press *Ctrl* and drag and drop the **Number of Records** pill from Rows to **Label** in the **Marks** card.
7. Click on the **Sheet 6** tab at the bottom of the page and enter Reading labels by Age:

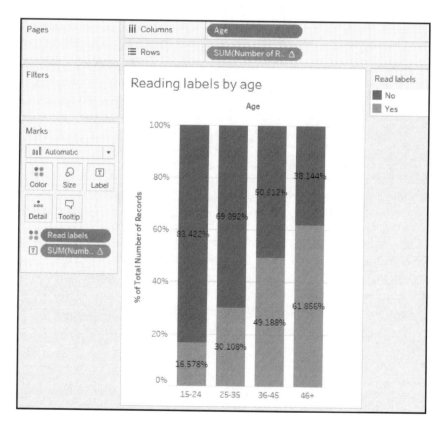

How it works...

In the climax phase, we are connecting the dots:

- The youngest purchasers are the least aware of the recycling possibility
- Those who do not regularly read labels on packaging are also not informed about the recycling possibility
- The youngest purchasers (the 15-24 group) do not regularly read labels (at least most of them)

By linking these findings, we can arrive at a conclusion. The youngest purchasers are the least aware of the recycling possibility, mainly because they do not regularly read the labels on packaging.

Here, we can point out the main difference between findings and insights. In a nutshell, a finding just informs us about the facts, while an insight provides an explanation of those facts. Findings give us the answer to the *what*, while insights answer the *why*. The crucial difference is that insights enable us to speculate about the underlying mechanism of a phenomenon, and put us in a position to make an impact on the situation and to change the facts.

Resolution

In the Resolution phase, we should properly articulate and communicate results to the relevant audience.

How to do it...

1. Open a blank worksheet and drag and drop **Age** from **Dimensions** into the **Column** shelf.
2. Drag and drop **Milk cartons disposal** from **Dimensions** into the **Column** shelf, to the right of the **Age** pill.
3. Drag and drop **Number of Records** from **Measures** into the **Rows** shelf.
4. Drag and drop **Aware of recycling possibility** from **Dimensions** to **Color** in the **Marks** card.
5. Hover over the **Number of Records** pill in the **Marks** card so that a small downward arrow appears and click on it.
6. Navigate to **Quick table calculation** | **Percent of Total**. Then, choose **Edit Table Calculations** and click on **Table (down)**.

7. Press *Ctrl* and drag and drop **Milk cartons disposal** from **Column** into the **Filters** shelf.

8. Deselect the box in front of the **Recycling garbage can** and click OK.

9. Press *Ctrl* and drag and drop **Number of records** from **Rows** into the **Label** in the **Marks** card.

10. Click on the **Sheet 7** tab at the bottom of the page and enter `Potential for recycling`:

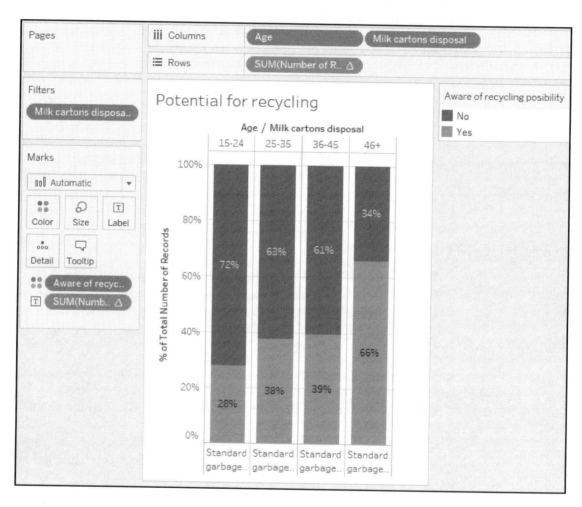

How it works...

In this recipe, we compared the age groups and then focused only on those who currently do not recycle. We can see that among 15-24 year olds, we have the smallest percentage (28%) of those who know about the possibility of recycling but do not use it. Based on that, we can conclude that within the 15-24 age group, we have the smallest percentage of buyers who are resistant to our promotional efforts. Accordingly, we can assume that we have a good potential for recycling within this group! Now, we have all the elements. In the following sections, we will learn how to connect them in a story.

There's more...

The names of the phases in storytelling we use throughout this chapter are just one of the many ways to conceive the storytelling process. In other sources, you might encounter phases that are a bit different or have different names for similar phases. However, the basic structure of a story is universal, and there is always an introduction, a problem, attempts to solve the problem, the moment of arriving at a solution, and a conclusion.

See also

- **The Anatomy of a Story**: *22 Steps to Becoming a Master Storyteller*, by John Truby

- **Resonate**: *Present Visual Stories that Transform Audiences*, by Nancy Duarte

- **Long story short**: *The Only Storytelling Guide You'll Ever Need*, by Margot Leitman

Choosing the right charts

Once we make the basic narrative, we need to pick up the crucial moments to present in a Story. When we were speaking about the development phase of storytelling, we said that we should inform our listener about the hypothesis that we tested. However, this does not mean that we need to describe every step that we made in detail and every dead end that we encountered. Like a movie director who cuts the frames of scenes when editing a movie, we also need to crop only those elements that are important for our Story. All the other things should be mentioned, but in a way that they do not draw attention away from the main plot of the Story.

Getting ready

For this recipe, we will need all the sheets that we have made so far:

- Awareness
- Recycling
- Aware but not recycling
- Awareness by Age
- Awareness by reading labels
- Reading labels by age

How to do it...

1. Go to the main menu at the top of the screen and navigate to **Story | New Story**.
2. Drag and drop **Recycling** from the left sidebar to the **Drag a sheet here** placeholder in the canvas:

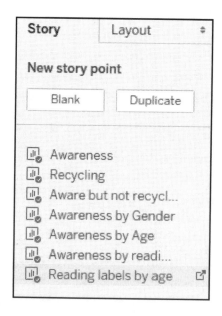

3. In the **Story** tab on the left-hand side, click on the **Blank** button.
4. Drag and drop **Awareness** into the canvas.

5. Repeat the same procedure for the following sheets in the proposed order:
   - `Aware but not recycling`
   - `Awareness by Age`
   - `Awareness by reading labels`
   - `Reading labels by age`

6. Double-click on the **Story 1** tab and rename it `Promotion of milk carton recycling among buyers in Serbia`

How it works

As you've probably noticed, we have skipped `Awareness by Gender`. In the following analysis, we are focusing on the differences between age groups, not on gender differences. Information about gender differences is not a crucial part of understanding the main plot of the Story:

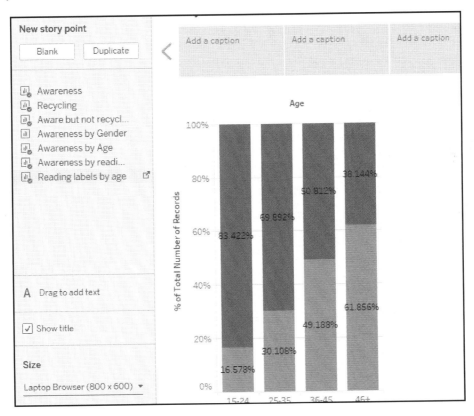

There's more...

Sometimes, it isn't easy to decide which finding is important for the Story and which is not. In such cases, you can rely on a simple rule of thumb: if a finding is not going to be mentioned again, it is probably not crucial.

See also

- Interested readers can find more information about how to communicate effectively with data in the following book: **Storytelling with data:** *a data visualization guide for business professionals,* by Cole Nussbaumer Knaflic

Writing effective headlines

As mentioned earlier, our presentation should always be adjusted for the audience we are presenting it to. In business, stakeholders to whom we are presenting our findings often have limited resources in terms of the time and attention that they can devote to our presentation. With that in mind, we should do our best to make our captions short and precise.

Getting ready

Follow the previous recipes, *Creating a Tableau Story, Setting the narrative of the Story,* and *Choosing the right charts* recipes to create the sheets we will be using in this recipe.

How to do it...

1. Open the **Promotion of milk carton recycling among buyers in Serbia** Story that we made in the previous recipe, *Choosing the right charts*.
2. Click on the left arrow in the navigation and go to the first textbox in the row. It should be the **Milk cartons disposal** sheet:

3. Double-click on the **Add a caption** placeholder, and then type `We come to know that 8 in 10 buyers do not use recycling garbage bins:`

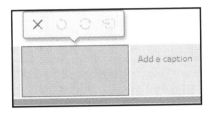

4. Go to the first textbox on the right-hand side (it should be the **Awareness** sheet), double-click on it, and type `Almost 1/2 do not even know about the recycling possibility.`

5. Double-click on the **Aware but not recycling** text-box sheet and type `1/3 are aware, but not use recycling garbage bins.`

6. In the **Awareness by Age** textbox, type `Buyers in the 15-24 age group are the ones least aware of recycling possibility.`

7. In the **Awareness by reading labels** text-box sheet, type `Those who do not read labels on packaging's are less aware of the recycling possibility.`

8. In the **Reading labels by age** text-box sheet, type `Buyers in the 15-24 age group least likely to read labels:`

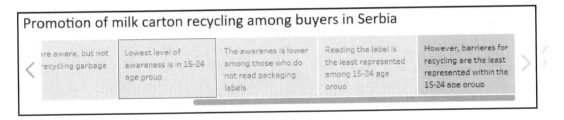

How it works...

Writing effective headlines is a skill that requires some practice. Luckily, there are some tips that we can use to make them better.

When writing headlines, we must make sure that they meet the following requirements:

- They clearly communicate the most important finding
- They are not data chart titles
- They do not repeat the figures from the charts
- They should use a verb
- They should use transitional words (such as *but, moreover,* and *in addition to*)
- They are no longer than five lines

Recommendation and executive summary

Writing the executive summary is probably the most intimidating phase of the whole analytical process. When we need to give concrete advice for an action, we are always on a slippery slope, because it involves a prediction of future events. However, our task is to be as objective as possible and to provide the most useful business advice, based on the data that we have.

Getting ready

It's time to wrap up our Story, so we will need all the sheets that we have made in this chapter so far:

- Awareness
- Recycling
- Aware but not recycling
- Awareness by Age
- Awareness by reading labels
- Reading labels by age

How to do it...

1. Open a new dashboard.
2. Drag and drop **Potential for recycling** from the list of sheets that are on the left-hand side of the **Drag a sheet here** placeholder in the canvas.

3. Drag and drop **Awareness by Age** from the list of sheets to the canvas that is to the right side of **Potential for recycling**.

4. Drag and drop **Reading labels by age** from the list to the canvas under **Potential for recycling**.

5. Drag and drop **Text** from the **Objects** card at the left-hand side to the bottom of the canvas:

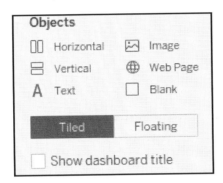

Then type the following paragraph:

Based on the results of our study, we can expect that promotional activities focused on the 15-24 age group can have a significant effect on their recycling habits. Because of that, our recommendation is to launch a promotional campaign that would be specifically designed in accordance with the media consumption habits of younger buyers. In this age group, we found that those who know about the possibility of recycling use it to a greater extent than the other groups. However, the awareness of the possibility of recycling milk cartons is lowest in this group. The current campaign was unsuccessful in raising awareness about recycling because it used a channel of communication that doesn't reach young people. We can conclude that milk buyers within the 15-24 age group are responsive to the appeal to recycle, but we have to find a way to get the message across.

6. Double-click on the **Dashboard 1** tab at the bottom of the screen and rename it `Executive summary`:

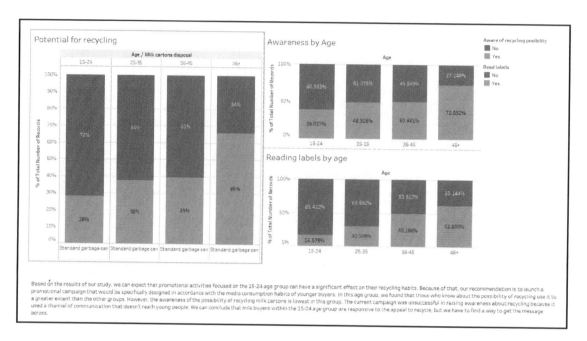

7. Open the **Promotion of milk carton recycling among buyers in Serbia** Story.
8. In the **Story** tab on the left-hand side, click on the **Blank** button.
9. Drag and drop **Executive summary** from the list on the left-hand side to the **Drag a sheet here** placeholder in the canvas.
10. Double-click on the **Add a caption** placeholder in the gray box that appeared at the top.

11. Type Launch a campaign focused on young buyers:

Promotion of milk carton recycling among buyers in Serbia

How it works...

Our Story has, so far, been built by connecting individual conclusions. But when we are writing an executive summary, we need a reverse, **top-down** approach. When we are giving advice for the concrete course of action, we need to be concise and get to the point. First, we give the recommendation about what should be done, and then elaborate on it with arguments—why it should be done. Your listeners will appreciate your effort to save their time and you will sound much more confident.

There's more...

This way of communicating recommendations, which advocates a top-down approach, is known as the **Pyramid Principle**. The Pyramid Principle, designed by Barbara Minto, is one of the best-known concepts in modern executive communication. The main rationale behind this principle is that, when making decisions, people find it easier to focus on a specific course of action or recommendation first, and then consider all the pros and cons of it.

See also

- Check out Barbara Minto's website for more details about the Pyramid principle at `http://www.barbaraminto.com/`.

Formatting the Story

Although the content of the Story is essential, the importance of visual aspects of the Story's presentation should never be underestimated. If the visual layout of the presentation is sloppy, it can leave a bad impression on the audience and take away the credibility of the content of the Story. We certainly wouldn't want our hard work to be ignored due to bad formatting. So, let's pick up some tricks that can improve the visual identity of our presentation.

Getting ready

In this recipe, we are going to format the charts we've made so far. Follow the previous recipes from this chapter: *Creating a Tableau Story, Setting the narrative of the Story, Choosing the right charts, Writing effective headlines, Recommendation* and *executive summary* to create the Story that we are going to be working on.

How to do it...

1. Open the **Awareness by Age** chart.
2. Hover over the **Number of records** green pill in the **Marks** card, and when the small white downward arrow appears, click on it.
3. In the menu, choose **Format...**

4. In the **Pane** tab, under the section **Default**, go to the **Numbers** drop-down menu.

5. Choose **Percentage** and set the number of **Decimal places** to 0:

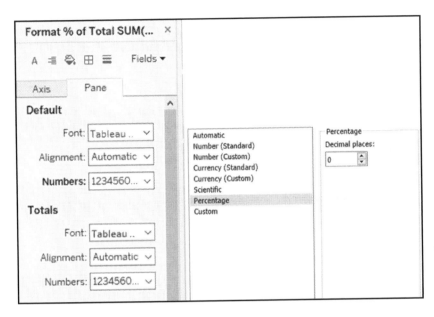

6. In the **Pane** tab, under the **Default** section, go to **Font**.

7. Increase the size of the font from **9** to **12**:

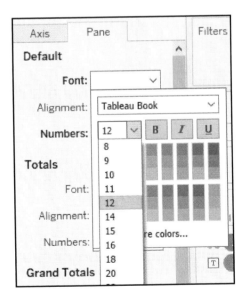

8. Choose the white color.
9. In the **Marks** card, click on **Color** and select the **Edit Colors** button.
10. In the **Select Color Palette** drop-down menu, choose **Traffic Light**.
11. Under **Select Data Item**, click on **No** and pick **Red** from the top of the **Select Color Palette** drop-down menu.
12. In the **Select Data Item** drop-down menu, click on **Yes**, pick **Green** from the top of the **Select Color Palette** drop-down menu, and click on **OK**:

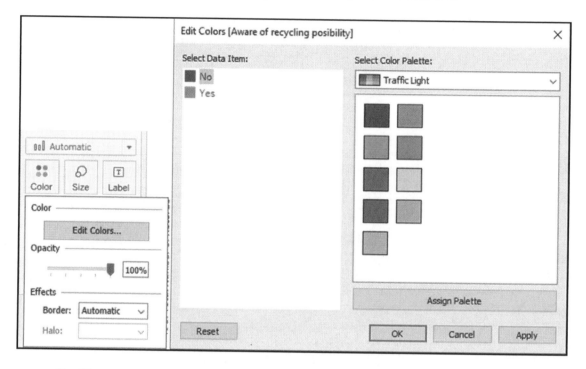

13. Hover over the vertical axis of the **% of Total Number of Records** chart and right-click on it.
14. Choose **Edit Axis** and in the **General** tab, delete **% of Total Number of Records** from the **Titles** option.

15. In the **Tick Marks** tab of the same window, choose **None** in both **Major tick marks** and **Minor tick marks**, and click on **OK**:

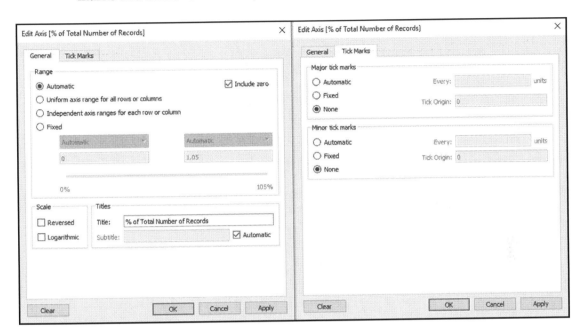

16. Hover over the horizontal axis of the chart (the **15-24, 25-35, 36-45, 46+** age categories), right-click on it, and choose **Format**.

17. In the **Header** tab on the left-hand side, under the **Default** section, click on the **Font** drop-down menu.

18. Increase the font size from **9** to **12**:

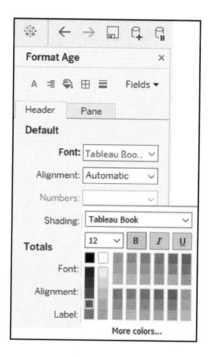

19. Right-click on **Age** at the top of the chart.
20. Choose **Hide Field Labels** for **Columns**:

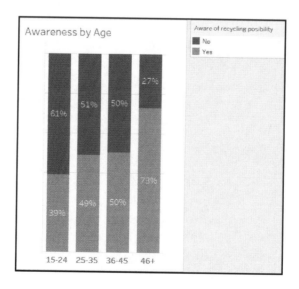

How it works...

First, we decreased the number of decimal places (in the *Formatting the Story* recipe, steps 1-5). Although in some cases the decimal places are necessary, in most cases, whole numbers are enough.

We then increased the font size. It is recommended to adjust the layout of the screen on which the results will be presented. However, we can't always know where they will be displayed, so to stay on the safe side, we need to use a larger font size.

After that, we adjusted the colors. Some colors have specific meanings, and it is always handy to go along with them when possible. In our case, relying on a traffic light analogy, we use red for "not aware" and green for "aware."

In the formatting phase, our goal is to eliminate all unnecessary elements from the sheet. In our case, we have labels with percentages on bars, tick marks, and also the title in the vertical axis is sufficient. Due to the fact that the "Awareness by Age" title says enough, the label of the "Age" columns is redundant.

When you are not sure whether an element is needed, ask yourself, "Does it carry unique information, or can we come to the same conclusion via another item?"

There's more...

A general rule to follow when we are making our visualization is to be consistent! Nothing makes our presentation sloppier than randomly using different formatting styles. Choose one formatting principle and stick to it throughout the Story.

In this recipe, we adjusted the format of only one of the sheets that makes our Story. Follow the given instructions to adjust the other sheets. When you open the Story again, you will find that it has been updated with the changes you made.

See also

- For more tips on how to make your presentation look stylish, check out https://www.tableau.com/about/blog/2017/10/7-tips-and-tricks-dashboard-experts-76821.

8
Tableau Visualization

In this chapter, we will cover the following topics:

- Dual axis waterfall charts
- Pareto charts
- Bump charts
- Sparkline charts
- Donut charts
- Motion charts

Technical requirements

We will use Tableau 2019.x and datasets about potholes, coal emissions, soccer rankings, alien sightings, avocado prices, and snowfall.

Introduction

We will go beyond **Show Me** and learn techniques to master visualizations in Tableau to make your dashboards stand out. In this recipe, we will cover detailed steps for creating visualizations that convey percentages, based on how a proportion relates to a whole, or how a value changes. The use cases vary from identifying elements in the data that create the biggest impact, creating ranks for different categories over a period of time, or tracking goals for organizations.

Dual axis waterfall chart

Waterfall charts show us how a series of positive or negative changes contribute to a final total. Waterfall charts can also be used to show the composition of a measure with categorical values, resulting in the cumulative amount. The **Dual Axis** waterfall charts illustrate changes more elegantly than color alone.

Getting ready

In this recipe, we will create a dual axis waterfall chart, using a line chart as the base.

How to do it...

We're using data from the city of Chicago to see how many potholes are identified and how many are fixed. Use `Waterfall.tbwx` and `Potholes.csv` to follow along:

1. Create a line or bar chart with one dimension and one measure—**Activity Date** and **Potholes**—as follows:

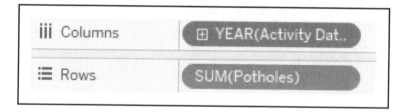

2. Apply a **Running Total** measure under **Quick Table Calculation** for **Potholes**, as shown in the following screenshot:

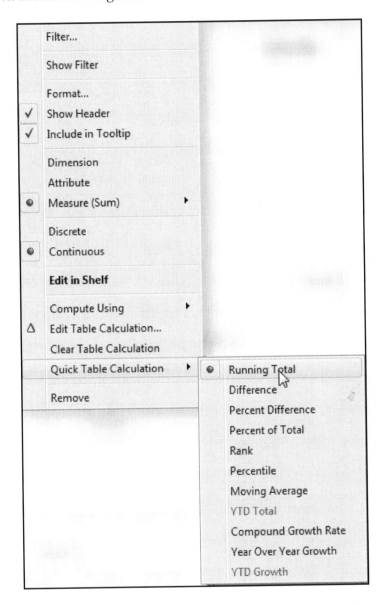

3. Change the **Marks** type to **Gantt Bar**, as shown in the following screenshot:

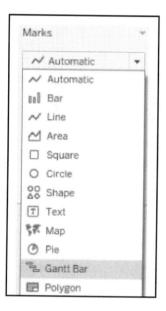

4. Create bars by sizing the mark with a negative version of the same measure. Sizing by a negative version allows the start of each bar to line up with the end of the previous bar. We illustrate one method by applying negative **Potholes** to **Size,** as shown in the following screenshot:

5. At this point, we should have a single axis waterfall chart, as follows:

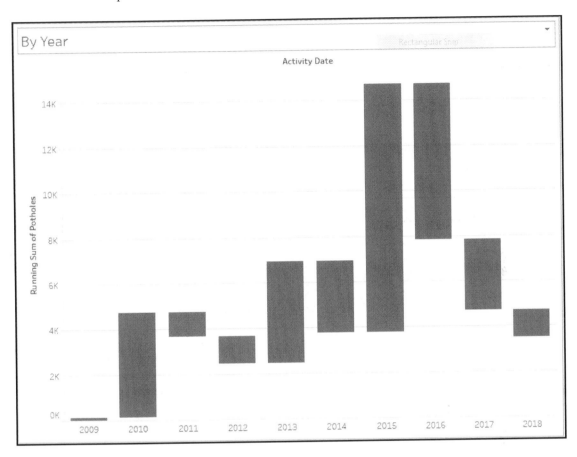

Waterfall charts can be used with time and categorical dimensions. The order of the categories can impact the story. Color can be used to show negative and positive values. We can have more options with shapes using a dual axis waterfall chart.

6. Duplicate the pill by pressing the *Ctrl* key and selecting **SUM(Potholes)** and placing to the right, as shown in the following screenshot:

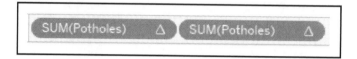

7. Clear the size from the **Marks** card for the second measure, as shown in the following screenshot:

8. Right-click on the second green pill and choose **Dual Axis**, as shown in the following screenshot:

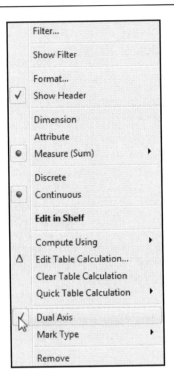

9. Click on the second axis, select **Synchronize Axis**, and hide the headers, as shown in the following screenshot:

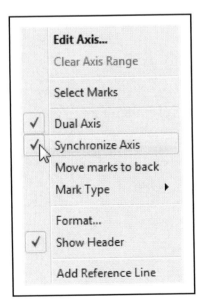

10. Add **Totals** from the **Analysis** menu. Navigate to **Totals** | **Show Row Grand Totals**, as shown in the following screenshot:

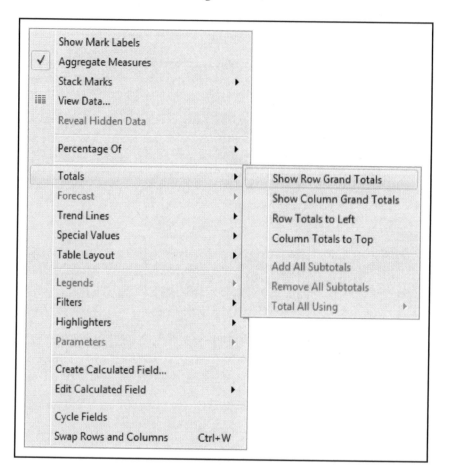

11. In the **Marks** card, change the default mark or modify the color of the mark based on whether a value is negative or positive. We use **Gantt Bar** to create lines at the end of each bar, as shown in the following screenshot:

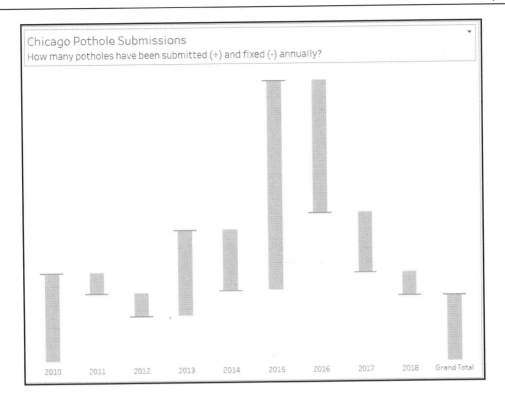

How it works...

In *step 1*, we create a line chart with one dimension and one measure and then apply **Running Total Table Calculation** in *step 2*. In *step 3*, we then change the mark type to **Gantt Bar**. In order to create bars, in *step 4*, we negate the measure so each column can grow to the previous mark. This creates the stair step effect, so the end of one mark is the beginning of the previous one. We see in *step 5* that we've created a basic waterfall chart.

In order to highlight the positive or negative change, we create a **Dual Axis** chart. In *step 6*, we duplicate the same measure on the **Rows** shelf. We clear the size from the second **Marks** card in *step 7*, which will emphasize the ending value when we make the dual axis in *step 8*—causing the marks to overlay. In *step 10*, we add a total to show the cumulative impact of all values. Finally, in *step 11*, we change the default mark type to **Gantt Bar** to emphasize the negative or positive change.

There's more...

We can also use shapes to indicate positive or negative values by taking the following steps.

1. Create calculations for positive and negative values, as follows:

2. Apply **Arrow Direction** to **Shape** (and optionally **Color** for both **SUM(Potholes)** and **SUM(Potholes) (2)**, as follows:

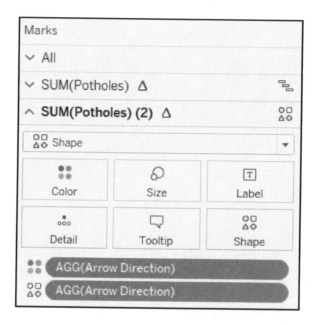

3. Click on **Shape**, select **Filled**, and choose the up and down triangles, as follows:

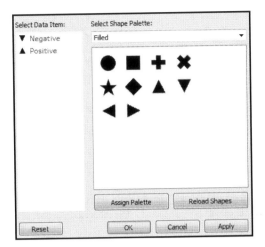

Our final visualization can be seen in the following screenshot:

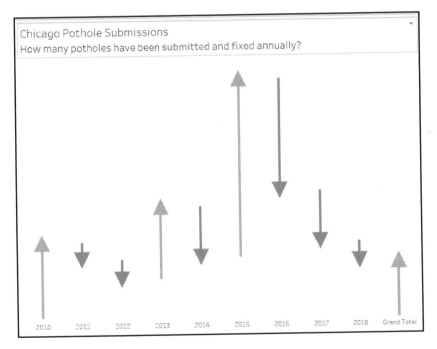

See also

- See VizWiz's blog post, **How to Create Waterfall Chart in Tableau** under **Tableau Tip Tuesday** at http://www.vizwiz.com/2015/05/waterfall.html.

Pareto chart

Pareto charts are best used when you want to identify the biggest contributing factors to a measurable outcome. They help with identifying priorities and are often used in risk management. The name comes from Vilfredo Pareto, the originator of the 80/20 Rule, or the Pareto Principle, which roughly states that 80% value comes from 20% of a factor. An example would be 80% of sales comes from 20% of our customers.

Getting ready

In this section, we will use a bar chart with reference lines to create a Pareto chart.

How to do it...

In this example, we are looking at CO2 emissions data. Open the packaged workbook `Pareto.twbx` to follow along:

1. Create a bar chart with **Emission Type** on **Columns** and **Value** on **Rows**, as follows:

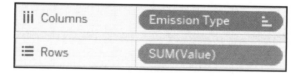

2. Order the chart in descending order according to the measure, as follows:

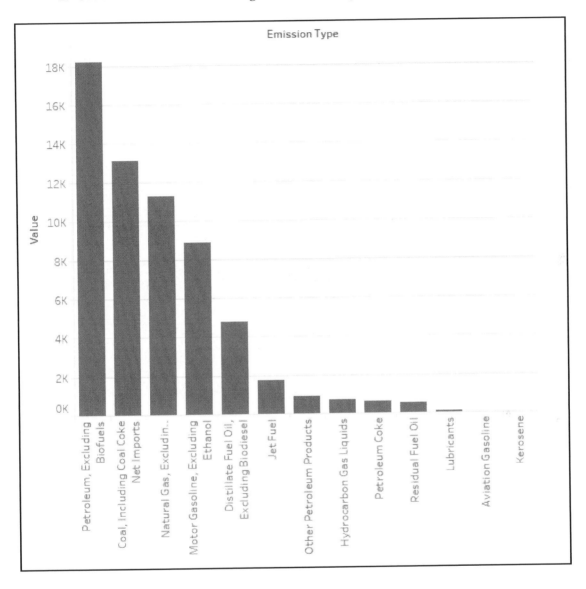

3. Add a primary and secondary table calculation for **Running Total** and **Percent of Total**. Modify **Compute Using** to **Specific Dimensions**, as depicted in the following screenshot:

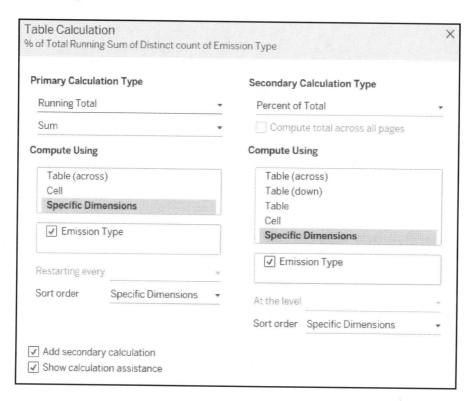

4. Add a **Reference Line** at 80%, as follows:

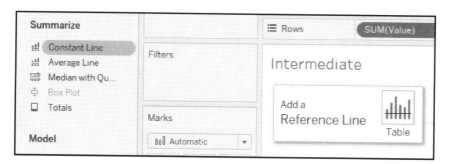

In the following screenshot, we can see our basic **Pareto** chart:

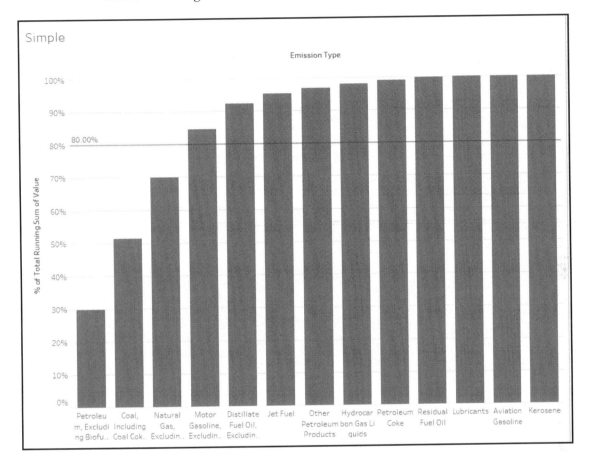

How it works...

In *step 1* and *step 2*, we create a bar chart using one dimension and one measure sorted in descending order. For *step 3*, we apply the **Running Total** and **Percent of Total Table Calculation**. In *step 4*, we use reference lines at 80% and a simple bar chart to allow us to see what categories have the biggest impact.

There's more...

We can also create a more advanced version of the Pareto chart that shows the actual 80% and 20% values. We can start with the simple version created in the previous steps, and use the advanced worksheet to see the end product, by taking the following steps.

1. Add **Emission Type** to the **Detail** section of the **Marks** card. We do this because our table calculation for **Sum(Value)** is referencing a specific dimension **Emission Type**, as follows:

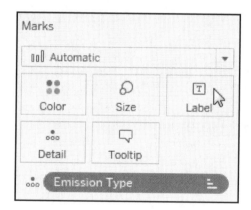

2. On the **Columns** shelf, modify **Emission Type** to be a **Count (Distinct)**, as follows:

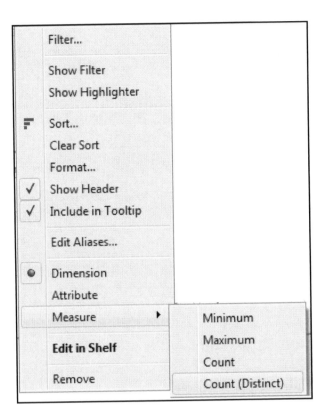

3. Apply the **Running Total** and **Percent of Total** table calculation to it, as follows:

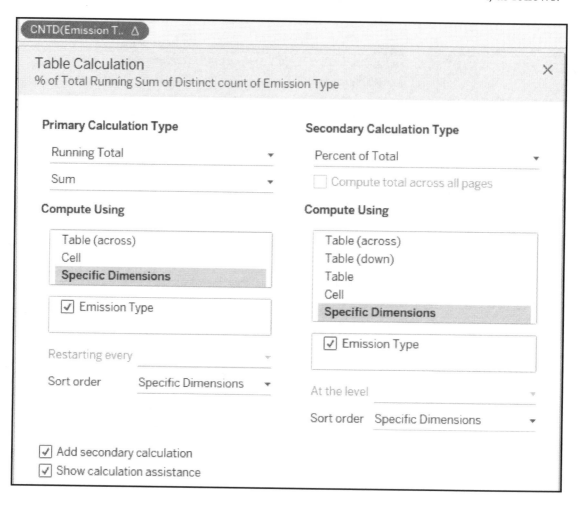

4. Change the **Mark** type to **Line**, as follows:

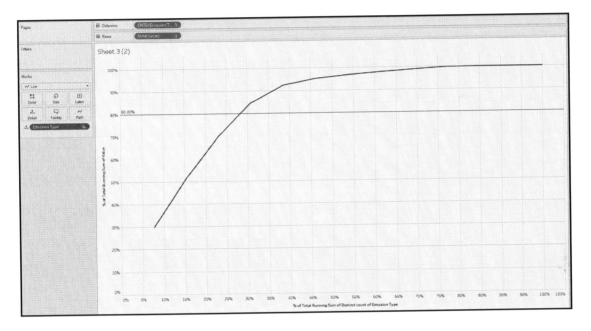

5. Add value to **Rows** to begin making a **Dual Axis** chart and change the mark type to **Bar**, as follows:

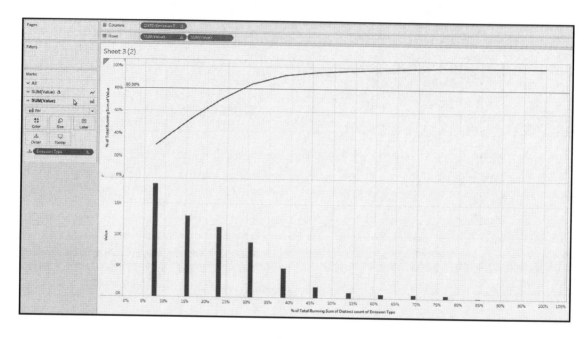

6. When you switch the newly placed green pill to dual axis, it'll change the line chart to a scatter plot as a result of having essentially a measure in the columns and rows, as shown in the following screenshot:

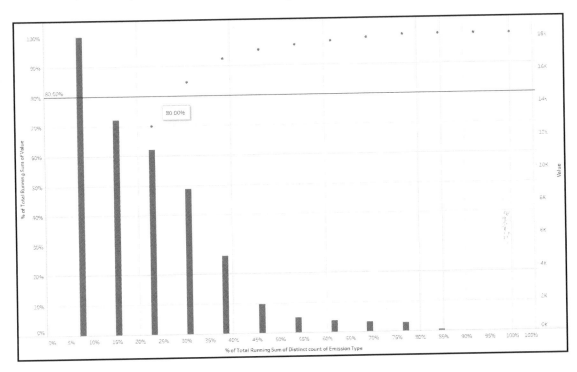

7. Change the dots to a continuous line, and move **Emission Type** to **Path**. Make sure you are doing this for the first green pill, as follows:

8. Add a reference line for 20%, as follows:

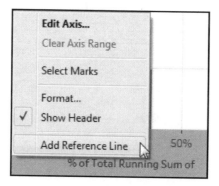

9. Right-click on the axis and select the option **Move marks to back**, which allows the reference lines to sit on top of the visualizations, as follows:

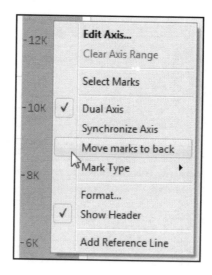

After some cleanup, it should look like the following screenshot:

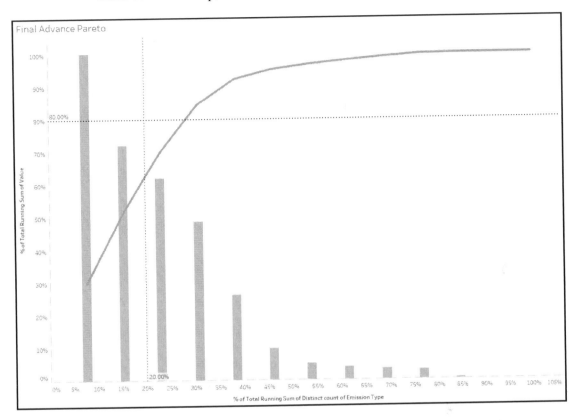

See also

- Please see Tableau's help page for another great resource for creating `Pareto` `charts`.

Bump chart

We will use the bump chart to compare two dimensions against each other using a single value of measurement. They are great for examining rank changes.

Getting ready

For the bump chart recipe, we will use a line chart with the rank table calculation.

How to do it...

In this example, we are ranking the teams of the South American Soccer Confederation. Use the `Bump Chart.twbx` workbook to follow along:

1. Since we want to color our visualization lines by country, put **Country Full** on **Color**, as follows:

2. Add **Rank Date** and **Rank** to the **Columns** and **Rows** shelves. Set **Rank Date** to **Year** and **Rank** to **Sum**, as follows:

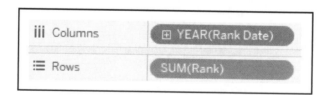

3. Rank in our current dataset is the actual global ranking of each soccer team. Because we want these to show up as 1-10 instead of their country rankings, we apply the **Rank Table Calculation** to the rank field, as follows:

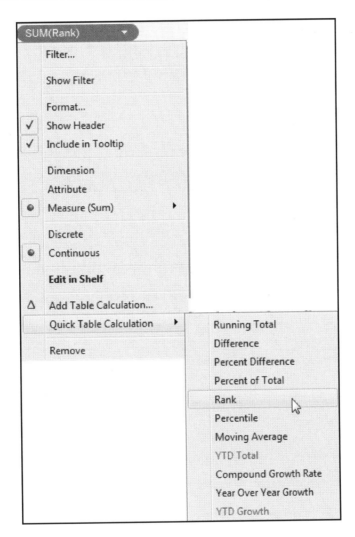

4. Edit the **Table Calculation** to **Rank** in **Ascending** order, and under **Compute Using**, select **Country Full**, as follows:

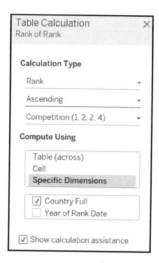

5. Reverse the axis of rank so our top performer is first, as follows:

6. Duplicate **Rank** on the **Rows** shelf to create the dot points in our visualization, and make this a dual axis by right-clicking and choosing the option, as follows:

7. Change the default mark for the second rank to **Circle**, as follows:

8. Reverse the axis.

9. We now have a basic bump chart, which we can see in the following screenshot:

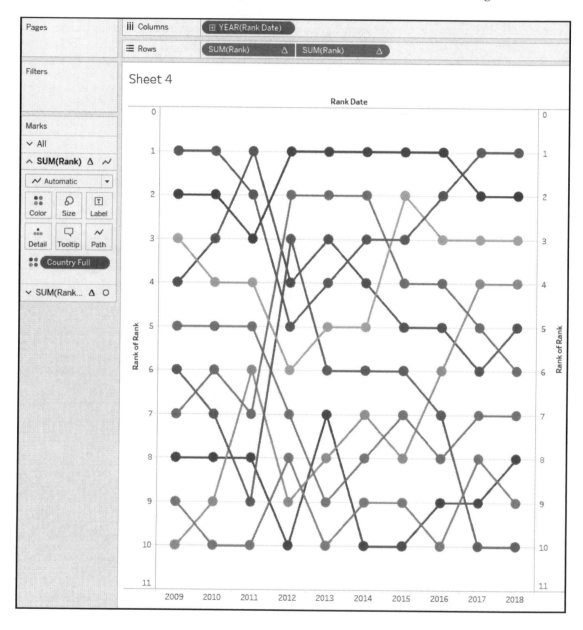

How it works...

In *step 1*, we put **Country Full** on **Color** in the **Marks** card, which groups and colors the values by **Country**. In *step 2*, we use a basic line chart for **Rank Date** and **Rank** by putting them on the **Columns** and **Rows** shelves. In *step 3* and *step 4*, the rank needs to be modified so that we see a sequential order rather than the rank in the dataset. In order for first place to show at the the top of the chart, we reversed the axis in *step 5*. Next, in *step 6* and *step 7*, we duplicate rank on the **Columns** shelf and change the **Mark** type to **Circle** to emphasize each yearly rank. In *step 8*, we reverse the axis as in *step 5*. In *step 9*, we merge the line (**Automatic**) and **Circle** marks by using dual axis, and, after some formatting and size changes, we have a basic bump chart.

There's more...

We can label the start and end of the lines by taking the following steps.

1. In order to easily see where a country starts and ends in the ranking, label the lines. While in the **SUM(Rank) Marks** card, move **Country Full** to **Label**, as follows:

2. Choose **Line Ends**. You may need to change the alignment or font sizes, as follows:

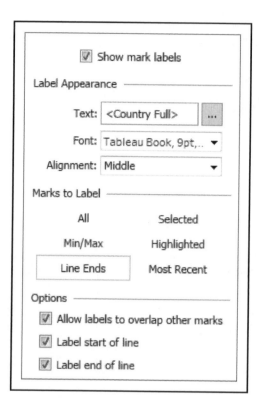

3. Match the text color with the line color, as follows:

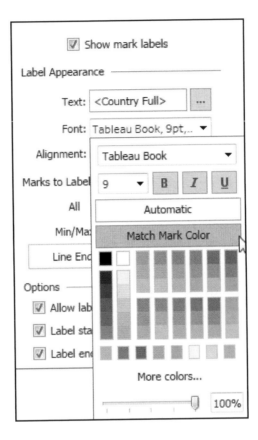

4. After the labels are applied and some additional cleaning up, here is our final chart:

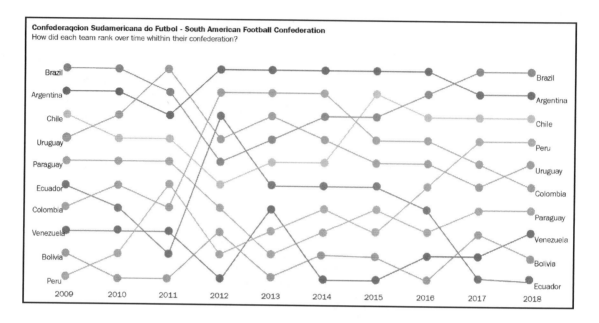

See also

- To make curved lines on your bump chart, see this blog post at `http://www.datatableauandme.com/2016/12/how-to-sigmoid-bump-chart-spline.html`.

Sparklines chart

Sparklines are compact visualizations. They show patterns over time and are essentially line charts without the axis. Edward Tufte explains that:

> *"Sparklines are datawords: data-intense, design-simple, and word-sized graphics."*

In other words, we recognize their form and the information being relayed as easily as we can words on a page—"word-like graphics".

Getting ready

In order to prepare for the Sparkline recipe, we will need a basic understanding of line charts. In this recipe, we rely heavily on the format lines menu and editing the axis.

How to do it...

In this section, we use UFO sighting data to make Sparklines. Open the Sparkline packaged workbook to follow along. To follow along, use `nuforc_events.csv` and `Sparklines.twbx`.

1. To begin, move the event date to **Columns** and shape to **Rows**. Because we have several years of data, we're filtering the dataset to 2010-2016 and displaying quarters, as follows:

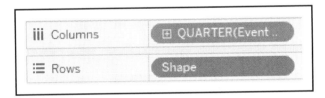

We use the green pill for **QUARTER(Event Date)** as opposed to the blue one because, in this scenario, the date is continuous rather than a discrete value. In other words, we want date to appear as a value on an axis rather than a value to be grouped.

2. Move the measure to the **Rows** shelf. For this dataset, we are using the number of records, as follows:

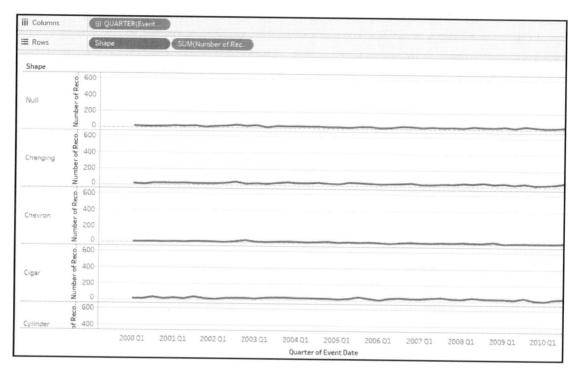

3. Create a measure called **Last Value** to indicate the final value in the Sparkline, as follows:

```
Last Value

Results are computed along Table (across).
IIF(LAST()=0, SUM([Number of Records]), NULL)
```

4. Move **Last Value** to the **Rows** shelf, as follows:

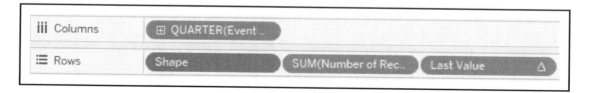

5. Right-click on **Last Value** and select **Dual Axis**, as follows:

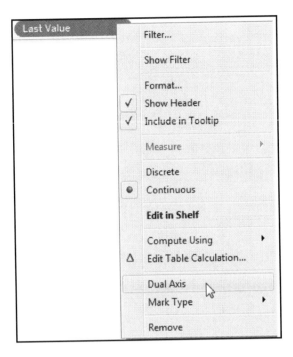

6. Right-click on the axis in the visualization and choose **Synchronize Axis**, as follows:

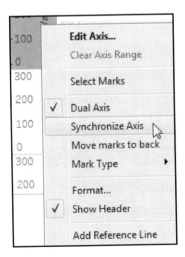

7. Edit the axis by deselecting the **Include Zero** option and choosing the **Independent axis ranges for each row or column** radio button, as follows:

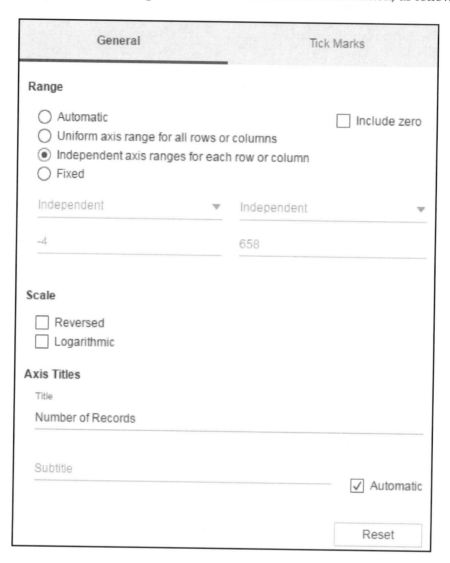

8. Remove all the headers by right-clicking on the visualization where each red x is located and deselecting **Show Header**, as follows:

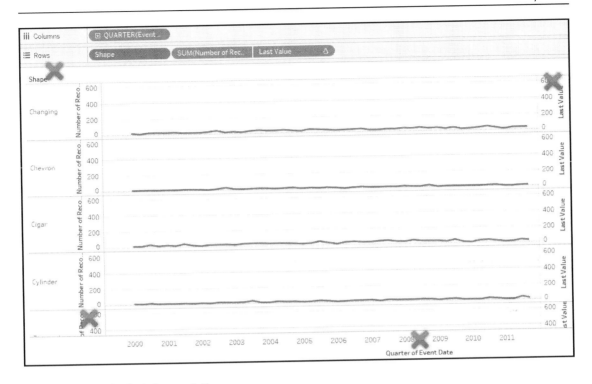

9. Fit the height, as follows:

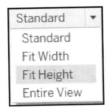

10. Manually resize the width by dragging the column ending inward, as follows:

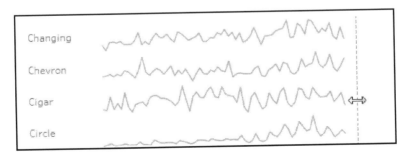

11. Remove all grid lines. From **Format Borders**, choose **Sheet**, and set **Column Divider** and **Row Divider Pane** to **None**, as follows:

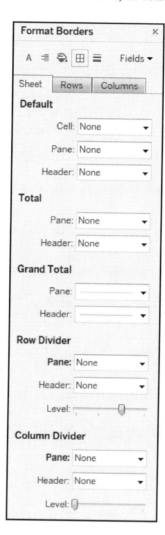

12. From **Format Lines**, choose **Rows**, and set **Grid Lines** and **Zero Lines** to **None**, as follows:

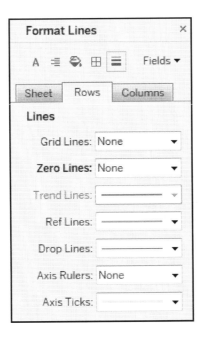

Tableau Visualization

13. Exclude null shapes by dragging **Shape** to the **Filters** card and select **Null** and **Exclude**, as follows:

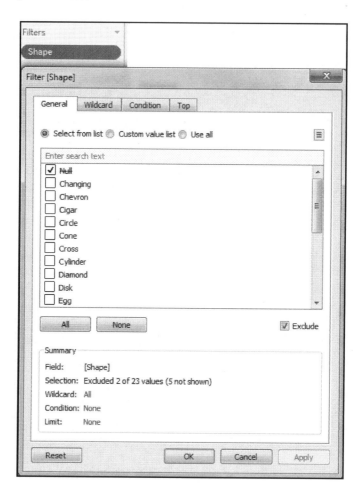

14. The Sparkline chart should appear as follows:

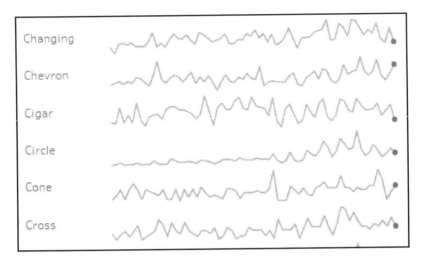

How it works...

In *step 1*, we put the event date on the **Columns** shelf and shape on the **Rows** shelf to create a long list of line charts. In *step 2*, we put the number of records on the **Rows** shelf. In order to highlight the final value in the Sparkline, we create a calculation for the final value in *step 3*, put it on the **Rows** shelf in *step 4*, and, in *step 5*, make it a synchronized dual axis chart. Each of the line charts should appear independent so we can see changes for each category relative to itself and not to each other. In *step 6*, we achieve this by editing the axis—excluding zero and making the axis independent for each row or column. In *step 7* to *step 10*, we remove and hide all the headers, all the grid lines, and shrink the width and height considerably. As a result of the formatting, we see the final Sparklines in *step 11*.

There's more...

Instead of adding a single color at the end of the Sparkline, we could make one that shows whether the last value is higher or lower than the one before, or even display the maximum values, by taking the following steps.

1. In order for the end of line indicator to change color, we need to make the calculation that we can see in the following screenshot:

Pos or Neg Change

Results are computed along Pane (across then down).
ZN(SUM([Number of Records])) - LOOKUP(ZN(SUM([Number of Records])), -1) < 0

2. Move this calculation to the **Marks** card, as follows:

3. Edit the **Color** option, as follows:

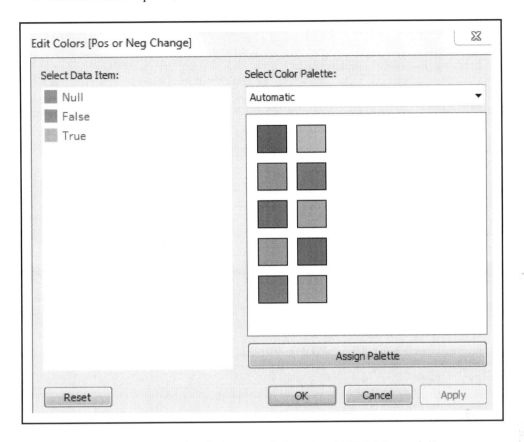

4. Format the title, by right-clicking and choosing **Edit Title**, as follows:

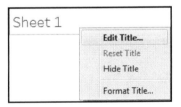

5. Type in the following text, and modify the size and colors as you would in any text editor:

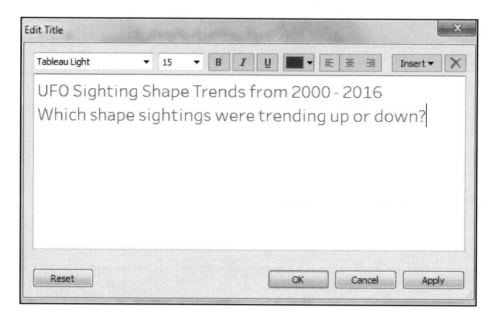

6. Finalize the formatting by further tweaking the sizes, colors, and transparencies, as follows:

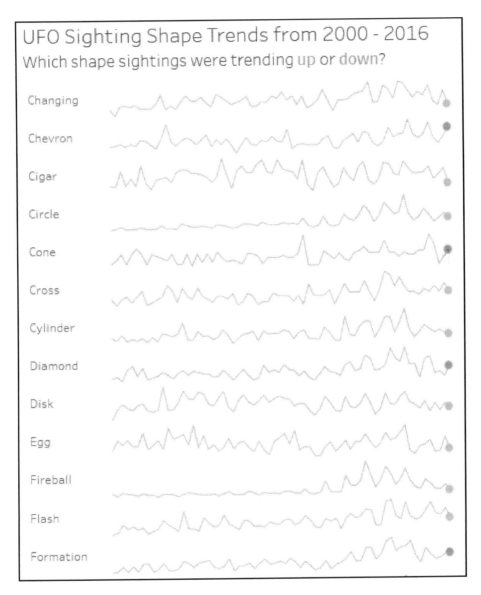

We can also highlight the maximum value instead of the final value.

7. Create the following calculation:

> **Max Sightings**
>
> Results are computed along Table (across).
> IF sum([Number of Records]) = WINDOW_MAX(sum([Number of Records]))
> then sum([Number of Records]) END

8. Substitute the final value measure with the max sightings one, as follows:

iii Columns	⊞ QUARTER(Event ..
≡ Rows ▼	Shape ▼	SUM(Number of Rec..	Max Sightings △

9. Format the color to fit your style, for example:

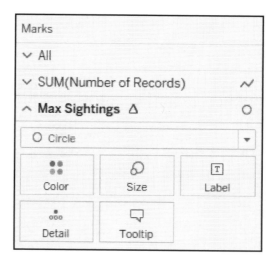

10. We can see the final Sparkline chart in the following screenshot:

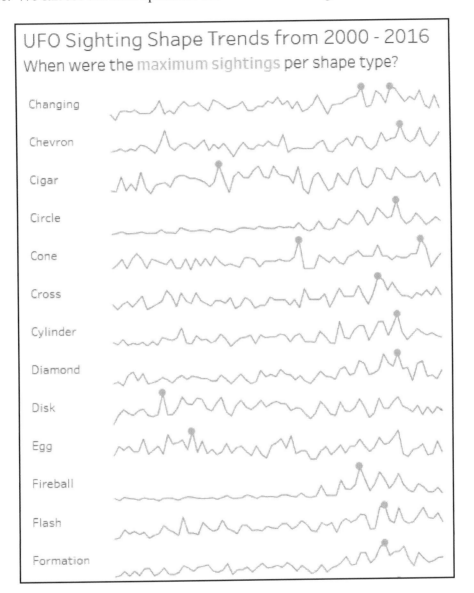

See also

- Read any of Edward Tufte's books. He is said to be the creator of the Sparkline.

Donut chart

Donut charts are pie charts with a hollow center. They are best used when communicating percentages, and can help the distinction of a few categories pop.

Donuts are best used when there are only a few categories to be displayed in the donut. There are other visualization types that would show many categories better, such as horizontal bars to name but one.

Getting ready

In this recipe, we extend the pie chart with a dual axis to create a donut chart.

How to do it...

In the next example, we're going to work with avocado data and show which cities eat a higher percentage of organic versus conventional. Use `Donut.twbx` to work through the example.

1. Create a calculation called `Donut` with zero hardcoded as the value, as follows:

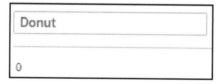

2. Place **Donut** on the **Rows** shelf twice, as follows:

3. In the **Marks** card for all values, change the default mark from **Automatic** to **Pie**, as follows:

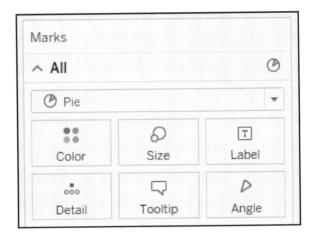

In the following screenshot, we can see how our chart should look:

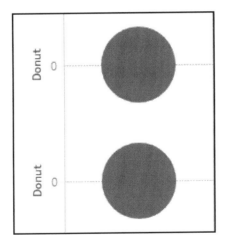

4. Next we will do some basic formatting by making the first donut larger, as follows:

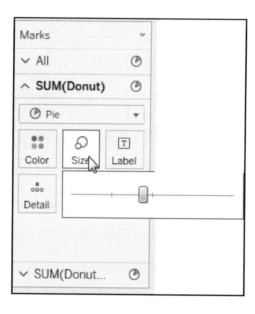

5. Change the color of the second donut to the background color, as follows:

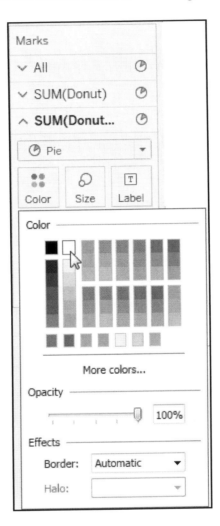

6. Create a dual axis chart by right-clicking on the axis and choosing **Dual Axis**, as follows:

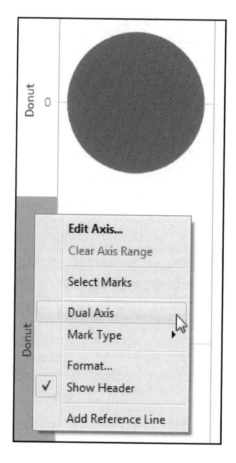

Right-clicking on the second donut pill and choosing **Dual Axis** is an alternative method.

At this point in the recipe, we now see a ring, as shown in the following screenshot:

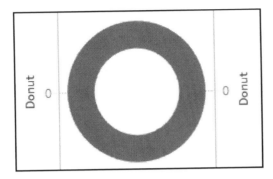

7. In the **Marks** card for the first donut, move the category you want to display as slices of your pie chart to color. In our example, that's type—organic or conventional. Because we haven't defined the angle, you should see an even split.
8. Next, we'll define the portion of each slice by moving the measure to **Angle**. In our example, this will be **Total Volume**:

9. To create the horizontal series, put a dimension in the **Rows**. In our example, this would be **Region**:

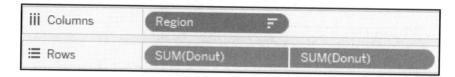

Because we have so many regions, I've also added a top rank filter so we only see a few, as follows:

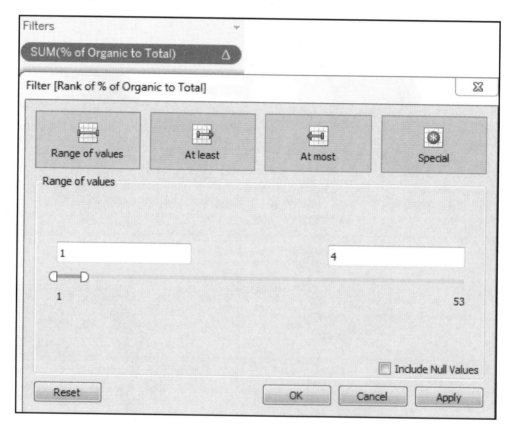

10. In the **Marks** card for the first donut chart, move **Region** to **Label** and change the alignment to be top and centered, as follows:

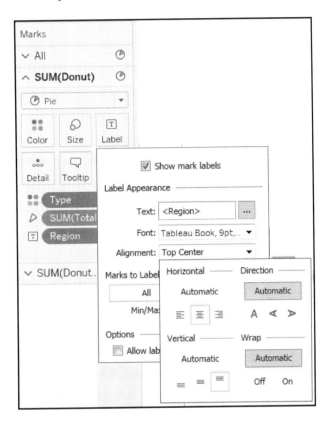

11. Remove the axis label, right-click on each donut pill, and deselect **Show Header**, as follows:

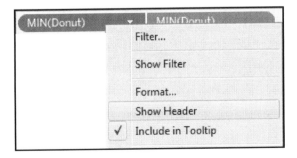

We can see our donut chart in the following screenshot:

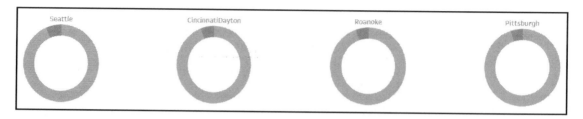

Donuts can be effective and fun when comparing two or three categories. Shy away from this chart type when comparing more.

How it works...

In *step 1*, we create a calculation called donut and place it on the **Rows** shelf twice in *step 2*. In *step 3*, we change the **Marks** card from **Automatic** to **Pie**. In *step 4*, we see that we have two pies. In *step 5*, we modify the format for one pie to be larger than the other pie. In *step 6*, to hollow out the center, the color of the smaller pie is set to match the background. In *step 7*, we create a dual axis chart that overlays the smaller circle onto the larger circle. In *step 8*, we should see a donut chart.

Next, in *step 9*, we create slices of the donut by moving the categorical dimension to **Color** on the **Marks** card (first donut measure). The angle shows how much each slice takes of the whole; in *step 10*, we put **Total Volume** on **Angle**. In *step 11*, we create a series of donuts by placing region on the **Columns** shelf. In *step 12*, we create titles for each donut by moving region onto **Label** within the **Marks** card. We format the text so its alignment is top and center. In *step 12*, we have our final donut chart.

There's more...

The hole of the donut can be used to display a value like the percent of the total.

1. Create a % of total metric, as follows:

2. Place the % of **Organic to Total** on to **Label** in the second donut's **Marks** card. Format **Alignment** to be **Middle Center** and modify the font size and color. Format the decimal places as follows:

The final chart can be seen in the following screenshot:

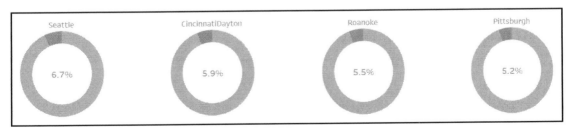

See also

- See stacked bar charts, and regular bar charts, or the section for waffle charts in the *Advanced Visualizations* chapter for alternatives to see the percent of totals.

Motion chart

This section highlights how to use Tableau to page through the data as a movie, frame by frame. Animated charts are useful in showing individual elements, as well as the big picture, in an immersive fashion.

Getting ready

In the motion chart recipe, we learn how to use **Pages**.

How to do it...

In this recipe, we're playing around with snow data for Snowbird, a ski resort in Utah. Open packaged workbook ski fall animation to follow along, ski fall animation.twbx and Snowbird - Utah.csv:

1. Drag a dimension with multiple values to the **Pages** shelf. In this example, we use **YEAR(Date)**. It works best when you have several values:

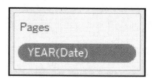

2. Move the date to **Columns** as **DAY(Date)** and **24 hour Snow** and **Base Depth** to **Rows**, as follows:

3. Within the **24 hr New Snow- Split 1 Marks** card, select **Shape** instead of **Automatic** and choose the star, as follows:

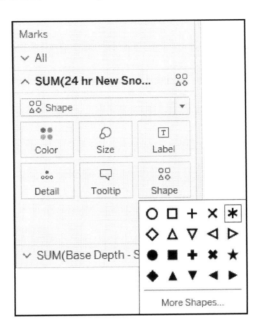

4. Within the **Base Depth - Split 1 Marks** card, select **Area**, as follows:

5. Change **Fit** to **Entire View**, as follows:

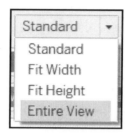

6. Remove all axis headers and grid lines.
7. Change the background to light blue, as follows:

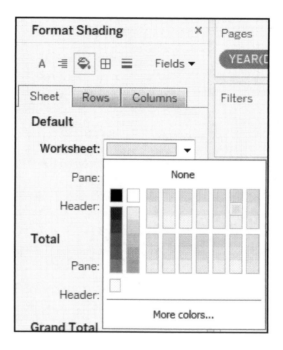

8. Select **All** and **Marks** to show all data points. Select the color grey and **Fade**, to create visual layers, as follows:

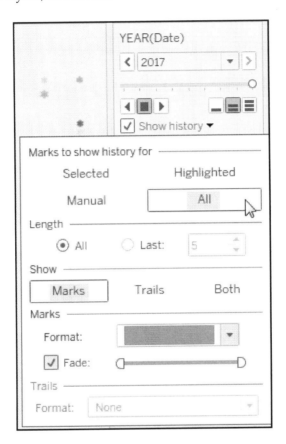

Make sure to continue using split axis, not dual axis. The lines control the speed. The play and stop buttons are intuitive. The part that makes this visualization fun is the history.

9. Here's the first page after we hit play:

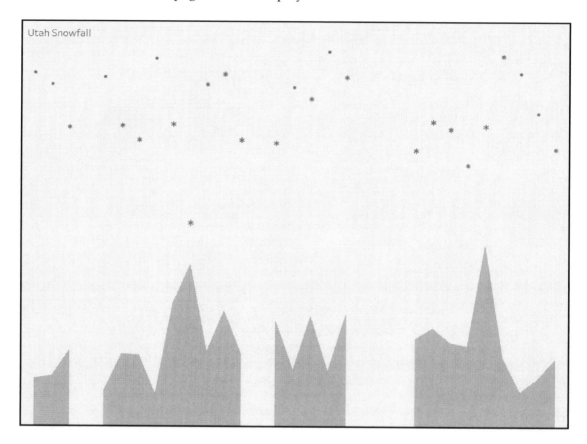

10. This is the last page after we hit play:

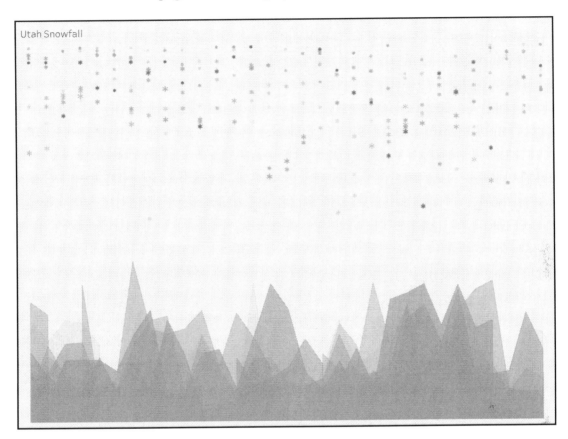

How it works...

In *step 1*, we use a time element in the **Pages** shelf to make an animated flip book. The history, illustrated in *step 3*, allows us to show changes in time or position relative to the previous data point. Because we chose to see all marks with fading, we're able to see a layered ghostly effect.

There's more...

In order to animate automatically when it is published to the server, you must make an animated GIF. You may check the tutorials for your favorite photo editing tool. Here is an example using GIMP, `https://www.digitalcitizen.life/how-create-animated-gif-using-your-own-pictures-gimp`. Also, play around with trail marks, which will give different effects.

See also

* Please watch any of Hans Rosling's *Ted Talks* videos and check out the Gapminder blogs. These videos are famous and fun. Hans Rosling is credited with being the creator of the motion chart.

9
Tableau Advanced Visualization

In this chapter, we will cover the following recipes:

- Lollipop charts
- Sankey diagrams
- Marimekko charts
- Hex-Tile maps
- Waffle charts

Technical requirements

We will use Tableau 2019.x, and data about mass transit complaints, beer, education, commuter times, and Lord of the Rings.

Introduction

In this chapter, we will learn more chart types that go beyond **Show Me**. We will use external data sources to provide a plotting frame and, in many cases, use advanced calculations to draw our visualizations. In these recipes, we will show how data elements relate to each other or how they are related to the whole.

Lollipop charts

Lollipop charts get their name from their shape. These charts can offer visual variety. We would typically use lollipops in place of bar charts or dot plots, which also happen to be construction components.

Getting ready

We will learn how to successfully combine a bar chart and a dot plot to create a lollipop chart.

How to do it...

We will open the packaged workbook lollipop to work through the recipe. We will examine the NYC mass transit customer complaints by complaint subject matter; use MTA_Customer_Feedback_Data_Beginning_2014.csv and MTA complaints.twbx:

1. Place **Subject Matter** and **Number of Records** on the **Columns** and **Rows** shelves:

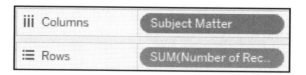

2. Duplicate the **Number of Records** pill on the **Rows** shelf:

3. Modify the chart to be **Dual Axis**:

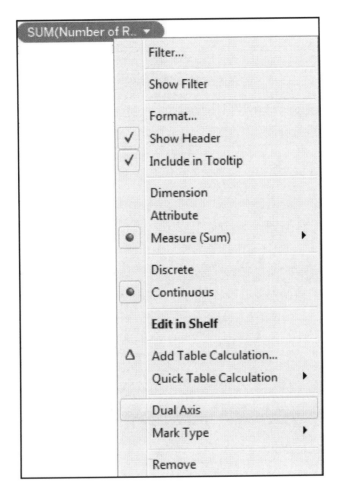

4. Change the mark type of **Sum(Number of Records)** to **Bar**:

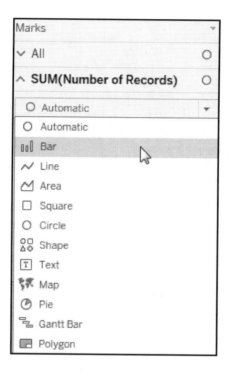

5. Make the **Size** of the bar smaller:

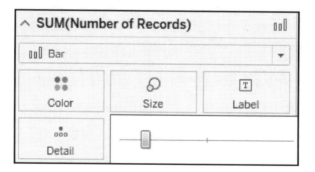

6. Make the **Size** of the circle larger:

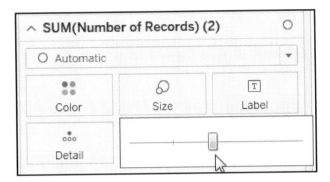

7. Sorting **Subject Matter** in descending order by **Number of Records**:

We now have the following example:

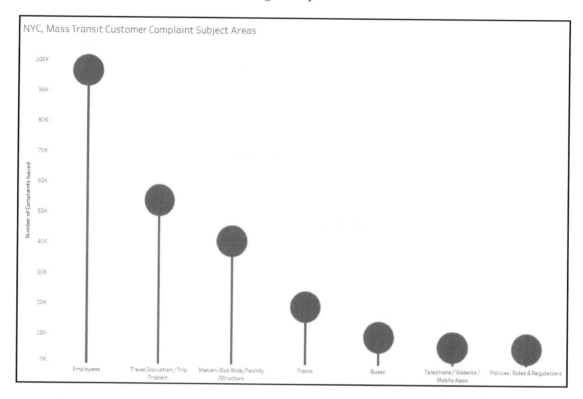

 Because there were many different **Subject Matter**, we filtered **Subject Matter** to the top seven based on the **Number of Complaints** issued.

How it works...

We placed the **Subject Matter** on the **Columns** shelf and **Number of Records** on the **Rows** shelf twice. Next, we made this a **Dual Axis** chart. We modified the mark type to be **Bar** and made the size smaller for the first **Number of Records**. We left the mark type for the second **Number of Records** as **Circle** and increased the **Size**. Finally, we combined a skinny bar chart with a dot plot chart.

There's more...

We can place a value in the center of the dot plot:

1. Place **Number of Records** onto the **Marks** card to create **Number of Records 2**:

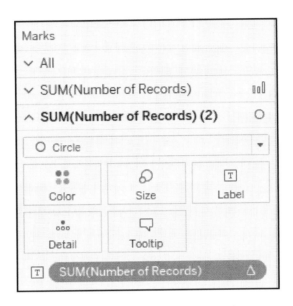

2. Right-click on **SUM(Number of Records),** choose **Add Table Calculation**, and choose **Percent of Total**:

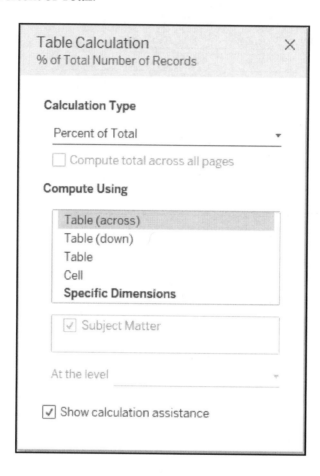

3. Format the text size, alignment, and color in order to create a similar chart:

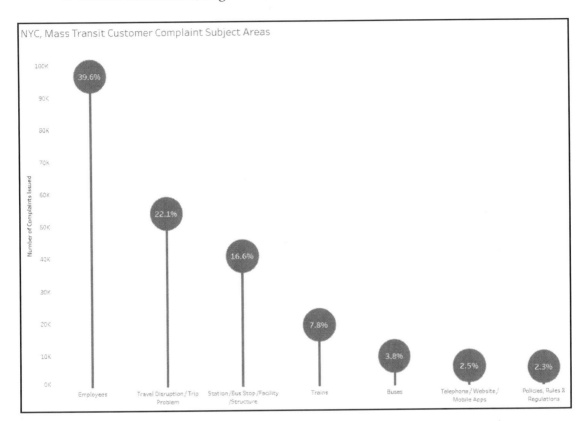

See also

To learn more about dot plots, use the following links as a starting point:

- `https://uc-r.github.io/cleveland-dot-plots`
- `https://en.wikipedia.org/wiki/Dot_plot_(statistics)`
- `http://www.storytellingwithdata.com/blog/2018/8/1/swdchallenge-lets-plot-with-a-dot`

Sankey diagrams

A Sankey diagram is a tool used to show the flow from one dimension to another.

Getting ready

In this recipe, we will create a Sankey diagram using a web extension provided by Infotopics. Web extensions are a new feature in 2018.2.

How to do it...

In 2018.2, we can use web extensions to build a Sankey chart. To follow along, use `Beer 2018.2.twbx`, `beers.csv`, and `breweries.csv`.

1. Create the `Select Dimension Left` parameter:

2. Create the `Select Dimension Right` parameter:

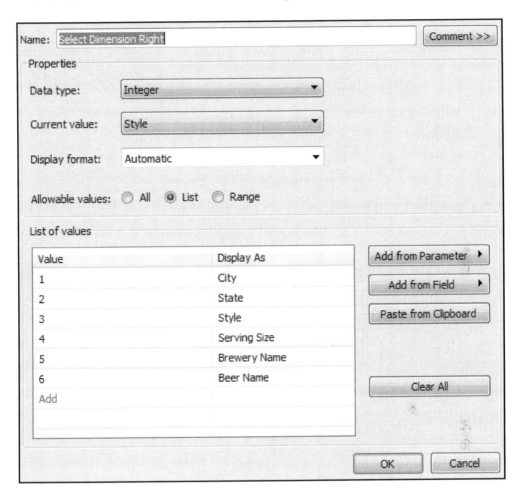

3. Create the `Dimension Left` parameter:

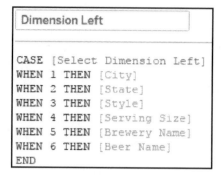

4. Create the `Dimension Right` parameter:

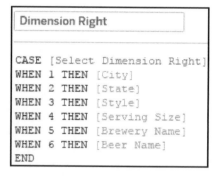

5. Create the `Chosen Measure` parameter:

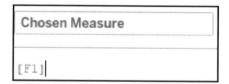

6. Create the `Top Dimension Values` parameter:

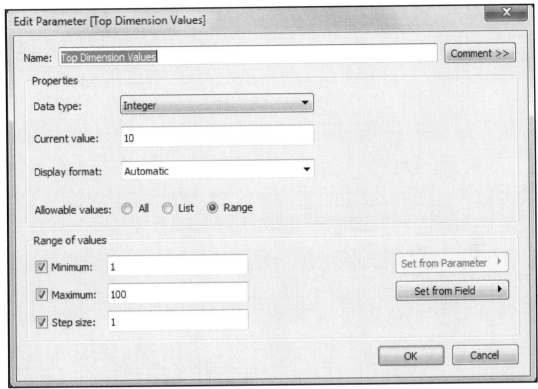

The first six steps are not required, but they give the visualization some fun flexibility. The user can select which categories appear on the left-hand side and the right-hand side of the chart. Also, because there are so many values, which can make the Sankey chart look busy, we've added a top value to filter the dimension values. For this Sankey recipe, we actually only need to create a sheet with two dimensions and one measure.

7. Add **Dimension Right** to the **Columns** shelf and the **Filters** shelf.
8. Add **Dimension Left** to the **Rows** shelf and the **Filters** shelf.

9. Right-click **Dimension Right** and **Dimension Left** in the **Filters** shelf, select **Edit Filter**, and set as follows:

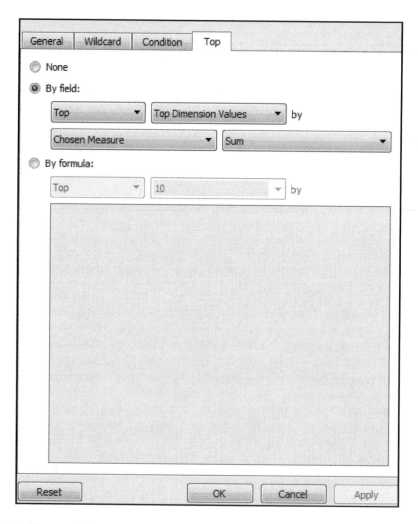

10. Add **Chosen Measure** to **Text** in the **Marks** card.

11. Add a **Percent of Total** option in **Table Calculation**:

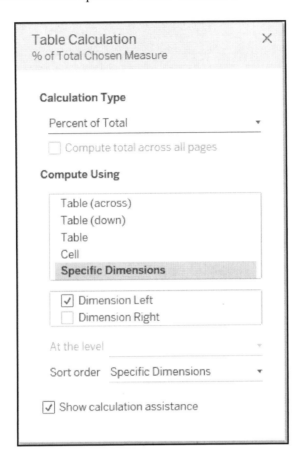

The cross-tab should appear as follows:

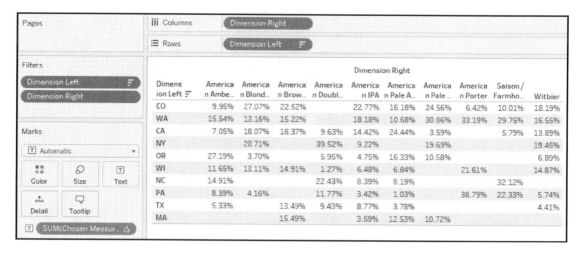

12. Add the sheet to a dashboard, as shown in the following screenshot:

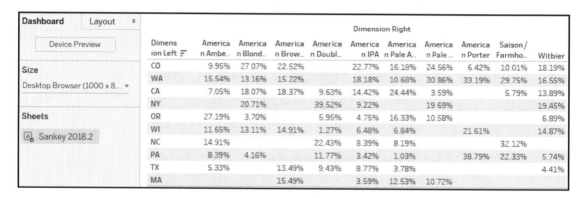

13. Make the sheet **Floating** and then minimize it. In this example, we don't want to see the cross-tab. However, the **Show Me More** extension requires it to be on the dashboard in order to work:

14. Use the **Extension** object:

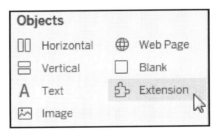

15. When prompted for the first time, download the **Show Me More** web extension by visiting **Extension Gallery**:

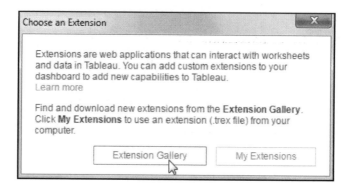

16. You can go to **My Extensions** and navigate to your extensions library to choose **Show Me More**:

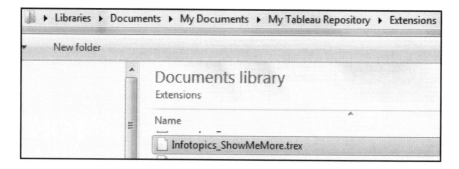

17. Click on **Use configure to get started.** to begin the configuration:

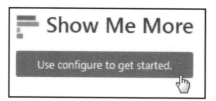

18. Choose **Sankey Diagram**:

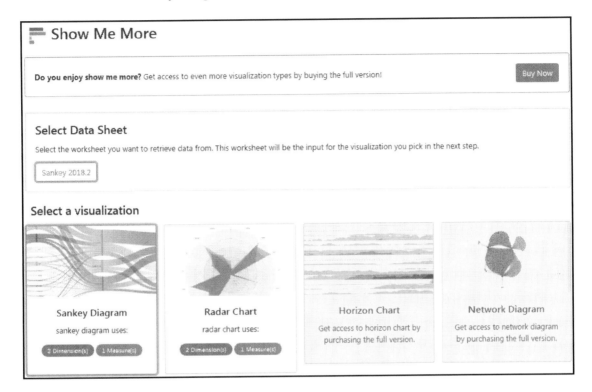

19. Select the dimensions and measures as shown in the following screenshot:

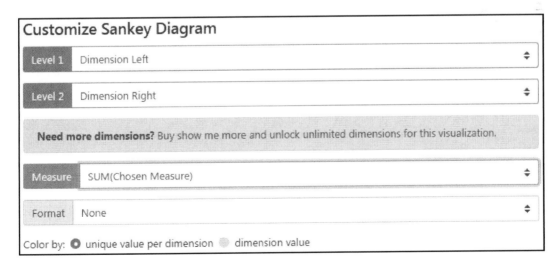

We can see the final visualization in the following screenshot:

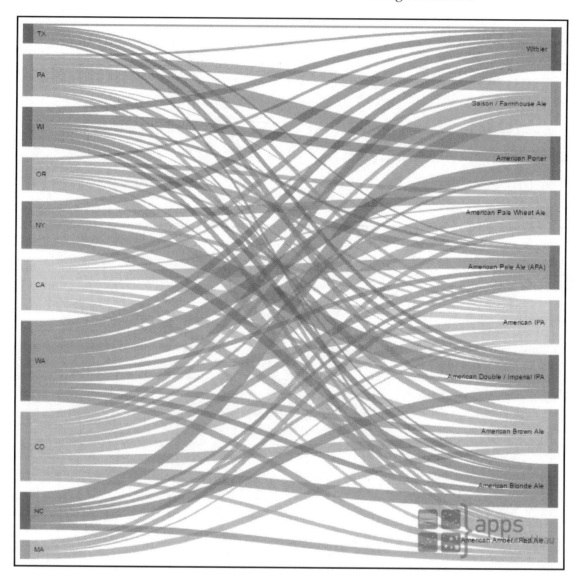

How it works...

We created a cross-tab with two dimensions and one measure. We then added this to a dashboard. Because we only wanted to see the Sankey chart and the extension requires that the cross-tab be on the dashboard, we "hid it" by making it very small and floating. Using the extension object, we chose the **Show Me More** extension. We configured it for **Sankey Diagram**.

See also

There are several ways to create a Sankey chart published on various blogs. Ian Balwin's post on *Information Lab* is excellent because it is flexible and does not require outside data prep. However, there are many calculations, which can make it hard to follow. But once it's set, there is a great deal of flexibility because of how the dimensions and measures have been created. The following directions are taken from his blog post at `https://www.theinformationlab.co.uk/2018/03/09/build-sankey-diagram-tableau-without-data-prep-beforehand/`.

Use `Beer.twbx`, `beers.csv`, and `breweries.csv` to work through this example:

1. Create the `Select Dimension Left` parameter or use the same one from the previous recipe:

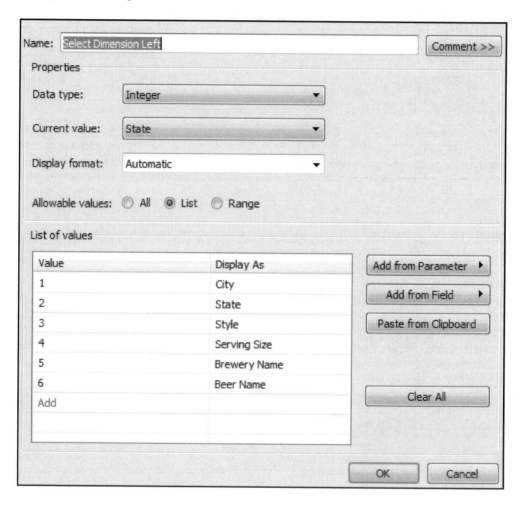

2. Create the `Select Dimension Right` parameter or use the same one from the previous recipe:

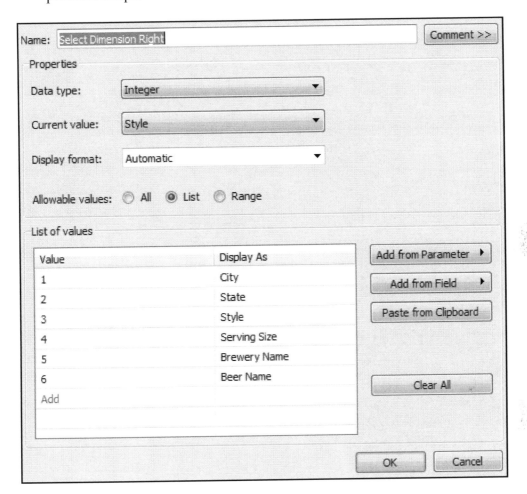

3. Create the `Dimension Left` parameter or use the same one from the previous recipe:

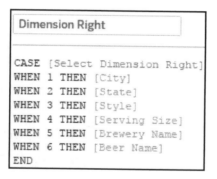

```
Dimension Left

CASE [Select Dimension Left]
WHEN 1 THEN [City]
WHEN 2 THEN [State]
WHEN 3 THEN [Style]
WHEN 4 THEN [Serving Size]
WHEN 5 THEN [Brewery Name]
WHEN 6 THEN [Beer Name]
END
```

4. Create the `Dimension Right` parameter or use the same one from the previous recipe:

```
Dimension Right

CASE [Select Dimension Right]
WHEN 1 THEN [City]
WHEN 2 THEN [State]
WHEN 3 THEN [Style]
WHEN 4 THEN [Serving Size]
WHEN 5 THEN [Brewery Name]
WHEN 6 THEN [Beer Name]
END
```

5. Create the `Chosen Measure` parameter or use the same one from the previous recipe:

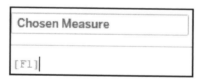

```
Chosen Measure

[F1]
```

6. Create the `Top Dimension Values` parameter or use the same one from the previous recipe:

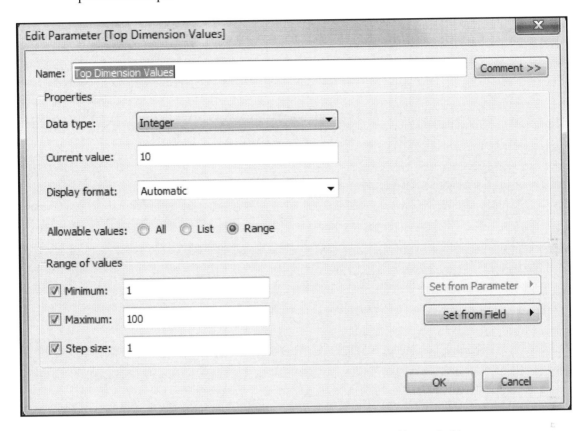

7. Add **Dimension Right** and **Dimension Left** to the **Filters** shelf.

8. Right-click **Dimension Right** and **Dimension Left** in the **Filters** shelf, select **Edit Filter**, and set it as follows:

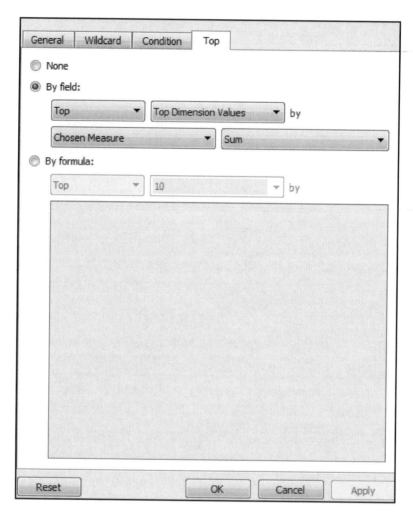

9. Create the `Path Frame` parameter:

10. Create a `Path Index` parameter:

11. Create the `T` parameter:

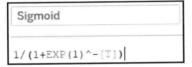

12. Create the `Sigmoid` function:

13. Create the `Sankey Arm Size` parameter:

14. Create all the following calculations for the top of the Sankey Arm:
    - `Max Position Left`
        - `RUNNING_SUM([Sankey Arm Size])`
    - `Max Position Left Wrap`
        - `WINDOW_SUM([Max Position Left])`
    - `Max Position Right`
        - `RUNNING_SUM([Sankey Arm Size])`
    - `Max Position Right Wrap`
        - `WINDOW_SUM([Max Position Right])`

15. Create all of the following calculations for the bottom of the Sankey Arm:
    - `Max for Min Position Left`
        - `RUNNING_SUM([Sankey Arm Size])`
    - `Min Position Left`
        - `RUNNING_SUM([Max for Min Position Left])-`
          `[Sankey Arm Size]`
    - `Min Position Left Wrap`
        - `WINDOW_SUM([Min Position Left])`
    - `Max for Min Position Right`
        - `RUNNING_SUM([Sankey Arm Size])`
    - `Min Position Right`
        - `RUNNING_SUM([Max for Min Position Right])-`
          `[Sankey Arm Size]`
    - `Min Position Right Wrap`
        - `WINDOW_SUM([Min Position 2]`

16. Create the `Sankey Polygons` calculation as follows:

17. Create the **Left Side** sheet:

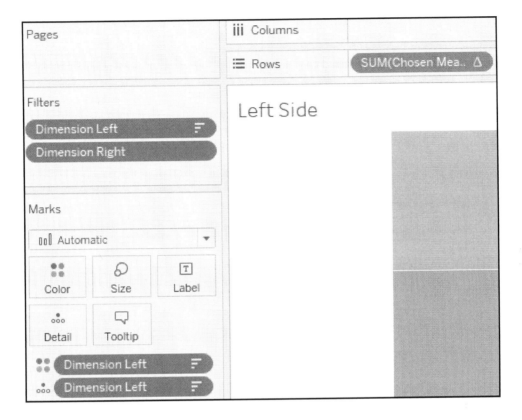

18. Apply a **Percent of Total** option in **Table Calculation** to **Chosen Measure**:

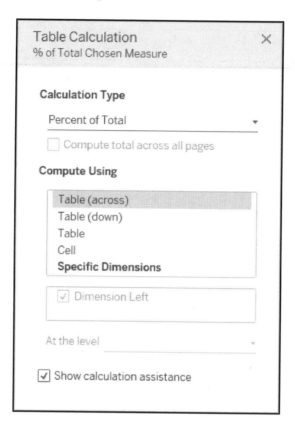

19. Create the **Right Side** sheet:

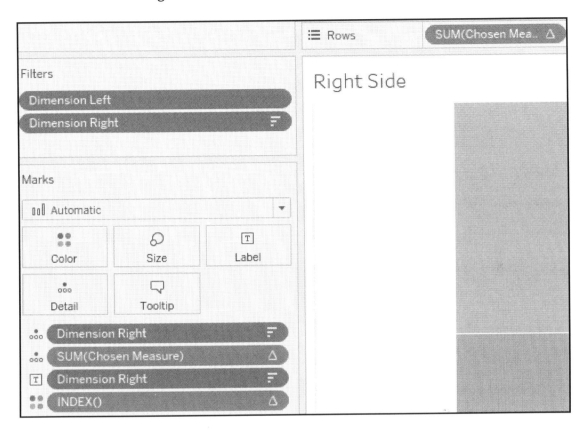

20. Apply a **Percent of Total** option under **Table Calculation** to **Chosen Measure**:

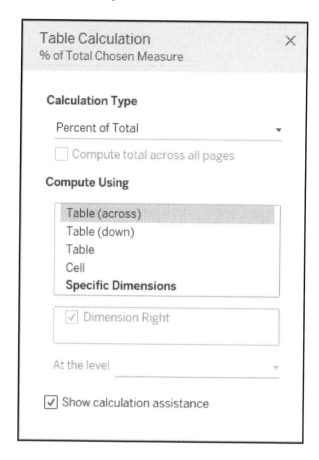

21. Create `INDEX()` by double-clicking in the **Marks** card and typing `INDEX()`:

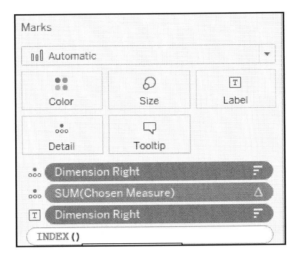

22. Apply **INDEX()** to the **Color** card:

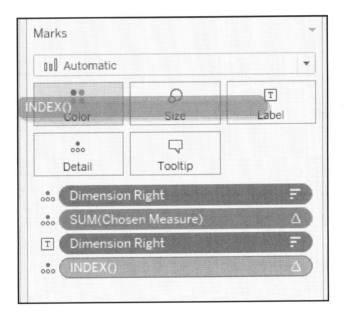

23. Apply a table calculation to **INDEX()**, as shown in the following screenshot:

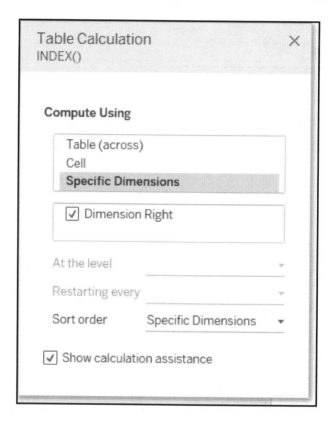

24. Create the **Sankey** sheet:

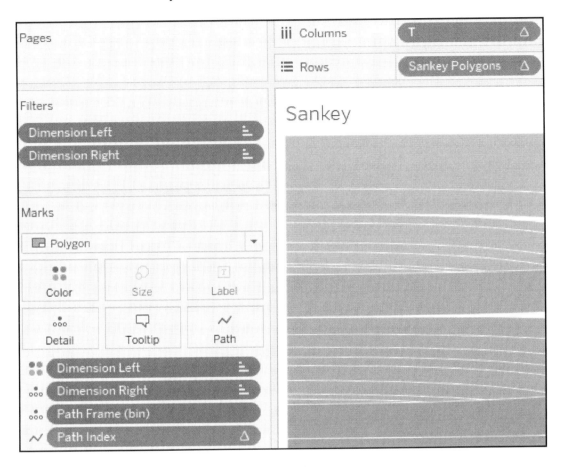

25. **Table Calculation** for **Sankey Polygons**:

   - These are all the table calculations we will need to configure for the **Sankey Polygons**:

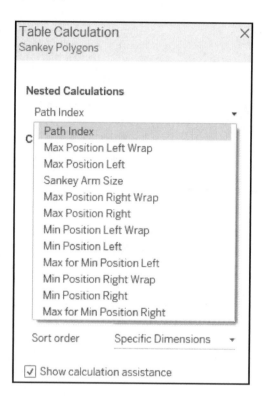

- **Path Index**:

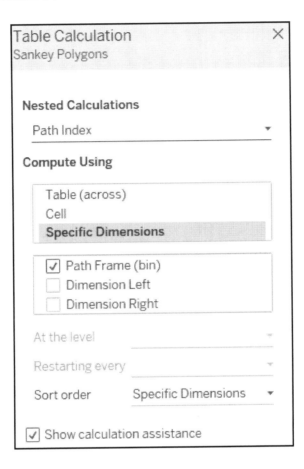

- **Max Position Left Wrap**:

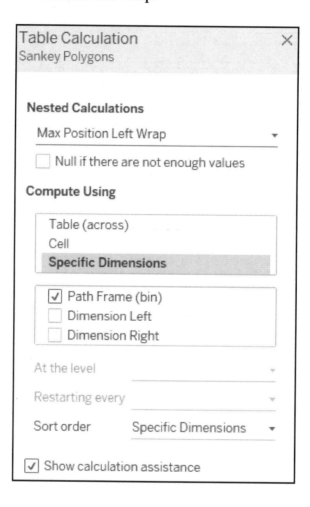

- **Max Position Left**:

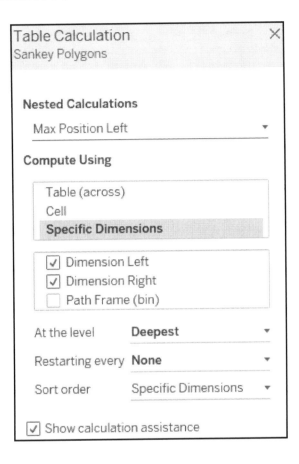

- **Sankey Arm Size:**

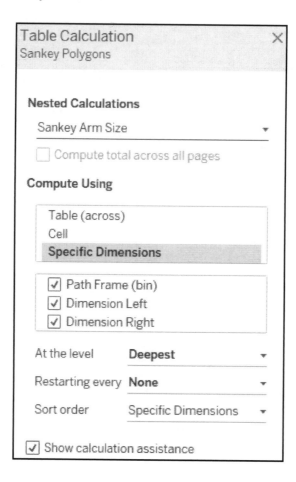

- **Max Position Right Wrap:**

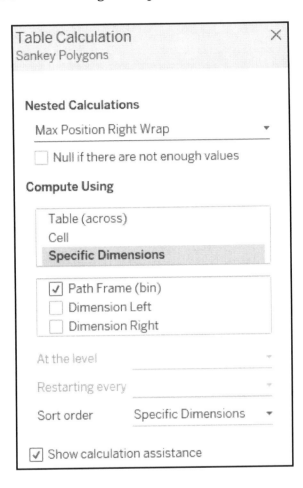

- **Max Position Right**:

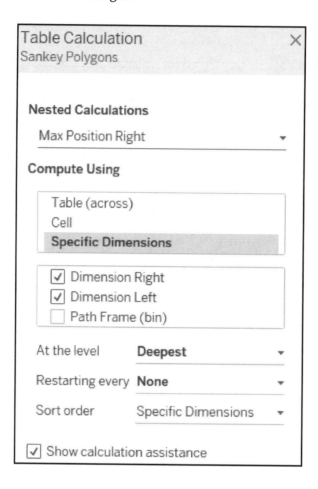

- **Min Position Left Wrap**:

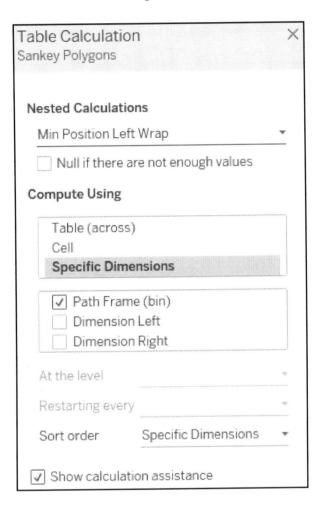

- **Min Position Left**:

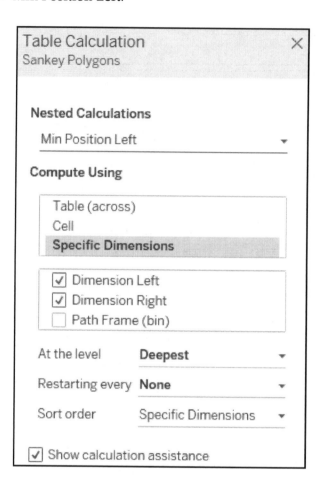

- **Max for Min Position Left:**

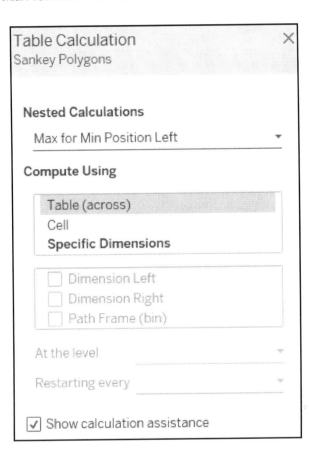

- **Min Position Right Wrap**:

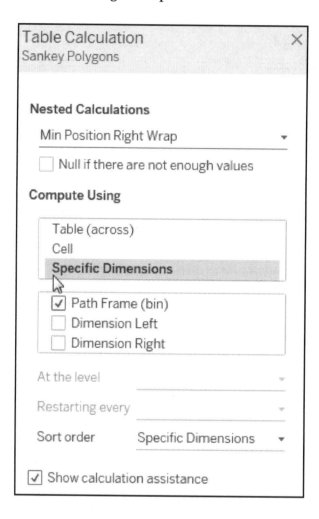

- **Min Position Right:**

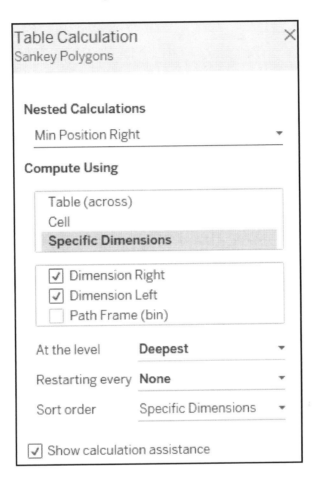

- **Max for Min Position Right:**

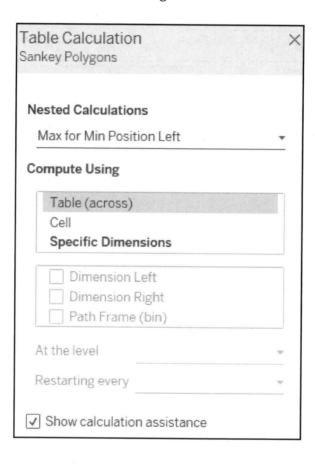

You will see the final dashboard in the following screenshot:

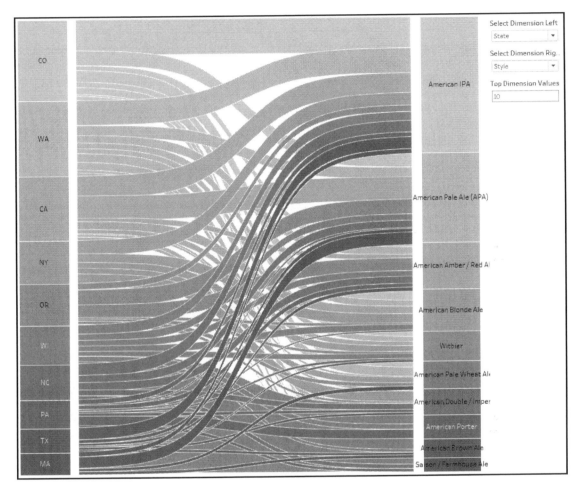

Marimekko charts

Marimekko charts go by many names: mekko, mosaic, or matrix, to name a few. It is a two-dimensional stacked chart. They are used to analyze data composition or distribution across two variables at once. Each axis represents 100%.

Getting ready

In this recipe, we use complex calculations to build the Marimekko chart.

How to do it...

To follow along, open the Marimekko packaged workbook: `Mekko.twbx` and `xAPI-Edu-Data.csv`. We are going to compare gender, parent satisfaction with school, and student participation by raised hands.

It is recommended you start with a text table to get the calculations correct.

1. Add the dimensions of interest to the **Rows** shelf. We are going to add **Grade ID**, **Gender**, and **Parentschool Satisfaction**.
2. Add the **Raised Hands** to the **Text** shelf in the **Marks** card:

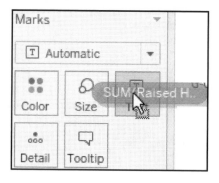

3. Add the **Percent of Total** option in **Table Calculation**, and under **Compute Using** select **Parentschool Satisfaction**:

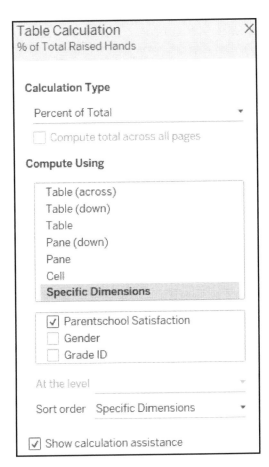

4. Double-click on **Measure Values**:

5. Add the **Raised Hands** to the **Measure Values** card:

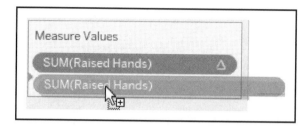

6. Create calculation `Raised Hands per Column`:

7. Add **Raised Hands per Column** to the **Measure Values** card:

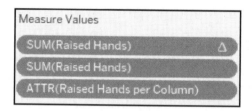

8. Create **Calculation # of Raised Hands, Grade, Gender ID, Parentschool Satisfaction** and add it to the **Measures Value** card. This calculation creates somewhat of a running total summary for grades and genders. This value will be the *x* axis:

```
Results are computed along Table (across).
//If it's the first row in parition
IF FIRST()==0 THEN
     //return this value
     MIN([Raised Hands per Column])

//check if this grade is NOT the same as the previous one
ELSEIF MIN([Grade ID]) != LOOKUP(MIN([Grade ID]),-1) THEN
     //Add the previous value of raised hands per column to this one
     PREVIOUS_VALUE(0) + MIN([Raised Hands per Column])

//check if gender is NOT the same as the previous one
ELSEIF MIN([Gender]) != LOOKUP(MIN([Gender]),-1) THEN
     //add the previous value of raised hands per column to this one
     PREVIOUS_VALUE(0) + MIN([Raised Hands per Column])

ELSE
     //it's the same grade and gender, show the same raised hands value
     PREVIOUS_VALUE(0)

END
```

9. We've completed the calculation work in order to make the visualization. Your grid should look as follows:

Grade ID	Gender	Parentschool Satisfaction	Raised Hands	% of Total Raised Hands along Parents..	Raised Hands per Column	# of Raised Hands, Grade, Gender ID, Pa..
G-02	F	Bad	499	20.18%	2,473	2,473
		Good	1,974	79.82%	2,473	2,473
	M	Bad	1,072	37.00%	2,897	5,370
		Good	1,825	63.00%	2,897	5,370
G-04	F	Bad	272	24.46%	1,112	6,482
		Good	840	75.54%	1,112	6,482
	M	Bad	345	30.50%	1,131	7,613
		Good	786	69.50%	1,131	7,613

10. Move **Measure Values** from **Text** to **Detail**:

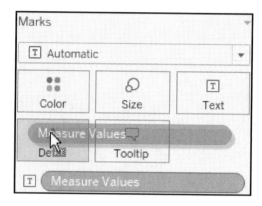

11. Move **Grade ID**, **Gender**, and **Parentschool Satisfaction** to **Detail**:

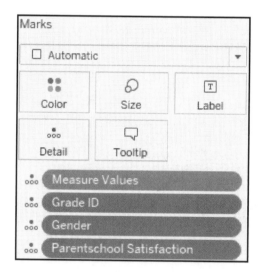

12. Move **Sum(Raised Hands)** with the **Percent of Total** calculation to the **Rows** shelf:

13. Remove **Measure Names** from the **Columns** shelf:

14. We have a stacked bar at this step:

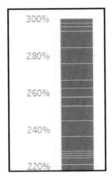

15. Move # **of Raised Hands, Grade, Gender ID, Parentschool Satisfaction** to the **Columns** shelf:

16. Change the **Scatter Plot** mark type to **Bar**:

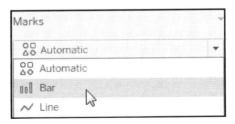

17. Move **Raised Hands per Column** from **Measure Values** to **Size**:

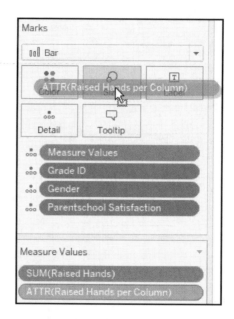

18. Set **Size** to **Fixed** and **Alignment** to **Right**:

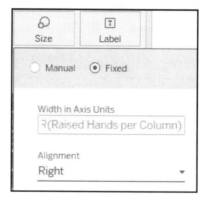

19. Create a **Gender** and **Parentschool satisfaction** combined field, as shown in the following screenshot:

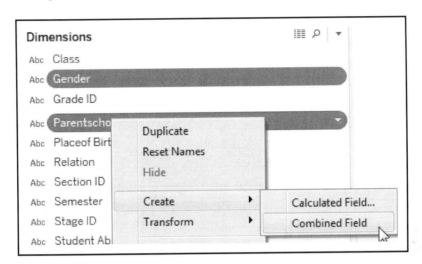

20. Add the combined field to **Color**:

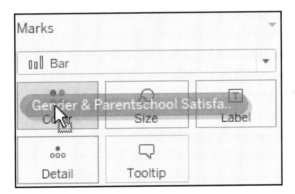

21. Manually sort by **Gender & Parentschool Satisfaction**:

- Right-click on this dimension in the marks card and select **Sort**:

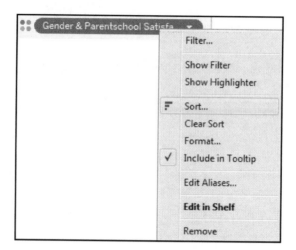

- Choose **Manual Sort** and make it appear as follows:

22. This should produce the following chart. Second, seventh, and eighth graders raise their hands more in class than other grades. Parents with students who raise their hands in class were generally happier with the school. High school students do not raise their hands in class, as shown in the following screenshot:

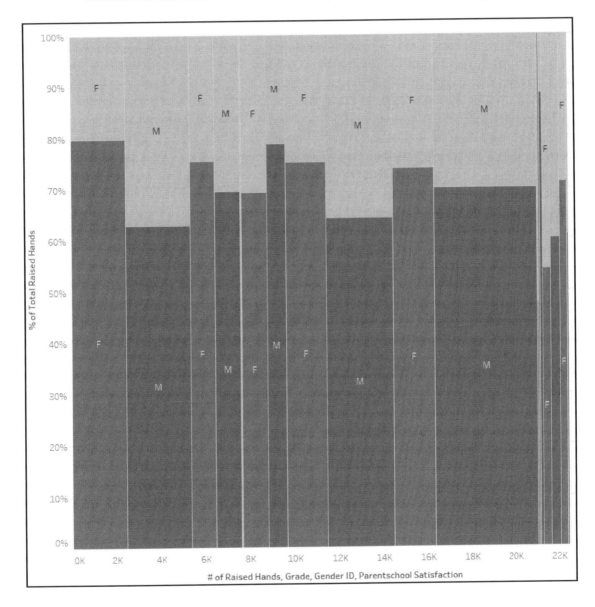

How it works...

First, we created a text table to work through our calculations. We then added the dimensions of interest to the **Rows** shelf and the measure of interest to the **Text** shelf.

For column height, we created `Percent of Total for Raised Hands`, which we compute by using **Parentschool Satisfaction**. This allows us to see 100% for each **Gender** and **Grade** combination, which is our column height. We add this calculation to the **Measure Values** card.

In order to get our column widths, we created the **Raised Hands per Column** calculation, which calculates the sum for all hand raises for each combination of **Gender** and **Grade**. We then add the calculation to the **Measure Values** card.

Next, we created # **of Raised Hands, Grade, Gender ID, Parentschool Satisfaction** to help order the columns of each grade and gender correctly along the x-axis. This calculation is building a running total based on raised hands per column.

It does this math by going through the following checks:

- Is it the first row in the partition then return this value?
- Has the grade changed then add this value and the previous value?
- Has the gender changed? If it has, add this value and the previous value; otherwise we have to return the previous value.

Then we began to create the visualization. We moved **Measure Values** from **Text** to **Detail**; move **Grade ID**, **Gender**, and **Parentschool Satisfaction** to **Detail**. We moved Sum(Raised Hands) with the percent of total calculation to the **Rows** shelf, and removed **Measure Names** from the **Columns** shelf. At this point, we have a stacked bar.

We moved # **of Raised Hands, Grade, Gender ID, Parentschool Satisfaction** to the **Columns** shelf. Next, we changed the **Scatter Plot** mark type to **Bar**. To get the column widths, we move **Raised Hands per Column** from **Measure Values** to **Size** and set it to **Fixed** and **Alignment** to **Right**.

In order to color our visualization, we created a **Gender** and **Parentschool Satisfaction** combined field that we add to **Color**. Finally, to make **Gender** more visible, we added it to **Label**.

There's more...

We can create a header visualization to use in a dashboard so that the grades are labelled better:

1. Add **Raised Hands** to the **Column** shelf:

2. Add **Grade ID** to **Label**:

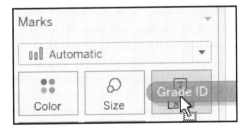

3. Add the **Marimekko** chart to a dashboard:

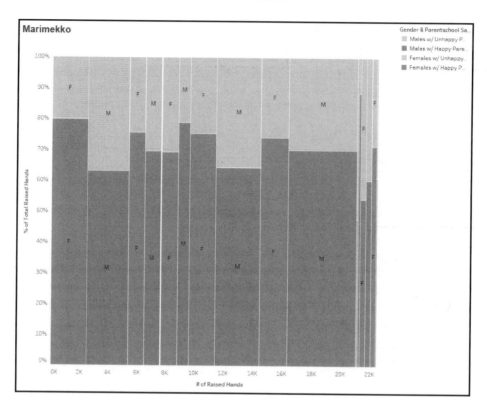

4. Add the **Header** visualization to the dashboard as a floating object and resize it:

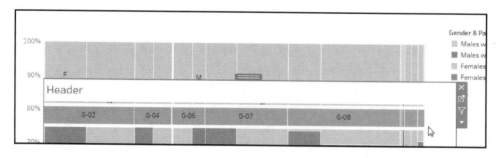

5. After some formatting and resizing, we can view our final visualization in the following screenshot:

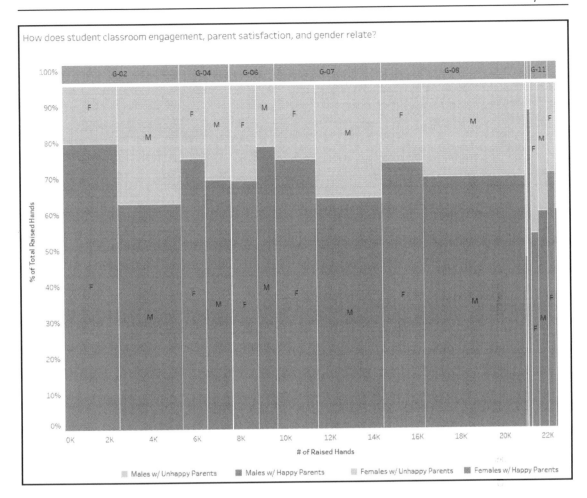

Hex-Tile maps

Here, you will learn how to eliminate the visual perceptions that occur due to different sizes of different states or countries and focus on showing more actionable trends.

Getting ready

In this recipe, we will create a Hex-Tile map using a scatter plot as a base.

How to do it...

Follow along using the `Hexmap.twbx`, `hexmap_plots.xlsx`, and `Data USA - Map of Commuting Alone over 30 Minutes by State.csv` datasets:

1. Choose the `hexmap_plot.xlsx` file.

2. Join **Data USA - Map of Commuting Alone over 30 Minutes by State** to the **hexmap_plot** data using the State and Geo Name columns as the join condition:

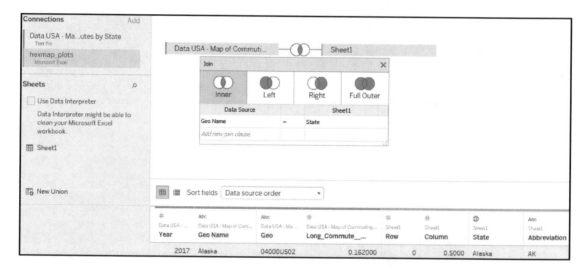

3. Add **Column** to the **Columns** shelf, add **Row** to the **Rows** shelf, and use **AVG** for the aggregation:

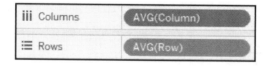

4. Use **Abbreviation** as the **Label**:

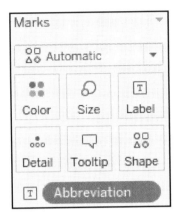

5. Edit the row axis and reverse the scale:

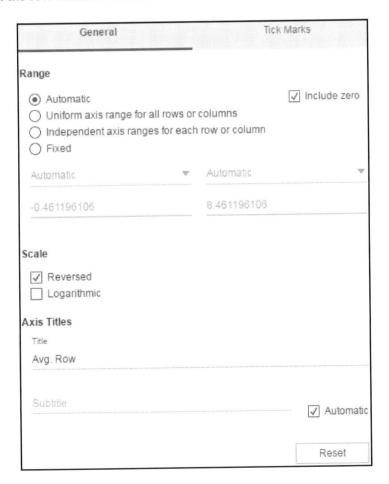

6. Use the `inverted_hex.png` image as a custom shape:

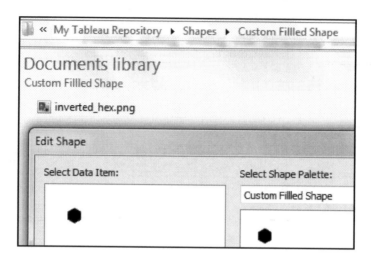

Save the `inverted_hex.png` image to your `Tableau Repository` | `Shapes` | `Custom Filled Shape` folder.

7. Adjust the **Size**:

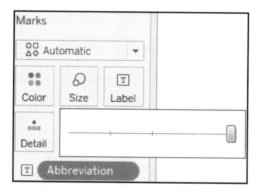

8. Color and shade the tiles by a measure in your data file. In our visualization, we're using **Longest_Commute_Driving_Alone**:

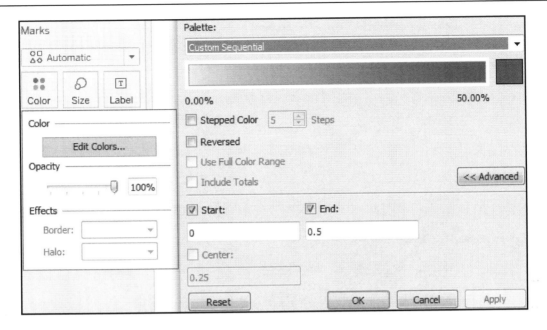

9. Add state labels, by putting **Abbreviation** on **Label**:

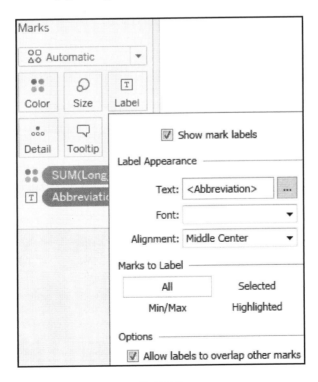

After some formatting, we can see the final visualization in the following screenshot:

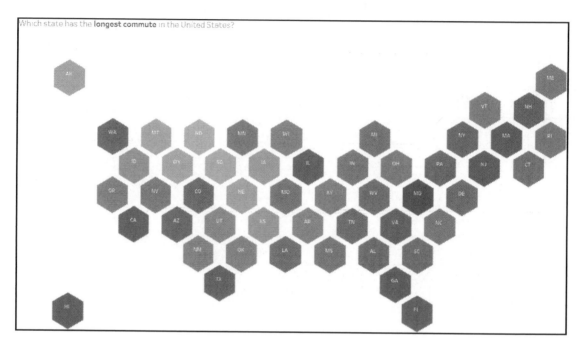

How it works...

The key to the *Hex-Tile maps* recipe was using the `hexmap_plot` data and the tile image. The column and row values position the tiles so they were arranged in a similar, relative place as each state. The custom shape helped tie the visualization together in a compact way.

See also

Here are some examples of user community hexmap plots for other countries:

- `https://revizited.com/how-to-create-hex-tile-map-for-india-in-tableau/`
- `https://www.sportschord.com/single-post/2018/02/12/Maps-in-Tableau-Part-1---UK-Hex-Tile-Map`

Waffle charts

Waffle charts have almost similar use cases to Donut charts. They are used to show how items contribute to a whole. They are best used when comparing only a few categories.

Getting ready

In this recipe, we will create a Waffle chart using a text table as the foundation.

How to do it...

To follow along, open the Waffle chart packaged workbook. In this example, we are looking at word counts for each Lord of the Rings character by race:

1. Use the `Waffle frame` Excel sheet:
   - This Excel sheet is 100 rows representing each percentage point. Because we want to create a frame of 100 squares in a 10 x 10 frame, we have columns called `Rows`, `Columns`, and `Percentage`. Each row and column has a value of 1 through 10, repeating. This creates a 10 row x 10 column square. The first 20 are displayed in the following screenshot:

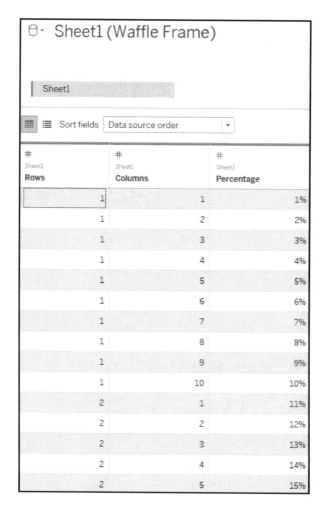

2. Add **Columns** to the **Columns** shelf and **Rows** to the **Rows** shelf. Because we want these values to be grouped in discrete buckets, we have set these to discrete. This can be achieved by right-clicking and choosing discrete, as opposed to continuous:

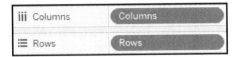

3. Add percentage to **Label** to see the layout:

						Columns				
Rows		1	2	3	4	5	6	7	8	9	10
10		91%	92%	93%	94%	95%	96%	97%	98%	99%	100%
9		81%	82%	83%	84%	85%	86%	87%	88%	89%	90%
8		71%	72%	73%	74%	75%	76%	77%	78%	79%	80%
7		61%	62%	63%	64%	65%	66%	67%	68%	69%	70%
6		51%	52%	53%	54%	55%	56%	57%	58%	59%	60%
5		41%	42%	43%	44%	45%	46%	47%	48%	49%	50%
4		31%	32%	33%	34%	35%	36%	37%	38%	39%	40%
3		21%	22%	23%	24%	25%	26%	27%	28%	29%	30%
2		11%	12%	13%	14%	15%	16%	17%	18%	19%	20%
1		1%	2%	3%	4%	5%	6%	7%	8%	9%	10%

4. Order the **Rows** column in descending order:

						Columns		
Rows		1	2	3	4	5	6	7
10		91%	92%	93%	94%	95%	96%	97%
9		81%	82%	83%	84%	85%	86%	87%

5. Remove the percentage from **Label** and change the mark type to **Square**:

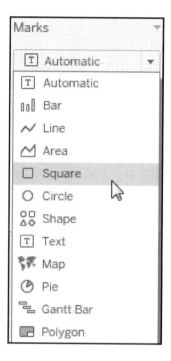

6. Create the actual share of words spoken by the Hobbits. Go the
    WordsByCharacter dataset and create a Hobbit calculation based on Race =
    Hobbit for percent of total spoken words:

7. Create a true/false calculation to indicate whether the Hobbit is greater than or
    equal to each square in the Waffle chart. The **Hobbit Percentage** calculation
    allows us to color each square:

8. Apply **Hobbit Percentage** to **Color**:

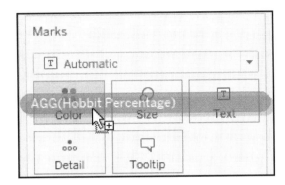

9. Adjust the color so that false is faint and subtle:

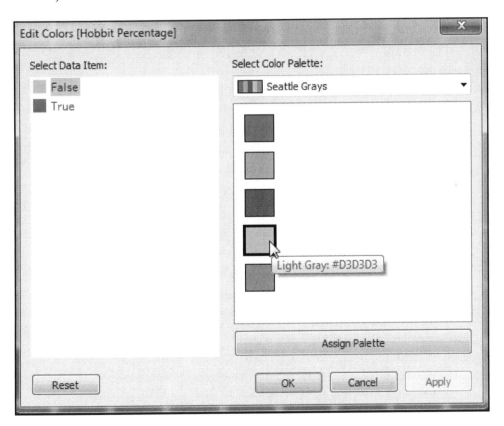

10. Adjust the mark size as follows:

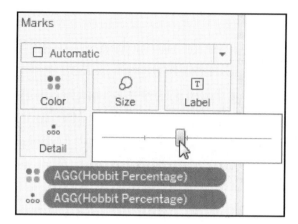

11. Adjust the chart size by manually adjusting the columns and rows:

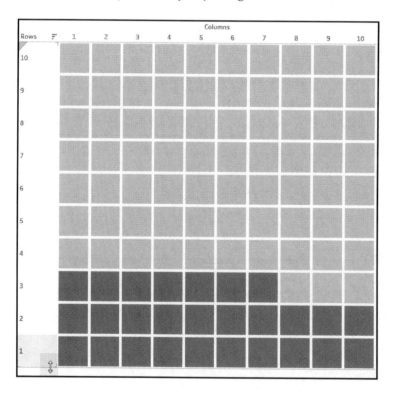

12. Add **Hobbit** to details, so we can annotate the chart:

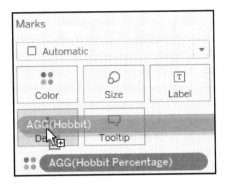

13. Annotate the Waffle chart as follows:

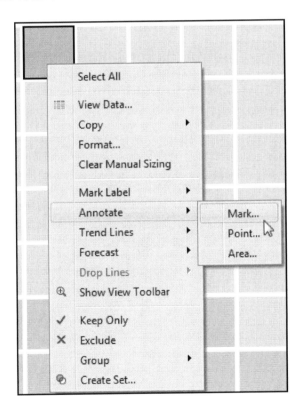

14. Modify the annotation as shown in the following screenshot:

15. After formatting and hiding headers, the final Waffle chart should look like this:

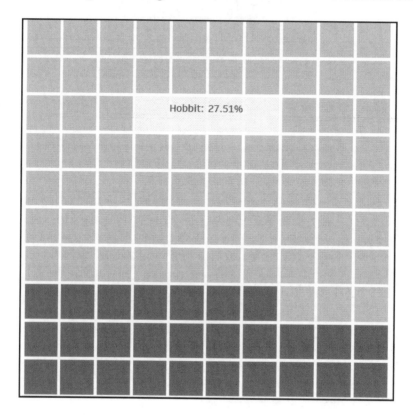

How it works...

We used the Excel 10 row x 10 column grid to represent a 100% grid, and put columns and rows on their respective shelves. We then changed the mark type to **Square**. We colored the tiles by creating percent of total for each category, in this case for race. In order to emphasize each category, we checked whether the value is less than the percentage value in our Waffle frame, which drives the color. We also changed the size of each square to get a nice waffle shape. Finally, we annotated the Waffle chart to make it easier to read.

There's more...

We can create more complicated calculations to represent more than one category in each Waffle chart. In a new sheet, starting with columns and rows in their respective shelves, continue with the following steps:

1. Create a calculation that will color every square in the Waffle chart depending on what percentage of words came from which movie:

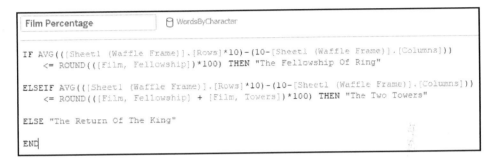

2. Add this calculation to **Color**:

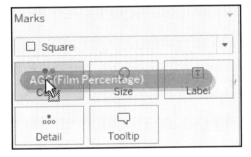

3. Annotate the chart:

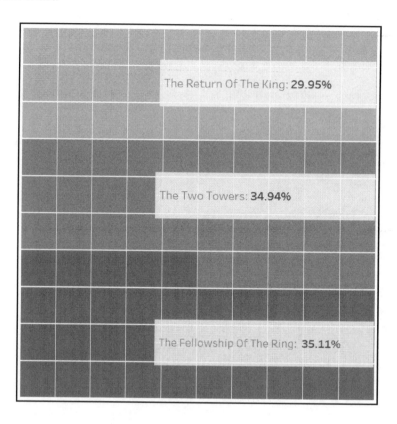

An example of a dashboard, after some cleanup and formatting, can be seen in the following screenshot:

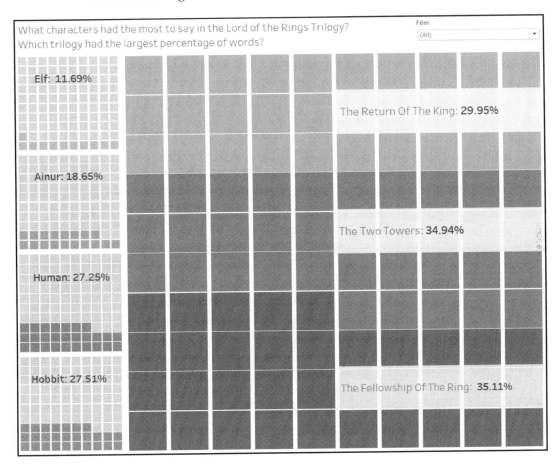

See also

- See use cases for Pie charts (`https://onlinehelp.tableau.com/current/pro/desktop/en-us/buildexamples_pie.htm`) and Bar charts (`https://onlinehelp.tableau.com/current/pro/desktop/en-us/buildexamples_bar.htm`), or the chapter for Donut charts. They are used in a similar manner to Waffle charts.

10
Tableau for Big Data

Nowadays, we have a lot of popular data platforms, for instance, Google BigQuery, Azure Data Warehouse, Hadoop, and Snowflake. In this chapter, we will integrate Tableau Desktop with the most popular among them.

In this chapter, we will cover the following topics:

- Connecting with Amazon Redshift
- Launching an Amazon Redshift cluster
- Connecting a Redshift cluster
- Loading sample data into the Redshift cluster
- Connecting Redshift with Tableau
- Creating a Tableau report
- Tuning Redshift for efficient Tableau performance
- Connecting to Amazon Redshift Spectrum
- Connecting to Snowflake
- Using SnowSQL CLI
- Connecting Tableau to Snowflake
- Connecting big data
- Accessing semi–structured data
- Connecting Amazon Elastic MapReduce with Apache Hive
- Creating sample data
- Connecting Tableau with Apache Hive

Technical requirements

To perform the recipes in this chapter, you will need to have Tableau Desktop 2019.x installed. Moreover, you need internet access to register and download the trial versions of the products required. We will create an AWS account and launch AWS EMR, Redshift, and Spectrum. Finally, we will launch a Snowflake instance.

Introduction

Nowadays, almost all organizations are trying to become data-driven. Organizations collect data about sales, customer behavior, user experience, inventory, clickstream, marketing activity, and more. As a result, the data volume is huge and can't fit in a single computer. There are also other attributes of big data such as velocity, variety, and value. BI and data engineers should use different analytics platforms that are able to process big volumes of data, often unstructured or streaming in real time.

Another important trend in the industry is shifting to the cloud. There are multiple leaders such as AWS, Google, and Azure, which offer cloud infrastructure, high availability, and security of the data. The cloud gives us a lot of advantages and also gives us more time to focus on data processing and analysis.

Tableau supports more than 40 different data sources. There are plenty of data sources available for big data ecosystems, as follows:

- **Cloud Data Platforms**: Snowflake, Amazon Redshift, AWS Spectrum, Amazon Athena, Google BigQuery, and so on
- **Hadoop**: Cloudera, Hortonworks, Hive, Presto, and so on
- **MPP databases**: Teradata, Oracle Exadata, HP Vertica, Exasol, SAP HANA, and many more

In this chapter, we will learn how to connect the most popular big data platforms, such as Amazon Redshift, Snowflake, and Hadoop to Tableau. Moreover, we will look into the data lake concept and will connect our raw data to Tableau using Amazon Spectrum.

It is important to understand that the key element for working with massive datasets in Tableau is good data engineering execution, to make sure that all heavy lifting is performed by the big data systems. Tableau will just render the query results.

Connecting with Amazon Redshift

Amazon Web Services (**AWS**) completely changed the way that IT infrastructure is deployed. It is available on demand and is cost-effective. Amazon Redshift is one of the hundreds of AWS services and it is one of the most popular cloud data warehouses. It is fast, secure, and petabyte-scale. Redshift combines the following two important technologies:

- Columnar data store or column-oriented database
- **Massively parallel processing (MPP)**

You can learn more about MPP and column databases on the Internet. You can find more information about Redshift at AWS's documentation: `https://docs.aws.amazon.com/redshift/index.html`

Getting ready

Before we start, we need to create an AWS account or use an existing one. AWS offers us a two month free trial, and then we can spin up the smallest Redshift cluster and do important network settings to open access from our local machine to Amazon Redshift. Finally, we will load some sample data into Redshift from an S3 bucket, and then we will query and connect Tableau Desktop.

In this section, we will go deep into data engineering design to show you the main principles of working with big data, so that we can use the strength of each tool. These patterns could be applicable to any other big data platform.

How to do it...

To launch an Amazon Redshift cluster, we should have an AWS account. Then, we need to set up security with AWS **Identity and Access Management (IAM)**.

Creating an AWS account

Go to `https://aws.amazon.com/account/` and sign in to an existing account, or create a new account.

Creating an IAM role

We should create an **IAM** role to get access to data for another AWS resource, such as Amazon S3 buckets because our cluster needs some permissions to access the resources and the data. You can learn more about IAM and permissions to access other AWS resources here: https://docs.aws.amazon.com/redshift/latest/dg/copy-usage_notes-access-permissions.html

Follow these steps to create an IAM role:

1. Go to **IAM** and choose **Roles**.
2. Click **Create Role**.
3. Under **AWS services**, choose **Redshift**.
4. Under **Select your use case**, choose **Redshift Customizable**, and then click **Next**.
5. Attach **AmazonS3ReadOnlyAccess** and click **Next**.
6. Type the role name, **RedshiftS3Access**, and click **Create**.
7. Open the role that we just created and copy the **Amazon Resource Name (ARN)**:

Let's view the results of the steps we carried out in the following screenshot:

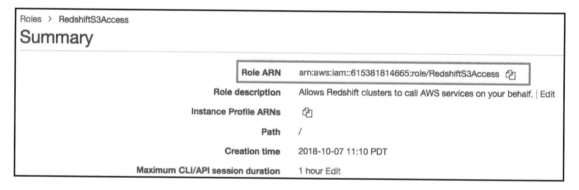

We will need this later in this chapter.

How it works...

AWS gives us an account for free where we can explore all the available services and features. In addition, AWS provides us with AWS Free Tier. You can learn about it here: `https://aws.amazon.com/free/`. In addition, we created an IAM role, to allow our Redshift cluster access the S3 bucket with data.

Launching an Amazon Redshift cluster

AWS allows us to create a powerful analytical data warehouse with just multiple clicks. In this recipe, we will create an Amazon Redshift cluster using AWS Free Tier. AWS provides us with two months of free usage of the basic cluster, which is still powerful and good for our purpose.

How to do it...

We should launch an Amazon Redshift cluster, as shown via the following steps:

1. Let's find **Amazon Redshift** among **AWS services**, as follows:

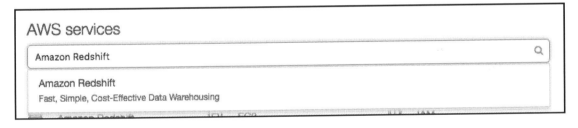

2. Click on **Quick Launch Cluster**.

3. Fill the options for the cluster, as shown in the following screenshot:

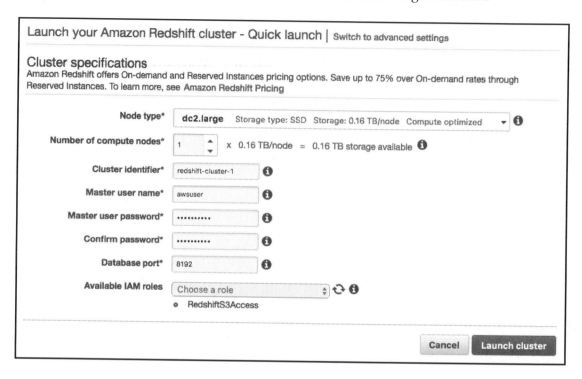

4. We should choose the smallest cluster if we want to use the trial version of AWS. We will choose our IAM roles and enter the password.
5. We should keep the password in a secure place, as we will need this for the Tableau connection. In this example, we are going to use a more powerful cluster `ds2.xlarge`, but we can work with the smallest available cluster.
6. Click on **Launch cluster**.

How it works...

As you might have noticed, the launching of Redshift is a very simple and straightforward approach. It is very important to decide what size cluster we want and give write permissions to AWS resources with IAM.

There's more...

You can learn more about the available sizes of clusters at `https://aws.amazon.com/redshift/pricing/`.

Connecting a Redshift cluster

The cluster should be created by now, and we should test that we can connect to the cluster from our local machine. The best way to do this is to download the SQL client and connect to it using the JDBC driver. It is the common pattern for databases or analytics tool connections.

The cluster should be created and we should test that we can connect to the cluster from our local machine. The best way to do this is to download an SQL client and connect using the JDBC driver. It is the common pattern for database or analytics tool connection.

How to do it...

We will connect the Redshift cluster using the following steps:

1. Let's download the Redshift SQL client. There are many available clients. Some of them are free, while others aren't. We will download the DBeaver SQL client. Go to `https://dbeaver.io/download/` and download the lastest available package for your OS from `https://www.sql-workbench.eu/downloads.html`. In my case, I will use macOS X (pkg installer + JRE).

2. We will now install DBeaver and launch it. It will offer us the option to create a new database connection. We should use **AWS Redshift**. The connection window will ask us about **Host**, **Database**, **Port**, **User**, and **Passwords**. We should copy them from the AWS console under our cluster properties.

3. By default, any resource in AWS is closed. We should adjust the security settings to allow access to the Redshift cluster from local machine. Among the **AWS Services**, find **EC2** and click on it.

4. On the left sidebar, click on **Security Groups**.

5. Edit your **VPC group**. In my case, I have only one default group. If you have more than one group, you can check for, the VPC group associated with your cluster.

6. Click **Edit inbound rules** and add a new rule. From the **Source**, you can choose **My IP**. Let's take a look at the results, which are shown in the following screenshot:

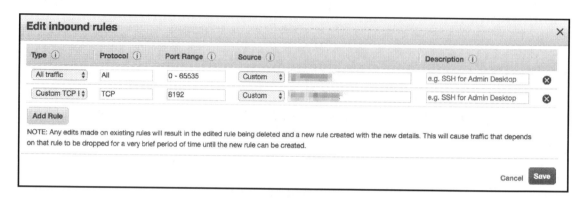

7. Now, we can go back to **DBeaver** and enter our credentials for a new Redshift database connection. We should copy these credentials from the AWS console under the Redshift properties, as shown in the following screenshot:

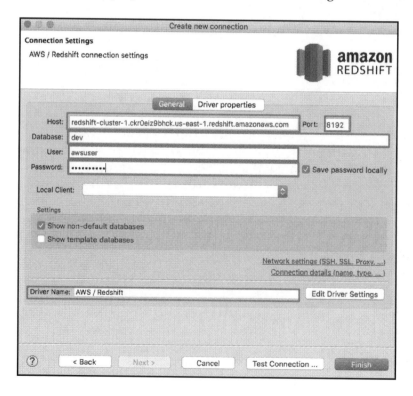

DBeaver will offer us the ability to download the Redshift JDBC driver. We will accept it and install the driver.

As a result, we have now connected to the Amazon Redshift cluster, and our next step is to get the sample data.

How it works...

To connect any data platform, we should obtain a driver and adjust the firewall. In our case, we've got an Amazon Redshift native JDBC driver. In addition, we had to use the SQL client to connect Redshift and query it. We used open source DBeaver, which served well for our purpose and works perfectly in real life.

There's more...

We might use a native PostgreSQL driver because Amazon Redshift was originally based on PostgreSQL. You can learn more about this at the following link:

```
https://docs.aws.amazon.com/redshift/latest/dg/c_redshift-postgres-jdbc.html
```

Moreover, you might consider the internal AWS SQL client—Query Editor.

You can also read about it at the following link:

```
https://aws.amazon.com/about-aws/whats-new/2018/10/amazon_redshift_announces_
query_editor_to_run_queries_directly_from_the_aws_console/
```

In our case, it was important to demonstrate how Tableau Desktop can communicate with Redshift clusters remotely.

Loading sample data into the Redshift cluster

We should load sample data into Redshift to demonstrate how Tableau Desktop will connect to a huge dataset and query it.

How to do it...

To load data into the Redshift cluster, we should use Amazon S3 buckets, which consist of folders with files. We will use AWS samples and utilize the `COPY` command to load data into a cluster, as follows:

1. Copy and paste the SQL code from the `Create_Statement_Redshift.sql` file that is available for this chapter.

2. Run these statements and the tables should be created, as seen in the following screenshot:

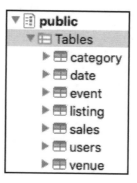

3. Then, we should load the data using the `copy` command. We will copy the commands from the `COPY` data to the `Redshift.txt` file and insert our ARN for each statement. Let's look at my example, in the following code block:

```
copy dwdate from 's3://awssampledbuswest2/ssbgz/dwdate'
credentials
'aws_iam_role=arn:aws:iam::615381814665:role/RedshiftS3Access'
gzip compupdate off region 'us-west-2';
```

4. Run some sample queries to see a number of rows, as shown in the following screenshot:

```
select count(*) from customer; --3000000 rows
select count(*) from dwdate; --2556 rows
select count(*) from lineorder; --600037902 rows
select count(*) from part; --1400000 rows
select count(*) from supplier; --1000000 rows
```

The biggest table has 600 million rows, which is a huge amount of rows. The question is, is this big data or not? You can answer this question for yourself.

How it works...

Using the COPY command, we were able to load 600 million rows in seconds.

There's more...

The COPY command is a game changer for your data ingesting processes because it can instantly load big volumes of data into Redshift using a bulk methodology. You can learn about the COPY command here:

```
https://docs.aws.amazon.com/redshift/latest/dg/r_COPY.html
```

Connecting Redshift with Tableau

This is the main part of this chapter. We are going to connect our huge sample dataset with Tableau Desktop. Moreover, we will tune Redshift to get the best possible performance from Tableau.

How to do it...

During this part of this chapter, we will measure our performance based on the following three metrics:

- Load time
- Storage use
- Query performance

Let's see how it is done by performing the following steps:

1. Open Tableau Desktop and click on **Connect to Amazon Redshift**. Fill in the credentials and click on **Sign In**:

Basically, we have now connected to Amazon Redshift. If you get an error, you should check your Firewall settings and make sure that you can connect with a SQL client to the cluster.

Now, we can choose the tables and create a Tableau data source. However, this isn't a true case. We need to make sure that we get the best possible performance. As a result, we need to learn more about our data usage, that is, SQL queries, patterns, tables, and joins.

2. We should turn off Amazon Redshift caches to make accurate performance comparisons. In the following code block, we will run the following command:

```
set enable_result_cache_for_session to off;
```

3. Let's finish our Tableau Data Source. We should use the following tables:

   - customer
   - lineorder
   - supplier
   - dwdate

The following screenshot depicts the preceding listed tables:

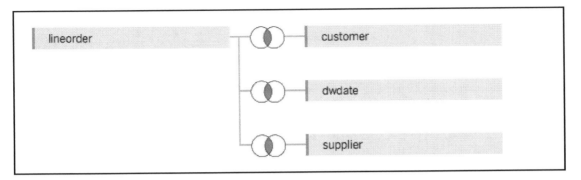

There are joins too, as shown in the following list:

- `lineorder.lo_custkey = customer.c_custkey`
- `lineorder.lo_suppkey = supplier.s_suppkey`
- `lineorder.lo_orderdate = dwdate.d_datekey`

4. Finally, go to **Sheet 1**, and you will see that our data source has been created and is ready to use.

How it works...

When Tableau Desktop establishes a live connection, it acts in the same way as the SQL client. The difference is that Tableau Desktop will generate an SQL query based on our Tableau Data Source and query Redshift every time we have updated the Tableau View by dragging and dropping the new object or changing filters.

Creating a Tableau report

Let's ask questions with Tableau. For example, we want to know the revenue in specific cities (UNITED KI5, UNITED KI1) in December 1997. Moreover, we want to order the result by revenue amount in descending order.

How to do it...

1. We are using a live connection, which means that each interaction with a report will generate an SQL query and we should wait. To avoid this, we will pause Tableau Auto Updates, as shown in the following screenshot:

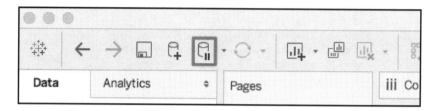

2. Now, we can craft our report by dragging and dropping **Dimensions** and **Measures** to the canvas, as follows:

3. You should add the following filters:

   - **C City**: UNITED KI1 or UNITED KI5
   - **S City**: UNITED KI1 or UNITED KI5
   - **D YEAR**: Dec1997

   Moreover, we should convert **D Year** into discrete and sort by **Revenue**.

4. We should unpause auto updates and run our query. It takes ~18 seconds for my cluster. If we missed the time, we can log in to the **AWS Console** and navigate to the **Redshift cluster** | **Queries Tab** and see all executed queries, their time, and plan. You might see that, in the case of Tableau, we don't have actual queries; instead, we have something like **fetch 10000 in SQL_CUR7**. Tableau is using cursors and we can run the following query to see queries for currently active cursors:

```
SELECT
    usr.usename AS username
  , min(cur.starttime) AS start_time
  , DATEDIFF(second, min(cur.starttime), getdate()) AS run_time
  , min(cur.row_count) AS row_count
  , min(cur.fetched_rows) AS fetched_rows
  , listagg(util_text.text)
    WITHIN GROUP (ORDER BY sequence) AS query
FROM STV_ACTIVE_CURSORS cur
    JOIN stl_utilitytext util_text
```

```
        ON cur.pid = util_text.pid AND cur.xid = util_text.xid
    JOIN pg_user usr
        ON usr.usesysid = cur.userid
 GROUP BY usr.usename, util_text.xid;
```

5. Let's run one more system query that will help us to identify the size of tables we are using in our Tableau data source, as follows:

```
select stv_tbl_perm.name as table, count(*) as mb from
stv_blocklist, stv_tbl_perm
where stv_blocklist.tbl = stv_tbl_perm.id
and stv_blocklist.slice = stv_tbl_perm.slice and stv_tbl_perm.name
in ('lineorder','part','dwdate','supplier')
group by stv_tbl_perm.name
order by 1 asc;
```

We can notice the size of the tables:

- lineorder=34311mb
- part=92mb
- dwdate=80mb
- supplier=76mb

Finally, we can tune our cluster to improve the performance of the queries.

How it works...

We've built a new report and analyzed the SQL query that was generated by Tableau Desktop. In addition, we measured the performance and size of the tables.

There's more...

You can learn more about Redshift cursors at the following URL:

https://docs.aws.amazon.com/redshift/latest/dg/declare.html

Tuning Redshift for efficient Tableau performance

Every big data platform has special settings for tuning. For example, in our case, Redshift we will focus on the following three options:

- Sort keys
- Dist keys
- Compression

You can learn more about Redshift tuning here:

```
https://aws.amazon.com/blogs/big-data/top-10-performance-tuning-techniques-for-
amazon-redshift/
```

How to do it...

We will adjust our tables to get the maximum from Redshift in terms of a place for computing, and, allow Tableau to efficiently render the results and visualize it as follows:

1. To choose the right sort key, we should evaluate our queries to find a date column that we are using for filters (the WHERE condition in SQL). For our huge fact table, it is the lo_orderdate column. For the remaining dimension tables, we will use their primary key as a sort key: p_partkey, s_supkey, d_datekey.
2. Then, we will choose candidates for the sort key. The following are the three types of distribution available in Redshift:

   - The key distribution
   - The all distribution
   - The even distribution

   You can learn more about Redshift distribution at the following URL:

   ```
   https://docs.aws.amazon.com/redshift/latest/dg/c_best-practices-best-
   dist-key.html
   ```

3. To find the best distribution style, we need to analyze the SQL query that is generated by Tableau and executed by Redshift. We should use the preceding query to extract the SQL from the cursor. Then, we should look to the execution plan by running our query with the word EXPLAIN, as follows:

```
explain
SELECT "customer"."c_city" AS "c_city", "dwdate"."d_year" AS
"d_year", "supplier"."s_city" AS "s_city",
SUM("lineorder"."lo_revenue") AS "sum_lo_revenue_ok"
FROM "public"."lineorder" "lineorder"
INNER JOIN "public"."customer" "customer" ON
("lineorder"."lo_custkey" = "customer"."c_custkey")
INNER JOIN "public"."supplier" "supplier" ON
("lineorder"."lo_suppkey" = "supplier"."s_suppkey")
INNER JOIN "public"."dwdate" "dwdate" ON
("lineorder"."lo_orderdate" = "dwdate"."d_datekey")
WHERE (("customer"."c_city" IN ('UNITED KI1', 'UNITED KI5'))
AND (("supplier"."s_city" IN ('UNITED KI1', 'UNITED KI5'))
AND ("dwdate"."d_yearmonth" IN ('Dec1997'))))
GROUP BY 1, 2, 3
```

We will get the plan as follows:

	ᴬᴮᶜ QUERY PLAN
1	XN HashAggregate (cost=8838907488.18..8838907488.19 rows=1 width=36)
2	-> XN Hash Join DS_BCAST_INNER (cost=60110.78..8838907483.69 rows=449 width=36)
3	Hash Cond: ("outer".lo_orderdate = "inner".d_datekey)
4	-> XN Hash Join DS_BCAST_INNER (cost=60078.75..8833946984.65 rows=37002 width=36)
5	Hash Cond: ("outer".lo_custkey = "inner".c_custkey)
6	-> XN Hash Join DS_BCAST_INNER (cost=15019.67..2216602842.55 rows=4697040 width=26)
7	Hash Cond: ("outer".lo_suppkey = "inner".s_suppkey)
8	-> XN Seq Scan on lineorder (cost=0.00..6000378.88 rows=600037888 width=16)
9	-> XN Hash (cost=15000.00..15000.00 rows=7868 width=18)
10	-> XN Seq Scan on supplier (cost=0.00..15000.00 rows=7868 width=18)
11	Filter: (((s_city)::text = 'UNITED KI1'::text) OR ((s_city)::text = 'UNITED KI5'::text))
12	-> XN Hash (cost=45000.00..45000.00 rows=23633 width=18)
13	-> XN Seq Scan on customer (cost=0.00..45000.00 rows=23633 width=18)
14	Filter: (((c_city)::text = 'UNITED KI1'::text) OR ((c_city)::text = 'UNITED KI5'::text))
15	-> XN Hash (cost=31.95..31.95 rows=31 width=8)
16	-> XN Seq Scan on dwdate (cost=0.00..31.95 rows=31 width=8)
17	Filter: ((d_yearmonth)::text = 'Dec1997'::text)

I've highlighted BS_BCAST_INNER. It means that the inner join was broadcasted across all slices. We should eliminate any broadcast and distribution steps. You can learn more about query patterns here:

```
https://docs.aws.amazon.com/redshift/latest/dg/t_evaluating_query_
patterns.html
```

In our case, we should look at the join between the fact table with 600 mln and dimension tables. Based on fairly small rows in the dimension tables, we can distribute the dimension tables SUPPLIER, PART, and DWDATE across all nodes. For the LINEORDER table, we will use lo_custkey as a distribution key and for the CUSTOMER table, we will use the c_custkey as the distribution key.

4. Next, we should compress our data to make sure that we can reduce storage space, and also, reduce the size of the data that is read from storage. It decreases I/O and improves query performance. By default, all data is uncompressed. You can learn more about compression encodings here: https://docs.aws.amazon. com/redshift/latest/dg/c_Compression_encodings.html. We should use system tables in order to research the best compression encoding. Let's run the following query:

```
select col, max(blocknum)
from stv_blocklist b, stv_tbl_perm p
where (b.tbl=p.id) and name ='lineorder'
and col < 17
group by name, col
order by col;
```

It will show us the highest block number for each column in the LINEORDER table. Then, we can start to experiment with different encoding types in order to find the best. In addition, we should always analyze the table after changes in order to update table statistics. However, in our case, we can simply execute the COPY command with the auto compression parameter.

5. Let's apply the changes to our tables and run the same report. Copy the queries from the Create_Statementv2_Redshift.sql file and run them.

6. Then, we should reload data with autocompression. Run SQL from the COPY data to Redshiftv2.txt file. Don't forget to insert your ARN.

7. Let's refresh our Tableau workbook and see the improvements. Moreover, we can check the query plan and see the changes. In my case, it took 8 seconds.

How it works...

As you can see, the secret of working with big volumes of data is in good design patterns of the Data Platform. In the case of Redshift, we analyze the data structure, volume, and query patterns, and then apply the best practices of using sort keys, distribution styles, and compression encoding. It is obvious that we are depending on query patterns, and we can keep high performance for any queries. As a result, we should be very careful with the preceding options.

There's more...

It is important for cost-based optimization databases such as Redshift to keep table statistics up-to-date in case of any changes or updates by using the ANALYZE and VACUUM commands.

See also

- You can learn more about options for loading data into Redshift at https://docs.aws.amazon.com/redshift/latest/dg/t_Loading_data.html

Connecting to Amazon Redshift Spectrum

In this section, we will upgrade our Redshift data warehouse by enabling Redshift Spectrum, which plays the role of a data lake and compliments our data warehouse. It gives us a powerful and serverless architecture and can handle a tremendous volume of data, which is true big data.

Amazon Spectrum extends Redshift data warehouse out to the Exabytes website. You can get all the benefits of open data formats and inexpensive storage, and we can easily scale out to thousands of nodes. Another benefit is the cost; we pay only for usage and storage using S3, which is fairly small in comparison with an analytical data warehouse.

Getting ready

We should update our IAM roles for Redshift by adding the following additional policies:

- **AmazonS3FullAccess**
- **AmazonAthenaFullAccess**
- **AWSGlueConsoleFullAccess**

Spectrum will use the Glue or Athena data catalog. It is important to have the data in the region as our Redshift cluster. That's why we are going to use the UNLOAD command: so that we have the data in the same network with our Redshift. In real life, we can query data from other VPC in the same region.

How to do it...

1. Let's create an S3 bucket for our data. Go to **S3** and click on **Create new bucket**. Type the name cookbook-spectrum.

2. Now, we can unload data into this bucket and run this command, as shown in the following code block:

```
unload ('select * from lineorder')
to 's3://cookbook-spectrum/
iam_role 'arn:aws:iam::615381814665:role/RedshiftS3Access'
delimiter '\t'
```

3. Let's create the external schema, as follows:

```
create external schema datalake
from data catalog
database 'spectrumdb'
iam_role 'arn:aws:iam::615381814665:role/RedshiftS3Access'
create external database if not exists;
```

4. Let's create an external table in this schema, as follows:

```
create external table datalake.lineorder
(
  lo_orderkey INTEGER
  ,lo_linenumber INTEGER
  ,lo_custkey INTEGER
  ,lo_partkey INTEGER
  ,lo_suppkey INTEGER
  ,lo_orderdate INTEGER
  ,lo_orderpriority VARCHAR(15)
  ,lo_shippriority VARCHAR(1)
  ,lo_quantity INTEGER
  ,lo_extendedprice INTEGER
  ,lo_ordertotalprice INTEGER
  ,lo_discount INTEGER
  ,lo_revenue INTEGER
  ,lo_supplycost INTEGER
  ,lo_tax INTEGER
  ,lo_commitdate INTEGER
  ,lo_shipmode VARCHAR(10)
)
row format delimited
fields terminated by '\t'
stored as textfile
location 's3://cookbook-spectrum/
table properties ('numRows'='172000');
```

5. We can test this table by running queries against it, such as SELECT * FROM
    datalake.lineorder, or we can adjust our Tableau Data Source and use a
    Spectrum table instead of the initial one. However, it is better to tune the external
    table before use, otherwise Spectrum will scan the full table.

How it works...

The main benefit of Spectrum for the end user is that there are no changes; they can still use SQL, and query the same tables as well, for BI or ETL use. The following diagram demonstrates the life of a Spectrum query:

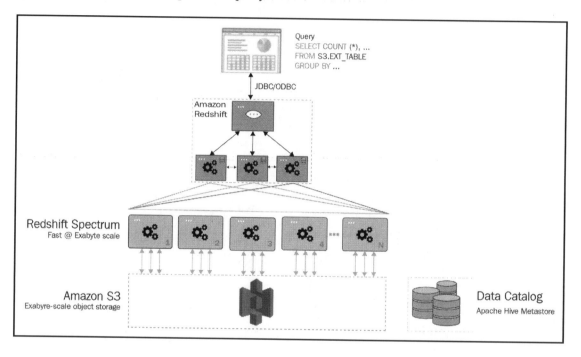

There's more...

By default, Spectrum will scan all your rows, which could become expensive. There is a good explanation about improving Spectrum performance at the following link:

```
https://docs.aws.amazon.com/redshift/latest/dg/c-spectrum-external-performance.
html
```

We can learn more about the usage of Amazon Redshift Spectrum with this article: *10 Best Practices for Amazon Redshift Spectrum*, which can be found at `https://aws.amazon.com/blogs/big-data/10-best-practices-for-amazon-redshift-spectrum/`.

Moreover, you can learn about Glue at `https://docs.aws.amazon.com/glue/latest/dg/what-is-glue.html` and Amazon Athena at `https://docs.aws.amazon.com/athena/latest/ug/what-is.html`.

Finally, you can drop your cluster if you no longer need it.

See also

- *Amazon Redshift Spectrum—Exabyte-Scale In-Place Queries of S3 Data* with 6+ billions of rows at `https://aws.amazon.com/blogs/aws/amazon-redshift-spectrum-exabyte-scale-in-place-queries-of-s3-data/`

Connecting to Snowflake

Snowflake is the leading cloud data warehouse platform. Moreover, it is the first data warehouse that was created for the cloud. In this section, we will launch a Snowflake instance and connect to it with Tableau. Currently, Snowflake is available for AWS and Azure. We are going to use the AWS version of Snowflake.

Snowflake has a multi-cluster shared architecture, and it separates storage and computes. This allows it to easily scale up and down on the fly without any disruption.

Snowflake is an SQL data warehouse that supports structured and semi-structured data, such as JSON, AVRO, or XML.

The Snowflake architecture consists of the following three layers:

- **Cloud services**: This is a collection of services such as authentication, and so on
- **Query processing**: Snowflake executes queries using a virtual warehouse, for example, an MPP cluster with multiple compute nodes using Amazon EC2 or Azure virtual machines
- **Database storage**: Snowflake stores optimized data in Amazon S3 or Azure Blob Storage

Let's take a look at the following diagram that depicts the preceding mentioned layers:

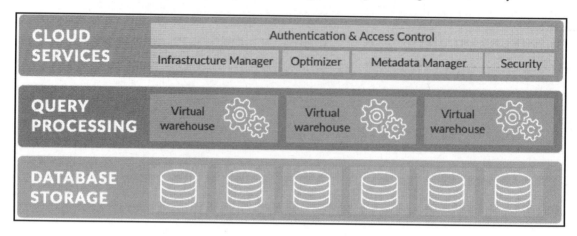

There is the same principle when we allow Snowflake to do the heavy lifting and then, Tableau renders the results. As a result, we don't need to use Tableau extracts.

With a live connection, we should avoid a custom SQL data source because often it is counterproductive, and could be run multiple times on the dashboard. Tableau itself can generate much more efficient queries.

Getting ready

We should start the free trial of Snowflake. We can choose either AWS or Azure. In my case, I will use AWS. After that, we will launch the cluster, and then, we can load sample data and connect the Tableau Desktop using a built-in Snowflake connector.

How to do it...

Let's begin with logging into Snowflake, and carrying out the following steps:

1. Go to the Snowflake, `https://www.snowflake.com/`, and click on **START FOR FREE**. Fill in the form and you'll get an email about Snowflake.
2. You will get an email with the link. Click the link and you will create the user and password. Then, you will see the worksheet of Snowflake. In my case, it was `https://<account name>.snowflakecomputing.com`.

3. After successful activation, you can go to `https://<account name>.snowflakecomputing.com`, where you can find a web-based GUI where you can create and manage all Snowflake objects. You can learn more here: `https://docs.snowflake.net/manuals/user-guide/snowflake-manager.html`.

How it works...

- Snowflake provides a free trial and gives you 400 credits. You can learn more about Snowflake Trial at `https://www.snowflake.com/trial_faqs/`

Using SnowSQL CLI

One of the common ways of interacting with the database is CLI. Let's do a quick exercise to load data into the Snowflake and then connect Tableau.

How to do it...

1. At the GUI, you can click on **Help** and choose **Download**.
2. Download the CLI client (`snowsql`) for your OS. In my case, I am using macOS.
3. Install the file.
4. Connect the Snowflake instance. In our case, we are using macOS. Open a command line and run the following command:

```
/Users/anoshind/Applications/SnowSQL.app/Contents/MacOS/snowsql -a
<account name> -u <user name>
```

In our case, we have `-a DZ27900 -u tableaucookbook`. It will ask for a password. After successful authentication, we connected to Snowflake.

5. Now, we can start to create Snowflake objects:
    1. Run this command to create a database:

    ```
    create or replace database sf_tuts;
    ```

2. Run this command to create a target table:

```
create or replace table emp_basic (
first_name string, last_name string, email string,
streetaddress string,  city string    ,  start_date date );
```

3. Run this command to create our computing DW. Depending on the size, you can choose the power of your cluster:

```
create or replace warehouse sf_tuts_wh with
 warehouse_size='X-SMALL'    auto_suspend = 180    auto_resume = true
 initially_suspended=true;
```

You can learn more about pricing options at:

```
https://docs.snowflake.net/manuals/user-guide/credits.html
```

6. Next, load the files into Snowflake. You should download files from the chapter bundle (five `.xls` files) and put them into any directory, where `snowsql` can access it. In our case, we will copy them into `/tmp`.

7. Put file: `///<path>/employees0*.csv @sf_tuts.public.%emp_basic;`.

8. The Windows syntax will be different: put file `//C:\<path>\employees0*.csv @sf_tuts.public.%emp_basic;`.

9. This operation will upload and compress (`.gzip`) files into the stage for our table, `emp_basic`.

10. Now, we can copy data into the target table by executing the following command:

```
copy into emp_basic
  from @%emp_basic
  file_format = (type = csv field_optionally_enclosed_by='"')
  pattern = '.*employees0[1-5].csv.gz'
  on_error = 'skip_file';
```

We can see the output in the following screenshot:

```
tableaucookbook#SF_TUTS_WH@SF_TUTS.PUBLIC>copy into emp_basic
                        from @%emp_basic
                        file_format = (type = csv field_optionally_enclosed_by='"')
                        pattern = '.*employees0[1-5].csv.gz'
                        on_error = 'skip_file';
+------------------+--------+-------------+-------------+-------------+-------------+-------------+------------------+-----------------------+------------------------+
| file             | status | rows_parsed | rows_loaded | error_limit | errors_seen | first_error | first_error_line | first_error_character | first_error_column_name|
+------------------+--------+-------------+-------------+-------------+-------------+-------------+------------------+-----------------------+------------------------+
| employees03.csv.gz | LOADED |      5 |      5 |      1 |      0 | NULL |              NULL |                  NULL | NULL |
| employees05.csv.gz | LOADED |      5 |      5 |      1 |      0 | NULL |              NULL |                  NULL | NULL |
| employees02.csv.gz | LOADED |      5 |      5 |      1 |      0 | NULL |              NULL |                  NULL | NULL |
| employees01.csv.gz | LOADED |      5 |      5 |      1 |      0 | NULL |              NULL |                  NULL | NULL |
| employees04.csv.gz | LOADED |      5 |      5 |      1 |      0 | NULL |              NULL |                  NULL | NULL |
+------------------+--------+-------------+-------------+-------------+-------------+-------------+------------------+-----------------------+------------------------+
5 Row(s) produced. Time Elapsed: 3.128s
```

As a result, we successfully loaded data from the local machine. Moreover, we can load huge datasets from S3 into Snowflake or other source systems.

How it works...

We used internal Snowflake storage in order to upload data into Snowflake and we used the Snowflake CLI tool to work with the Snowflake cluster remotely.

Connecting Tableau to Snowflake

We can connect Snowflake with Tableau in the same way as any other data warehouse. Let's do this!

How to do it...

1. First, we need to download and install the Snowflake ODBC Driver. We can download it from the same place that we downloaded snowsql.

2. After a successful installation, we create a new data source by filling in the connection details, as follows:

3. Then, we can choose the following:
   - **Warehouse**: SF_TUTS_WH
   - **Database**: SF_TUTS
   - **Schema**: PUBLIC

As usual, we can drag and drop the table and see the data.

How it works...

It works in the same way as we connect Amazon Redshift or any other database by using the specific driver and our credentials. You can learn about other ways of connecting Snowflake here:

https://docs.snowflake.net/manuals/user-guide-connecting.html

Connecting big data

Now, we can try to query a bigger dataset and see how Tableau will work with big data. We shouldn't avoid Tableau Extracts, because our data size is huge. This is the great thing about the cloud. We can orchestrate with big data without loading it into our machine.

How to do it...

1. We can create a new data source and specify the following options:
   - **Warehouse**: COMPUTE_WH
   - **Database**: SNOWFLAKE_SAMPLE_DATA
   - **Schema**: TPCH_SF1000

   You can learn more about the TPC sample dataset at http://www.tpc.org/tpc_documents_current_versions/pdf/tpc-ds_v2.5.0.pdf.

2. When we are choosing **Warehouse**, we are choosing to compute resources for our DW. In our case, COMPUTE_WH is a X-Large. We also have SF_TUTS_WH that is X-Small.

3. Build the data model, as shown in the following screenshot:

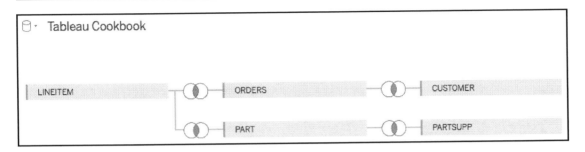

4. Let's answer the following business question: List the totals for the extended price, discounted extended price plus tax, average quantity, average discount, and average extended price, and group the result by **Return Flag** and **Line Status**. Using Tableau, we can drag and drop the following object. Do not forget to pause Auto Updates. In addition, we should create the following calculation fields:

   - **Extended Discounted Price**: `[L Extendedprice]*(1-[L Discount])`
   - **Extended Discounted Price with Tax**: `[L Extendedprice]*(1-[L Discount])*(1+[L Tax])`

Here is the screenshot showing the end result:

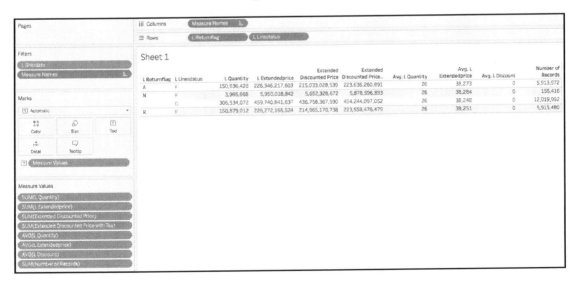

5. We can check with Snowflake GUI about the actual plan by going to **History** and finding our **Query**. Because we are using a live connection, Tableau generates a query and uses only one table, LINEITEM, instead of the whole data model, which saves us time and money.

How it works...

We've created new Tableau data source based on Snowflake sample data. In addition, we had to specify a Virtual Warehouse (our horsepower) and source dataset.

There's more...

We can use Tableau Initial SQL to create temporary or aggregation tables. This can significantly improve performance in case if we are using custom SQL logic or want to use aggregate tables by materializing the result into a temp table.

Accessing semi–structured data

In the modern world, often we can meet unstructured data that is generating by machines, apps, sensors, and so on. There are the following two main attributes of semi-structured data that differ it from structure data:

- Semi-structured data can contain n-level hierarchies of nested information
- Structured data always needs a defined schema before loading it. Semi-structured data doesn't need this, so as a result we can create the schema on the fly

Despite the fact that Tableau supports direct connection to the JSON format, we still have the same issue with big data, when we need more compute resource than Tableau allows us to use and also, we can collect data types such as Avro, ORC, Parquet, and XML.

Usually, we should parse unstructured data and write into the table. But not with Snowflake; it has a special data type VARIANT that allows us to store semi-structured data. Moreover, we can easily parse key-value pairs. You can run the following SQL and check how it looks:

```
select * from "SNOWFLAKE_SAMPLE_DATA"."WEATHER"."WEATHER_14_TOTAL" limit 1
```

Let's try to use the Snowflake sample database in order to see how it looks. Unfortunately, Tableau can't parse `VARIANT` data type, which is why we should create the SQL for Tableau based on a `VARIANT` column.

How to do it...

Let's create a Tableau workbook based on semi-structured data. At the Snowflake sample database we have a table `HOURLY_16_TOTAL` with 392 mln rows and 322 GB. This dataset keeps the last four days of hourly weather forecasts for 20,000+ cities.

1. Create a new Tableau data source with a Snowflake connection:
   - **Warehouse**: `COMPUTE_WH`
   - **Database**: `SNOWFLAKE_SAMPLE_DATA`
   - **Schema**: `WEATHER`

2. Drag and drop custom SQL element and use this query, that will parse the `VARIANT` data type, as follows:

```
select (V:main.temp_max - 273.15)::FLOAT * 1.8000 + 32.00 as
temp_max_far,      (V:main.temp_min - 273.15)::FLOAT * 1.8000 +
32.00 as temp_min_far,
  cast(V:time as timestamp) time,
      V:city.coord.lat::FLOAT lat,
      V:city.coord.lon::FLOAT lon,
      v:city.name::VARCHAR,
      v:city.country::VARCHAR,
      v:city:id,
      V
```

From `"SNOWFLAKE_SAMPLE_DATA"."WEATHER"." HOURLY_16_TOTAL"` you can use another table that is much smaller, such as `DAILY_14_TOTAL` (37 mln rows). In addition, you can always specify `LIMIT` at the end of the query in order to limit you output.

3. Then we can build the dashboard in order to see the minimum temperature in Fahrenheit across the world, as follows:

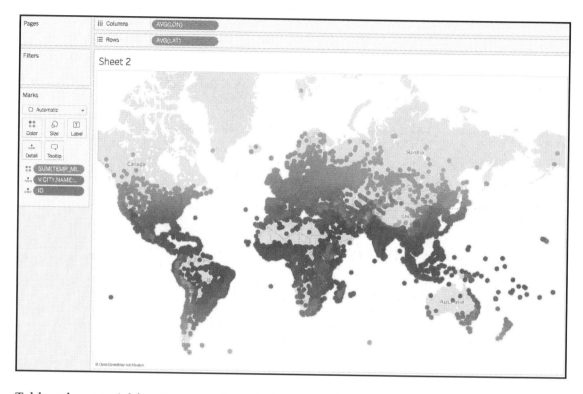

Tableau has special function pass-through functions that can send SQL expressions to the database, without being interpreted by Tableau. In our case with weather data, we can create a new calculated field WIND SPEED:

RAWSQL_REAL("v:wind.speed::float",[V]) and it will add wind speed to our dataset.

How it works...

Tableau on top of Snowflake is fast because it is utilizing Snowflake's computing power and just renders the result in Tableau.

There's more...

According to the best practices, if our semi-structured data schema is static, we can parse it and load it into the Snowflake tables. We can use SQL queries from the Snowflake GUI or SnowSQL CLI, or we can use the ELT tool such as Matillion ETL. You can learn more about Snowflake and Matillion ETL here:

`https://www.matillion.com/etl-for-snowflake/`

See also

- There are couple more great features of Snowflake that can be handy for Tableau users. The first one is **Snowflake Time Travel**. Imagine the situation where your business dashboard gives your wrong metrics, but you feel that yesterday or last week the numbers were different? There is no way to check this. However, with the Time Travel feature we can easily query tables from the past. You can adjust the existing data source with custom SQL and travel back in time. You can learn more here `https://docs.snowflake.net/manuals/user-guide/data-time-travel.html`

- The second feature is **Snowflake Data Sharing**. This feature allows us to enable data consumers with access read-only copies of live data that's in a data provider account. You can think about creating a virtual copy of a database with special permissions. You can learn more here: `https://docs.snowflake.net/manuals/user-guide-data-share.html`

Connecting Amazon Elastic MapReduce with Apache Hive

Amazon Elastic MapReduce (EMR) is a true big data platform. It provides a managed Hadoop framework that can process a huge volume of data across dynamically scalable Amazon EC2 instances. It allows us to run popular distributed frameworks with it, such as Presto, Hive, Spark, and others. This is a short video about Amazon EMR: `https://youtu.be/S6Ja55n-oOM`.

Organizations use Hadoop for big data use cases, such as clickstream analysis, log analysis, predictive analytics, data transformation, data lake, and many more. Often, business users need to work with raw data that is stored in Hadoop, in our case Amazon EMR. There are multiple ways to connect Hadoop with Tableau, such as Presto, Hive, and more.

Getting ready

We should launch the cluster, get sample data, and connect it via Tableau Desktop using Hive. Let's do this! But be aware, EMR cluster isn't free and you might spend $20-$30 in order go through scenarios.

How to do it...

Let's create our EMR cluster.

1. Go to the AWS account: `https://aws.amazon.com/console/` and sign in.
2. Follow the instructions present here: `https://docs.aws.amazon.com/emr/latest/ManagementGuide/emr-gs.html` in order to launch a cluster. You should perform the following three steps first:
    1. Set up prerequisites
    2. Launch the cluster
    3. Allow SSH access

We used the following names:

Bucket name	tableau_cookbook
Folder name	tableau-cookbook-query-result
Key pair name	tableau-cookbook.pem
Cluster name	My Cluster for Tableau Cookbook
Cluster parameters	Core Hadoop: Hadoop 2.8.4 with Ganglia 3.7.2, Hive 2.3.3, Hue 4.2.0, Mahout 0.13.0, Pig 0.17.0, and Tez 0.8.4

As a result, we should be able to successfully launch the EMR cluster. In addition, we can connect our cluster via SSH using the `tableau-cookbook.pem` key.

3. Let's connect the cluster by running the following command:

    ```
    ssh -i ~/.ssh/tableua-cookbook.pem
    hadoop@ec2-18-215-157-216.compute-1.amazonaws.com
    ```

 I saved my key in the `.ssh` folder and the key should have 400 permissions.

In the following screenshot we can see the following output:

```
[f45c89c859a9:.ssh anoshind$ ssh -i ~/.ssh/tableua-cookbook.pem hadoop@ec2-18-215-157-216.compute-1.amazonaws.com
Last login: Sat Oct 13 16:46:34 2018

    __|  __|_  )
    _|  (     /   Amazon Linux AMI
    ___|\___|___|

https://aws.amazon.com/amazon-linux-ami/2018.03-release-notes/
15 package(s) needed for security, out of 28 available
Run "sudo yum update" to apply all updates.

EEEEEEEEEEEEEEEEEEEEE MMMMMMMM          MMMMMMMM RRRRRRRRRRRRRRRR
E::::::::::::::::::::E M:::::::M        M:::::::M R::::::::::::::R
EE:::::EEEEEEEEE:::::E M::::::::M      M::::::::M R:::::RRRRRR:::::R
  E:::::E       EEEEE M:::::::::M    M:::::::::M RR::::R      R::::R
  E:::::E             M::::::M:::M  M:::M::::::M   R:::R      R::::R
  E:::::EEEEEEEEEE    M:::::M M:::M M:::M M:::::M   R:::RRRRRR:::::R
  E:::::::::::::::E    M:::::M  M:::M:::M  M:::::M   R:::::::::::RR
  E:::::EEEEEEEEEE    M:::::M   M:::::M   M:::::M   R:::RRRRRR::::R
  E:::::E             M:::::M    M:::M    M:::::M   R:::R      R::::R
  E:::::E       EEEEE M:::::M     MMM     M:::::M   R:::R      R::::R
EE:::::EEEEEEEE::::E M:::::M             M:::::M   R:::R      R::::R
E::::::::::::::::::::E M:::::M             M:::::M RR::::R      R::::R
EEEEEEEEEEEEEEEEEEEEE MMMMMMM             MMMMMMM RRRRRRR      RRRRRR

[hadoop@ip-172-31-17-64 ~]$
```

How it works...

Using AWS, we launched EMR cluster. In addition, we accessed it with SSH using key. You can learn more about EMR in AWS documantation: `https://docs.aws.amazon.com/emr/latest/ManagementGuide/emr-gs.html`

Creating sample data

Next, we want to create a Hive external table on top of S3 logs and use EMR to compute the results. We can do this using the following three different methods:

- Using EMR CLI
- Using EMR console
- Using web GUI

How to do it...

It depends on your preferences. In my example, I will use EMR CLI. We should already be connected to the EMR cluster via SSH. Let's start to work with Hive:

1. In EMR CLI type `hive` and it will launch Hive.

2. Next, we can execute SQL commands. Let's create the table on top of the CloudFront logs that are stored in the S3 bucket. We will run this DDL, as follows:

```
hive>CREATE EXTERNAL TABLE IF NOT EXISTS cloudfront_logs (
    DateObject Date,
    Time STRING,
    Location STRING,
    Bytes INT,
    RequestIP STRING,
    Method STRING,
    Host STRING,
    Uri STRING,
    Status INT,
    Referrer STRING,
    OS String,
    Browser String,
    BrowserVersion String
)
ROW FORMAT SERDE 'org.apache.hadoop.hive.serde2.RegexSerDe'
WITH SERDEPROPERTIES (
    "input.regex" = "^(?!#)([^ ]+)\\s+([^ ]+)\\s+([^ ]+)\\s+([^
]+)\\s+([^ ]+)\\s+([^ ]+)\\s+([^ ]+)\\s+([^ ]+)\\s+([^ ]+)\\s+([^
]+)\\s+[^\(]+[\(]([^\;]+).*\%20([^\/]+)[\/](.*)$"
) LOCATION 's3://us-
east-1.elasticmapreduce.samples/cloudfront/data';
```

It is important that region location is in the same region as where we have the EMR cluster, that is in my case it is `us-east-1`.

3. We can test our new table, by running the following simple query:

```
Hive>SELECT os, COUNT(*) count FROM cloudfront_logs GROUP BY os;
```

Let's look at the results in the following screenshot:

```
hive> SELECT os, COUNT(*) count FROM cloudfront_logs GROUP BY os;
Query ID = hadoop_20181013171623_9c7dfe43-9086-47c6-8e36-4ab61d56630e
Total jobs = 1
Launching Job 1 out of 1
Tez session was closed. Reopening...
Session re-established.
Status: Running (Executing on YARN cluster with App id application_1539374666378_0006)

----------------------------------------------------------------------------------------
        VERTICES      MODE        STATUS   TOTAL  COMPLETED  RUNNING  PENDING  FAILED  KILLED
----------------------------------------------------------------------------------------
Map 1 .......... container      SUCCEEDED    1        1         0        0        0       0
Reducer 2 ...... container      SUCCEEDED    1        1         0        0        0       0
----------------------------------------------------------------------------------------
VERTICES: 02/02  [==========================>>] 100%  ELAPSED TIME: 25.50 s
----------------------------------------------------------------------------------------
OK
Android 855
Linux   813
MacOS   852
OSX     799
Windows 883
iOS     794
Time taken: 32.262 seconds, Fetched: 6 row(s)
```

You can see that the query works. Despite the fact that it has a fairly small amount of data, the query took 32 seconds. This is how Hadoop works, it takes a long time for initialization and other complementary steps. This is true for any big data system and should work for big data. You can also experiment with other SQL-friendly Hadoop tools, such as Impala, Presto, and so on. For us, the main feature of these guys is their connection to the Tableau via the ODBC driver.

4. Let's create one more table, using the *Google Books N-grams* dataset. It is an AWS public dataset available for everyone. You can read more about it here: `https://registry.opendata.aws/google-ngrams/`. Let's create the Hive table for 1-gram, as follows:

```
hive> CREATE EXTERNAL TABLE eng_1M_1gram(token STRING, year INT,
frequency INT, pages
 INT, books INT) ROW FORMAT DELIMITED FIELDS TERMINATED BY 't'
STORED AS SEQUENCEFILE
  LOCATION
's3://datasets.elasticmapreduce/ngrams/books/20090715/eng-1M/1gram'
;
```

As a result, we will get one more table. This table has 261,823,186 rows.

How it works...

We used Apache Hive that was deployed on top of an EMR cluster. In addition, we queried two datasets using Hive SQL.

There's more...

You can learn more about Apache Hive here: `https://docs.aws.amazon.com/emr/latest/ReleaseGuide/emr-hive.html`

See also

- You can visit the official page for Apache Hive at `https://hive.apache.org/`

Connect Tableau with Apache Hive

The fastest way to connect Tableau to AWS EMR via Hive JDBC is to open an SSH tunnel to the master node. Let's connect.

How to do it...

1. Open Terminal and run the following command:

```
ssh -o ServerAliveInterval=10 -i ~/.ssh/tableau-cookbook.pem -N -L
10000:localhost:10000
hadoop@ec2-18-215-157-216.compute-1.amazonaws.com
```

   But this could be a different command in your case.

2. Open Tableau Desktop and create a new connection using Amazon Hadoop
   EMR Hive.

3. Download and install ODBC drivers for your OS from: `https://docs.aws.`
   `amazon.com/emr/latest/ManagementGuide/emr-bi-tools.html`

4. Now, we can connect Hive, as follows:

5. Then choose **default** as a schema and **cloudfront_logs** as a table and go to the sheet. As you know, every drag and drop will initialize the SQL query and will trigger our EMR. In order to avoid this, we should pause Auto Updates and create our report, then run the final query, as follows:

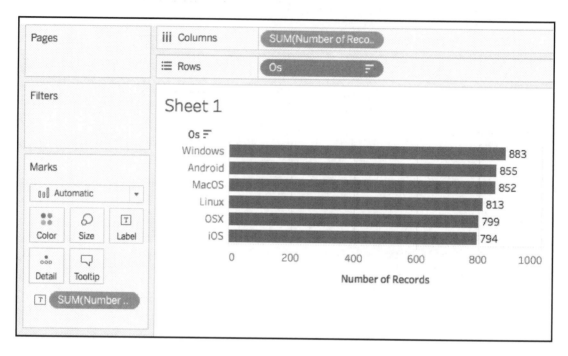

As a result, we were able to connect to Tableau. You can connect to the bigger `eng_1M_1gram` table as well. There are lots of different techniques for accessing data from Hadoop, and often it depends on use case.

How it works...

In our scenario, we connected Tableau Desktop to EMR cluster via Apache Hive. As usual, we left all the heavy work to ERM cluster and used Apache Hive in order to get an SQL interface to the Hadoop cluster.

There's more...

You can also use Impala. It is also an open-source tool in the Hadoop ecosystem. Instead of using MapReduce, as Hive does, it is using MPP (similar to the analytical data warehouse), which gives us a better query performance but requires additional steps. Hive and Impala both use Hive Metastore, but Hive requires more time to process the query and it isn't very efficient for improvised analyses. Impala requires data to be stored on HDFS. Moreover, it depends on the memory resource of clusters. As a result, every tool has its own pros and cons. You can read more here:

`https://vision.cloudera.com/impala-v-hive/`

See also

- There is a good article about designing for performance using Hadoop Hive at `https://community.tableau.com/docs/DOC-10244`
- You can learn more about Hive at `https://cwiki.apache.org/confluence/display/Hive/Tutorial`
- You can learn more about Amazon EMR in the following video link: *A technical Introduction to Amazon EMR,* `https://youtu.be/WnFYoiRqEHw`
- *Amazon EMR Deep Dive & Best Practices* at: `https://youtu.be/4HseALaLllc`

11
Forecasting with Tableau

In this chapter, we will cover the following recipes:

- Basic forecasting and statistical inference
- Forecasting on a dataset with outliers
- Using R within Tableau
- Forecasting based on multiple regression
- Regression with random forest
- Time series forecasting

Technical requirements

To follow the recipes from this chapter, you will need to have Tableau 2019.1 installed. You will also need to install the latest version of R software for statistical computing. R software is free and can be downloaded from `https://cran.r-project.org/`.

In the following recipes, we will be using the `hormonal_response_to_excercise.csv` and `stock_prices.csv` datasets, which you can download from the following URLs:

- `https://github.com/SlavenRB/Forecasting-with-Tableau/blob/master/hormonal_response_to_excercise.csv`
- `https://github.com/SlavenRB/Forecasting-with-Tableau/blob/master/stock-prices.txt`

Please make sure you have a local copy of the dataset saved to your device before we begin.

Introduction

In this chapter, we will learn how to perform forecasting, using real-life data from health behavior research and from stock market prices. We are going to discover Tableau built-in functions for linear regression and learn how to correctly interpret the results of statistical tests. Also, this chapter will cover the integration of R in Tableau. Using R functionality, we will be able to deal with slightly more complex datasets and perform more sophisticated forecasting.

"Prediction is difficult, especially if it's about the future."

– Niels Bohr

Basic forecasting and statistical inference

The aim of this recipe is to introduce a basic forecasting method that relies on linear regression. We are going to use a built-in Tableau facility for linear regression. Simply put, regression analysis helps us discover predictors of a variable that we are interested in. We model the relationship between potential predictors and our variable of interest. Once we establish the model of the relationship between predictors and our variable, we can use it for further predictions.

To perform for casting, we will use the `hormonal_response_to_excercise.csv` dataset. This dataset comes from a health behavior study that aimed to explore the factors influencing cortisol response while exerting the maximal, peak effort during physical exercise (the `Cortmax` variable in our dataset).

Our first task is to explore how effectively we can predict the level of cortisol response in the point of maximal effort during physical exercise, based on the cortisol level at rest (the `Cortrest` variable). So, in this example, our variable of interest (variable we are trying to predict) is `Cortmax` (cortisol level during maximal effort), while our predictor variable (the one that we are using to make a prediction) is `Cortrest` (cortisol level during rest). We will try to model the relationship between these two variables.

Getting ready

To perform the steps outlined in this recipe, you will need to connect to the `hormonal_response_to_excercise.csv` dataset.

How to do it...

1. Open a blank worksheet and drag and drop **Cortmax** from **Measures** into the **Columns** shelf.
2. Drag and drop **Cortrest** from **Measures** to the **Rows** shelf.
3. In the main menu toolbar, navigate to **Analysis** and in the drop-down menu deselect **Aggregate Measures**:

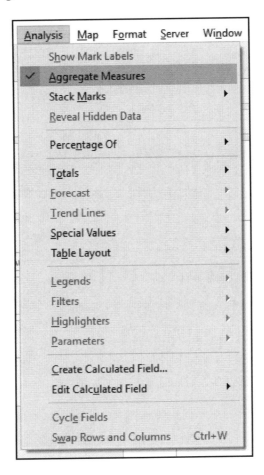

4. In the main menu toolbar, navigate to **Analysis** and in the drop-down menu, under **Trend Lines**, select **Show Trend Lines**:

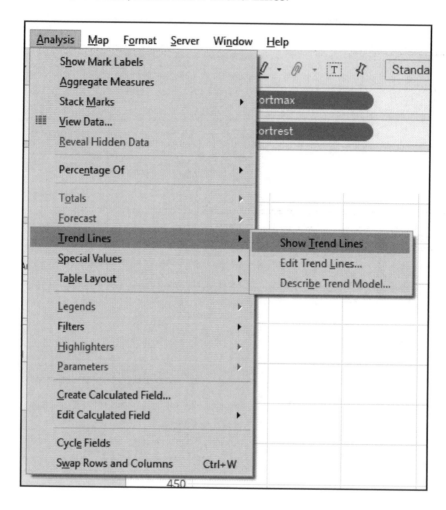

5. Once again, navigate to **Trend Lines** under **Analysis** in the main menu toolbar, and select **Describe Trend Model...**:

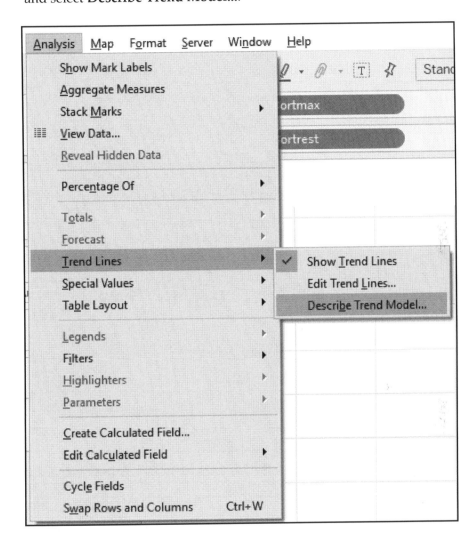

The following is the output:

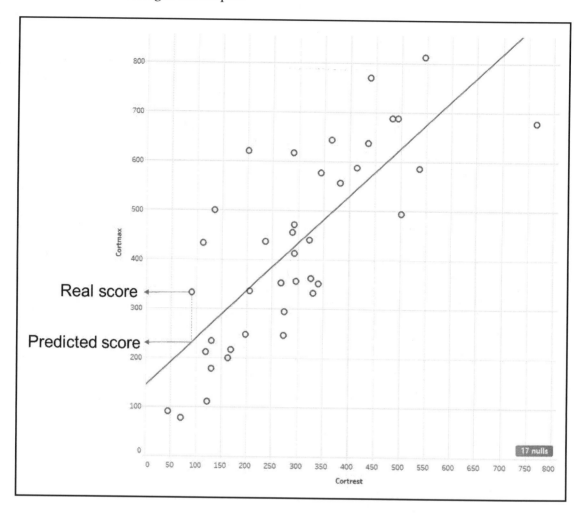

In the following screenshot, we can see that we have successfully modeled the relationship between these two variables:

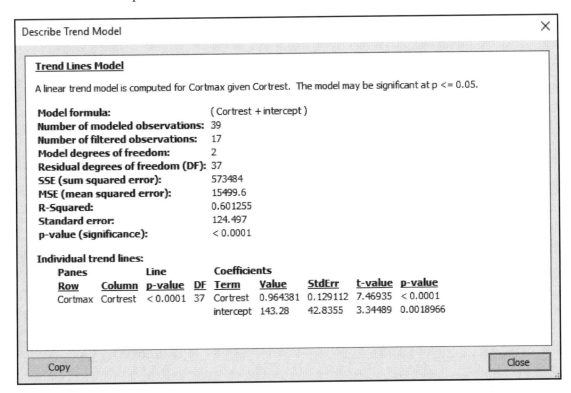

How it works...

We have created a regression model. Now, we are going to interpret the results, which tell us how successful our model is. But first, we need to get familiar with some basic statistics. In the broadest terms, the aim of each model is to represent real-life phenomena. All models differ in accuracy, or how well they depict reality. In statistics, we call the accuracy of the model its fit. The fit of a model is better if the difference between real data (that we measured) and predicted data (based on our model) is smaller.

We tried to predict cortisol level during maximum effort based on cortisol level during rest. Actual data points are represented with the circles, and the predictions that we made based on our model are vertically projected on the line (shown in the previous screenshot). As you can see, some circles lie almost on the line, some are above, and some are below the line. But the line is positioned so that these differences are minimized. If we want to estimate how good our model is, we should estimate the size of these differences. But, since the differences have both positive and negative values (some points are above and some are below the line), we can not just simply sum it up because they would cancel out. That's why we first need to square each difference and then sum it up. The result is **sum squared error (SSE)**—that is a measure of our model's error, or how much it deviates from actual data. In order to estimate the goodness of our model's fit, we need to compare the size of that deviation with a benchmark. The most commonly used benchmark is the simple average of y value or the flat, horizontal line. Comparison of our model and baseline gives us R-squared. The bigger the R-squared is, the smaller the probability that we obtained it by chance. The conventionally accepted threshold of the probability is 0.05 and is denoted by the p-value (significance) in our output. If our p-value is smaller than the threshold, we can conclude that we have enough evidence to believe that our model is good enough. In our case, the p-value is much smaller than the mentioned threshold, so we can assume that the cortisol level during the maximum effort can be reasonably well predicted based on the cortisol level at rest. We can conclude that we have created a successful model of the relationship between these two variables. In the next chapter, we are going to use it to create predictions.

There's more...

The regression that we presented in this example is linear because we assumed that the relationship between our variables was linear – an assumption that turned out to be correct. However, other types of models are also available in Tableau. They can be accessed by navigating to **Analysis | Trend Lines | Edit Trend Lines...**. In the **Trend Lines Options** window, we can choose other models such as **Logarithmic**, **Exponential**, **Power**, or **Polynomial**. A good way to choose the model is to first plot the data and visually inspect it.

See also

- Since statistical regression is a broad topic that greatly exceeds the scope of this book, if you are interested in learning more about the analysis itself, we highly recommend the following course: `https://onlinecourses.science.psu.edu/stat501/`

Forecasting on a dataset with outliers

In this recipe, we are going to learn how to deal with outliers. Outliers are data points that are very unusual, atypical, and deviate from the trend present in the majority of the dataset. Outliers can be dangerous if not dealt with appropriately because they can significantly skew the results of an analysis. In this recipe, we will explore ways of detecting outliers in Tableau. We are going to perform a regression analysis and see how the regression line is affected by these cases.

Getting ready

For this recipe, we need the `hormonal_response_to_excercise.csv` dataset. We are going to use the `Achtp` and `Achtmax` variables. The `Achtp` variable is the level of adrenocorticotropic hormone at the beginning of the test, while `Achtmax` is the level of adrenocorticotropic hormone at the maximum effort during physical exertion.

How to do it...

1. Drag and drop **Achtp** from **Measures** into the **Columns** shelf.
2. Drag and drop **Achtmax** from **Measures** into the **Rows** shelf.
3. In the main menu toolbar, in the **Analysis** drop-down menu, deselect **Aggregate Measures**.

4. In the main menu toolbar, in the **Analysis** drop-down menu, navigate to **Trend Lines | Show Trend Lines**:

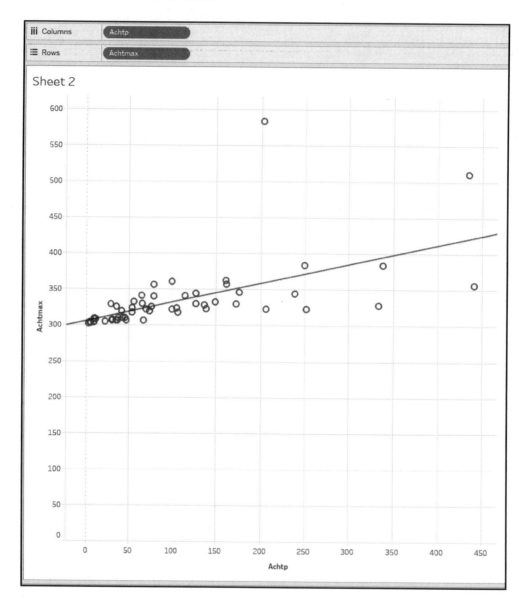

5. Rename the sheet to `Outliers included`.
6. In the main menu navigate to **Analysis** | **Create Calculated Field...**.
7. Rename the calculated field from **Calculation 1** to `Average`, and in the formula space, type the following expression:

```
WINDOW_AVG(SUM([Achtmax]))
```

The calculation field shows the preceding expression in the following screenshot:

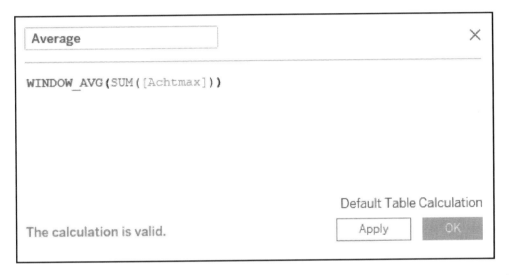

8. Click on **OK** to save and exit the calculated field editor window.
9. Repeat *step 7* to create another calculated field. Name the field `Lower` and in the formula space type the following expression:

```
[Average] - 2.5*WINDOW_STDEV(SUM([Achtmax]))
```

10. Save and exit by clicking **OK**.
11. Repeat *step 7* to create yet another calculated field. Name the field `Upper` and in the formula space, type the following expression:

```
[Average] + 2.5*WINDOW_STDEV(SUM([Achtmax]))
```

12. Save and exit by clicking on **OK**.

13. Repeat *step 7* one last time to create our final calculated field. Name this field `Outliers` and in the formula space, type the following expression:

```
SUM([Achtmax])> [Upper] or SUM([Achtmax]) < [Lower]
```

14. Save and exit by clicking on **OK**.

15. Right-click on the **Outliers included** sheet tab at the bottom of the workspace and select **Duplicate** as seen in the following screenshot:

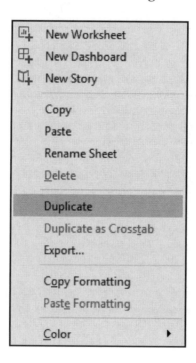

16. This will create an identical sheet named **Outliers included (2)**. Rename this sheet `Outliers excluded`.

17. Drag and drop **Outliers** from **Measures** to **Color** in the **Marks** card:

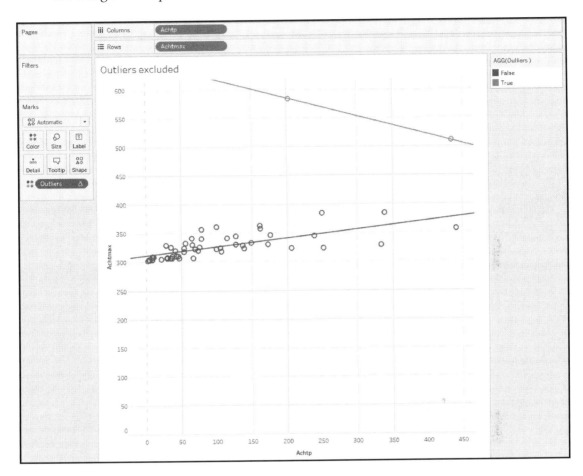

18. In the main menu toolbar, navigate to **Dashboard | New Dashboard**.
19. Drag and drop **Outliers included** sheet from the **Sheets** section of the **Dashboard** pane into the canvas.

20. Drag and drop the **Outliers excluded** sheet from the **Sheets** section of the **Dashboard** pane into the canvas, to the right of the **Outliers included** sheet in the chart:

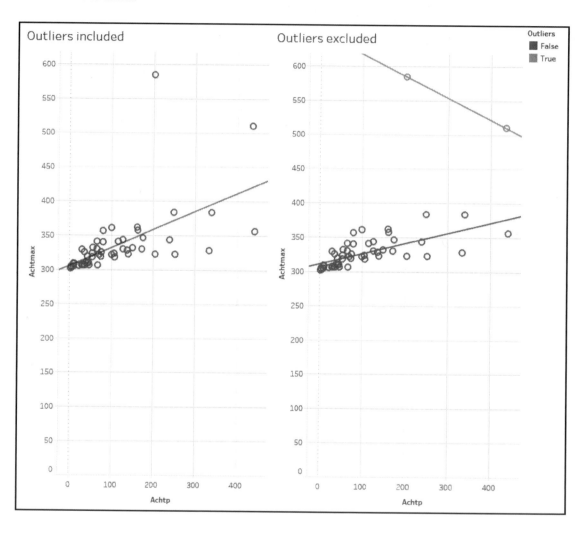

How it works...

In this recipe, we learned how to detect outliers. Outliers are extreme values that stand out from the other values in the sample. In order to detect outliers, we relied on a commonly used conventional rule—outliers are all values that deviate from the mean more than +/-2.5 standard deviations, which excludes around 1% of our sample.

In this example, we are able to see how outliers can influence statistical models. We can see that the model that includes outliers has a much steeper slope than the model that excludes outliers, meaning that they have pulled our linear model away from the majority of data, giving us skewed results. When interpreting results, we have to pay special attention to this (so-called leverage) effect. Otherwise, we risk declaring a statistical effect significant even when it does not actually exist.

There's more...

In our example, we were dealing with univariate outliers, which means that we tried to identify outliers along one variable. In multivariate cases, this task can be much more difficult. It is not always enough to look for outliers in each variable separately. Sometimes, you will also need to estimate all included variables at once. A particular data point doesn't have to have stood out on any single one of the variables, but its combination of positions on multiple variables can deem it an anomaly. Detecting multivariate outliers requires different resources, but you should keep in mind that you might encounter cases where you will need to undertake this task.

See also

- For more information about identifying multivariate outliers, read Chapter 12,
  Advanced Analytics with Tableau of this book and visit https://www.tableau.com/
  learn/tutorials/on-demand/r-integration?signin=
  c24f9d48d1fdda75861e6bce39b92f99

Using R within Tableau

The main goal of this recipe is to demonstrate how R can be used in conjunction with Tableau. R is a popular statistical language that can be used to perform sophisticated statistical analysis and predictive analytics. R is open source and free. It is supported by a community of contributors who continually create new packages.

Getting ready

Make sure that you have installed the most recent version of R on your computer. If not, go to `https://cran.r-project.org/` and download the latest version adequate for your operating system and follow the instructions for the installation. The default settings are just fine.

> When installing R, it is important to run it as administrator (right-click on the **Setup** icon). Otherwise, you may encounter problems with the access to folders and having permissions to conduct specific tasks.

Take a look at the following screenshot for better understanding:

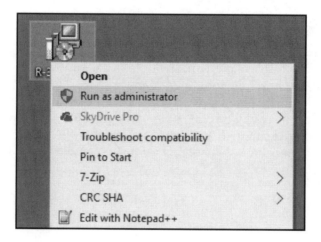

How to do it...

1. Click on the icon at your desktop and run R as shown in the following screenshot:

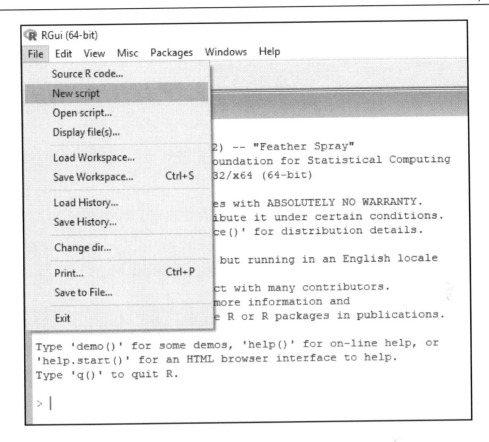

2. When the script is opened, type the following
   code `install.packages("Rserve",`

   `repos='http://cran.us.r-project.org')`, select it and click on  or
   press *Ctrl + R*:

```
install.packages("Rserve", repos='http://cran.us.r-project.org')
```

3. When the installation is completed you will receive the message that the `Rserve` package is successfully unpacked:

```
Type 'demo()' for some demos, 'help()' for on-line help, or
'help.start()' for an HTML browser interface to help.
Type 'q()' to quit R.

> install.packages("Rserve", repos='http://cran.us.r-project.org')
Installing package into 'C:/Users/Slaven/Documents/R/win-library/3.5'
(as 'lib' is unspecified)
trying URL 'http://cran.us.r-project.org/bin/windows/contrib/3.5/Rserve_1.7-3.zip'
Content type 'application/zip' length 638205 bytes (623 KB)
downloaded 623 KB

package 'Rserve' successfully unpacked and MD5 sums checked

The downloaded binary packages are in
        C:\Users\Slaven\AppData\Local\Temp\Rtmps3yCfk\downloaded_packages
>
```

4. Get back to script and type the following code:

```
library(Rserve)
Rserve()
```

5. Select the code and click on or press *Ctrl + R*.

6. Open Tableau and in the main menu toolbar navigate to **Help | Settings and Performance | Manage External Service Connection...** as shown in the following screenshot:

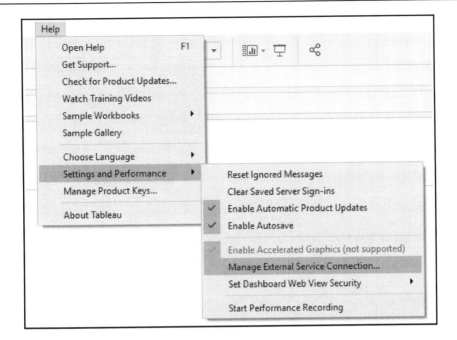

7. In the **External Service Connection** dialog box, from the **Server** drop-down menu, choose **localhost.** The **Port** field should contain the value of **6311.** Click on the **Test Connection** button:

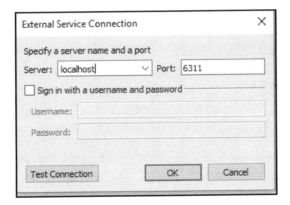

8. If you went through all of the steps outlined above you will get the message that the connection between Tableau and R is successful:

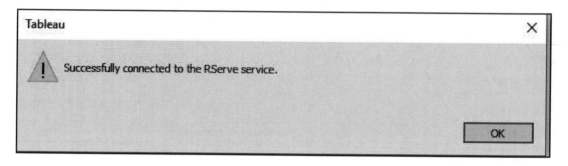

9. Click on **OK** to exit the **External Service Connection** dialog box.

How it works...

In this recipe, we installed the R software on our computer. Also, we installed the Rserve package, loaded its library, and initialized it. Essentially, Rserve is a connector between R and Tableau Desktop.

After that, we configured and tested the Rserve connection. When all of this was done, we were ready to write R syntax in Tableau calculated field. We have the following four different scripts at our disposal:

- SCRIPT_REAL: This script returns real numbers
- SCRIPT_INT: This script returns integers
- SCRIPT_STR: This returns strings
- SCRIPT_BOOL: This script returns Boolean

Within this script, we are allowed to write regular R syntax and the result of the calculation will be saved in a calculated field. This calculated field can be further used in the same manner as any other calculated field in Tableau.

In order to use R functionality in a workbook, the reader needs to have an R Tableau connection. This holds for locally shared workbooks and for workbooks published on Tableau Server. As of 2019, Tableau supports RSserve connections, which means secure Rserve is being hosted remotely from Tableau Server, and the data is protected in transit.

There's more...

- A concrete example of performing analysis that requires writing R syntax will be covered in the next recipes, *Forecasting based on multiple regression* and *Regression with random forest*, and other recipes in Chapter 12, *Advanced Analytics with Tableau*. However, any of these chapters do not have the ambition to serve as an introduction in R language. Because of that, readers are encouraged to learn R in parallel by referring to the following links:
- https://www.statmethods.net/index.html
- https://www.r-bloggers.com/

However, readers without any previous experience in R should be able to perform all the recipes.

See also

See more about R and Tableau integration at:

- https://www.tableau.com/learn/whitepapers/using-r-and-tableau
- https://www.tableau.com/solutions/r

Forecasting based on multiple regression

In the first recipe of this chapter, *Basic forecasting and statistical inference*, we learned how to perform forecasting with simple linear regression. In this recipe, we will learn how to perform forecasting based on multiple regression. Multiple regression is a type of forecasting procedure in which we use more than one variable to predict the outcome variable that we are interested in. In this recipe, our goal is to predict the level of cortisol at the highest effort during the physical exercise, based on cortisol level at rest and cortisol level at the beginning of the test. In the dataset that we are going to use, we have some respondents with missing data for cortisol level during physical exertion. Our aim is to use the result of our regression analysis to approximate cortisol level for those respondents and use these predicted values for further analysis. For this recipe, we need to employ R functionality in Tableau.

Getting ready

For this recipe, we will need the `hormonal_response_to_excercise.csv` dataset. Variables that we are going to use are `Cortmax` (the level of cortisol at the maximum level of physical excretion), `Cortrest` (cortisol level at rest), `Cortp` (the level of cortisol at the beginning of the test), and `Achtmax` (the level of adrenocorticotropic hormone at the beginning of the test). Before the start, make sure that R is installed on your machine, that `Rserve` is installed, loaded and initialized, and that connection between R and Tableau is configured. For detailed instruction on this, please refer to the *Using R within Tableau* recipe.

How to do it...

1. In the main menu toolbar, navigate to **Analysis | Create Calculated Field...** and type the following code:

```
SCRIPT_REAL('
mydata <- data.frame(y=.arg1, x1=.arg2, x2=.arg3);
reg <- lm(y ~ x1 + x2, data = mydata);
save(reg, file = "C:/Users/Slaven/Documents/mymodel.rda")
prob <- predict(reg, newdata = mydata, type = "response")'
,
AVG([Cortmax]),AVG([Cortrest]), AVG([Cortp]))
```

2. Name the field `CortmaxPred` as shown in the following screenshot:

```
CortmaxPred                                                    ×

Results are computed along Table (across).
SCRIPT_REAL(
'
mydata <- data.frame(y=.arg1, x1=.arg2, x2=.arg3);
reg <- lm(y ~ x1 + x2, data = mydata);
save(reg, file = "C:/Users/Slaven/Documents/mymodel.rda")
prob <- predict(reg, newdata = mydata, type = "response")'
,
AVG([Cortmax]),AVG([Cortrest]), AVG([Cortp]))
```

3. Drag and drop **CortmaxPred** from **Measures** to the **Columns** shelf.
4. Drag and drop **Achtp** from **Measures** to the **Rows** shelf.
5. In the main menu, go to **Analysis** and deselect **Aggregate Measures**.
6. In the same menu, choose **Trend Lines** and select **Show Trend Lines** and you will see the following output:

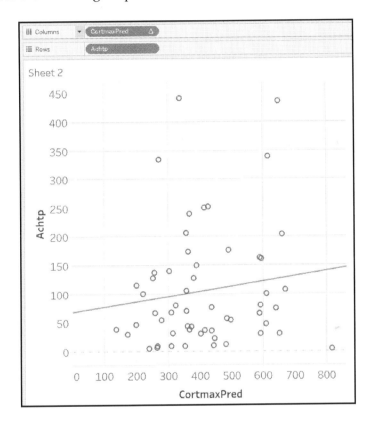

How it works...

In this recipe, we learned how to utilize R facility within Tableau. If you have some experience with R, you might notice that the syntax looks pretty standard with an exception at the beginning and at the end. Actually, the R syntax is wrapped, so that Tableau can be used to recognize it.

Also, it is important to notice that we need to assign arguments that are going to be used. `.arg1` represent the first variable from the left-hand side mentioned in the bottom line of the syntax (in our case, it is `Cortmax`), the `.arg2` variable represent the second one (`Cortrest`), and so on.

There's more...

In the syntax for this recipe, you might have noticed the following line of code:

```
save(reg, file = "C:/Users/Slaven/Documents/mymodel.rda")
```

This line created a `.rda` file on your hard drive, witch contains our regression model. Once you have saved the model, you can reuse it with another data set. Let's say we receive a new data set with data which contains information about cortisol level at the beginning of the test and at rest, but no information on the cortisol level at the point of maximum exertion. Thanks to our model, which predicts the level of cortisol at the point of maximum exertion, we can estimate its value for the new subjects. We just need to load our model by creating a calculated field with the following line of code:

```
SCRIPT_REAL('
mydata <- data.frame(y=.arg1, x1=.arg2, x2=.arg3);
load ("C:/Users/Slaven/Documents/mymodel.rda")
prob <- predict(reg, newdata = mydata, type = "response")'
,
AVG([Cortmax]),AVG([Cortrest]), AVG([Cortp]))
```

The new calculated field will contain the predicted values of `Cortmax`. However, keep in mind that the new data set has to contain a field named the same as the variable we were predicting in the original data set (in this case, `Cortmax`) for the script to work, even if it is completely empty. Also, make sure that all the other fields are also named exactly the same as in the original data set, where the model was created.

See also

- An excellent explanation can be found at `https://onlinecourses.science.psu.edu/stat501/node/283/`

Regression with random forest

In the previous recipe, *Forecasting based on multiple regression*, we learned how to use multiple variables in order to predict the variable that we are interested in. Sometimes, we have a lot of variables and we are not sure which ones we should choose as predictors. Also, predictor variables can be related among themselves in different ways, which complicates the setup of the model and the interpretation of the results. In recent years, random forest algorithm has gained popularity among analysts and data scientists, as they provide a solution to these problems. The random forest algorithm is based on decision tree approach. This approach can be used to predict both discrete class membership (classification) and exact values of a continuous variable (regression). In this recipe, we will cover the latter. Regression-based on decision tree works by iteratively splitting cases in the dataset into increasingly homogeneous groups. Looping through all variables the algorithm searches for the one that splits cases into the groups. so that cases within each group are as similar as possible with regards to the predicted variable. This process continues, resulting in the three with more and more branches and data that is partitioned into smaller and smaller subsamples. Random forest is an enhanced version of the decision tree algorithm that builds many decision threes using randomly selected subsamples of both variables and cases.

Results obtained by each of the trees are compiled into a final single solution. Visualized in R, a random forest model looks like this:

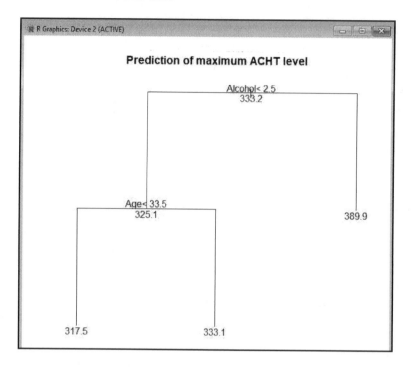

It is not possible to create a tree chart like the one shown above in Tableau—it is possible to create it directly in R though. You can learn how in the next chapter, *Advanced Analytics with Tableau*.

We will use the `hormonal_response_to_excercise.csv` dataset. Our main task will be to predict the level of adrenocorticotropic hormone at the maximum level of physical exertion. In order to take into consideration different factors that can influence an ACHT spike during exercise, we are going to include the following variables in our model: cortisol level at rest, alcohol and tobacco consumption, height, age, and weight. This variable can be also interrelated: for example, smoking and drinking, height, and weight. Baseline cortisol may be also related to tobacco and alcohol consumption. For this reason, the random forest can make our life easier.

Getting ready

In order to perform this recipe make sure that you installed R, and that you have activated the `Rserve` package and connect it to Tableau (for detailed instruction see the recipe, *Using R within Tableau*). You will also need to connect to `hormonal_response_to_excercise.csv` and open a new blank worksheet.

How to do it...

1. Launch R, open a new script and type `install.packages("rpart", repos='http://cran.us.r-project.org')`.

2. Select the text, and click on ▣ or press *Ctrl + R*.

3. When the installation process is completed, load the package by typing the following line:

```
library(rpart)
```

4. Select the text, and click on ▣ or press *Ctrl + R*.

5. In Tableau, in the main menu toolbar, click on **Analysis** and then click on **Create Calculated Field...**.

6. Rename the field from **Calculation 1** to `Random Forest` and type the following expression into the formula space:

```
SCRIPT_REAL('library(rpart);
fit = rpart(Achtmax ~ Cortrest + Alcohol + Tobacco + Height + Age +
Weight,
method="anova", data.frame(Achtmax = .arg1, Cortrest =.arg2,
Alcohol=.arg3, Tobacco =.arg4, Height =.arg5, Age =.arg6,
Weight=.arg7));
t(data.frame(predict(prune(fit,0.05), type = "vector")))[1,]',
AVG([Achtmax]),
AVG([Cortrest]),
AVG([Alcohol]),
AVG([Tobacco]),
AVG([Height]),
AVG([Age]),
AVG([Weight]))
```

The preceding code is shown in the following screenshot:

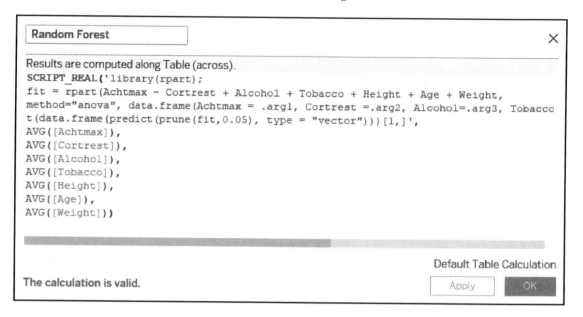

7. Click **OK** to exit the editor window and save the calculated field.
8. Drag and drop **Random Forest** from **Measures** into the **Rows** shelf.
9. Drag and drop the **ID** variable from **Dimensions** into the **Columns** shelf.
10. In the **Marks** card, change the mark type from **Automatic** to **Circle** using the drop-down menu.
11. Drag and drop **ID** from **Dimensions** to **Label** in the **Marks** card.
12. Drag and drop **Random Forest** from **Measures** to **Color** in the **Marks** card.
13. Rename the sheet to **Random Forest Regression**:

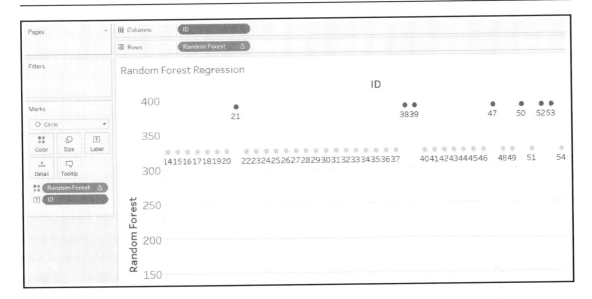

How it works...

In this recipe, we used the random forest algorithm to predict the level of ACHT during exercise. The subjects with high values of ACHT (389.86) are represented with dark blue circles at the top of the chart, while the rest of the respondents (with the average value of 325.14) are at the bottom of the chart (light blue cycles).

There's more...

In this recipe, we have created a model, and we can now save it and apply it to another dataset (for detailed explanation and instructions, see the recipe *Forecasting based on multiple regression*). You might also want to try further evaluation the model by splitting the data into a training and a test set. It is a common practice in data modeling to use a part of the data set as the training set, on which the model is built (fitted). The model is then evaluated on the test set. If the fit that is observed for the training set is preserved in the test set, it is an indication that we did a good job. Otherwise, we need to reconsider our model.

See also

- For more information about the random forest in Tableau, check out this resource at `https://www.packtpub.com/big-data-and-business-intelligence/advanced-analytics-r-and-tableau`
- To learn more about the random forest algorithm, you might want to start at this link: `https://www.stat.berkeley.edu/~breiman/RandomForests/cc_home.htm`, belonging to the authors of the algorithm, Leo Breiman, and Adele Cutler

Time series forecasting

Tableau has excellent capabilities for dealing with time series data. One of them is time series forecasting – extrapolating values for points in time that are outside our dataset, based on the time points in our dataset for which we have the recorded values.

In this recipe, we will be using stock market prices of a soft drink company shares, stored in the `Stock_prices.csv` dataset.

Getting ready

To perform the steps in this recipe, make sure you are connected to the `Stock_prices.csv` dataset and open a new blank worksheet.

How to do it...

1. Right-click on the **Date** field under **Dimensions** and from the drop-down menu select **Convert to Continuous**:

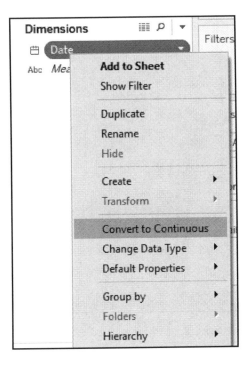

2. Drag and drop **Date** from **Dimensions** into the **Columns** shelf.
3. Drag and drop **Adj.Close** from **Measures** into the **Rows** shelf.

4. In the main menu toolbar, click on **Analysis**, navigate to **Forecast** and select **Show Forecast**:

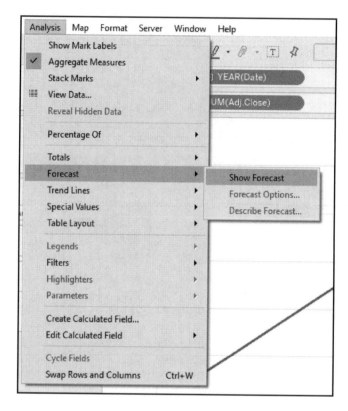

5. Tableau will automatically place the **Forecast indicator** field in **Color** in the **Marks** card. However, we can remove it from there:

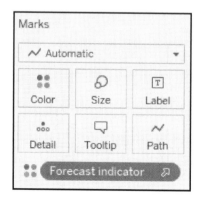

6. Once again, navigate to **Analysis** in the main menu toolbar and under **Forecast** select **Forecast Options...**.

7. **Forecast Length** is automatically set to **Next 5 quarters**, but we can change it by selecting **Exactly** or **Until** and selecting the desired period. Try changing the **Forecast Length** period and notice how the shaded area around the line expands as you increase the **Forecast Length**. However, let's leave it at 5 quarters:

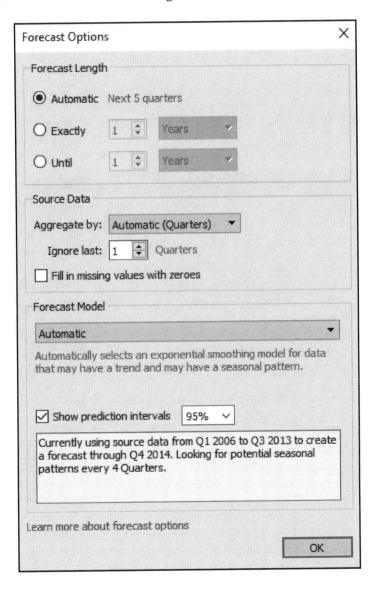

8. Click **OK** to exit the **Forecast Options** window:

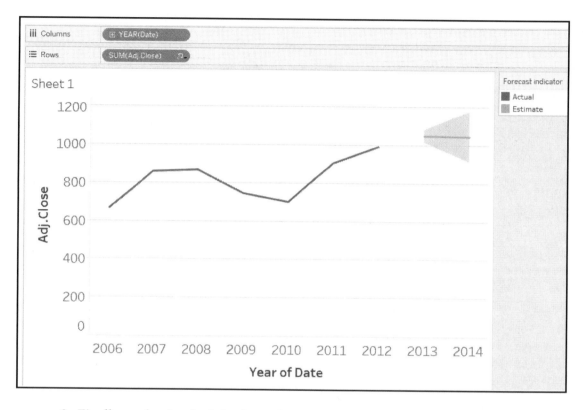

9. Finally, under **Analysis** in the main menu toolbar, navigate to **Forecast** and select **Describe Forecast** to see the performance of the forecast we have created:

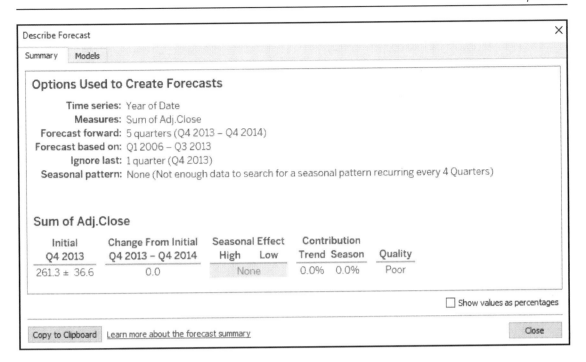

How it works...

We have extrapolated the closing prices of the company's shares based on the prices we have recorded in our dataset. Let's explore the characteristics of the model we have created, by inspecting the content of the **Describe Forecast** window.

In the **Summary** tab, we can see some basic information describing our forecast. The most important of these is quality—it describes how well the forecast fits our actual data and can take values of `Good`, `Ok`, and `Poor`.

In the **Models** tab, we can see the role of the **Level**, **Trend**, and **Season** components of our model. We can also see the quality metrics that provide information about the statistical quality of our model—**root mean squared error (RMSE)**, **mean absolute error (MAE)**, **mean absolute percentage error (MAPE)**, and **Aikake Information Criterion (AIC)**. Finally, in the **Models** tab, we can get the information about smoothing coefficients that were used to weight the data points according to their how recent they are, so that forecast errors are minimized as shown in the following screenshot:

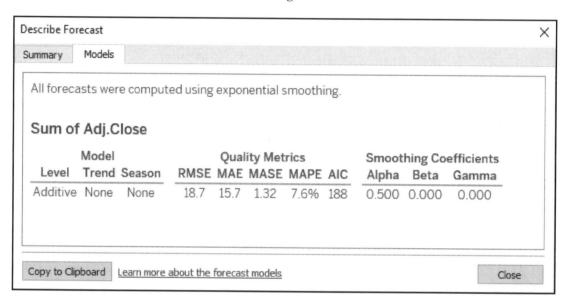

Tableau allows us to choose the time period for which we wish to predict the values. We have chosen 5 quarters, but we can increase the period further. However, note that the precision of our prediction becomes smaller as our forecasting length period becomes longer. This is reflected by the prediction interval (the shaded area around the line), which becomes larger as we make our prediction period becomes longer.

There's more...

In the **Forecast Options** window, Tableau provides us with various option for customizing our forecast. We can choose how to aggregate our data under **Source Data**. By default, it is aggregated by **Quarters**, but in the drop-down menu, we can choose to aggregate across different time periods, such as **Year** or **Month**. Under **Data Source**, we can also choose how many time points to ignore. Finally, we can replace the null (missing) values with zeros if desired.

Under **Forecast Model**, we can change our model from **Automatic** to **Automatic without Seasonality**, or **Custom model**, in which case we can manually choose the trend and season.

Finally, we can select or deselect the box in front of **Show prediction intervals** in order to turn the prediction intervals on or off. We can also choose among the 90%, 95%, and 99% prediction intervals.

See also

- For more information on forecasting in Tableau, see this excellent Tableau help resource at `https://onlinehelp.tableau.com/current/pro/desktop/en-us/forecast_create.html`.

12
Advanced Analytics with Tableau

This chapter will cover the following topics:

- Running segmentation analysis
- Discovering the latent structure of the dataset
- Extracting the structure beneath discrete variables
- Data mining with tree-based models
- Identifying anomalies in data

Technical requirements

To follow the recipes from this chapter, you'll need to have Tableau 2019.1 installed. You will also need to have R installed, as well as the `Rserve` library. To install the `Rserve` library, open a new R script by navigating to **File** | **New script**:

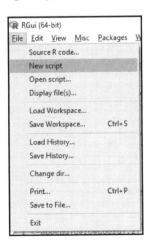

Run the following code:

```
install.packages('Rserve',repos='http://cran.us.r-project.org')
```

You can run the code by selecting it and clicking the **Run** button ![run button] or by pressing *Ctrl + R* on your keyboard.

Introduction

In this chapter, you'll learn how to utilize joined capabilities of Tableau and R in order to perform some more advanced analytical tasks. This will enable us to dive below the surface and to discover hidden underlying patterns in our data. We'll learn how to identify and interpret latent dimensions of our dataset, to group similar cases, and to detect and interpret unusual cases and anomalies in data.

> *"Hiding within those mounds of data is knowledge that could change the life of a patient, or change the world."*
>
> *–Atul Butte*

Running segmentation analysis

Cluster analysis is one of the most popular data analysis techniques. It allows us to find patterns or segments in our data, which we can then interpret in order to gain a more in-depth understanding of its underlying structure. Tableau has a built-in clustering functionality, which means we'll not be using R in this recipe—we'll perform the entire analysis through Tableau only.

Getting ready

In this recipe, we'll be using the mtcars.csv dataset. It contains characteristics of various car models, such as the number of horsepowers, number of cylinders, miles per gallon, and so on. Before we dive into the recipe, make sure you have the dataset saved to your device and open Tableau and connect to it.

How to do it...

1. After connecting to the `mtcars.csv` dataset, open a new blank worksheet.
2. Drag and drop **Qsec** from **Measures** into the **Rows** shelf.
3. Drag and drop **Mpg** from **Measures** into the **Columns** shelf.
4. In the main menu toolbar, navigate to **Analysis** and, in the drop-down menu, deselect **Aggregate Measures**:

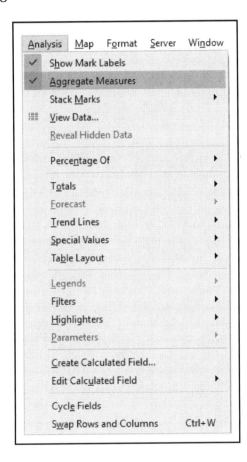

5. We've now produced a scatter plot of the car models. Let's add the clusters! In the **Data** pane, navigate to **Analytics**:

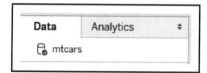

6. Drag and drop **Cluster** from **Model** into the view we have created:

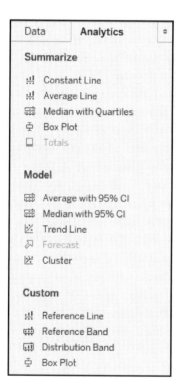

7. A dimension, **Clusters**, has been created and placed onto **Color** in the **Marks** card:

8. In the **Clusters** window that opened, we can see two measures that we previously placed into the scatter plot. Navigate back to the **Data** pane and, under **Measures**, select the remaining measures (**Am** through **Wt**), by clicking on them while holding the *Ctrl* key on your keyboard:

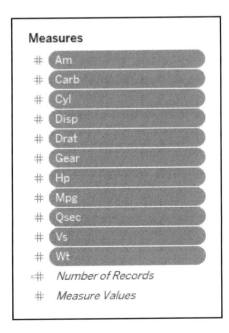

9. Drag and drop all of the selected measures into the **Clusters** window, under **Variables**:

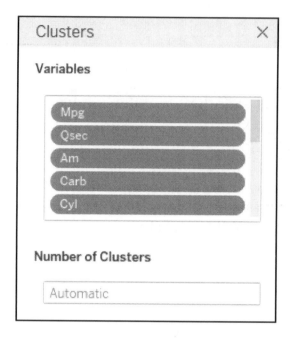

10. Click on **X** to close the **Clusters** window.
11. Drag and drop **Model** from **Dimensions** onto **Label** in the **Marks** card:

How it works...

Cluster analysis works by grouping cases (in our example, car models) into clusters based on a complex underlying pattern of scores on multiple measures. When setting up the cluster analysis, we entered all of the measures we wanted the cluster based on into the **Clusters** window, and Tableau automatically detected the optimal number of clusters. There are many clustering algorithms—the one implemented in Tableau is called k-means.

But this is just the beginning of the analysis. The next step is to interpret the clusters. We can use the **Describe Clusters** function to aid the interpretation. We'll access it by right-clicking on the **Clusters** pill in the **Marks** card and selecting **Describe Clusters** from the drop-down menu, as shown in the following screenshot:

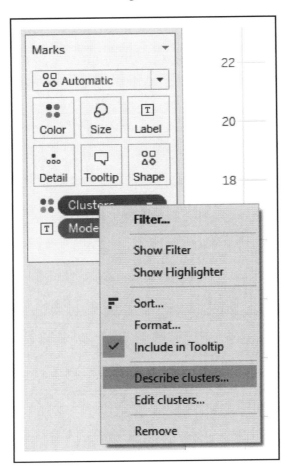

This will launch the **Describe Clusters** window. Under **Summary**, we can see what variables entered into the cluster analysis, as well as **Summary Diagnostics**, which includes the description of the model itself, as well as that of the individual clusters. The **Summary** tab is shown in the following screenshot:

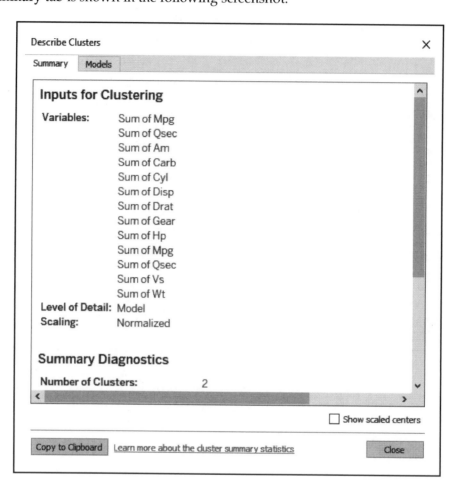

Chapter 12

If we navigate to the **Models** tab, we'll see the results of the **Analysis of Variance,** showing us which variables actually differentiate the clusters. The **Models** tab is shown in the following screenshot:

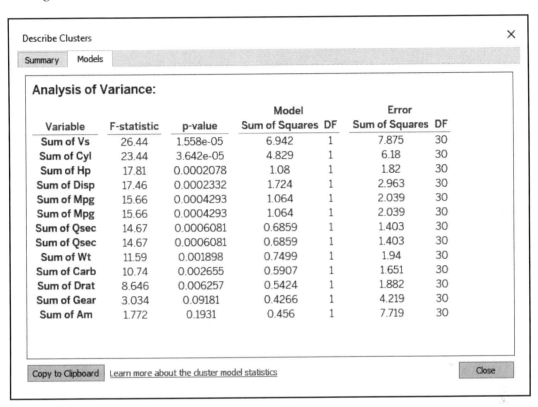

In in the preceding screenshot, we can see that all of the variables, except for **Sum of Vs** and **Sum of Gear**, are significant by looking at their associated values in the **p-value** column. A **p-value** that is less than or equal to 0.05 is usually considered significant. To gain more insight into how these variables differentiate the clusters, we can compare the values of different variables for each of the clusters in the **Summary** tab, under **Summary Diagnostics**. We can also create new scatterplots by placing various measures into the **Rows** and **Columns** shelves, so we can gain a better sense of how the clusters are distributed.

There's more...

In the following example, we'll let the Tableau clustering algorithm automatically determine the number of clusters—in this case, two. However, it's also possible, and sometimes desirable, to set the number of clusters ourselves. Let's change the number of clusters by performing the following steps:

1. Right-click on the **Clusters** pill in the **Marks** card.
2. From the drop-down menu, select **Edit clusters...**:

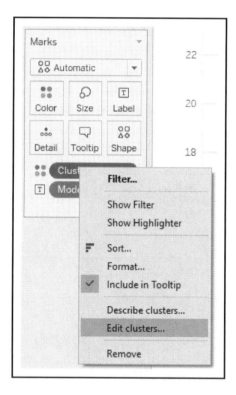

This will launch the **Clusters** window that we already encountered when we were creating the initial clusters.

3. Under **Number of Clusters**, type in the desired number of clusters. This time, let's go with 3:

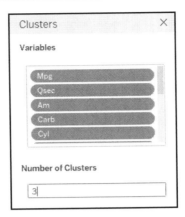

4. Click on **X** to close the **Clusters** window. We've now created a three-cluster solution:

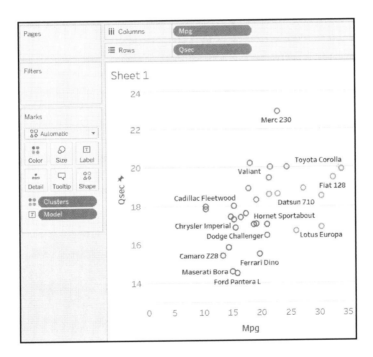

Always be careful with setting the number of clusters and don't increase it unless you have a good reason to do so. Simpler solutions are usually better!

See also

- To learn more about k-means clustering, start here: `https://en.wikipedia.org/wiki/K-means_clustering`
- For more information about running cluster analysis in Tableau, feel free to visit the **Tableau Help** page on the topic: `https://onlinehelp.tableau.com/current/pro/desktop/en-us/clustering.htm`

Discovering the latent structure of the dataset

When dealing with complex topics, we usually end up with a dataset with a large number of variables. To find meaning in this kind of dataset is typically a tricky task. Luckily, there are some analytical techniques that can help us. One of those techniques is **principal component analysis (PCA)**, which is a data reduction technique. Mathematical transformation in this analysis enables us to derive the most informative dimensions of our dataset. The mathematics underlying the analysis **singular value decomposition (SVD)** is somewhat complex, so we won't go into too much detail in this recipe. The basics of PCA can be described like this: you start with a dataset with many variables, then you simplify that dataset by turning your original variables into a smaller number of **principal components** in a way that guarantees that you'll preserve as much information as possible. Those components can be used for further analysis as well and provide insight into the underlying structure of our data, helping us make sense of our data and see the forest among the trees.

Getting ready

The dataset that we're going to use for this recipe comes from a psychological survey. A group of people was assessed using a psychological test. The result of the assessment is psychological profile composed of numerical scores representing following personality traits: anxiety, hostility, self-consciousness, assertiveness, sensation seeking, positive emotions, aesthetics, ideas, values, fairness, altruism, gentleness, competency, achievement, and discipline. Since simultaneously interpreting the results on various variables is a difficult task, we want to reduce the number of variables, but in a way that preserves the most information from the original dataset.

For that task, we'll use the `prcomp` function that's built-in R.

How to do it...

1. Launch R and open a new script by selecting **File** and then **New script**.
2. In the **R Editor** window, enter the following code and make sure to replace all of the file paths with the paths leading to the appropriate locations on your device. After pasting the paths, make sure to replace the backslashes with double backslashes, as seen in the following code:

```
pt <-read.table ("C:\\Users\\Slaven\\Desktop\\personality_
traits.csv", header=T, sep=",")
pt.pc <- prcomp(pt, scale = TRUE)
X1 <- pt.pc$x [, 1]
X2 <- pt.pc$x [, 2]
X3 <- pt.pc$x [, 3]
X4 <- pt.pc$x [, 4]
X5 <- pt.pc$x [, 5]
scores <- cbind(pt, X1, X2, X3, X4, X5)
colnames(scores)[17] <- "X1"
colnames(scores)[18] <- "X2"
colnames(scores)[19] <- "X3"
colnames(scores)[20] <- "X4"
colnames(scores)[21] <- "X5"
write.csv (scores, "C:\\Users\\Slaven\\Desktop\\scores.csv")
loadings <- as.data.frame(pt.pc$rotation)
loadings <- loadings[2:16, 1:5]
loadings$trait <- row.names(loadings)
rownames(loadings) <- c()
path <-matrix(1,15,1)
up <- cbind(loadings,path)
zero <-matrix(0, 15, 6)
trait <- as.data.frame(loadings [,6])
down <-cbind (zero, trait)
colnames(down) <- c("PC1","PC2","PC3","PC4","PC5", "path", "trait")
pt.loadings <- rbind(up, down)
write.csv (pt.loadings,
"C:\\Users\\Slaven\\Desktop\\pt.loadings.csv")
```

3. Select the entire code and click the **Run** icon 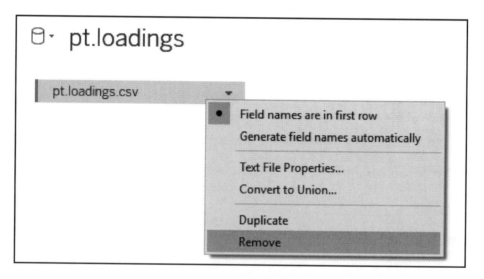. Alternatively, use *Ctrl+R* to run the code.

4. Two files have now been created at the location you specified: pt.loadings.csv and scores.csv. We'll now use them to create a visualization in Tableau. Launch Tableau.

5. From the **Connect** pane, select **Text file** and navigate to either of the files you have created—pt.loadings.csv or scores.csv. Select it and click **Open**.

6. In the **Data Source** page, remove the file you've connected to by right-clicking on it and selecting **Remove** from the drop-down menu:

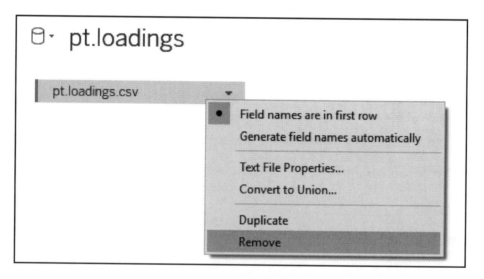

7. From the **Files** pane, drag and drop **New Union** into the whitespace. The **Union** window will open.

8. Drag and drop scores.csv and pt.loadings.csv from the **Files** pane into the **Union** window, one by one. Click on **Apply**, and then click on **OK** to exit the window:

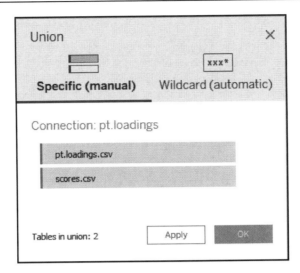

9. Navigate to **Sheet 1**.
10. Drag and drop **X1** from **Measures** into the **Columns** shelf.
11. Drag and drop **X2** from **Measures** into the **Rows** shelf.
12. Drag and drop **PC1** from **Measures** into the **Columns** shelf, to the right of the **SUM(X1)** pill.
13. Drag and drop **PC2** from **Measures** into the **Rows** shelf, to the right of the **SUM(X2)** pill:

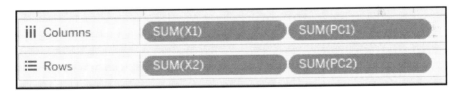

14. In the **Marks** card, click on the second **SUM(PC1)** chart in order to expand it:

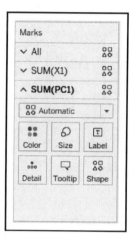

15. Click on the **Automatic** drop-down menu and change the mark type to **Line**.
16. Drag and drop **path** from **Measures** onto **Path** in the **Marks** card.
17. Drag and drop **trait** from **Dimensions** onto **Label** in the **Marks** card:

18. In the main menu toolbar, navigate to **Analysis** and, from the drop-down menu, deselect **Aggregate Measures**:

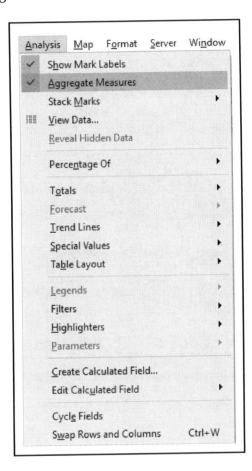

19. Right-click on the **PC1** pill in the **Columns** shelf and select **Dual Axis** from the drop-down menu:

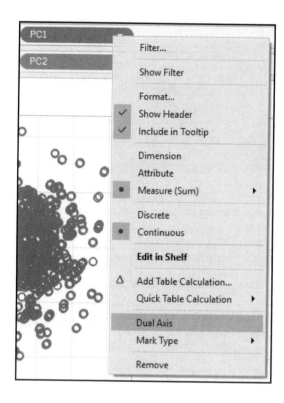

20. Right-click on the **PC2** in the **Rows** shelf and select **Dual Axis** from the drop-down menu. We've finished our PCA and created a chart to visualize it:

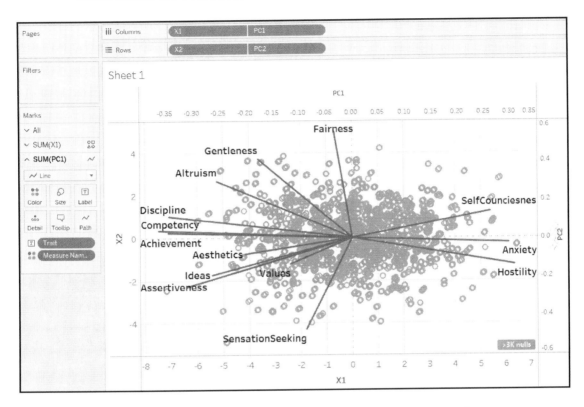

In order to make the chart more appealing and easier to read, you can adjust the formatting in a way that emphasizes the most important elements. In the preceding screenshot, we've increased the label font and made it bold, while at the same time changing the color of circles from orange to gray and decreasing opacity. Feel free to explore the formatting options that work best for you!

How it works...

We've just performed a PCA and created a plot showing data points in a swarm and our original personality dimensions as lines radiating from the center of the chart. Values on x and y-axes are actually the first and the second principal components, respectively. By definition, the first two components explain the largest proportion of variability in the original data, which is why we use them in our chart. Points represent individual people (cases) from our original data file but, instead of showing scores on the different personality traits, we're charting the scores on the first two principal components. Through our R script, we wrote a new file, `scores.csv`, where we recorded the scores of individuals on each of the principal components. We saved those values (scores on principal components) as measures: X1, X2, and so on. On the other hand, the lines represent our original dimensions—personality traits. In the chart, we're showing their loadings on, or correlations with, the first two principal components. Those values are also saved as measures: PC1, PC2, and so on. We used them to interpret our principal components—the higher the loading, the more important that original dimension is for defining the principal component. We created this part of the chart using the `pt.loadings.csv` dataset, where we recorded loading of each trait on each of the principal components.

Based on the length and direction of lines, we can conclude that the first principal component, which carries the most information, differentiates people based on their emotional stability, ranging from emotionally stable (on the left-hand side), characterized by high **Discipline**, **Competency**, and **Achievement**, to emotionally unstable (on the right-hand side), characterized by high **Self-consciousness**, **Anxiety**, and **Hostility**.

The second principal component, which is shown on the y-axis, is defined by **Fairness**, **Gentleness**, and **Altruism** on one side, and **Sensation-seeking** and **Assertiveness** on the other side. This dimensions can be interpreted as speaking about cooperativeness versus competitiveness.

 Always be mindful of the fact that interpretation of the components goes beyond interpreting the data at hand and relies heavily on domain-specific knowledge about the topic of research.

There's more...

Visualizing the first and the second principal component is the usual way to go since these two components carry the most information. However, sometimes we might wish to see the third, fourth, and so on, principal component.

A handy way to allow for this is to create a parameter that would enable users to switch between principal components they wish to see in the plot.

See also

- For more information on PCA, you may want to start here: `https://en.wikipedia.org/wiki/Principal_component_analysis`
- To find out more about the `prcomp` function that we used to implement the analysis, see the documentation: `https://www.rdocumentation.org/packages/kazaam/versions/0.1-0/topics/prcomp`
- Since the book is not meant to provide a comprehensive introduction to R language or data science reader is encouraged to refer the following links:
    - `https://www.statmethods.net/index.html`
    - `https://www.r-bloggers.com`
    - `https://www.datacamp.com`

Extracting the structure beneath discrete variables

This recipe will guide you through the process of performing and visualizing the results of correspondence analysis. Correspondence analysis is a data reduction technique frequently used in brand image studies, but also in other types of research, because it allows us to neatly map brands on a map formed by brand attributes.

Getting ready

In this recipe, we'll use `telco_image.csv`, a dataset coming from a market research survey. Cell phone users were asked to rate the three biggest mobile network providers in their country on a list of attributes. For each attribute, they chose one brand they felt best fit that description. Before we begin, make sure you've saved the `telco_image.csv` dataset to your device.

How to do it...

1. Launch R, and open a new script by selecting **File** and then **New script**.

2. In the **R Editor** window, enter the following code. Make sure to replace all of the file paths with the paths leading to the appropriate locations on your device. After pasting the paths, make sure to replace the backslashes with double backslashes, as seen in the following code block:

```
install.packages('ca',repos='http://cran.us.r-project.org')
library(ca)
df <- read.table("C:\\Users\\Slaven\\Desktop\\telco_image.csv",
header=T, sep=",")
n <-ncol(df)
blank <-matrix(NA, 1 ,n)
blank$brands <- c(colnames(df))
brands <- as.data.frame(blank$brands[-1])
names(brands) <- "labels"
labels <-df [ ,1]
labels <- as.data.frame(labels)
labels.df <- rbind(labels,brands)
type1 <-as.data.frame(rep("Brand", nrow(brands)))
names(type1) <- "Type"
type2 <-as.data.frame(rep("Feature", nrow(labels)))
names(type2) <- "Type"
type.df <- rbind(type2, type1)
num.df<- df[,-1]
c<-ca(num.df)
X <-append(c$rowcoord[,1],c$colcoord[,1], )
Y <-append(c$rowcoord[,2],c$colcoord[,2], )
axes <- data.frame(cbind(X,Y))
fin.data <- cbind(axes,type.df,labels.df)
write.csv(fin.data,
"C:\\Users\\Slaven\\Desktop\\CA_input_data.csv")
```

3. Select the entire code and click on the **Run** icon . Alternatively, use *Ctrl + R* to run the code.

4. A new file, `CA_input_data.csv`, has now been created at the location you specified. We'll now use it to create a visualization in Tableau. Launch Tableau.

5. From the **Connect** pane, select **Text file** and navigate to `CA_input_data.csv`, then select it and click on **Open**.
6. Navigate to **Sheet 1**.
7. Drag and drop **X** from **Measures** into the **Columns** shelf.
8. Drag and drop **Y** from **Measures** into the **Rows** shelf.
9. Drag and drop **Labels** from **Dimensions** onto **Label** in the **Marks** card.
10. Drag and drop **Type** from **Dimensions** onto **Color** in the **Marks** card.
11. Drag and drop **Type** from **Dimensions** onto **Shape** in the **Marks** card:

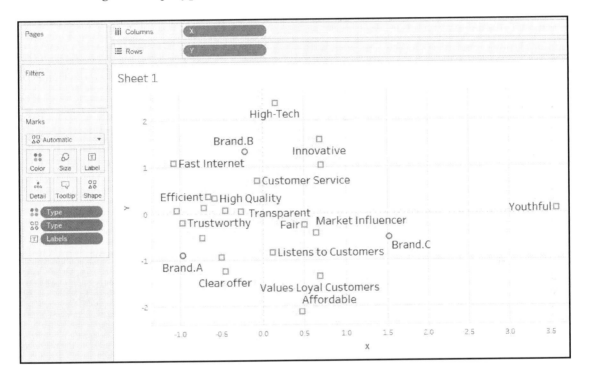

12. Click on the **Shape** button in the **Marks** card:

13. Assign the shapes you like to the brand and feature by clicking on the desired value (**Brand** or **Feature**) under **Select Data Item**, and choosing the desired shape from the **Select Shape Palette** drop-down menu. Let's choose the shapes shown in the following screenshot:

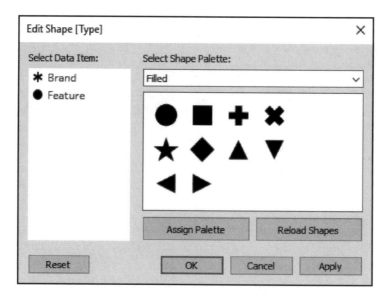

14. When you are done with choosing the shapes, click on **OK** to exit the **Edit Shape [Type]** window. Our correspondence analysis is done:

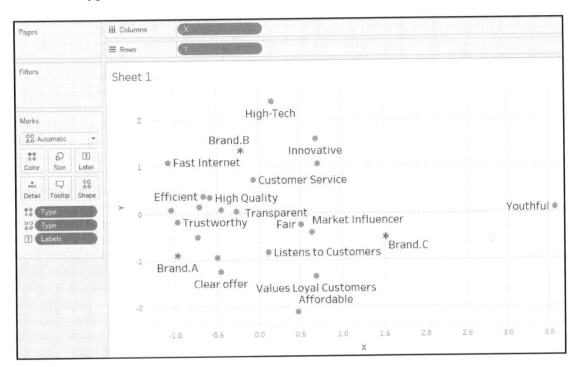

How it works...

Correspondence analysis works similarly to PCA, which we covered in the first recipe, Discovering latent structure of the dataset, of this chapter. It reduces the number of dimensions that differentiate our cases (in this example, brands) so we have a clearer overview of how each of the brands is positioned. On the x and y axes, we plotted the first two dimensions extracted by correspondence analysis, which have the same function as the first two principal components in the principal components analysis.

Both the brands and the attributes describing them are plotted in the space created by the first two dimensions. We interpret the results, or read the map, by looking at the spatial relationship of attributes and brands. In our example, we see that **Brand.B** is perceived as **High-Tech** and **Innovative**, offering **Fast Internet** and a good choice of smartphones. On the other hand, it's on the opposite side of the spectrum from the attributes **Affordable**, **Values Loyal Customers**, and **Clear offer**, which are more representative of **Brand.A** and **Brand.C**. Additionally, **Brand.A** is also seen as **Trustworthy** and having professional staff, while **Brand.C** has an image of a **Youthful** and **Fair** brand that is a strong market influencer. Overall, the map helps us form a well-rounded image of how customers perceive each of the brands.

There's more...

Just as with the PCA, we can also use the positions of attributes on the plot to interpret the dimensions created by them. In our example, the y axis could be interpreted as ranging from affordable/simple offer to high-tech/innovative, while the x axis could be interpreted as being trustworthy/friendly/transparent on one pole, and youthful on the other.

See also

- If you're interested in gaining a more in-depth understanding of the correspondence analysis itself, you may want to start with this article: https://en.wikipedia.org/wiki/Correspondence_analysis
- For more information on the R ca package that we used to run the analysis, you can refer to this link: https://cran.r-project.org/web/packages/ca/index.html

Data mining with tree-based models

Classification of cases in groups is one of the most important tasks in data mining and analytics. In the previous recipe, *Clustering*, we made clusters of similar cases based on measures by letting Tableau discover groups and patterns in the data. However, there are also situations where we already have a dimension labeling certain groups in our data, and we want to create a model that will predict group membership using other fields in our dataset. For this task, we can use a tree-based model. By the end of this chapter, you'll have built a decision tree using a classification algorithm, while retaining a focus on a real-life business question.

Getting ready

In this recipe, we'll be using the `new_or_used_car.csv` dataset. It contains data on people planning to buy a car in the next 12 months. We have some demographic data on them, such as age, gender, and income, and some data about the car they're currently driving—whether it was bought as new or used and its date of manufacture. Finally, we have a dimension, `Future Purchase`, which lets us know whether they're planning to buy a new or used car.

Before we dive into the recipe, please make sure you have the `new_or_used_car.csv` dataset saved to your device.

How to do it...

1. Launch R and open a new script by selecting **File** and then **New script**.
2. In the **R Editor** window, enter the following code. Make sure to replace all of the file paths with the paths leading to the appropriate locations on your device. After pasting the paths, make sure to replace the backslashes with double backslashes, as in the following code block:

```
install.packages('rpart',repos='http://cran.us.r-project.org')
library(rpart)
cars <- read.table("C:\\!Slaven\\6 KNJIGA\\4 Advanced analytics\\4
decision tree\\new_or_used_car.csv", header=T, sep=",")
fit <- rpart(FuturePurchase ~ Age + Gender + Education +
FamilyStatus + CurrentCar + AgeOfCurrentCar + MunicipalityType,
method="class", data=cars)
plot(fit, uniform=TRUE, main="Classification of new cars buyers")
text(fit, all=TRUE, cex=.8)
```

3. Run the entire block of code by selecting it clicking the **Run** button or by pressing *Ctrl + R* on your keyboard.
4. In order to make the connection with Tableau possible, call the `Rserve` library by running the following code:

```
library(Rserve)
Rserve()
```

5. Open Tableau and connect to the `new_or_used_car.csv` dataset.

6. In the main menu toolbar, navigate to **Help** and, from the drop-down menu, select **Settings and Performance**. From the additional drop-down menu that will open, select **Manage External Service Connection**...:

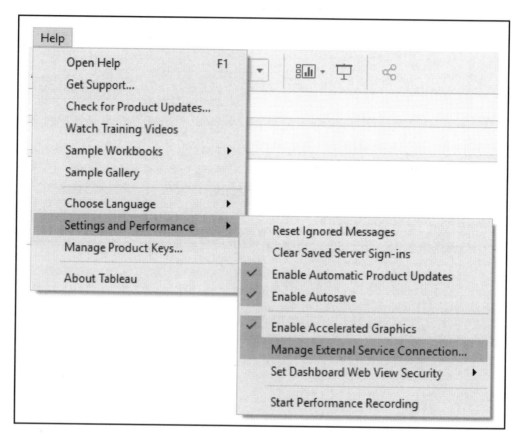

7. In the **Server** field, enter `localhost`.

8. In the **Port** field, enter `6311`.

9. Click on the **Test Connection** button:

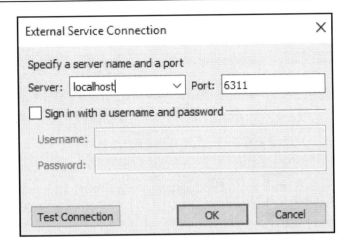

10. After receiving the message that you're successfully connected to the `RServe` service, click on **OK** to exit the notification, and then click on **OK** again to exit the **External Service Connection** window:

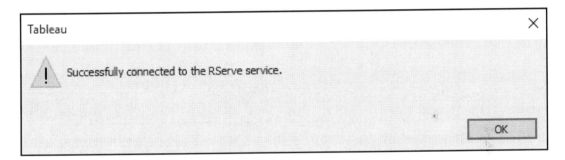

11. Open a new sheet.
12. Drag and drop **Future Purchase** from **Dimensions** into the **Columns** shelf.
13. Drag and drop **Id** from **Dimensions** onto **Tooltip** in the **Marks** card.
14. In the main menu toolbar, navigate to **Analysis** and, from the drop-down menu, select **Create Calculated Field...**.

15. Rename the new calculated field to **Prediction** and enter the following code block:

```
SCRIPT_STR
('library(rpart);
fit = rpart(FuturePurchase ~ Age + Gender + Education +
FamilyStatus + CurrentCar + AgeOfCurrentCar + MunicipalityType,
method="class",
data.frame(FuturePurchase = .arg1,
Age =.arg2,
Gender =.arg3,
Education =.arg4,
FamilyStatus =.arg5,
CurrentCar =.arg6,
AgeOfCurrentCar =.arg7,
MunicipalityType=.arg8));
io<-predict(fit, type =
"prob");colnames(io)[apply(io,1,which.max)]',
ATTR([Future Purchase]),
AVG([Age]),
ATTR([Gender]),
ATTR([Education]),
ATTR([Family Status]),
ATTR([Current Car]),
AVG([Age Of Current Car]),
ATTR([Municipality Type]))
```

16. Click **OK** to exit the calculated field window.

17. Drag and drop **Predictions** from **Measures** onto **Color** in the **Marks** card.

18. In main menu toolbar, go to **Analysis** and deselect **Aggregate Measures**.

19. In the drop-down menu, change **Standard** to **Entire View**:

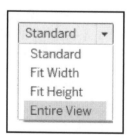

In the following screenshot, we can see that we finished our chart showing the actual and predicted classification of customers:

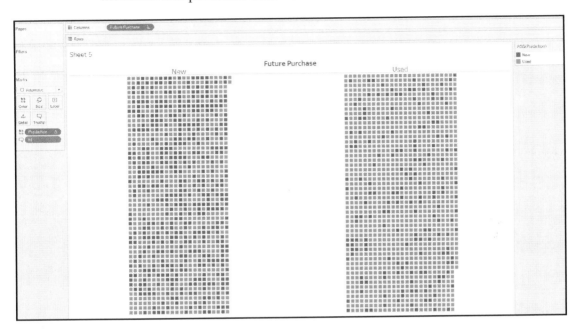

How it works...

Decision trees utilize the approach of repetitively dividing cases into smaller, more homogeneous groups. Finally, we end up with a classification tree which can be effectively visualized and easily interpreted. In our example, we're trying to answer the question based on the data we have. The question that arises is: can we effectively predict who's going to buy a new car and who's going to buy a used car? As it turns out, we can. We've created a predictive model using the previous R script, and we recorded the predicted values for each case in the new field called **Prediction**. We've then created a visualization comparing the actual values of the **Future Purchase** dimension and the values we predicted. We can clearly see that, although there are some misclassifications, our model performs pretty well!

There's more

After having developed your model, you can save it as the .rda file at your computer and reuse it with a new dataset. Let's say you receive some more data about consumers, and you want to see how many of them you can expect to go for a new car—you can just feed that data into the model you've already developed and get an estimate. For more details on how to do this, you can refer to the *Forecasting based on multiple regression* recipe in Chapter 11, *Forecasting with Tableau*.

See also

- If you're interested in learning more about tree-based models, you may want to start at the following link: https://en.wikipedia.org/wiki/Decision_tree_learning#General
- For more information about the rpart library we used in this recipe, start here: https://cran.r-project.org/web/packages/rpart/rpart.pdf

Identifying anomalies in data

When analyzing data we'll frequently encounter unusual cases, outliers, and anomalies. Those cases are different from the majority and they don't match the pattern that the rest of the cases fit in. Sometimes, we might want to identify them in order to remove them from the analysis, because they can skew our results. In other cases, we might be interested in analyzing them. Either way, it's very important to know how to deal with them properly. In Chapter 11, *Forecasting with Tableau*, the *Forecasting on a dataset with outliers* recipe taught up how to deal with outliers on one dimension, which is relatively simple. But when we have more than one dimension, things get much more complicated. In this recipe, we'll learn how to deal with multidimensional outliers.

Getting ready

In our recipe, we'll use a dataset from a health study of blood pressure, `age_and_blood_pressure.csv`. It contains information on the age of participants and their blood pressure. Before we begin, make sure you have the dataset saved to your device.

How to do it...

1. Start R, open a new script and run the following code block:

```
install.packages('mvoutlier',repos='http://cran.us.r-project.org')
library(Rserve)
Rserve()
```

2. Open Tableau and connect to the `age_and_blood_pressure.csv` file.

3. In the main menu toolbar, navigate to **Help** and, from the drop-down menu, select **Settings and Performance**. From the additional drop-down menu that will open, choose **Manage External Service Connection...**.

4. In the **Server** field, enter `localhost`.

5. In the **Port** field, enter `6311`.

6. Click on the **Test Connection** button.

7. After receiving a message that you're successfully connected to the `RServe` service, click on **OK** to close the notification, and then click on **OK** again to exit the **External Service Connection** window.

8. Drag and drop **Age** from **Measures** into the **Columns** shelf.

9. Drag and drop **Blood Pressure** from **Measures** into the **Rows** shelf.

10. In the main menu toolbar, navigate to **Analysis** and, from the drop-down menu, select **Create Calculated Field...**.

11. Rename the new calculated field `Outliers` and enter the following code:

```
IF SCRIPT_REAL("library(mvoutlier);sign2(cbind(.arg1,
.arg2))$wfinal01", AVG([Age]), AVG([Blood Pressure])) == 0 THEN
"Outlier" ELSE "OK" END
```

12. In the main menu toolbar, navigate to **Analysis** and, in the drop-down menu, deselect **Aggregate Measures**.

13. Drag and drop **Outliers** from **Measures** onto **Color** in the **Marks** card. Our chart clearly shows the multidimensional outliers now, as shown in the following screenshot:

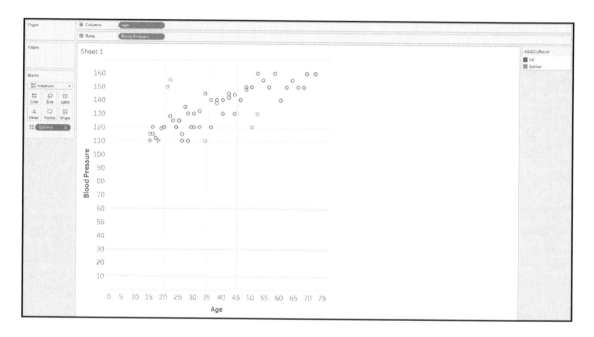

How it works...

In this recipe, we created a scatter plot showing the multidimensional outliers. We did this because, sometimes, we can't simply isolate outliers on each dimension. Multivariate outliers are defined by their position on more than one variable, so it is important to observe them simultaneously. Certain cases don't have to be outliers on any one of the dimensions considered separately but are outliers if we observe their pattern of values on multiple dimensions.

In our example, we've flagged two people with a respective blood pressure of 150 and 155 as outliers, circled in the following screenshot:

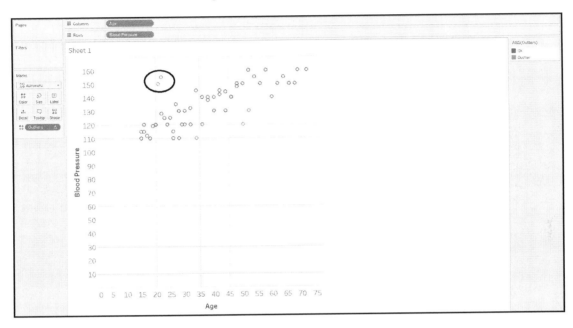

However, these values of **Blood pressure** do not make them extreme—there are some subjects with much higher blood pressure. With reference to the preceding screenshot, we can see that other subjects who have blood pressure this high are also considerably older than the ones we marked—they are in their forties, or older, while our two flagged cases are in their early twenties! We can see that their peers have much lower blood pressure. So, while neither the values of **Blood pressure** nor the values of **Age** taken in isolation make this two cases extreme, when considered together, we see that these two subjects are unusual because they have unusually high blood pressure for their age. The opposite is true for other flagged cases—they are flagged because they have unusually low blood pressure for their (older) age. So, had we done a simple, one-dimensional, outlier analysis, we would have never detected these unusual cases.

There's more...

To keep our example clear and illustrative, we used a two-dimensional dataset (and two-dimensional outliers). However, you'll usually deal with datasets that have more than two dimensions. Nevertheless, the general approach you'll use to detect the multidimensional outliers will be the same. You can use the same syntax as the one we've used in this example, but simply add as many arguments as needed. The script will run in the same manner and detect the outliers.

However, when operating with more than two dimensions, you won't be able to visualize the multidimensional outliers on a scatter plot as easily, since the pattern of values that makes them extreme is spread across various dimensions. If you wish to represent them visually, you can check out the `uniplot` function (https://www.rdocumentation.org/packages/mvoutlier/versions/2.0.9/topics/uni.plot) from the `mvoutlier` package in R, which allows you to unfold the pattern of values into a series of unidimensional projections. Although it isn't as neat as Tableau visualizations, it'll provide some insight on how the outlier values can be interpreted.

See also

- To find out more about the `mvoutlier` package we used in this chapter and the detection of multivariate outliers in general, visit this page: https://cran.r-project.org/web/packages/mvoutlier/index.html.

13
Deploy Tableau Server

.In this chapter, we will cover the following recipes:

- Deploying Tableau Server in Windows
- Deploying to Tableau Server
- Deploying Tableau Server on Linux using AWS
- Getting started with Tabcmd

Technical requirements

There are multiple ways available to get the Tableau Server, namely:

- Deploy on-premise
- Deploy on cloud using AWS, Azure, or Google Cloud Platform
- Get a preconfigured Tableau Server at the Cloud Marketplace
- Use Tableau Online

In our case, we will be using AWS, and we will deploy Tableau Server on top of an EC2 instance, to get the advantage and flexibility of the cloud, and to demonstrate the main concepts of Tableau Server.

We will use the same AWS account as we used in `Chapter 10`, *Tableau for Big Data*. We should launch EC2 instances for both Linux and Windows.

Introduction

Tableau Server is a core element of any analytical solution. It helps to share insights across organizations and allows end users to access enterprise data. It is secure and scalable. Moreover, the recently released Tableau Server is available on Windows and Linux.

It is good to know how Tableau licesing their Server. There are two options available:

- User-based - you need license for every user who access Tableau Server. In addition, user based licnes has different options such as Viewer, Exploer and Creater.
- Core-based - you license total number of cores for your entire Tableau Server implementation.

When you start to plan your Tableau Server implementation, you shoud start from planning hardware and licesnes based on business needs, such as:

- How many users does your organization have?
- How fast does your organization grow?
- What is the level of Tableau knowledge of users?
- How big is your Data Warehouse?
- and so on.

You might learn more about license types here `https://onlinehelp.tableau.com/ current/server/en-us/license_server_overview.htm`. It is applicable for Linux and Windows implementations. In addition, you may leran about the prices for license: https://www.tableau.com/pricing/teams-orgs.

This chapter will guide you through the Tableau Server deployment on both Linux and Windows to give you an idea of the differences. In addition, it will cover key concepts of Tableau Server and best practices of deployment using AWS.

Deploying Tableau Server in Windows

In this recipe, we will learn how to self-deploy Tableau Server on AWS using Windows. Self-deploy offers the most flexibility in security, scaling, and capacity. Also, the total cost of ownership and the amount of time to deploy in the cloud versus on-premise solutions should be much less.

Getting ready

To complete this recipe, please have an AWS account and the Tableau Server product key.

For a single production instance, please be prepared to build an EC2 instance using the recommended resource requirements:

- Windows Server 2012 R2, 64-bit or Windows Server 2016, 64-bit
- 16+ vCPU
- 64+ GB RAM (4 GB RAM per vCPU)
- 30-50 GB for the the OS
- 100+ GB for Tableau Server
- EBS Storage type (SSD (gp2) or provisioned IOPS)
- Less than or equal to 20 milliseconds

 The minimum hardware requirements are 64-bit processor, 16 vCPU, 32 GB RAM, 50 GB disk space. If the server does not have the minimum hardware requirements you will not be able to install Tableau Server.

How to do it...

To begin the recipe, we need to log into AWS and take the following steps:

1. Create a **Virtual Private Cloud** (**VPC**).
2. Navigate to the Amazon VPC console.

3. Click on **Launch VPC Wizard**, as follows:

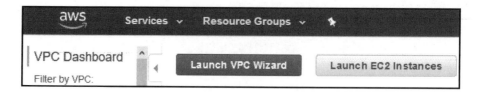

4. Select **VPC with a Single Public Subnet**, as follows:

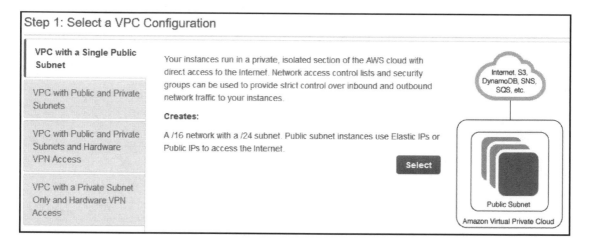

Note: When we are creating VPC we should make sure, that we have Public Subnet with Internet Gateway and Router table. Otherwsise, you will be able access Tableau Server GUI only from VPC. You can read more about this at AWS documentation: `https://docs.aws.amazon.com/vpc/latest/userguide/what-is-amazon-vpc.html`. In this chapter, we didn't focus on creating Internet access for the server and used RDP and Private DNS to access Tableau Server.

5. Give the VPC a name and click **Create VPC**, as follows:

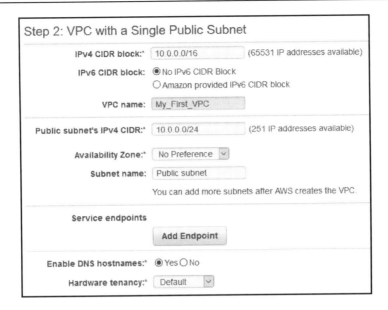

6. We will see our VPC created, as follows:

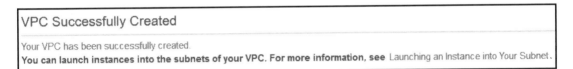

7. The next step will be to configure the networking and security. To configure networking and security, we will use the following steps:
   - Go to the EC2 console.
   - Ensure your region is in the same location as the VPC we just created.
   - Click **Security Groups** in the **Navigation** pane.
   - Click on **Create Security Group**.
   - Fill in the security group name, description, and select the VPC we created in the previous steps, as follows:

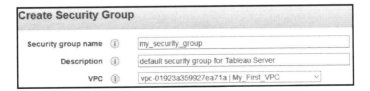

8. Create the inbound rules, by clicking on **Add Rule**, as follows:

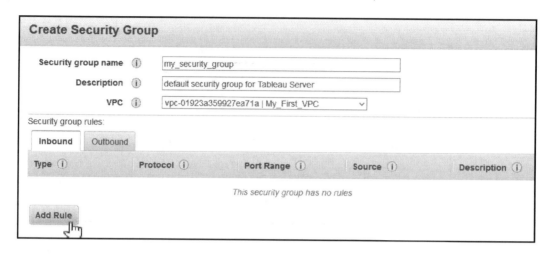

9. Create the inbound traffic rules for **HTTP**, **HTTPS**, and **RDP**. Then, click on **Create**, as follows:

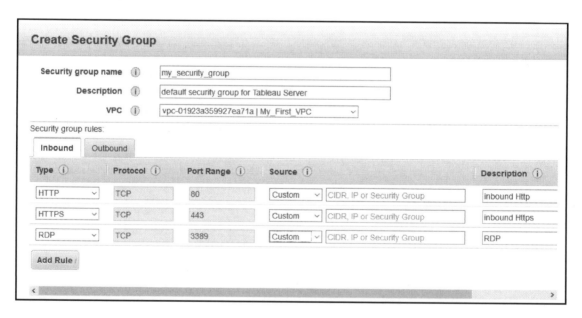

10. Use **Custom** to specify an IP range or another security group. For production environments, it is important to limit who has access to your environment. In addition, we should add SSH port 22 for the Linux environment. Finally, we need to add port 8850 for the Tableau Service Manager (TSM) web interface.
11. Launch an Amazon EC2 instance.
12. Navigate to the EC2 console.
13. Verify you are in the same region as the VPC created previously.
14. Under **Create Instance**, Click on **Launch Instance**, as follows:

15. Select an Amazon Machine image for Windows Server 2012 R2, 64-bit or Windows Server 2016, 64-bit, as follows:

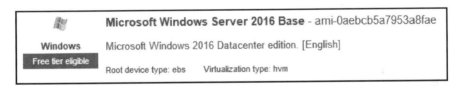

16. Within the **Choose an Instance Type** menu, scroll down to select an instance that meets the recommended requirement for Tableau Server: 16+ vCPU and 64+ GB RAM (4 GB RAM per vCPU), as follows:

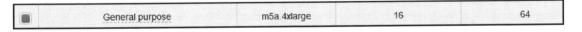

Installing Tableau on Amazon EC2 T2 instances are not supported. Typical environment types and sizes for development, test, and production are as follows: c5.4xlarge, m5.4xlarge, r5.4xlarge

17. Configure the instance type by choosing the VPC created in the previous steps, as follows:

1. Choose AMI	2. Choose Instance Type	3. Configure Instance	4. Add Storage	5. Add Tags	6. Configure Security Group	7. Review

Step 3: Configure Instance Details

Configure the instance to suit your requirements. You can launch multiple instances from the same AMI, request Spot instances to take advantage of

Number of instances	1	Launch into Auto Scaling Group
Purchasing option	☐ Request Spot instances	
Network	vpc-01923a359927ea71a | My_First_VPC ˅	C Create new VPC
Subnet	subnet-00be4dd887e442110 | Public subnet | us-ea ˅ 251 IP Addresses available	Create new subnet
Auto-assign Public IP	Use subnet setting (Disable) ˅	
Placement group	☐ Add instance to placement group	
Capacity Reservation	Open ˅	C Create new Capacity Reservation
Domain join directory	No directory	C Create new directory
IAM role	None ˅	C Create new IAM role
CPU options	☐ Specify CPU options	
Shutdown behavior	Stop ˅	
Enable termination protection	☐ Protect against accidental termination	
Monitoring	☐ Enable CloudWatch detailed monitoring Additional charges apply.	
EBS-optimized instance	☑ Launch as EBS-optimized instance	

18. Add another 100 GB of storage as a separate drive. You may have to partition and mount this drive, as follows:

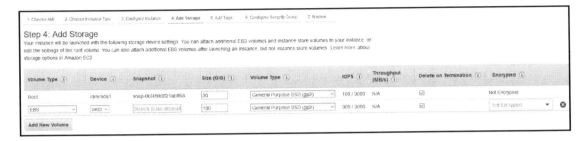

19. In the **Configure Security Group** menu, choose the security group we created in the previous recipe steps, as follows:

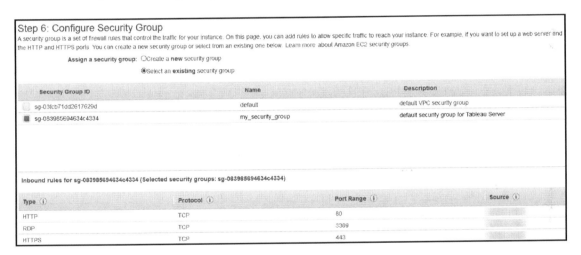

20. Review the instance you created and then launch it.

21. Create a key pair file (or use an existing one). We need to create this `.pem` file in order to log in to the server remotely, as follows:

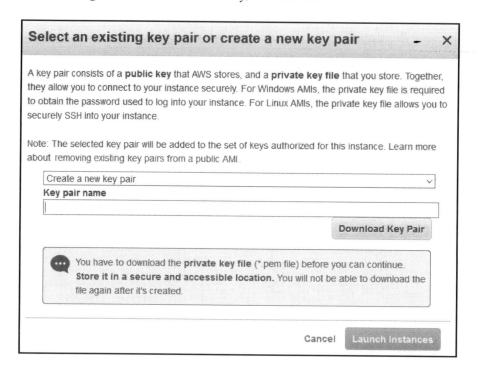

22. It can take a few minutes to launch the instance. While it is initializing, copy the instance ID for the next step, as follows:

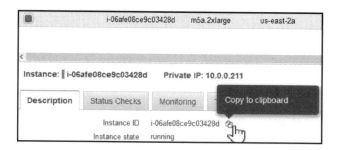

23. Create an elastic IP address for the VPC:

- Navigate to the Amazon VPC console
- Use the same region as the VPC created in earlier steps
- In the **Navigation** pane, choose elastic IP, as follows:

24. Click on the **Allocate new address** button and then click on **Allocate** in the next screen, as follows:

25. Once created, click on the **Actions** menu, and select **Associate address**, as follows:

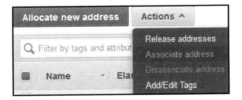

26. In the **Associate address** window, choose the **Instance** resource type and the server/instance you created in the earlier steps, as follows:

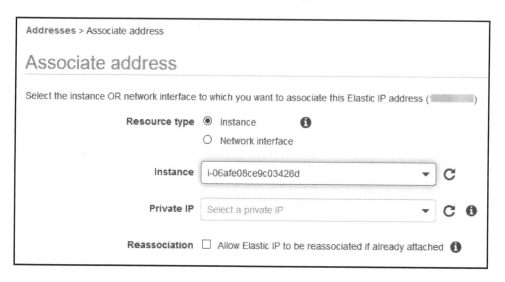

27. Log into Amazon EC2 using remote desktop:
    - Navigate to the EC2 console.
    - Select the region where we launched the instance.
    - In the EC2 dashboard, click on Instances.
    - Select the instance, click on **Actions**, and choose **Connect**, as follows:

28. In the **Connect To Your Instance** dialog box, click on **Download Remote Desktop File**.
29. Click on **Get Password** and select the .pem file created earlier.
30. Click on **Decrypt Password**, when it's displayed copy it and keep it, as follows:

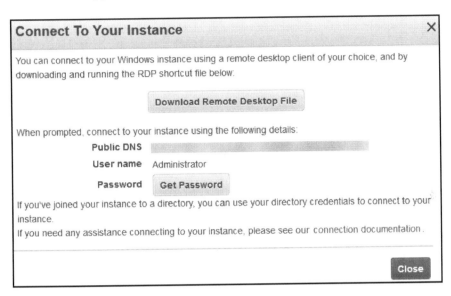

31. Log in using the .rdp file saved earlier and ignore any messages or warnings about unknown publishers or unknown connections.
32. Install Tableau Server as follows:
    - Download the installer for Tableau Server 2019.x and save it locally
    - For a single node, guided install, double-click on the installer and follow the instructions to create a new Tableau Server installation. Rather than installing onto the C drive, it is best practice to install the application on a separate drive. We added this in the previous steps for setting up an EC2 instance

33. Once Tableau Server has been installed, you must use an account with local administrator rights to run **Tableau Services Manager** (**TSM**) Web UI, and CLI tools. Follow the guided instructions to activate and register Tableau Server. Go through the following setups in the following screenshot:

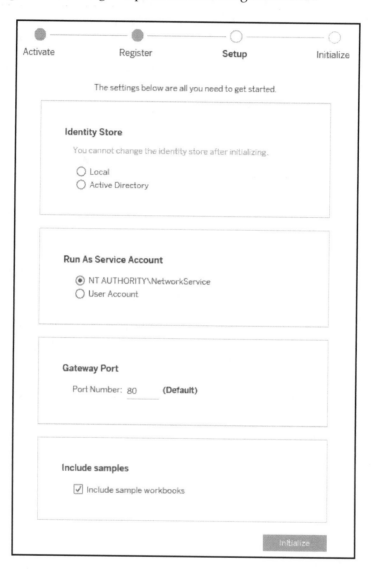

34. Click

35. on **Initialize**:

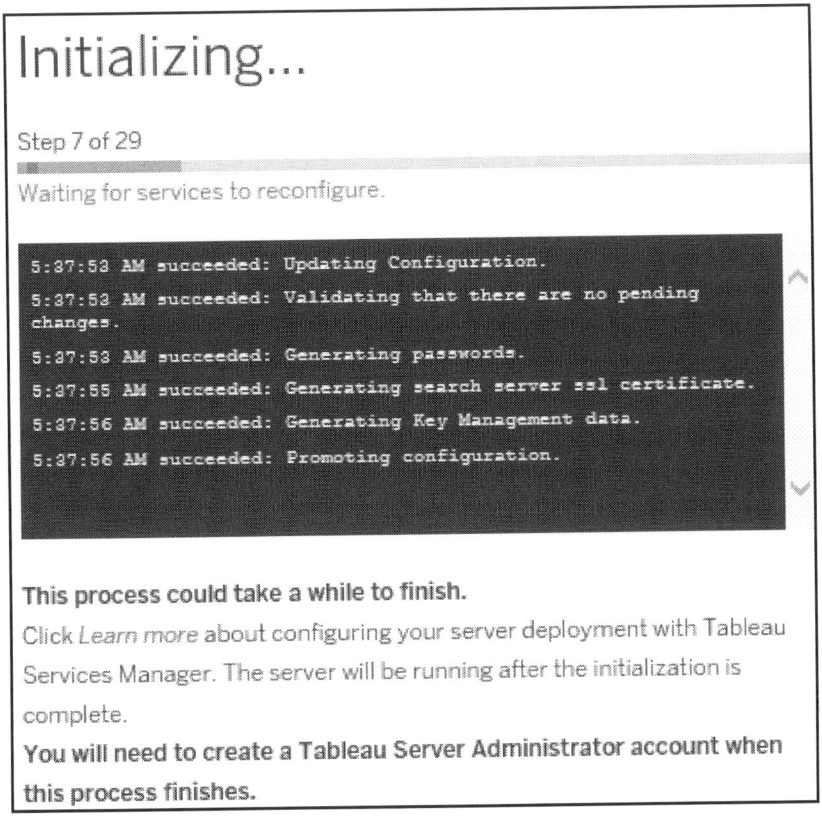

Initializing...

Step 7 of 29

Waiting for services to reconfigure.

```
5:37:53 AM succeeded: Updating Configuration.
5:37:53 AM succeeded: Validating that there are no pending
changes.
5:37:53 AM succeeded: Generating passwords.
5:37:55 AM succeeded: Generating search server ssl certificate.
5:37:56 AM succeeded: Generating Key Management data.
5:37:56 AM succeeded: Promoting configuration.
```

This process could take a while to finish.

Click *Learn more* about configuring your server deployment with Tableau
Services Manager. The server will be running after the initialization is
complete.

**You will need to create a Tableau Server Administrator account when
this process finishes.**

36. Click on **Continue**:

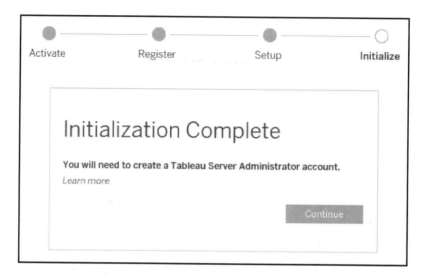

37. Create a tableau administrator account, as follows:

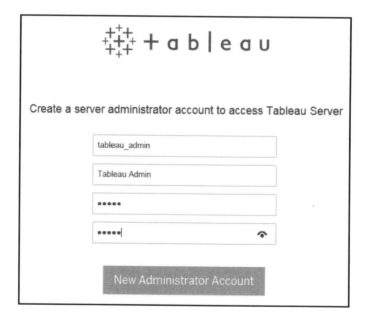

Note: By default, Tableau will using Local Authentification method. However for the Production purpose it is good to use another authentification methods such as AD, Kerberos and so on. You might learn more about it using Tableau documentation: `https://onlinehelp.` `tableau.com/current/server/en-us/security_auth.htm`. You may use TSM CLI or TSM GUI in order to setup authentification method and you should do it during initializing of Tableau Server. You can't switch later to another method.

38. You can validate the install by going to the built-in administrative views in Tableau, as follows:

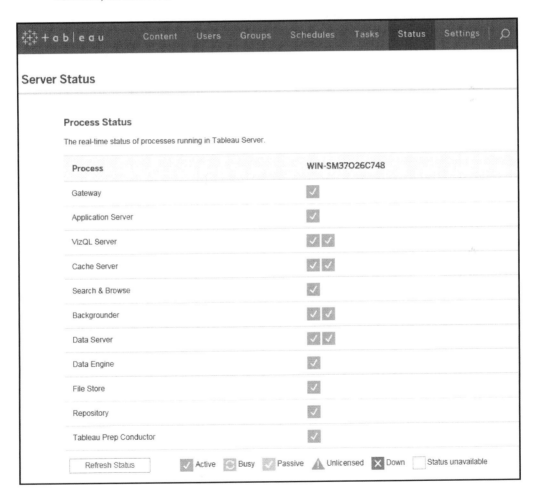

Note: This is default Tableau Server configuration for Single node. You may increase number of backgrounders, for example if you have enought capasity. This is advance topic and it depends on organization needs. You may learn more about sizing of Tableau Server in White Paper Tableau Server Scalability - A Technical Deployment Guide for Server Administrators
Read more at https://www.tableau.com/learn/whitepapers/tableau-server-scalability-technical-deployment-guide-server-administrators#OcvXkMS7csDuTIRu.99

How it works...

With AWS we created the infrastructure and server we needed for Tableau Server. We created a virtual private cloud with a private subnet. We created a security group within our VPC, so we can accept web requests and remote desktop into the server. We configured an EC2 instance and launched it. Next, we downloaded the Tableau Server installer and executed it. We used the new TSM to configure Tableau Server.

There's more...

We can use an automated installer SilentInstaller.py. It's written in Python and community supported. Automated installers are great to use when you need multiple servers or environments to have the same configuration. See Tableau's online help for more instructions at https://onlinehelp.tableau.com/current/server/en-us/automated_install_windows.htm.

In addition, we want to mention TSM. It is a new feature that was introduced with version 2018 R2 on Windows and with version 10.5 on Linux. It serves the configuration and administration purpose of Tableau Server. You can learn more about TSM here:

- **Windows**: https://onlinehelp.tableau.com/current/server/en-us/tsm_overview.htm.
- **Linux**: https://onlinehelp.tableau.com/current/server-linux/en-us/tsm_overview.htm.

The downside of this tool is, that if you have Tableau Server without TSM (older version) and want to upgrade, you have to install Tableau Server and install a fresh copy of new version with TSM, as explained here:

`https://onlinehelp.tableau.com/current/server/en-us/sug_pretsm_to_tsm.htm.`

Read more about coordination services and configuring processes in the second and third nodes in the online Tableau help document at `https://onlinehelp.tableau.com/current/ server/en-us/distrib_ha_install_3node.htm.`

See also

There are other methods that we can use to install Tableau Server. One way is to build a clustered environment. This architecture is great for systems that have 24 hours service level requirements or to optimize performance.

This recipe assumes you've stood up the correct architecture components in AWS and followed the best practice guidelines for network security and load-balancing:

1. When installing Tableau on the first node (referred to as instance 1), use the **Create new Tableau Server installation** option. When installing Tableau Server on the redundant nodes (referred to as instance 2), click on the additional node to existing Tableau Server cluster option, as follows:

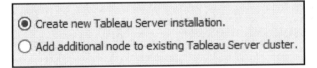

2. Create a bootstrap file from instance 1, by logging into the TSM.

3. Go to **Configuration** and click on **Download Bootstrap File**, as follows:

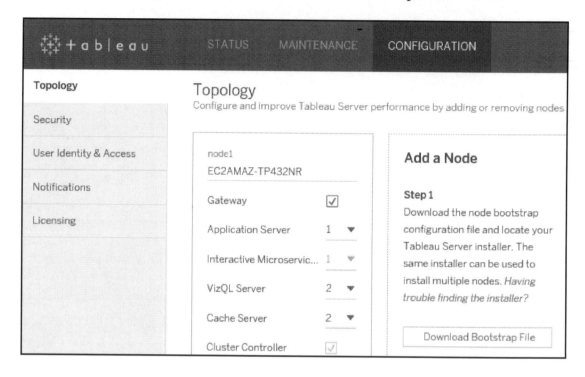

4. Copy the `bootstrap.json` file to instance 2, execute the installer, and fill in the node configuration as follows:

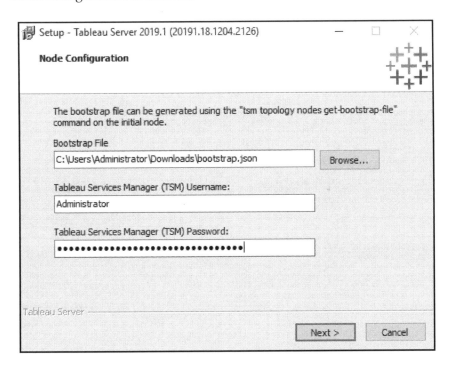

5. When prompted, log in to the TSM and you will see a message showing that node 2 was added to the cluster. Click on **Continue**. Take a look at the **Pending Changes** and **Apply Changes** tabs and click on **Restart** and then **Confirm**, as follows:

6. If you install a total of three or more nodes, you should also deploy a co-ordination service ensemble.

Read more about Coordination Services and configuration processes in the second and third nodes in the online Tableau help document. There are more materials about high availability and redundancy in the online Tableau help document. https://onlinehelp.tableau.com/current/server/en-us/distrib_ha _install_3node.htm

Deploying to Tableau Server

In this recipe, we illustrate how to configure our newly configured Tableau Server for security and usability. Tableau Server is the most secure way of sharing insights at an enterprise level. Users sign in with a login and each user must have permission to view or work with content. We will build a framework for content management.

Getting ready

Have a Tableau workbook and the Tableau Server URL ready.

To set up the framework for your users correctly, we need to be grounded in the following three concepts:

- **Groups**: Sets of users who have the same access. It's best practice to set permissions at the group level and assign users to the group. Also, it is recommended that a user belong to one group as best practice for better user manageability.
- **Projects**: Folders and sub-folders for workbooks and data sources. It's recommended to separate content by role, function, or audience.
- **Permissions**: The actions that can be executed on the server and what they can impact.

How to do it...

In this recipe, we will create some projects, groups, users, and set permissions.

1. Create two new projects, one for `Marketing` and `Finance`, by navigating to **Create | Project**, as follows:

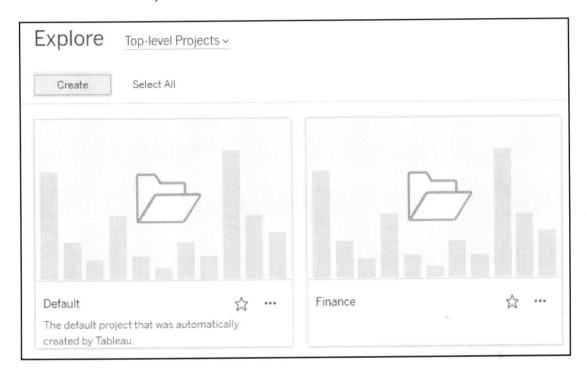

2. Create the following three groups for **Finance** as shown in the following screenshot:

- Owner
- Developers
- Viewers

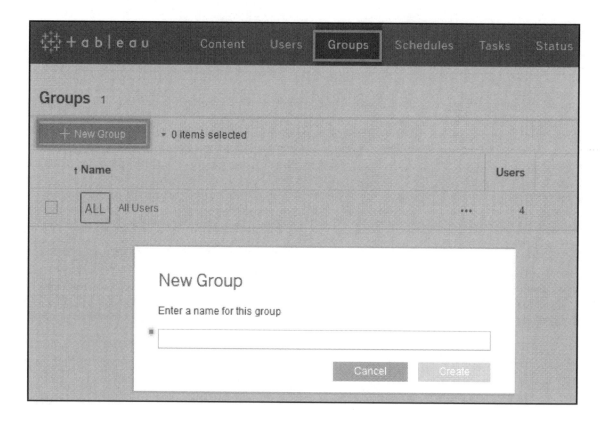

3. We create the following five local users:
   - Lisa: `Finance Site Administrator Creator`
   - Mike: `Finance Explorer(publish)`
   - Eric: `Finance Explorer(publish)`
   - John: `Finance Viewer`
   - Satu: `Finance Viewer`

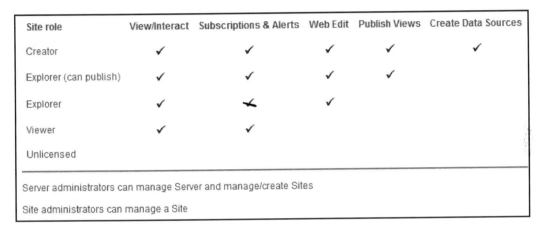

Site role	View/Interact	Subscriptions & Alerts	Web Edit	Publish Views	Create Data Sources
Creator	✓	✓	✓	✓	✓
Explorer (can publish)	✓	✓	✓	✓	
Explorer	✓	✗	✓		
Viewer	✓	✓			
Unlicensed					

Server administrators can manage Server and manage/create Sites

Site administrators can manage a Site

4. Add those users to their respective groups. We are considering developers are those who can publish views and data source.

5. Within the **Content** page, add the groups to their respective projects by clicking on the ellipse and selecting **Permissions**, as follows:

6. Add the groups to the projects and assign each group with the permissions roles. These roles act as a template to help make setup easier. To see each capability, expand the section. The permissions we set allow the content developers to manage all assets in their project, whereas the viewers can only view what's been published, as shown in the following screenshot:

New in 2019.1, we have the ability to manage Tableau Prep flows via Tableau Prep Conductor.

7. Lock the permissions so that content publishers cannot deviate from the default permissions we set on the server, as follows:

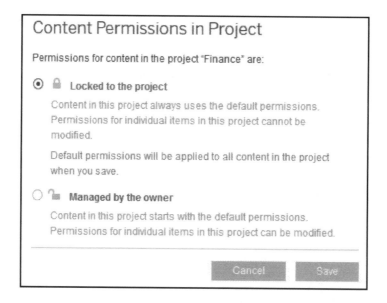

Because we made these test users, we can try publishing to the server using one account with those permissions; we can also try publishing to the server using an account without publishing access.

8. In Tableau Developer, open the **Superstore** sample workbook and go to the **Server** menu and select **Publish Workbook...** as follows:

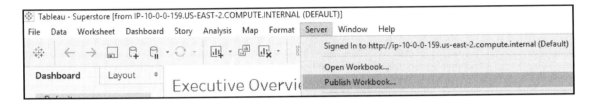

9. Publish this to the **Finance** project, as follows:

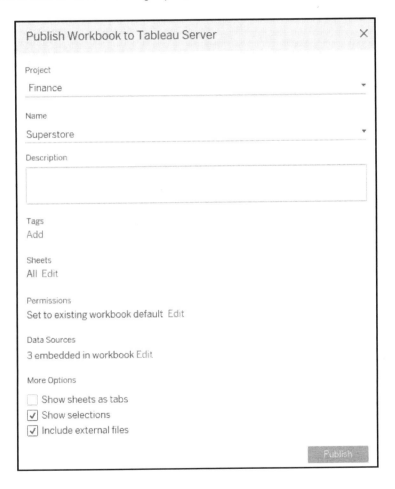

10. In Prep, open a sample flow from the beta site and go to the **Server** menu and select Publish Flow, as follows:

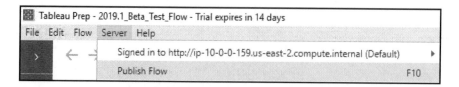

11. Publish this to the **Finance** project, as follows:

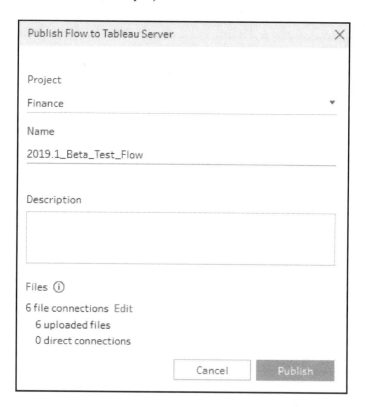

12. Log into the server to access the published content. Try this as different users.

How it works...

We created a project for our **Finance** team and created groups based on the activities of the users. In our prototype exercise, we created users and added these users to each group. Next, we assigned permission templates to the groups at the project level. Finally, we locked the permissions to ensure our model stays intact. We illustrated that the permissions worked by uploading one of the sample workbooks and sample flows to the server.

There's more...

There are some items to be aware of for permissions. You can only assign permissions to content. Individual permissions will take priority over any group permissions. Every user is added in the All Users group. It's important to delete this group so it doesn't cause conflicts with the other group permissions.

See also

A big part of server administration is monitoring and tuning an environment. It is important to ensure that Tableau Server is healthy. Tableau has published a great guide for setting up notifications, monitoring, and tuning. Refer to `https://onlinehelp.tableau.com/current/guides/everybody-install/en-us/everybody_admin_monitor.htm`.

Deploying Tableau Server on Linux using AWS

For a long time Tableau Server was available only for Windows platforms. But with the Tableau version 10.5 there was an introduction of Tableau Server on Linux. Basically, now you have more flexibility with Tableau Server. Some organizations prefer Windows, whereas others consider only Linux. In addition, it depends on the culture of the organization and the available resources to maintain and support Linux or Windows servers. For sure, using a cloud environment will simplify this.

Tableau Server on Linux makes Tableau products more agnostic. Moreover, it increases the security of deployment and decreases the cost of ownership.

Getting ready

In this recipe, will will download the last available Tableau Server for Linux and deploy it in our AWS account on top of EC2 Linux Instance.

We can use the same VPC that we used for the Windows recipe, or we can deploy new from scratch. In this recipe we will:

- Launch EC2 Linux instance
- Download Tableau Server for Linux distribution
- Install Tableau Server and access it via SSH

Before you start, you also may refer to *Everybody's Install Guide*, which will give you a more detailed explanation behind the server installation at https://onlinehelp.tableau.com/current/guides/everybody-install-linux/en-us/everybody_admin_intro.htm.

How to do it...

Let's start our journey. This process should be straightforward and I hope you have some Linux experience. We are going to use CLI. We can choose from Ubuntu, **Red Hat Enterprise Linux** (RHEL), CentOS 7, Amazon Linux 2, and Oracle Linux. You should check with the documentation before installing in order to use the last available version of Linux that supports Tableau.

For our purpose we will use RHEL, but you can choose any other Linux distribution. Let's do it:

1. Log in to AWS and go to the EC2 dashboard. In the previous recipe, we created VPC and a security group that we will use for this recipe as well.
2. Now, we need to launch EC2 with RHEL 7. Go to the Amazon EC2 Console and under **Create Instance**, click on **Launch Instance**.
3. Select an **Amazon Machine Image (AMI)** that will meet your performance requirements. In our case, I will use m4.xlarge. It has 16 GB RAM and it should be enough for learning purposes. You can refer to Tableau recommendation documentation at https://onlinehelp.tableau.com/current/server-linux/en-us/ts_aws_virtual_machine_selection.htm.

We should create EC2 in the same region as we created VPC.

4. Then we should configure the instance details, as follows:

Network	My_First_VPC
Storage Size	100 GiB
Security Group	my_security_group

5. Then click on **Launch**. It will allow you to create a key pair or use an existing one. We need this for SSH to our Linux box, where we can download and install Tableau Server.

6. Let's create a static Elastic IP for our EC2 instance. We should navigate to the Amazon VPC console, go to **Elastic IP**, and click **Allocate new address**. Use all settings by default. Then, we need to associate our new Elastic IP with our EC2 instance. As a result, our EC2 instance got new IPs that we will use for connection to the host. You can refer to the following screenshot for clarity:

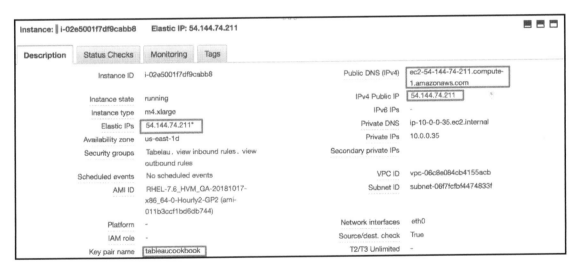

7. Next, we should SSH to our Linux box. If you are using macOS or Linux, then you can use CLI, but if you are using Windows, you should use Putty. In our case, we are using macOS and will open Terminal. We need to use our private key and execute the following commands:

```
cd ~/.ssh
chmod 400 tableaucookbook.pem
ssh -i ~/.ssh/tableaucookbook.pem ec2-
user@ec2-54-144-74-211.compute-1.amazonaws.com
```

Here the following commands are elaborated as follows:

- `ec2-user`: This represents the default user
- `tableaucookbook.pem`: This is from our key pair
- `ec2-54-144-74-211.compute-1.amazonaws.com`: This represents the public DNS of our EC2 instance

Now, we can install Tableau Server.

8. Let's download the installation file from Tableau Server. We could use the last available version of Tableau Server 2019.x. From the CLI, execute the following commands:

```
sudo yum update
sudo yum install wget
wget
"https://downloads.tableau.com/esdalt/2018.3.2/tableau-server-<tabl
eau version>.x86_64.rpm"
```

Here, you replace `<tableau version>` in order to specify the version of Tableau Server, for example 2019-1-1.

9. Then we can install Tableau Server. Execute the following command:

```
sudo yum install tableau-server-<tableau version>.x86_64.rpm
```

This will install you server very fast, much faster and easier than on the Windows platform!

10. The next step is the same as usual. We should initialize `tsm` and `accepteula`, as follows:

```
cd /opt/tableau/tableau_server/packages/scripts.<code version>/
sudo ./initialize-tsm --accepteula
```

It will create the `tsmadmin` group for admin authorization, create a Tableau user account, and set permissions. In addition, it will add our Linux `ec2-user` to the Tableau security groups `tableau` and `tsmadmin`. In addition, it initializes a web interface for the GUI and a REST API, and will provide a link to it. But this link will have private IP and we won't be able access it from the internet. We should use a public DNS instead.

11. In addition, we should create password for our `ec2-user`, as follows:

```
sudo passwd ec2-user
```

The preceding command will prompt us to enter a new password for the user. If you don't know what the admin user is, you can run the following command:

```
grep tsmadmin /etc/group
tsmadmin:x:994:ec2-user
```

We've created a password for this user and may use it for authentication.

12. Let's activate **Tableau Server Trial** and log in to TSM. Before you should re-log in to the EC2, as follows:

```
tsm login -u ec2-user
tsm licenses activate -t
```

13. Next we should register Tableau Server by generating JSON and send it to Tableau. In addition, we will add text editor for Linux: `nano`, as follows:

```
sudo yum install nano
tsm register --template > /tmp/tableaucookbook.json
```

Fill the file with your information, as follows:

```
{
  "zip" : "V1R2P5",
  "country" : "Canada",
  "city" : "Victoria",
  "last_name" : "Anoshin",
  "industry" : "Dmitry",
  "eula" : "yes",
  "title" : "Boss",
```

```
"phone" : "2508919300",
"company" : "Amazon",
"state" : "BC",
"department" : "Engineering",
"first_name" : "Dmitry",
"email" : "dmitry.anoshin@example.com"
}
```

14. Then execute the following command:

```
tsm register --file /tmp/tableaucookbook.json
```

You should get the message: `Registration Complete`.

15. Then we will configure `Identity Store` in order to specify the authentication method. We will use the `local` authentication. Let's create the script with config, as follows:

```
sudo nano /tmp/auth.json
{
"configEntities":{
"identityStore": {
  "_type": "identityStoreType",
  "type": "local"
  }
 }
}
```

16. Then we will import setting to Tableau, as follows:

```
tsm settings import -f /tmp/auth.json
```

If you need any other option, you can check templates here:

https://onlinehelp.tableau.com/current/server-linux/en-us/entity_
identity_store.htm

In addition we can configure SMTP (mail server), SSL, and so on. Moreover, we can use the TSM GUI and enter all these settings much more simply.

17. Let's apply changes, as follows:

```
tsm pending-changes apply
Starting deployments asynchronous job.
Job id is '1', timeout is 10 minutes.
6% - Retrieving the topology to deploy.
13% - Retrieving the configuration to deploy.
20% - Validating the new topology.
```

```
26% - Determining if server needs to be started.
33% - Disabling all services.
40% - Waiting for the services to stop.
46% - Updating nodes to new topology.
53% - Waiting for topology to be applied.
60% - Updating nodes to new configuration.
66% - Disabling all services.
73% - Waiting for the services to stop.
80% - Reconfiguring services.
86% - Waiting for services to reconfigure.
93% - Enabling all services.
100% - Waiting for the services to start.
Successfully deployed nodes with updated configuration and topology
version.
```

18. Then initialize the server by executing the following command line:

    ```
    tsm initialize --start-server --request-timeout 1800
    ```

    This process will take a while.

19. The final step is to add initial `Administrator` account. We will use `tabmcd` for this purpose, as follows:

    ```
    tabcmd initialuser --server localhost:80 --username 'Administrator'
    ```

    It will ask for passwords. We should get the following output:

    ```
    ===== redirecting to http://localhost/auth
    ===== Signed out
    ===== Creating new session
    ===== Server: http://localhost:80
    ===== Username: Administrator
    ===== Connecting to the server...
    ===== Signing in...
    ===== Succeeded
    ```

    As a result, we've got the `Administrator` account for Tableau Server and we can access it through the web.

20. Before moving to another topic, I want to highlight internal system reports for Tableau Server. Click on **Status** and scroll down.

This list of reports is created on top of Tableau Repository based on PostgreSQL. You can learn more about reports here: `https://onlinehelp.tableau.com/current/server/en-us/adminview_bucket.htm`

How it works...

We just finished the installation of Tableau Server on Linux. In order to access Tableau Server, we will go to the Windows EC2 client, open a browser, and type Private DNS of Linux EC2, as shown in the following screenshot:

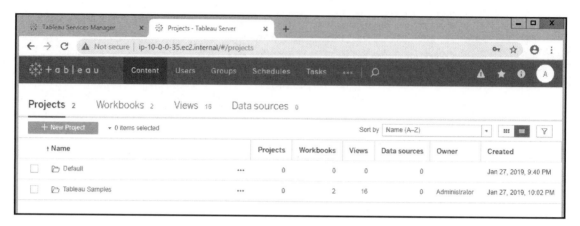

Here, `http://ip-10-0-0-35.ec2.internal/#/projects` is the private DNS of our server. In addition, we have a public DNS that can be used for accessing the Tableau Server, but we should make additional network settings.

In the following screenshot, you can see my current AWS account:

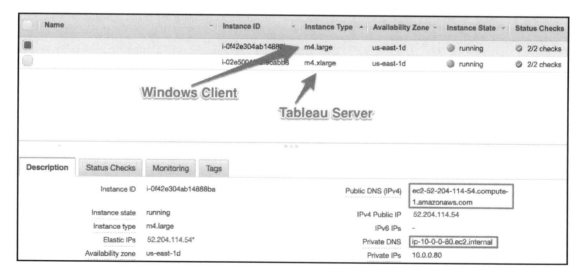

I highlighted the Public DNS that I am using for the RDP client and the Private DNS for internal usage, as well as a private IP.

There's more…

For the production version, you should consider using **Elastic Load Balancer** (**ELB**) that will serve as an end point for the Tableau Server. In addition, you can upload SSL certificates to ELB and make your connection secure. Finally, you can use the ELB logging option and collect web logs.

You can run Tableau Server on Linux with a distributed environment. There is good example of it at Tableau documentation, which can be found here:

`https://onlinehelp.tableau.com/current/server-linux/en-us/ts_aws_multiple_server.htm`.

See also

Before moving to the next recipe, I want to highlight one more useful option for you server. You can simply customize your server's appearance by adding your logo and company name. You should use this resource:

`https://onlinehelp.tableau.com/current/server/en-us/cli_customize.htm`

We have started to work with AWS and we have touched on a lot of AWS concepts. There are a couple of great AWS whitepapers you can refer to:

- *Architecting for the Cloud*: AWS Best Practices: `https://d0.awsstatic.com/whitepapers/AWS_Cloud_Best_Practices.pdf`.
- *AWS Well-Architected Framework*: `https://d1.awsstatic.com/whitepapers/architecture/AWS_Well-Architected_Framework.pdf`.

Getting started with Tabcmd

Tabcmd is great tool and it is the core component of your Business Intelligence solution, because it will help you with automation and integration with ETL and Data Warehouse. In this recipe, we will install Tabcmd on Windows and will learn how it can work with Tableau Server.

There are some common use case scenarios:

- Refresh Extract
- Generate Tableau Reader Book
- Generate Dashboards in PDF and upload to Shared drive or Amazon S3
- Export data from Tableau Server workbook and save in CSV or XLSX formats

You can think of Tabcmd as not only an administration tool, but also a kind of a self-service tool that may be used by end users for scheduling their dashboards, and so on.

Getting ready

We will download Tabcmd for Windows machines. In this recipe, I will use a Windows machine that is existing in the same VPC and will act as a client machine. It means that Linux EC2 and Windows EC2 are on the same network. All we need to do is adjust the security group to allow access from the Windows machine.

How to do it...

Let's download Tabcmd to our Windows EC2 machine and connect Tableau Server:

1. Go to Tableau Server Releases (https://www.tableau.com/support/releases/server) and download tabcmd for your version of the server and your desired OS. I will download tabcmd for the Windows client.

2. Install Tabcmd on your machine at C:\tabcmd\.

3. Next, we should log in to the Tableau Server. Open CMD and type the following commands:

```
cd C:\tabcmd\"Command Line Utility"
tabcmd login -s http://ip-10-0-0-35.ec2.internal -u Administrator -p Airmax86
```

The preceding command line generates the following output:

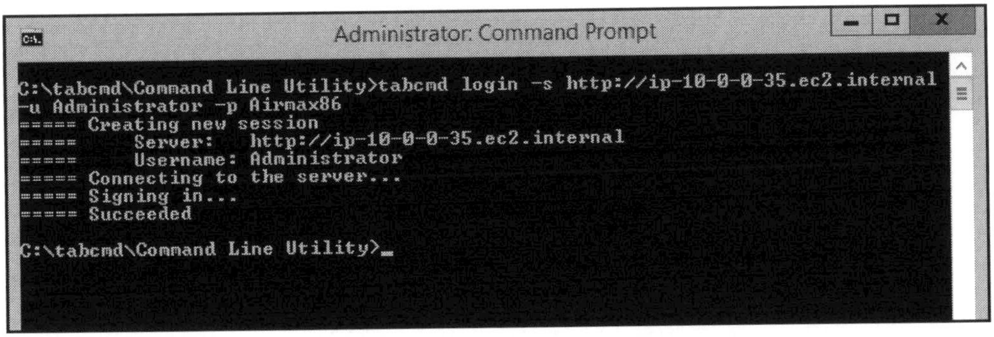

As a result, we connected to Tableau Server via Tabcmd.

4. Next, we will execute a command to export dashboard in PDF. Our Tableau Server has sample workbooks and we will use them. Let's open Regional Workbook and Obesity Map View. We need to copy the individual views' URLs to use it in Tabcmd script.

   In the following image I have highlighted the part of URL that we will use for the `tabcmd` command.

5. Let's execute the following command with Tabcmd:

```
tabcmd export "Regional/Obesity" --pdf --pagelayo
ut landscape -f "C:\Users\Administrator\Desktop\Obesity.pdf"
```

It will create a PDF file on your desktop, as follows:

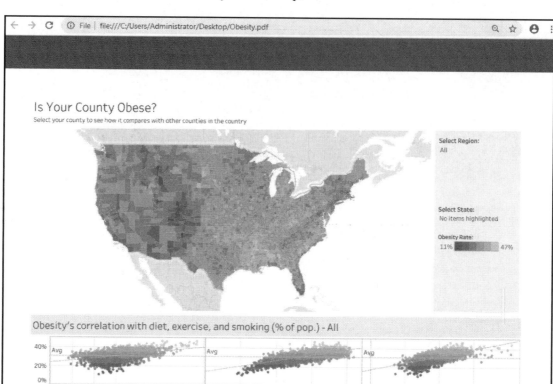

In the same way, we can generate Package Workbook or Refresh Extract. We can save this command as a batch file. We need to open notepad, put in all `tabcmd` commands, including authentication and export commands, and save this for future reference or use for automation.

How it works...

Tabcmd is a special utility for Tableau Server. It is a kind of client that can trigger Tableau Server and do lots of awesome and useful things. We just installed Tabcmd on our machine and connected Server. In addition, we've got a PDF from the Server. You may do many more actions with Tabcmd. This is a link with commands:

```
https://onlinehelp.tableau.com/current/server/en-us/tabcmd_cmd.htm
```

In a real-world scenario, Tabcmd is used for automation purposes and one script will include many commands, for example, you might refresh Tableau Extract first and then export a PDF of dashboards or generate Package Workbooks.

There's more...

Building automation with Tabcmd is awesome, but it has one missing element—notifications. In the real world, I am using an open source email client for CLI: `https://www.febooti.com/`.

You can download this tool and try it. All you need is to insert a snippet with the Febooti command and it will deliver you an email or attachment with the file. End users love it!

Finally, you should consider using internal Windows Task Scheduler to schedule Tabcmd scripts (Batch files) that can be found here: `https://en.wikipedia.org/wiki/Windows_Task_Scheduler`.

See also

- Finally, I wish to highlight a couple more server admin tools. First of all, you can check this GitHub repository for many useful utilities and try them in action at the following URL `https://github.com/tableau`.
- They are very handy when you are doing troubleshooting. Another resource is Tableau Server Client library for Python, which is available at the following URL: `https://tableau.github.io/server-client-python/#`.

14
Tableau Troubleshooting

In this chapter, we'll cover the following recipes:

- Performance recording
- Performance troubleshooting and best practices
- Troubleshooting through log files

Technical requirements

To follow the recipes outlined in this chapter, you'll need to have Tableau 2019.x installed on your device.

Introduction

When working with Tableau, we should always strive to optimize the performance of our workbooks. Even if we develop astonishing dashboards with great functionalities, our users' experience will not be optimal if our workbook works too slow. Especially in business, time is essential. Our stakeholders often don't have time to wait for our workbook to load. Despite all the effort we put into the workbook, the overall impression of our work would be tainted. To achieve the best possible results, it's important to test the performance of the workbook during development, and address issues that may appear. In this chapter, we'll learn some handy techniques for assessing and optimizing workbook performance, as well as for troubleshooting issues.

Performance recording

Anticipating possible performance issues, testing for them, and, if needed, solving solving them is important when creating a workbook. Poor performance can have a negative impact on the experience of our workbook users. In this recipe, you'll learn how to use Tableau's built-in performance-diagnostic tool: performance recording.

Getting ready

In this recipe, we'll test the performance of a dashboard. Follow the last recipe in `Chapter 6`, *Building Dashboards*, to create the dashboard we'll be working with in this recipe. When you're done, save the workbook to your device.

How to do it...

1. Launch Tableau.
2. In the main menu toolbar, select **Help**.
3. In the drop-down menu, go to **Settings and Performance**, and, from the additional drop-down menu, select **Start Performance Recording**:

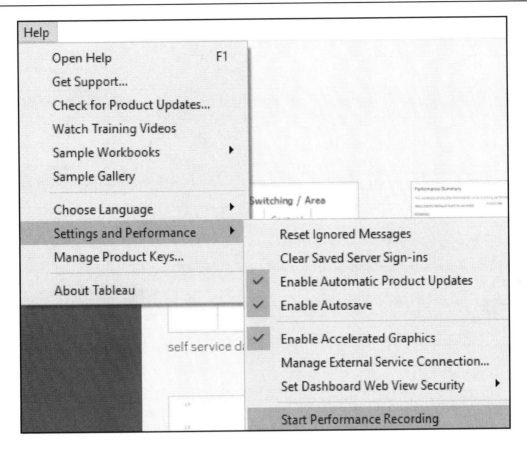

4. In the main menu toolbar, click on **File** and select **Open…**.
5. Navigate to the location on your device where you've saved the dashboard, select it, and click on **Open**.
6. Try playing around with the dashboard a bit—for example, filter different options.
7. In the main menu toolbar, navigate to **Help**.

8. In the drop-down menu, select **Settings and Performance** and in the additional drop-down menu, select **Stop Performance Recording**:

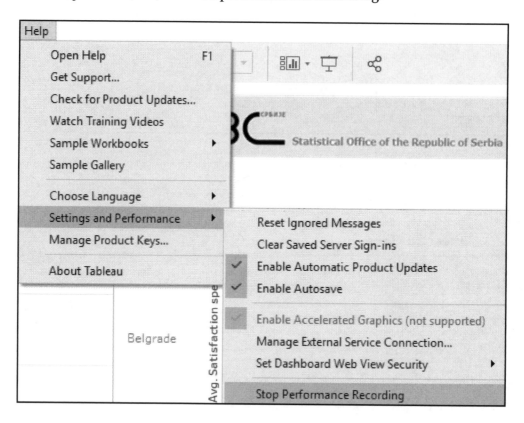

9. Once you've stopped the performance recording, you may need to wait a couple of seconds for Tableau to generate the performance recording report. Tableau will automatically open a new read-only workbook, called **PerformanceRecording**. In the following screenshot, you can examine the visualizations to see how various actions you've taken impact your workbook's performance:

How it works...

The Tableau performance recording functionality is a built-in tool that can help you assess the performance of your workbook and identify processes that might be slowing it down. In this recipe, we started the performance recording, and performed some actions, such as filtering. After we finished recording, Tableau automatically generated a read-only workbook that contains a dashboard with the processes that have taken place since we started recording, and the respective times they took to run.

The dashboard contains the **Timeline**, **Events**, and **Query** views, which are described here:

- **Timeline**: This view shows the processes that have taken place during the recording in chronological order. The processes are ordered from left to right along the *x*-axis, which represents the time since Tableau started. The view also provides information on the context of the events (**Workbook**, **Dashboard**, and **Worksheet**) and the nature of the event itself (**Event**). If you noticed performance issues with your workbook, this view is useful in exploring where the bottleneck occurs. Let's look at the processes that took place in the **Timeline** view, in the following screenshot:

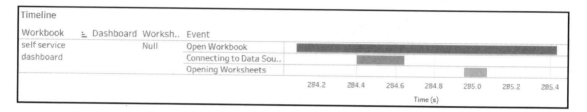

- **Events**: This view also shows the processes (events), but sorted by their duration, which is shown on the *x* axis. This view is very helpful because it highlights the processes that are taking the longest to run, making it easier to identify where the performance issue might be. In the following screenshot, we can see the processes of the **Events** view:

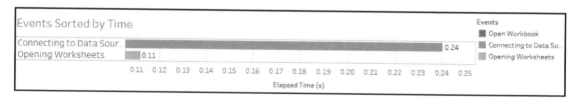

Both of the preceding views can be adjusted by using the **Show Events taking at least (in seconds):** filter, located in the top of the dashboard. By default, events taking less than **0.10** second are filtered out of both views, but shorter events can also be displayed by moving the filter slider to the left. In the following screenshot, we can see how the views can be adjusted:

- **Query**: The view is, by default, empty. However, it will be populated when you select an **Executing Query** event in either the **Timeline** or **Events** view. Let's look at the **Query** view in the following screenshot:

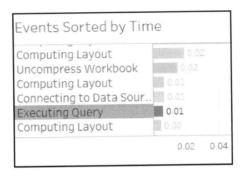

When you select a query event, the SQL or XML text (depending on whether you're connected to a data source directly or to a published data source, respectively) of that query will be displayed in the **Query** view. You can then use the text of the query to optimize it. We can view the result in the following screenshot:

```
Query

SELECT "Usage"."Area" AS "Area",
  "Usage"."Settlement type" AS "Calculation_858217245440413696",
  AVG(CAST("Usage"."Internet penetration" AS DOUBLE PRECISION OR NULL)) AS "avg:Internet penetration:ok"
FROM "TableauTemp"."Usage$" "Usage"
GROUP BY 1,
  2
```

There's more...

Apart from Tableau's built-in functionality, some third-party tools geared toward the same purpose also exist. One of the more well-known ones is *Power Tools for Tableau – Performance Analyzer*. Feel free to check it out: http://powertoolsfortableau.com/performance-analyzer-comes-to-workbook-tools-tableau.

See also

- For more information about assessing workbook performance, check out the excellent **Tableau Help** section on optimizing workbook performance: `https://onlinehelp.tableau.com/current/pro/desktop/en-us/performance_tips.htm`.

Performance troubleshooting and best practices

After you've run the performance recording, you might have identified the processes that are slowing down your workbook's performance, or maybe you're just creating a workbook and would like to anticipate any potential issues. Either way, you'll want to implement some best practices in order to prevent or resolve any potential performance bottlenecks.

How to do it...

In the following sections, we'll look at the following topics:

- Limiting your data source
- Being cautious with filters
- Keeping an eye on the calculations
- Optimizing your visualizations

Limiting your data source

When we develop a workbook, we usually don't use all the data that we have in our database. In order to improve the performance of our workbook, it's always recommended to limit your data source to only the information that's needed.

Filtering out cases in the database

If you aren't going to use all the cases from your database, the best thing you can do is apply a filter to it:

1. Open any workbook that you want to improve, and go to the **Data Source** tab in the bottom-left corner:

2. In the top-right corner, you can see the **Filters** section. Select **Add**:

3. The list of all of the variables in the database will be presented.
4. Chose the variable that contains the values you want to filter out:

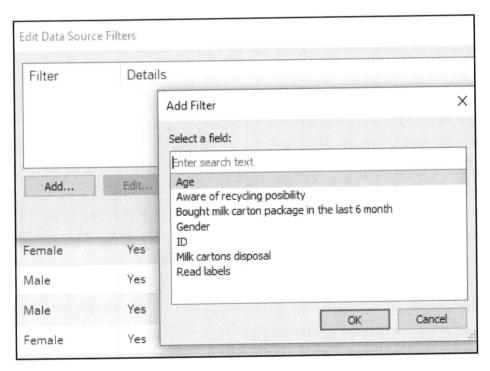

5. Select only those that you want to preserve (in our example, we want to keep only answers from female respondents), as shown in the following screenshot:

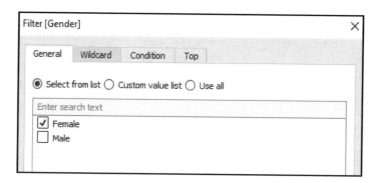

Filtering out variables

In most cases, we don't need all of the variables that we have in our database. In order to make our workbook run smoothly, we can hide variables that we don't need:

1. Open any workbook that you want to improve, and go to the **Data Source** tab in the bottom-left corner. Hover over the variable that you want to exclude until a black downward arrow appears.

2. Click on it and select **Hide**:

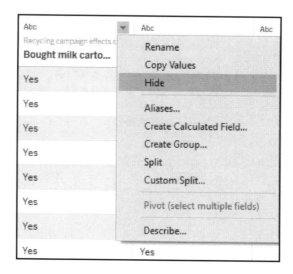

Making extracts

When we make a workbook that should communicate with a server, it's essential to decide how frequently our data should be refreshed. The default option is live. However, a live connection can be demanding and slow down your workbook. Luckily, in many situations, it isn't needed. In these situations, we can make extracts. For a detailed description of creating tableau extracts, see `Chapter 3`, *Tableau Extracts*.

Being cautious with filters

Filtering is, without a doubt, a fundamental feature of Tableau. However, in some cases, filters can have a negative effect on a workbook's performance. In order to keep your workbook running optimally, try to be mindful of the following things:

- Avoid applying filters to long lists. Querying for each option in your list can be a demanding task for Tableau. In cases where this might be an issue, consider creating a calculated field to shorten the list or use parameters.
- Filtering date fields can also be a demanding task for Tableau because individual dates can amount to a lot of data points for Tableau to process. However, we often don't need to filter on the lowest level of date granularity. So, when filtering dates, always try to think about the actual level of granularity you need to filter on and go with the highest level that you can. If you can - filter out years; if not, ask yourself if it is sufficient to filter out quarters, and so on. If possible, avoid filtering on the lower levels, such as days or hours.

- When adding a date field to the **Filters** shelf, you can choose the level of granularity you would like to use, as shown in the following screenshot:

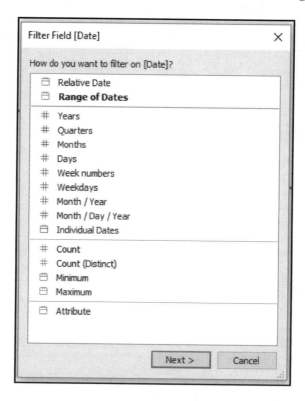

- In case you have smaller number of values in a dimension, then adding it to context can significantly improve the dashboard performance

Keeping an eye on the calculations

Calculated fields, especially when complex, can also give Tableau a hard time. However, you can counter this by trying to implement the following:

1. If there's a calculation metric that's frequently used in your workbook, consider creating it directly in the database, and not as a table calculation. This can save computational resources Tableau would otherwise have to invest in creating the views.

2. Disaggregated (row-level) calculations can be very demanding. Try to aggregate your measures when creating calculated fields.

3. When alternatives are available, consider using functions that are faster to execute in your calculated fields. For example:

- Try replacing IF-ELSE statements with CASE-WHEN statements
- Try to avoid nested IF statements
- Try to skip using LOD expressions if not necessary, since they can be computationally demanding

Optimizing your visualizations

Demanding visualizations can also create some trouble and slow down your workbook. If you encounter performance issues, or simply want to make sure your workbook is going to run smoothly, pay attention to the following:

- A visualization that shows many data points, such as the one shown in the following screenshot, can slow down performance of the workbook:

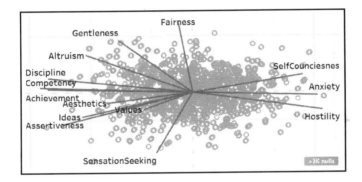

The number of marks in the view is visible in the very bottom-left corner of the workbook, as shown in the following screenshot:

 A large number of marks can make rendering the view a very demanding task for Tableau to process. So, make sure the number of marks in your view isn't excessive.

- Advanced visualizations aren't the only ones that give Tableau a hard time. Simple cross-tabs, especially with a higher number of rows and columns can also be very computationally demanding. Try to limit the number of rows and columns used in a single visualization—a table with too many rows and columns isn't easy to read anyway.

How it works...

All of these tips are about saving computational resources and minimizing the amount of interaction your workbook has to do with the database. For example, creating extracts minimizes the interaction of the workbook with the data base, which can be time consuming. On the other hand, creating frequently used calculations in the database minimizes the usage of computational resources.

There's more...

A range of third-party tools have been developed to help users assess and troubleshoot workbook performance. Some of them are geared specifically toward troubleshooting Tableau Server performance. Feel free to explore the options until you find the tool that addresses your needs the best.

See also

- For more tips and tricks, check out the **Tableau Help** page on performance tuning: `https://onlinehelp.tableau.com/current/server/en-us/perf_tuning.htm`.

Troubleshooting through log files

While running, Tableau records its activities in logs. If you encounter issues when working with Tableau, these logs can be extremely useful for troubleshooting.

How to do it...

In this section, we'll look at the following topics:

- Accessing logs
- Submitting logs to the support team

Accessing logs

1. To find your logs, in the main menu toolbar, navigate to **File** | **Repository Location...**:

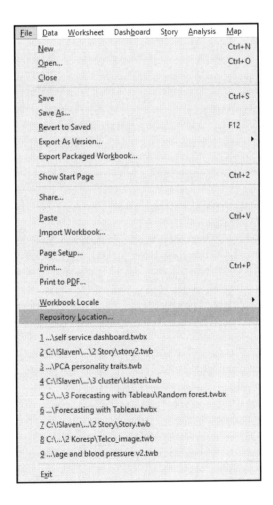

2. Alternatively, access the logs directly on your device. The default folder where the log files are saved is `/Users/<username>/Documents/My Tableau Repository`:

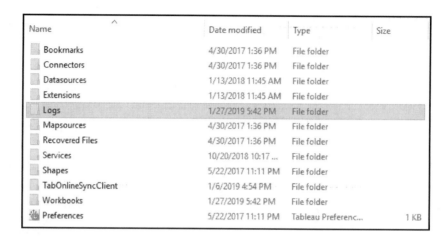

3. There's a wide range of issues that can occur, and it would be impossible to provide a comprehensive overview of them. However, once you've found the logs, you can use them to understand the nature of the issue you've experienced:

```
log_bk - Notepad                                                                                        –    □    ×
File  Edit  Format  View  Help
{"ts":"2019-01-14T22:57:49.067","pid":8944,"tid":"19d4","sev":"info","req":"-","sess":"-","site":"{CEBD4F2B-9C49-4059-A84D-FBAD487860BB}","user":
{"ts":"2019-01-14T22:57:49.067","pid":8944,"tid":"19d4","sev":"info","req":"-","sess":"-","site":"{CEBD4F2B-9C49-4059-A84D-FBAD487860BB}","user":
{"ts":"2019-01-14T22:57:49.067","pid":8944,"tid":"19d4","sev":"info","req":"-","sess":"-","site":"{CEBD4F2B-9C49-4059-A84D-FBAD487860BB}","user":
{"ts":"2019-01-14T22:57:49.069","pid":8944,"tid":"19d4","sev":"info","req":"-","sess":"-","site":"{CEBD4F2B-9C49-4059-A84D-FBAD487860BB}","user":
{"ts":"2019-01-14T22:57:49.070","pid":8944,"tid":"19d4","sev":"info","req":"-","sess":"-","site":"{CEBD4F2B-9C49-4059-A84D-FBAD487860BB}","user":
{"ts":"2019-01-14T22:57:49.105","pid":8944,"tid":"19d4","sev":"info","req":"-","sess":"-","site":"{CEBD4F2B-9C49-4059-A84D-FBAD487860BB}","user":
{"ts":"2019-01-14T22:57:49.105","pid":8944,"tid":"19d4","sev":"info","req":"-","sess":"-","site":"{CEBD4F2B-9C49-4059-A84D-FBAD487860BB}","user":
au\\Tableau 10.5\\bin","OS":"Windows_NT","OneDrive":"C:\\Users\\Slaven\\OneDrive","PATHEXT":".COM;.EXE;.BAT;.CMD;.VBS;.VBE;.JS;.JSE;.WSF;.WSH;.M$
es","QT_D3DCREATE_MULTITHREADED":"1","SESSIONNAME":"Console","SystemDrive":"C:","SystemRoot":"C:\\WINDOWS","TEMP":"C:\\Users\\Slaven\\AppData\\Lc
{"ts":"2019-01-14T22:57:49.107","pid":8944,"tid":"19d4","sev":"info","req":"-","sess":"-","site":"{CEBD4F2B-9C49-4059-A84D-FBAD487860BB}","user":
{"ts":"2019-01-14T22:57:49.107","pid":8944,"tid":"19d4","sev":"info","req":"-","sess":"-","site":"{CEBD4F2B-9C49-4059-A84D-FBAD487860BB}","user":
{"ts":"2019-01-14T22:57:49.108","pid":8944,"tid":"19d4","sev":"info","req":"-","sess":"-","site":"{CEBD4F2B-9C49-4059-A84D-FBAD487860BB}","user":
{"ts":"2019-01-14T22:57:49.108","pid":8944,"tid":"19d4","sev":"info","req":"-","sess":"-","site":"{CEBD4F2B-9C49-4059-A84D-FBAD487860BB}","user":
{"ts":"2019-01-14T22:57:49.109","pid":8944,"tid":"19d4","sev":"info","req":"-","sess":"-","site":"{CEBD4F2B-9C49-4059-A84D-FBAD487860BB}","user":
{"ts":"2019-01-14T22:57:49.110","pid":8944,"tid":"19d4","sev":"info","req":"-","sess":"-","site":"{CEBD4F2B-9C49-4059-A84D-FBAD487860BB}","user":
{"ts":"2019-01-14T22:57:49.110","pid":8944,"tid":"19d4","sev":"info","req":"-","sess":"-","site":"{CEBD4F2B-9C49-4059-A84D-FBAD487860BB}","user":
{"ts":"2019-01-14T22:57:49.111","pid":8944,"tid":"19d4","sev":"info","req":"-","sess":"-","site":"{CEBD4F2B-9C49-4059-A84D-FBAD487860BB}","user":
{"ts":"2019-01-14T22:57:49.111","pid":8944,"tid":"19d4","sev":"info","req":"-","sess":"-","site":"{CEBD4F2B-9C49-4059-A84D-FBAD487860BB}","user":
{"ts":"2019-01-14T22:57:49.112","pid":8944,"tid":"19d4","sev":"info","req":"-","sess":"-","site":"{CEBD4F2B-9C49-4059-A84D-FBAD487860BB}","user":
{"ts":"2019-01-14T22:57:49.113","pid":8944,"tid":"19d4","sev":"info","req":"-","sess":"-","site":"{CEBD4F2B-9C49-4059-A84D-FBAD487860BB}","user":
{"ts":"2019-01-14T22:57:49.113","pid":8944,"tid":"19d4","sev":"info","req":"-","sess":"-","site":"{CEBD4F2B-9C49-4059-A84D-FBAD487860BB}","user":
```

Submitting logs to the support team

If you have trouble diagnosing the problem, you can always contact Tableau support. In order to help them understand what has happened, you might be asked to provide log files where the issue has been recorded. Naturally, you'll want to provide log files in the manner that's most useful and informative for the Tableau support team.

If possible, you should create clean logs. But first, create a backup log. You can do this by following these steps:

1. Navigate to the folder where your logs are located.
2. Rename the folder from `Logs` to `Logs_Backup`:

Name	Date modified	Type	Size
Bookmarks	4/30/2017 1:36 PM	File folder	
Connectors	4/30/2017 1:36 PM	File folder	
Datasources	1/13/2018 11:45 AM	File folder	
Extensions	1/13/2018 11:45 AM	File folder	
Logs_Backup	1/27/2019 5:42 PM	File folder	
Mapsources	4/30/2017 1:36 PM	File folder	
Recovered Files	4/30/2017 1:36 PM	File folder	
Services	10/20/2018 10:17 ...	File folder	
Shapes	5/22/2017 11:11 PM	File folder	
TabOnlineSyncClient	1/6/2019 4:54 PM	File folder	
Workbooks	1/27/2019 5:42 PM	File folder	
Preferences	5/22/2017 11:11 PM	Tableau Preferenc...	1 KB

3. Create a new folder named `Logs`. `Logs` the new, clean folder where new logs will be stored, while the old folder, `Logs_Backup`, won't be used anymore.

Through the following steps, you will reproduce the issue that has occurred and send the logs to Tableau support:

1. Start Tableau and take the steps required to get to the point where the problem has occurred.
2. Close all Tableau Desktop sessions, so that the errors are recorded to the log file.

3. Compress the `Logs` folder by right-clicking on it, selecting **Send to**, and choosing **Compressed (zipped) folder**, as shown in the following screenshot:

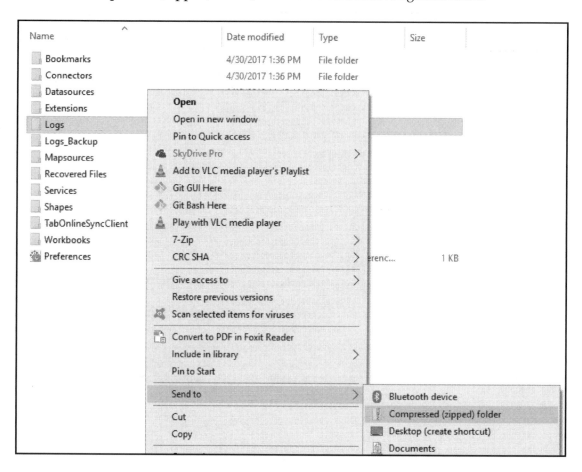

4. Send the compressed file to Tableau support.

There's more...

There are several open source applications that can make reading Tableau logs easier:

- `https://github.com/tableau/tableau-log-viewer`
- `https://github.com/tableau/Logshark`
- `https://github.com/tableau/TabMon`

Each of the mentioned third-party software provides clear guidance for installation and usage, so feel free to explore.

See also

- If you aren't sure how to reach Tableau support, you can find detailed instructions here: `https://kb.tableau.com/articles/howto/submitting-a-case-from-the-customer-portal`.

15
Preparing Data for Analysis with Tableau Prep

This chapter will cover the following recipes:

- Installing Tableau Prep
- Building the first flow with Tableau Prep
- Working with big data

Introduction

The main role of any business is bringing value to its customers, employees, and stakeholders. Every group needs to own a unique value, for example, stakeholders are interested in revenue growth and meeting KPIs. On the other hand, customers are expecting high-quality services and products.

In order to drive value, businesses need managers and employees to make the right decisions. They require clean and accurate data that enables sound decision-making and allows them to generate value for everyone.

Modern businesses generate tremendous volumes of data. Some data is available in data warehouses, some in **online Transaction processing** (OLTP) system, and some in third-party marketing applications. Tableau is a powerful tool that allows us to explore and visualize all this data, but sometimes it isn't enough. In some cases, data should be clean and transformed before analysis and usually it requires the help of data engineers or **extract, transform, load** (ETL) developers. As a result, this is a kind of bottleneck for the organization and slows down decision-making processes as well as value-generation.

With Tableau 2018.1, a new desktop tool - Tableau Prep- was announced. This is a self-service data tool that will help clean, transform, and reshape data for better analysis. It empowers business users with the ability to see and feel data and visually manipulate it in order to shape it into the correct form.

Technical requirements

For this chapter, we need to download and install Tableau Prep as well as a sample dataset from the chapter bundle. You might download it from Packt website.

Installing Tableau Prep

In the modern world, analysts and business users don't want to be block with IT any more. In other words, in traditional organizations all data work is done by IT stuff and business users have to wait, while IT solve their ticket. They demand data; they want to get all the data and analyze it in order to create vital insights that will help them to survive in this highly-competitive world. Around the globe, many people have adopted Tableau and they use for their day-to-day tasks.

Business users are becoming more and more proficient with technology and data. They are ready to learn new skills that help them get faster insights. As a result, Tableau released a new tool: Tableau Prep. It's an efficient and powerful desktop tool that's available for Windows and macOS and has a rich functionality for shaping data.

You might get questions about the use cases for Tableau Prep. There are lot of use cases for this tool. The main benefit of Tableau Desktop is that it empowers end users by giving them a powerful data-exploration tool. In most cases, business users with Tableau don't depend on IT any more. But they still need IT guidance when they want to prepare their data for analysis. By releasing Tableau Prep, Tableau is trying to solve one more challenge for business users, and offers them rich capabilities for local data transformation and preparation without IT involvement. For example, in a marketing team, you might have lots of data sources, and every month you need to bring in new data sources, so you have to move fast. Using Tableau Prep, you can set your own flow and bring all the data together. You can join, transform, reshape and clean your data, and generate a Tableau data source that will be ready for data analysis and exploration.

Getting ready

First of all, we should download Tableau Prep from the Tableau website and install it on our machine. All Tableau software releases can be downloaded from `https://www.tableau.com/support/releases/`.

How to do it...

Let's find Tableau Prep, download it, and install:

1. Go to `https://www.tableau.com/support/releases/prep`.
2. Find the most recent release of Tableau Prep and download it for your OS.
3. Install Tableau Prep and launch it:

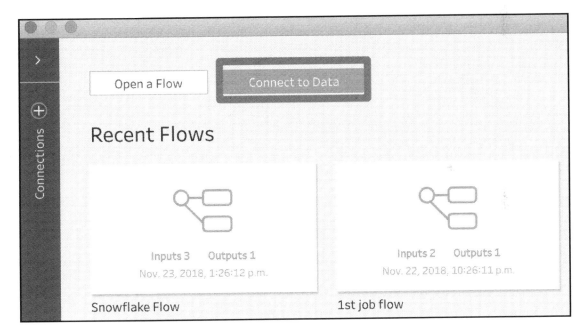

How it works...

Tableau Prep has a basic interface. You can discover **Sample Flows** or open your **Recent Flows** section. Flow means a sequence of steps (data transformations). Basically, we can think about Tableau Prep as a desktop ETL tool that allows us to connect and extract data, transform it, and publish it into a Tableau data source or write it to a file.

Currently, Tableau Prep supports fewer data sources than Tableau Desktop, but it offers over 40 different data sources, including Snowflake, an innovative analytical data warehouse.

There's more...

When we download Tableau Prep for the first time, we can start a free trial and we can use Tableau Prep for 14 days. Then, if we want to continue to use it, we need to buy a license. Tableau Prep isn't an individual product, it comes with Tableau Creator License and includes Tableau Desktop and one Tableau Server or Tableau Online. You can read more about licensing costs here: https://www.tableau.com/pricing/individual.

Building the first flow with Tableau Prep

After successfully installing and launching Tableau Prep, we can start to build our first data flow using the sample dataset. (Just an example, in this recipe, we'll cover how to connect the data, transfer it, and then publish the result.)

Getting ready

To proceed with this section, download the Microsoft Excel document, installs.xlsx, that's available for this chapter.

This dataset has data about a number of app installs for iOS and Android by date.

How to do it...

In the following section, we'll look at how to connect the data, transform it, and then publish the result.

Connecting the data

Tableau Prep supports lots of data sources and we can easily blend together multiple data sources, such as files and databases. Let's get started:

1. Navigate to **File** | **New** and create a new flow.
2. Click on the plus + sign near **Connections** and choose **Microsoft Excel**:

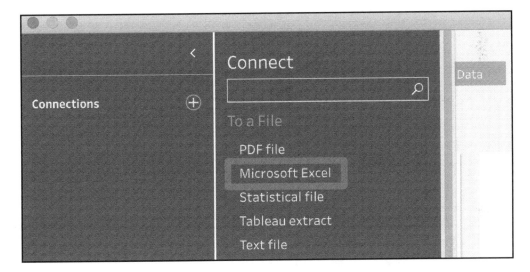

3. Choose the installs.xlsx file and click on **Open**. Connect the file and it will show us two available tables, **Android** and **IOS**, as shown in the following screenshot:

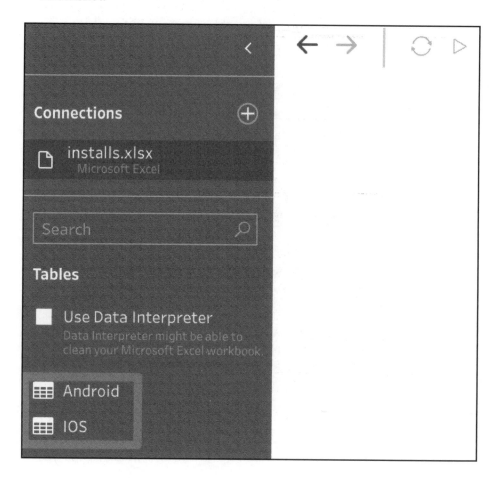

4. Using the drag-and-drop method, drag **IOS** to the canvas. Tableau Prep will create the **Input** step.

During the Input step, Tableau will read the file and learn about the structure of the file. For example, you can use the CSV or TSV file, and Tableau will automatically recognize the pattern and try to split into columns. We can also use the UNION operation by using the Wildcard union in order to read all the files and merge them into one. In addition, we can sample data in the case of a big dataset. Finally, we can apply filters.

5. Let's add one more dataset file with the Android `installs`. We have two ways of doing this: we can either drag and drop the **Android** sheet to the canvas or adjust the settings of **IOS** by enabling the Wildcard union.

6. We'll use the first method. Drag and drop **Android** to the canvas.

Transforming the data

Once we've successfully connected the data and added data sources to the canvas, we can start to build our flow:

1. Click on the + sign near the data source to choose the next step:

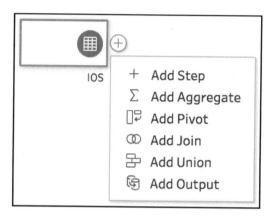

We have the following options:

Steps	Description
Add Step	This step will allow us to look at the data and modify it.
Add Aggregate	We can calculate a new measure, using functions such as SUM, AVG, and COUNT.
Add Pivot	We can transpose columns into rows. In other words, we can convert cross-table into a normal table.
Add Join	We can join data streams using the INNER, LEFT, RIGHT, and OUTER joins. Moreover, Tableau will visualize and color results on the fly.
Add Union	We can merge multiple streams into one.
Add Output	This is the final step, where we'll generate the result set. We can write into the CSV file or the Tableau data source. In addition, we can publish directly to the Tableau Server.

In our case, we will add the **Clean** step and learn about our dataset.

2. Click on the new step, **Clean 1**, and explore the **Profile** pane, as shown in the following screenshot:

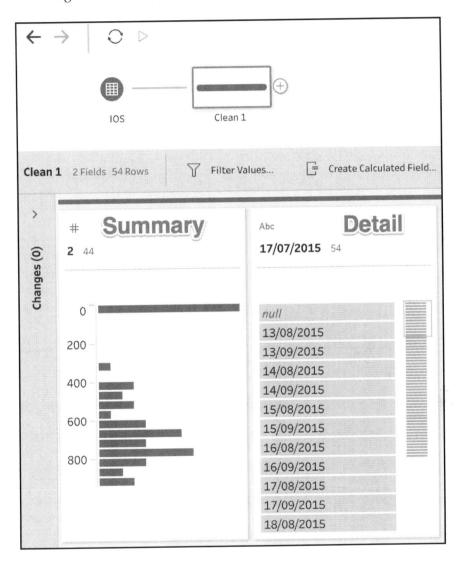

Tableau Prep creates cards for each column. At this step, we can modify our data by changing the data type, creating a new column, and filtering values. In addition, we can see the connection between values. For example, if we click to any value in the data card, it'll show us dependent values. Moreover, it'll show us a histogram of value distributions. Data card can have two **View States—Detail** (column #2) and **Summary** (column #1), that, is distinct values or grouped-by values.

3. Rename the columns. The first column should be **Number Installs** and the second should be **Install Date**.

4. Union the datasets. Click **+** after the **Clean 1** step and choose **Union**. Drag the **Android** data source and drop it on top of the **Union** step. At the same time, we can add **Union 1 step**, when we drag and drop the **Android** dataset on top of the **Clean** step, it will ask us to choose the appropriate step, such as **Join** or **Union**:

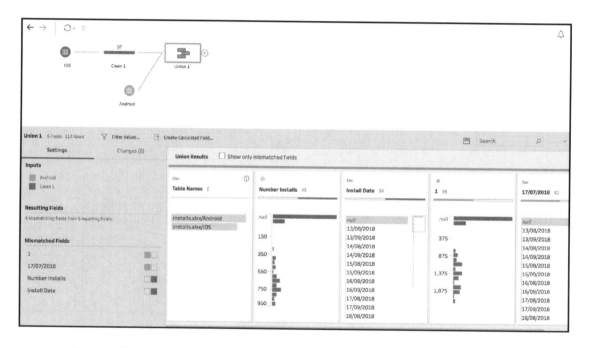

You will see that the result set doesn't look good in the **Profile** pane because we didn't rename the **Android** dataset column names and you can see the orange (Android) data still in different columns. Moreover, our date is in string format.

5. Click on the **Android** dataset and rename the column names the same way we did for **IOS**. Click on the **Android** Data Source Input and rename both `Field Name` to the **Install Date** and **Number Installs accordingly**:

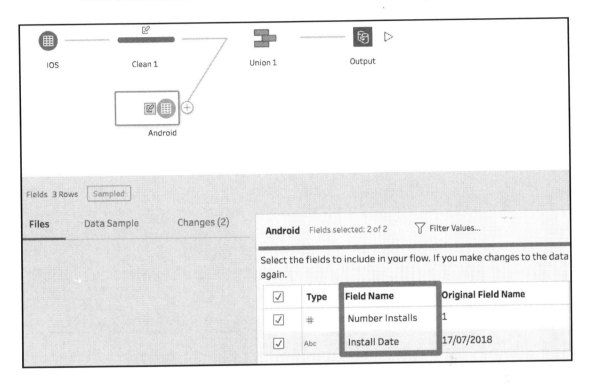

6. Click on the **Union** step and change the date format:

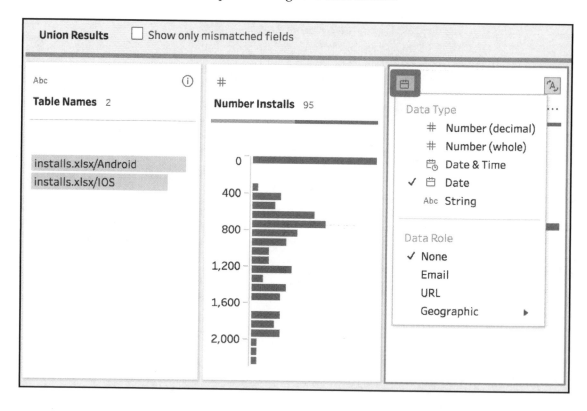

7. Let's also create new calculated fields. We don't have an OS name. We can use the **Table Names** system field in order to extract the phone's OS name. In order to create a new calculated field. In order to do it, click on the **Union 1** step and click on the **Table Names** pane and choose **Create Calculated Field...**:

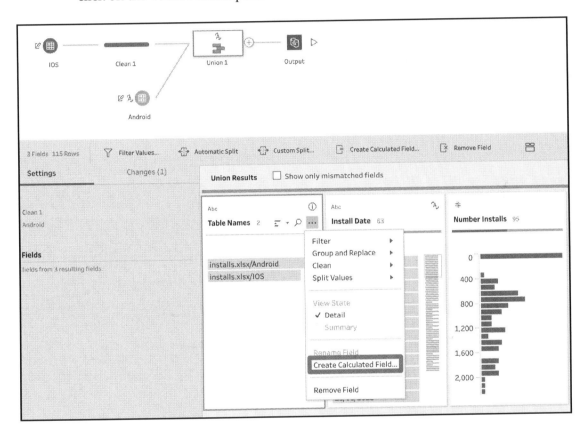

Then you can write this statement. Tableau Prep has the same syntax as Tableau Desktop.

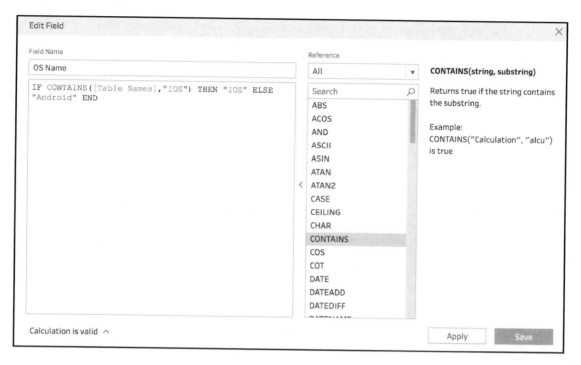

This will add one more field to our dataset. Now, we need to drop the original **Table Name** field. The calculated field won't disappear. In order to drop field, you should click on **Remove Field** at Data Pane of this field.

As a result, we've got the correct dataset for further analysis in Tableau.

Publishing the result

When we finish the transformation, we should publish our result using the **Add Output** step. Let's create the Tableau data source:

1. Click the **+** sign and choose **Add Output**. We have the option to save to a CSV file or to create Tableau Data Extract. Moreover, we can publish our data source right to the Tableau Server.

2. Create a Hyper data extract:

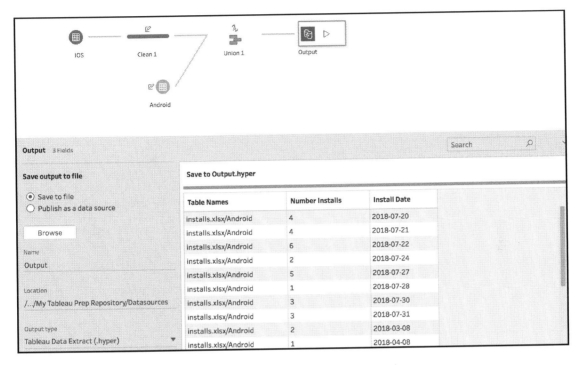

3. Click on the **Run Flow** button, this will find a new Tableau data source.

4. Open the new data source with Tableau Desktop:

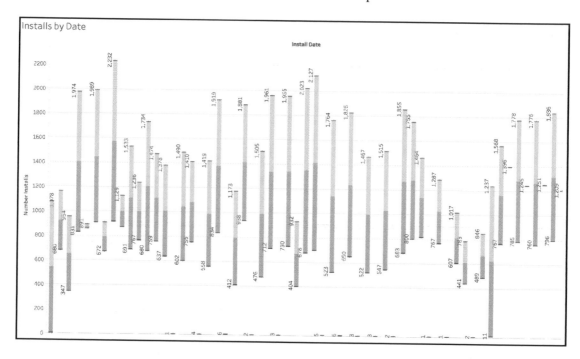

How it works...

Despite the fact that we performed a very simple task, we covered 80% of Tableau Prep's functionality. The main goal was to understand how the product works. Basically, Tableau Prep can connect to any data source and gives us the ability to fully control the data flow by transforming and merging the data. In addition, we can create calculated fields using the Tableau syntax. Finally, we store our results in CSV or Tableau Data Source.

There's more...

In this recipe, we got introduced Tableau Prep and learned the tool's main functionality. Here's a good resource for doing more complex work with Tableau Prep: `https://onlinehelp.tableau.com/current/prep/en-us/prep_dayinlife.htm`.

It has the following two use cases with a detailed step-by-step guide:

- *Hospital Bed Use with Tableau Prep*
- *Finding the Second Date with Tableau Prep*

Working with big data

Tableau Prep works with big data volumes and big data tools, such as Snowflake, Redshift, and Amazon EMR. You can refer to `Chapter 10`, *Tableau for Big Data* and connect existing accounts of Amazon Redshift, Amazon EMR, or Snowflake.

Tableau Prep allows us to work with big data sets by leveraging sampling. However, it processes data on your local machine and if you want to create, extract, or export data into a CSV using a huge dataset, it can fail due to lack of memory. We learned that Tableau Desktop works with big data by rendering results using a live connection. We don't want to create an extract when working with big data. In the case of Tableau Prep, we can learn our dataset and then use filters to split the dataset and work with part of it.

 Here's another solution: we can launch a powerful AWS EC2 instance and install Tableau Prep there, where it will use more resources.

Getting ready

In this recipe, we'll connect our Snowflake cluster and create a flow using Snowflake data in order to calculate metrics by marketing segment.

How to do it...

In Chapter 10, *Tableau for Big Data,* we used a trial version of Snowflake. Let's connect Snowflake and build our flow:

1. Click on **Connections** and choose Snowflake. Fill in the credentials:

We use the same credentials that we created in Chapter 10, *Tableau for Big Data.*

2. Choose the **Virtual Warehouse** (computing resource), **Database**, and **Schema** options. It's the same as we did in Tableau Desktop:

Warehouse	SF_TUTS_WH
Database	SNOWFLAKE_SAMPLE_DATA
Schema	TPCH_SF1

You might choose a different schema with a bigger dataset, such as TPCH_SF10, TPCH_SF100, or TPCH_SF1000.

3. Drag and drop tables onto the canvas. You should already know the differences between Desktop and Prep. Let's drag and drop the following tables:

- **LINEITEM**
- **ORDERS**
- **CUSTOMER**

We need to join them all together. In Tableau Prep, we can join only two streams at once. We should join the LINEITEM and ORDERS tables together. But before joining the dataset, we can learn more about tables and their data using the **Clean** step. If we don't want to change any data in the tables, the **Clean** step is optional. Anyway, it's a good practice to use the **Clean** step after every operation.

This is how it should look now:

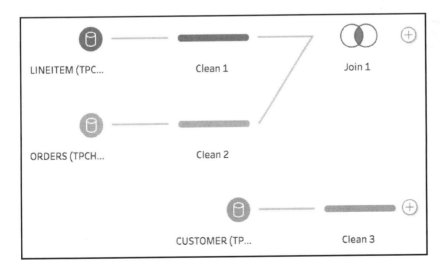

4. Click on **Join 1** and you'll see the **Profile** pane. It has nice visualization of the **JOIN** statement:

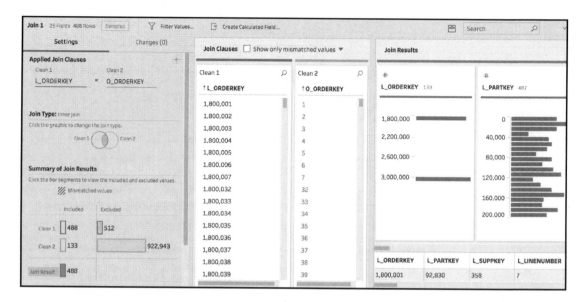

In the **O_ORDERKEY** data card, you might see lots of red values. It means these values aren't joined. Due to the sampling of **LINEITEM**, we don't have the full dataset here. If you want to check the full dataset, you should adjust the **LINEITEM** source table component and eliminate sampling. We will do this at the end of the flow.

 There's another trick to working with big datasets. You might apply filters for the **LINEITEM** data source and filter one or multiple. For example, you might add the **[L_ORDERKEY]=1]** filter.

It will bring us only three rows and add transparency.

5. Let's add the CUSTOMER table. Drag and drop the **CUSTOMER** object to **JOIN 1** and choose the **JOIN** operation. It will create **JOIN 2**. Because we filtered our **LINEITEM** table, we can check that we have only one customer in the flow.

6. Let's create some metrics. Add the **Add Aggregate** step by clicking the **+** sign. At the **Profile** pane, we have **Grouped Fields** and **Aggregated Fields**.

7. Drop **C_MKTSEGMENT** into **Grouped Fields** and then drop the metric fields into **Aggregated Fields**; in addition, we will rename them:

Original name	New name	Function
L_Quantity	Quantity	SUM
L_EXTENDEDPRICE	Base Price Amount	SUM
L_DISCOUNT	Discount Rate	SUM
L_TAX	Tax Rate	Sum
C_MKTSEGMENT	Marketing Segment	n/a

8. Let's calculate some additional metrics, such as amount with discount and tax. We can create calculated fields at the **Add Aggregate** step:

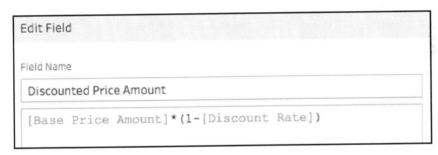

And then we can test the result of this job by adding the **Clean** step:

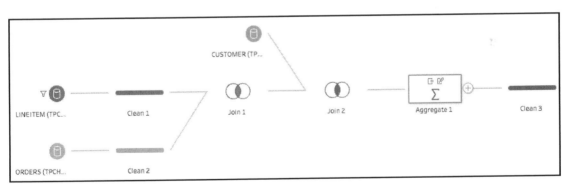

If we check `Discounted Price Amount` at the **Clean 3** step, we'll find that it's wrong because we broke the level of aggregation. Based on our dataset, we have a discount rate on the line-item level. This means we should calculate the **Discounted Price** on the **Item** level and then aggregate. We aggregated the discount on the **Marketing Segment** level (on the customer level because we have only one customer).

In order to fix this, we need multiple aggregate steps. We should change the existing one, and group by **Line Item**, **Order Key**, and **Marketing Segment**. Then we'll add one more aggregate step where we'll aggregate only on **Marketing Segment**:

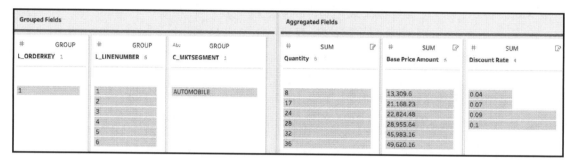

You can see that we have six line items and four different discount rates.

Add one more aggregation step and aggregate on **Marketing Segment**. As a result, we'll get the right discounted price.

9. Adjust the data type by changing it from **Number (decimal)** to **Number (whole)**. In order to do this, just click on data type symbol at data pane:

10. Create the final step by adding **Output**. Before running this, drop the filter and eliminate the sampling:

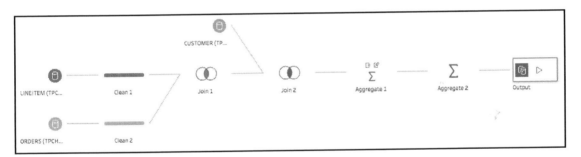

It took 36 seconds to run.

11. Test the result by opening the data source in Tableau Desktop. The data source was saved in My `Documents | Tableau Prep | Data Sources | Output.tde`. Open this with Tableau Desktop:

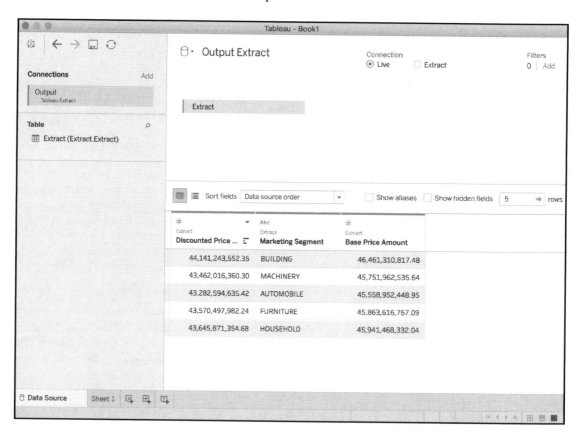

How it works...

We can go to the Snowflake console and see how Tableau Prep works under the hood:

✓	27b9f9fb-a...	SELECT "b15f6e92-e6c9-4137-a0a7-9c564c"."L_DISCOUNT" AS "L_DISCOUNT", "b15f6e9...	TABLEAUCOOKBOOK
✓	7aef9df4-f5...	SELECT "6d285608-20ca-4f84-b594-65f22f"."O_CUSTKEY" AS "O_CUSTKEY", "6d285608...	TABLEAUCOOKBOOK
✓	d584dff0-fd...	SELECT "edcd0042-63f1-4afb-b973-ee02b4"."L_ORDERKEY" AS "L_ORDERKEY", "edcd0...	TABLEAUCOOKBOOK
✓	edd60452-...	SELECT "287ec79d-633b-4e20-903d-22ef49"."C_CUSTKEY" AS "C_CUSTKEY", "287ec79...	TABLEAUCOOKBOOK

You can see that Tableau Prep ran multiple queries. The first three queries retrieved data from the tables. In the last one, we retrieved data for the first aggregate step. In other words, Tableau Prep is only partly using Snowflake to get the initial data. All other transformations are happening inside of Tableau Prep.

There's more...

You might think of this flow as the logic for a couple of metrics. With Tableau Prep, you can build as many streams as you want, then union them and create the Tableau Extract. For example, we could add a branch in the middle of my flow and start to create new metrics with different grouping options, and then Union with my initial flow and write to the extract. This gives us performance benefits because our dashboards work faster without complex calculations and filters. Moreover, it visualizes the flow and allows end users to quickly understand the logic or apply the changes. There is a link with more information about Tableau Prep steps: `https://onlinehelp.tableau.com/current/prep/en-us/prep_clean.htm`

See also...

With Tableau Prep 2019.1 was released new feature—Tableau Prep Conductor. Prep Conductor is that server integration, and it unleashes the full potential of Tableau Prep to operationalize your data prep experience. With Prep Conductor, you can schedule your flows to run, when, where, and how you want to. You can choose which outputs to schedule independently of one another. You can read more about this feature here `https://www.tableau.com/about/blog/2018/11/keep-your-data-fresh-tableau-prep-conductor-now-beta-97369`.

ETL Best Practices for Tableau 16

Tableau is a leader among BI tools and it brings great power to any organization. But with great power, there is great responsibility. Tableau is a tool that does what the end user wants. However, Tableau is at the top of the iceberg and it works with other tools, such as Data Warehouse and ETL (ETL allows us to load data into Data Warehouse or Data Platform). The key aspect of any Tableau implementation is quality analytics and actionable business insights that will drive business decisions and help the business grow. As a result, it is important to integrate Tableau with ETL and Data Warehouse.

In this chapter, we want to go through one of the most common problems that we spot on every project. Usually, organizations tend to use multiple independent vendors for their BI solution. As a result, there could be a gap, especially between a Data Warehouse and BI tool. We will cover the following topics:

- Getting started with Matillion ETL
- Deploying Tabcmd on Linux
- Creating Matillion Shared Jobs

Introduction

Let's understand this situation better through the following example. In one of our projects, a customer had a Cloud Data Warehouse and uses Matillion to load it. The customer was using Tableau as a primary BI tool.

Let's look at the ideal ELT, which is shown in the following screenshot:

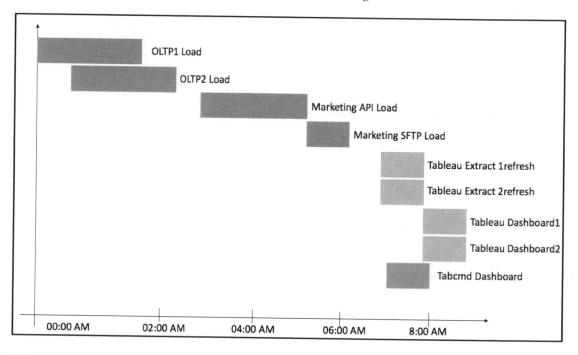

There are two individual processes here. The green one is Matillion, that is scheduled via Matillion Scheduler. The orange one is Tableau and it is scheduled via Tableau Server. Usually, we assume that ETL is done at 6 am and we scheduled Tableau extracts and dashboards a bit later. In our example, it is 7 am. In addition, we are using `tabcmd` and schedule Tableau Reports via **Windows Task Scheduler**.

As you might guess, the marketing data source isn't the most reliable. Let's consider a scenario, where SFTP was delayed files delivery.

As a result, the ELT job was failed and automatically restarted later at 7 a.m., as shown in the following screenshot:

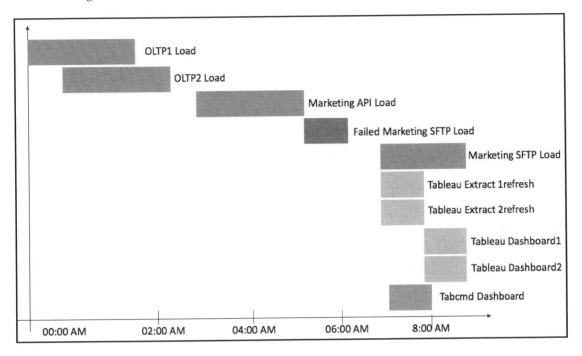

In our scenario, the ELT process was finished around 9 am. This should be the time of triggering BI reports and refreshing exports.

As a result, business users got their dashboards with inconsistent data and they usually send all ELT/DW emails into the spam folder. Based on our experience, around noon, users will realize that they spent half of the workday for nothing by working with inconsistent data.

We will simulate this issue and learn best practices for ETL and Tableau using Matillion ETL. You will learn the following topics:

- How to install Matillion ETL
- How to install Tabcmd for Linux
- How to create custom Tableau component for Matillion

Technical requirements

You may use Redshift or Snowflake from Chapter 10, *Tableau for Big Data*. We also need Matillion ETL from the AWS Marketplace.

Getting started with Matillion ETL

According to best practices, we should integrate our data pipelines with Tableau Server using tabcmd. The following diagram will show us the common architecture of a modern data warehouse project:

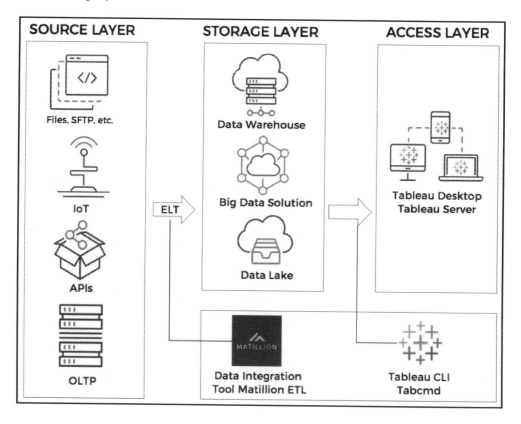

We will install the Linux version of Tabcmd on a Matillion EC2 instance and integrate with Tableau Server. We should be sure that our ETL and Tableau Server can talk with each other. In our case, we will use the same AWS account and region in order to use the same private network. In case you have Tableau Server on-premise, you should configure your firewall. We choose Matillion ETL because this is the leader among modern cloud ETL solutions and works with Redshift, Snowflake, and BigQuery.

How to do it...

Since we have already trialed Snowflake and Redshift, we should get Matillion ETL. In our example we will use Matillion ETL for Redshift. We will use free trial and get it from the AWS Market Place. There is detail information on how to launch Matillion for Redshift at:

```
https://redshiftsupport.matillion.com/customer/en/portal/articles/2487672-
launching-detailed-instructions.
```

Moreover, you may contact Matillion support and they will help you. They have awesome support and are happy to give a hand. We won't get into details about how to install Matillion ETL because it is quite simple and straightforward.

How it works...

By the end of the preparation, you should have running an Matillion ETL EC2 instance within your account. In addition, you should configure it to the Redshift instance, which we used in Chapter 10, *Tableau for Big Data*. Tableau will connect to the Redshift. We will use tabcmd for the following tasks:

- Triggering a refresh of Tableau Extract at the end of ETL
- Triggering an export of Tableau Workbook in order to generate a PDF and export to S3

There's more...

In our case, we were using Matillion ETL for Redshift, but you may use Matillion ETL for Snowflake as well as for Google BigQuery. You might apply these principles to any of data platforms.

Deploying Tabcmd on Linux

Since Tableau released Tableau on Linux, we don't need to spend any more time on converting Windows Tabcmd for Linux. We can simply download `tabcmd` from Tableau website and install it to the Linux box with Matillion ETL. We are going to use 2018.2 version for this recipe but you can use 2019.x `tabcmd` distributive.

 It is important that the `tabcmd` version was aligned with Tableau Server version. For example, if you have Tableau Server 2019.1 then you need to download Tabcmd 2019.1.

How to do it...

Let's download `tabcmd` and install it at Linux box:

1. First, we will go to the Tableau Releases website (`https://www.tableau.com/support/releases`) and download Tabcmd for Linux. We should download the same version as our Tableau Server. In our case, it is 2018.2, as shown in the following screenshot:

Download Files

Windows

- TableauServerTabcmd-64bit-2018-2-2.exe (86 MB)
- TableauServer-64bit-2018-2-2.exe (1460 MB)

Linux

- tableau-tabcmd-2018-2-2.noarch.rpm (5 MB)
- tableau-tabcmd-2018-2-2_all.deb (5 MB)
- tableau-server-2018-2-2.x86_64.rpm (1296 MB)
- tableau-server-2018-2-2_amd64.deb (1299 MB)

2. We will download RMP archive because Amazon Linux has lots in common with Red Hat.

3. Then we should, upload this into the EC2 instance with Matillion. There are multiple ways to do this. For example, the fastest way for us is to use AWS CLI S3. We will upload the file into the S3 bucket and then download it from EC2 instance.

4. Next, we should install this archive on the EC2. Go to the location of archive and execute the following command or specify the full path to the file:

```
sudo rpm -Uvh tableau-tabcmd-2018-2-2.noarch.rpm
```

5. As a result, we will have to install Tabcmd for our Linux system. Now, we want to make sure, that everything works as expected.

 It is important that Tableau and Matillion can see each other from the network point of view. We recommend that you deploy your data analytics solution using the same AWS account and the same region. In case you have to use other topology, you might need to configure access.

6. In order to test, we can do the following commands—login to Tableau Server and trigger extract. Also, you might to execute any other tabcmd command, as follows:

```
#matillion is running under tomcat user and we will switch to this
user
sudo -su tomcat
#go to tabcmd location
cd /opt/tableau/tabcmd/bin
#login tableau server
./tabcmd  login -u Admin -p 'p@ssword' -s https://myserver:443 --
no-certcheck --      accepteula
#refresh extract
./tabcmd refreshextracts --datasource "My Sexy Data Source" --
project "My project" --no-certcheck -synchronous
```

In the preceding command lines, we are using the following Tabcmd parameters:

- --no-certcheck: We need this in case of SSL.
- --accepteula: This is new parameter, that was introduced recently.
- -u: Tableau user name that has permissions to perform desired action.
- -p: This parameter represents the password.
- -s: Tableau host or load balancer endpoint.
- --datasource: Tableau data source.

- `--project`: Project where the data source is stored.
- `--synchronous`: This parameter will await feedback from the Tableau Server about the end of the Tableau Extract refresh. This allows us to execute jobs in chain.

As a result, we can trigger Tableau from Matillion EC2. We can even copy this logic into the Matillion Bash component, but it will be hard for business users to go through it and self-serve.

How it works...

Tabcmd is a command-line utility that automates site administration tasks on your Tableau Server site. In our case, we used the functionality of `tabcmd` to trigger Tableau Extracts.

There's more...

You can find the `tabcmd` list of commands at Tableau official documentation at `https://onlinehelp.tableau.com/current/server/en-us/tabcmd_cmd.htm`.

Creating Matillion Shared Jobs

In order to simplify the job of end users, we will leverage Matillion Shared Job (`https://redshiftsupport.matillion.com/customer/portal/articles/2942889-shared-jobs`) and Matillion variables (`https://redshiftsupport.matillion.com/customer/portal/articles/2037630-using-variables`).

The main purpose of Shared Jobs is to bundle entire workflows into a single custom component. We will create the following two custom components:

- Refresh Tableau Extract
- Export PDF dashboard to S3 bucket

How to do it...

Before we start, we should create a new Orchestration Job for each use case and then we can insert Matillion variables and create Shared Jobs.

1. Create new Orchestration Job with bash component and name it `Refresh Extract`, as follows

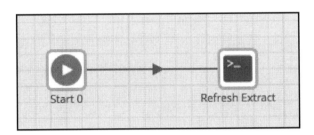

Bash component has the `timeout` parameter. By default, it is 1,000 seconds. For extract, we might increase this in order to wait while your biggest extract refresh.

2. Then paste the code that we tested already and replace Tableau objects with the Matillion parameters, as follows:

```
#go to tabcmd location
cd /opt/tableau/tabcmd/bin
#login tableau server
./tabcmd  login -u Admin -p '${password}' -s ${tableau_host} --no-
certcheck  --accepteula
#refresh extract
./tabcmd refreshextracts --datasource "${data_source_name}" --
project "${project_name}" --no-certcheck --synchronous
```

As a result, this component will refresh Tableau Extract based on value for variable.

3. In addition, we should create Matillion variable for our parameter. Click on the right button on canvas and choose **Manage Variables** as shown in the following screenshot:

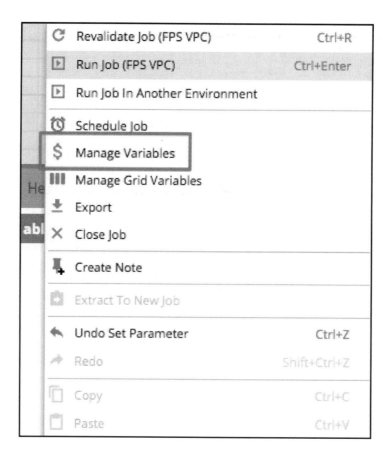

4. Then add three new variables that have to be public, as follows:

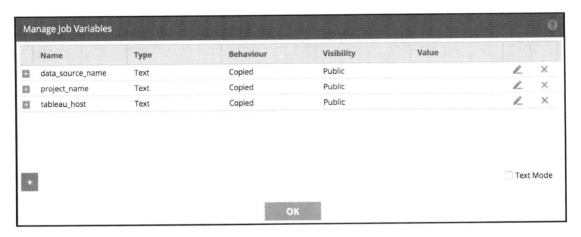

5. Create one more job or duplicate an existing one and name it `Tableau Export PDF`. Enter the following code with the Matillion parameters:

```
#go to tabcmd location
cd /opt/tableau/tabcmd/bin
#login tableau server
./tabcmd  login -u Admin -p 'p@ssword' -s ${tableau_host} --no-
certcheck  --accepteula
#export pdf from Tabelau Server
./tabcmd export "${tableau_view_name}" --pdf --pagelayout landscape
-f "/tmp/$(date +%Y%m%d)_${tableau_report_name}.pdf" --no-certcheck
#upload pdf to the S3
aws s3 cp /tmp/$(date +%Y%m%d)_${tableau_report_name}.pdf
s3://${bucket_name}/$(date +%Y%m%d)/$(date
+%Y%m%d)_${tableau_report_name}.pdf
#clean out
rm /tmp/$(date +%Y%m%d)_${tableau_report_name}.pdf
```

This script will export Tableau View into the `/tmp` location on our EC2 and then will upload to the Reporting Bucket via AWS CLI. Moreover, it will automatically create a folder in bucket with date. In addition, we specify the file name according with our naming convention.

6. Moreover, you should create the following variables in the same way as in step #1:

- `tableau_report_name`
- `tableau_view_name`
- `tableau_host`
- `bucket_name`

You can see how this solution is flexible and you can achieve many different use cases.

7. Now, we can create the Shared Jobs and wrap our Orchestration Jobs. Click on the right button on job name and choose **Generate Shared Job**, as follows:

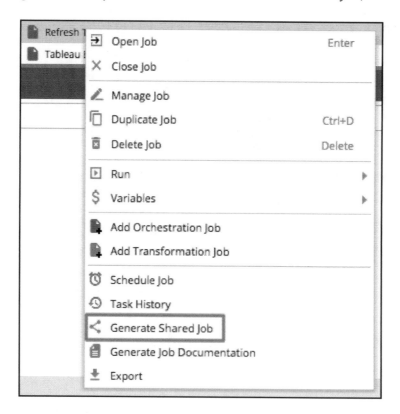

8. Then, we should fill in the form and choose the following mentioned options:

Package	Packt.tableau.refreshextract
Name	Refresh Tableau Extract
Description	This component refresh Tableau Extract

9. Click on **Next** and you will see the **Parameter Configuration** step. Then, click on **OK**.

10. Then, do the same for the second job **Tableau Export to PDF**, as follows:

Package	Packt.tableau.exporttopdf
Name	Tableau Export to PDF
Description	This component will export PDF report to S3 Bucket

11. Click on **Next**, fill in the **Parameter Configuration** page and click on **OK**. These parameters will be used for the data entry later.

12. Let's check out the jobs. Navigate to **Shared Jobs Pane** | **User Defined** | **Packt**, as follows:

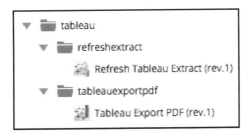

As a result, you'll see our new jobs.

13. Let's put it all together. Create a new Orchestration Job and drag and drop our new shared components, as follows:

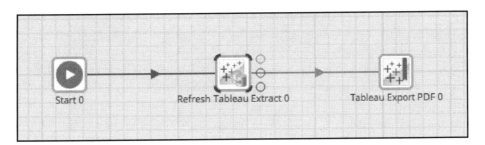

Usually, one extract can source many different workbooks. As a result, we can use another powerful feature of *Matillion—Fixed Iterator.* More information can be found here: https://redshiftsupport.matillion.com/ customer/en/portal/articles/2235536-fixed-iterator.

14. Let's add a fixed iterator on top of the job as it will allow us to specify multiple reports at once, as follows:

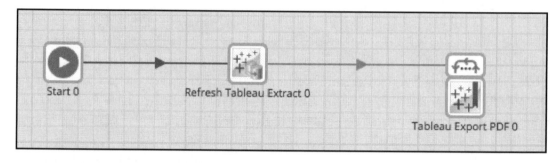

As a result, we have created new custom components that look very friendly and familiar for our end users. Using this approach, we can leverage any Tabcmd command and create a custom component for it.

How it works...

We used Tabcmd to manage Tableau Server and integrate it with data. Adding the Linux Tableau CLI tabcmd tool to EC2 Linux allows us to use Matillion components to plug Tableau into the data pipeline. And in case of a successful execution of ETL, we can easily trigger Tableau Extracts or perform any other actions.

Other Books You May Enjoy

If you enjoyed this book, you may be interested in these other books by Packt:

Getting Started with Tableau 2018.x
Tristan Guillevin, Recommended for You , Recommended for You , Learning, Recommended for You , Learning, Beginner's Guide, Recommended for You , Learning, Recommended for You , Recommended for You , Recommended for You , Learning, Recommended for You , Learning, Beginner's Guide

ISBN: 978-1-78883-868-9

- Discover new functionalities such as density, extensions, and transparency introduced in Tableau 2018.x
- Connect tables and make transformations such as pivoting the field and splitting columns
- Build an efficient data source for your analysis
- Design insightful data visualization using different mark types and properties
- Build powerful dashboards and stories
- Share your work and interact with Tableau Server
- Use Tableau to explore your data and find new insights
- Explore Tableau's advanced features and gear up for upcoming challenges

Advanced Analytics with R and Tableau
Jen Stirrup, Ruben Oliva Ramos

ISBN: 978-1-78646-011-0

- Integrate Tableau's analytics with the industry-standard, statistical prowess of R.
- Make R function calls in Tableau, and visualize R functions with Tableau using RServe.
- Use the CRISP-DM methodology to create a roadmap for analytics investigations.
- Implement various supervised and unsupervised learning algorithms in R to return values to Tableau.
- Make quick, cogent, and data-driven decisions for your business using advanced analytical techniques such as forecasting, predictions, association rules, clustering, classification, and other advanced Tableau/R calculated field functions.

Leave a review - let other readers know what you think

Please share your thoughts on this book with others by leaving a review on the site that you bought it from. If you purchased the book from Amazon, please leave us an honest review on this book's Amazon page. This is vital so that other potential readers can see and use your unbiased opinion to make purchasing decisions, we can understand what our customers think about our products, and our authors can see your feedback on the title that they have worked with Packt to create. It will only take a few minutes of your time, but is valuable to other potential customers, our authors, and Packt. Thank you!

Index

Made in the USA
Columbia, SC
09 March 2020